TEACHER EDUCATION POLICY

SUNY Series
FRONTIERS IN EDUCATION
Phillip G. Altbach, Editor

The Frontiers in Education Series draws upon a range of disciplines and approaches in the analysis of contemporary educational issues and concerns. Books in the series help to reinterpret established fields of scholarship in education by encouraging the latest synthesis and research. A special focus highlights educational policy issues from a multidisciplinary perspective. The series is published in cooperation with the Graduate School of Education, State University of New York at Buffalo.

Class, Race, and Gender in American Education
—Lois Weis (ed.)

Excellence and Equality: A Qualitatively Different Perspective on Gifted and Talented Education
—David M. Fetterman

Change and Effectiveness in Schools: A Cultural Perspective
—Gretchen B. Rossman, H. Dickson Corbett, and William A. Firestone

The Curriculum: Problems, Politics, and Possibilities
—Landon E. Beyer and Michael W. Apple (eds.)

The Character of American Higher Education and Intercollegiate Sport
—Donald Chu

Crisis in Teaching: Perspectives on Current Reforms
—Lois Weis, Philip G. Altbach, Gail P. Kelly, Hugh G. Petrie, and Sheila Slaughter (eds.)

*The High Status Track: Studies of Elite Schools and
   Stratification*
               —Paul William Kingston and Lionel S. Lewis (eds.)

*The Economics of American Universities: Management,
   Operations, and Fiscal Environment*
               —Stephen A. Hoenack and Eileen L. Collins (eds.)

*The Higher Learning and High Technology:
   Dynamics of Higher Education and Policy Formation*
                                        —Sheila Slaughter

Dropouts from Schools: Issues, Dilemmas and Solutions
               —Lois Weis, Eleanor Farrar, and Hugh G. Petrie (eds.)

*Religious Fundamentalism and American Education;
   The Battle for the Public Schools*
                                        —Eugene F. Provenzo, Jr.

Going to School: The African-American Experience
                                        —Kofi Lomotey (ed.)

*Curriculum Differentiation: Interpretive Studies in
   U.S. Secondary Schools*
                              —Reba Page and Linda Valli (eds.)

The Racial Crisis in American Higher Education
               —Philip G. Altbach and Kofi Lomotey (eds.)

The Great Transformation in Higher Education, 1960–1980
                                        —Clark Kerr

*College in Black and White: African-American Students
   in Predominantly White and in Historically Black
   Public Universities*
                              —Walter R. Allen, Edgar G. Epps,
                                  and Nesha Z. Haniff (eds.)

Textbooks in American Society: Politics, Policy, and Pedagogy
               —Philip G. Altback, Gail P. Kelly, Hugh G. Petrie,
                                  and Lois Weis (eds.)

Critical Perspectives on Early Childhood Education
               —Lois Weis, Philip G. Altbach, Gail P. Kelly,
                                  and Hugh G. Petrie (eds.)

Black Resistance in High School: Forging a Separatist Culture
                                        —R. Patrick Solomon

Emergent Issues in Education: Comparative Perspectives
  —Robert F. Arnove, Philip G. Altbach, and Gail P. Kelly (eds.)

Creating Community on College Campuses
  —Irving J. Spitzberg and Virginia V. Thorndike

Teacher Education Policy: Narratives, Stories, and Cases
  —Hendrik D. Gideonse (ed.)

TEACHER EDUCATION POLICY

Narratives, Stories, and Cases

Edited by
Hendrik D. Gideonse

STATE UNIVERSITY OF NEW YORK PRESS

Published by
State University of New York Press, Albany

© 1992 State University of New York

All rights reserved

Printed in the United States of America

No part of this book may be used or reproduced
in any manner whatsoever without written permission
except in the case of brief quotations embodied in
critical articles and reviews.

For information, address State University of New York
Press, State University Plaza, Albany, NY 12246

Production by Christine M. Lynch
Marketing by Fran Keneston

Library of Congress Cataloging-in-Publication Data
Teacher education policy : narratives, stories, and cases / edited by
　Hendrik D. Gideonse.
　　　p.　cm. — (SUNY series, frontiers in education)
　Includes bibliographical references and index.
　ISBN 0-7914-1055-2 (alk. paper) . — ISBN 0-7914-1056-0 (pbk. : alk. paper)
　　1. Teachers—Training of—United States. 2. Education and state-
-United States.　I. Gideonse, Hendrik D.　II. Series.
LB1715.T423　1992
370'.71'0973—dc20
　　　　　　　　　　　　　　　　　　　　　　　　　　　91-23032
　　　　　　　　　　　　　　　　　　　　　　　　　　　CIP

10 9 8 7 6 5 4 3 2 1

CONTENTS

Preface—Hendrik D. Gideonse   ix

Part I   *State Policy Development*

Chapter 1.   Teacher Education Policy:
The Texas Experience—Richard E. Ishler   1

Chapter 2.   New Mexico: Caps on Content—
David L. Colton and Barbara M. Simmons   27

Chapter 3.   The California Commission on
Teacher Credentialing:
Seeking the Ingredients for Change—
Richard K. Mastain and Ralph Brott   49

Chapter 4.   New Jersey's Alternate Route—Ken Carlson   73

Chapter 5.   Teacher Education in Ohio, 1960 to 1990:
Strong Paradigm; Emerging Anomalies—
Ellis A. Joseph and James Biddle   91

Chapter 6.   Turmoil in Teacher Education in Oregon—
Robert D. Barr   111

Chapter 7.   Restructuring Teacher Education in the
Old Dominion—James M. Cooper and
Philip M. Tate   133

Part II   *Higher Education Institutions*

Chapter 8.   The Struggle for Control of Teacher
Education: The University of
Wisconsin-Madison—Nona A. Prestine   159

Chapter 9.   Implementing the Holmes Agenda:
An Institutional Perspective—
Donald P. Anderson   181

Part III *Regional and National Influences*

Chapter 10. A Case Study in Teacher Education:
PL 94–142—Maynard C. Reynolds ... 201

Chapter 11. The Southern Regional Education Board
and Teacher Education Policy—
Richard Wisniewski ... 223

Chapter 12. The Redesign of NCATE 1980 to 1986—
Hendrik D. Gideonse ... 245

PART IV *Overview*

Chapter 13. Leadership in Policy Development by
Teacher Educators: Search for a
More Effective Future—David L. Clark ... 269

Notes On Contributors ... 297

Notes ... 303

References ... 313

ACKNOWLEDGMENTS

The editor gratefully acknowledges the permission granted by *Educational Evaluation and Policy Analysis*/American Educational Research Association to reprint the chapter by Nona A. Prestine which appeared in Fall, 1989, volume 11, number 3, pp. 285–300.

The chapters written by Richard Ishler, David Colton and Barbara Simmons, Richard Mastain and Ralph Brott, Ellis Joseph and James Biddle, Ken Carlson, Maynard Reynolds, James Cooper and Philip Tate, Richard Wisniewski, Hendrik Gideonse, and David Clark were presented in draft form at the annual meeting of the American Educational Research Association, April, 1990, Boston, Massachusetts.

*Dedicated to the enhancement of collegium
and the cultivation of leadership
among America's school-based and
pre-service teacher educators.*

Hendrik D. Gideonse

PREFACE

This collection of narratives, stories, and case studies seeks to inform teacher educators and related professionals about various kinds of policy processes that affect their aims, work, and accomplishments. Each chapter, while treating an event or process worth knowing in its own terms, is illustrative of the much larger set of policy initiatives in and out of the field that have come to impact upon us in the last decade or so. The basic purpose in commissioning this collection is to increase the awareness and sophistication of teacher educators in respect to such matters in hopes that we become, if not wholly in control of our destiny, much more effective participants in its determination. Impetus for this project came from two sources: first, my experience as a long-term participant in teacher education's policy processes in several different arenas and, then later, my experience as I sought to organize formal coursework for doctoral candidates with career aspirations in teacher education.

In the summer of 1989 the Teacher Education Council of State Colleges and Universities (TECSCU) invited me to address the lessons we in teacher education ought to have learned from the avalanche of recent state regulation of teacher education (Gideonse, 1990). I was asked to work from the perspective of opportunities which had arisen for me to address policy struggles in a number of individual states and also to study policy initiatives across the board in connection with several years of service on the Government Relations Task Force of the American Association of Colleges for Teacher Education (AACTE).

Over a couple of months I distilled my thoughts and then undertook a dialectic on them with colleagues across the country.[1] I ended up with a baker's dozen plus one of observations to share with the TECSCU membership.

Number 1: How Little We Know

An ironic conclusion is how little we know that satisfies others' policy queries of us. Teacher educators, the presumed repositories of the specialized knowledge pertaining to our field, are constantly being asked questions by policy makers to which we do not have ready answers. How many students in teacher education programs? How many different kinds of programs? How might the different kinds of programs be best characterized? How many states have alternative routes, and how many certificated teachers have taken those paths? What are the retention rates of different kinds of programs? How do the products of the different routes and programs differ from one another as input and as output?

In some states, progress is being made toward the collection of data that would begin to answer such questions. Organized teacher education (that is, AACTE) began a few years ago to address the demands of the policy processes at the state level,[2] but even the AACTE effort cannot do much more than generate and update the valuable compendia of state-level activities.

Part of our problem is that the kinds of things *we* consider knowledge are of lesser interest to legislators and policy makers, but our inability (and sometimes unwillingness) to provide what *they* consider knowledge actually undermines legislators' acceptance of our claims to know things of importance to teacher education. Our natural propensity to see the complexities of our work makes us reticent to make the simplifying assumptions legislators often feel necessary to the formulation of policy. Our difficulties are not eased by our own more-than-occasional assessment of the questions we receive from policy makers as ignorant, or our failure to keep that assessment to ourselves, a failure which sometimes leads policy makers to see us as arrogant or contemptuous.

Number 2: Different Rhythms

The rhythm of the work of state-level policy bodies is different from the rhythms with which college and university teacher educators are familiar. This is a reflection of two different cultures at work.

Policy bodies feel teacher educators drag their feet; teacher educators feel policy bodies move with inordinate speed. Different time frames and work structures are part of the explanation. Another is that policy makers seek to make decisions, but because of the collegial assumptions underlying academic enterprises, teacher educators strive for a more time-consuming aim—the development of consensus.

NUMBER 3: ORAL TRADITIONS VS. WRITTEN

While policy proposals and their results eventually get written down and teacher educators in the academy are no strangers to protracted discussion, there is an important truth in noting the oral character of much of what takes place in the processes by which policy is developed. While written analyses may be important and available (especially where policy staffs exist and are involved), legislators, particularly, tend to function most frequently and effectively in an oral mode, particularly when trading and testing ideas. The truism of "who you know" being important in politics is validated by the fact of the connections, yes, but also because it is an indication of whom you can and do *talk* to. The political process depends heavily on relatively brief, pertinent conversations among and between legislators and other policy makers and those in whom they have trust. Volumes of written material will not overcome distrust; where trust is present, however, very brief interactions can be almost unbelievably efficacious. Oral processes, however, are difficult to keep track of if one is unable to stay on top of them all the time.

NUMBER 4: THE HEAVY TIME DEMANDS OF PARTICIPATION IN POLICY PROCESSES

A crucial corollary of the different rhythms and the oral character of policy processes, therefore, is the heavy time demand of participation in the policy process. Keeping up with who knows or says what, what has happened most recently, and which directions protagonists are taking is incredibly taxing. And to play, one must keep up.

Active participants must stay in touch with one another, must dialogue continuously to assess what is happening, and must be prepared to be places or cover one another when needed, even on the day or two notice that a quick luncheon appointment or a swiftly scheduled (to say nothing of simultaneously scheduled) hearing may require.

When developments occur it is not unusual for protagonists to need to be on the phone with one another two or three times a day. On days during the most intensive activity dozens of such calls, many of them quite lengthy, may be exchanged. If teacher educator deans or faculty are to be involved, there are implications for prioritizing activities, availability, scheduling, and interruptions in addition to the issue of total amount of time involved.

NUMBER 5: BEING TOO LATE

When a disturbing policy proposal is first initiated by a key legislative or other policy official, teacher educators should view it as a signal not of the *starting* point of their involvement but of their *failure* to involve themselves in processes already ongoing. True, there have been more than a few successes in mounting holding actions to minimize harm from otherwise problematic initiatives. But the surprise appearance of an otherwise damaging or even outrageous policy proposal should be seen by teacher educators not as the start of their problems, but confirmation that they have existed for some time.

NUMBER 6: DISCOUNTING EXPERTISE AS VESTED INTEREST

A most disheartening realization of teacher education policy activists is the way many policy makers treat expressions of expertise as evidence not that we know something but that we seek only to protect our vested interests. The irony of the dismissal of expertise as mere defensiveness should not be lost. What teacher educators believe is the reason they should be listened to is the signal for policy makers to, as it were, mentally turn off our microphones!

NUMBER 7: SERENDIPITY

Many teacher educator policy activists report, with both surprise and relief, how important it has been that they found themselves in the right place at the right time. It is a rightness that they felt they could not have predicted before the fact, but that they clearly recognized after the fact. We can find a familiar analogy in our own scholarship. Every scholar has experienced reading a library shelf or browsing through a computerized index, in effect, being in "places" where our operant research and bibliographic search terms really didn't suggest we should be, and as a result finding a crucial citation that, perhaps, even changed the course of the quest on which we were embarked. The chance hall conversation outside a committee room as the bill is being marked up, seeing the respect accorded an "adversary" and the way she is questioned by a legislative committee (and thus coming to understand something about why the respect is there and what that might suggest about one's own stance), or actually being mistaken as an ally by an opponent and hearing the policy strategy unfold before your very eyes and ears—all these are real examples of events that made a difference in one or another policy context.

NUMBER 8: GEOGRAPHIC PROXIMITY

Given the rhythms and the oral character of policy formulation, individuals who are geographically closer to where policy is made are in a better position to be players than those who are more distant. That does not mean that distance cannot be overcome, but there is no substitute for being there when it counts. That places special burdens on those who are closer. Teacher educators who are in or near their state capital—or their president's or provost's office—have opportunities and obligations respecting policy formulation that it is difficult for others to assume.

NUMBER 9: DO WE FACE EVIL, IGNORANCE, OR SOMETHING ELSE?

Given the impulse to in some way label the latest policy struggle, assign the second greatest weight to ignorance, the least weight to the likelihood of evil, and the greatest weight to "something else," more than likely fragmentation of interest, different information, or competing purpose. The problem with attributing explanations to evil being visited on teacher education is not just that it is so often mistaken, but that it risks violating an important rule of politics: "Never make any permanent enemies."[3]

NUMBER 10: TOO FEW LEADERS

Many teacher educators believe that the burden of engagement in policy processes has fallen on a relatively small number of people. That may be because there are few leaders among us. It may be that there are few with the time and energy to devote after the on-campus requirements of their duties. It may also be that there are few who are willing to take the career or on-campus risks associated with such activity. Some faculty do not always understand or appreciate the importance of policy work. Provosts and presidents may not understand it either, and sometimes what they *think* they understand reflects a priority of the larger campus needs as contrasted with the needs of the teaching profession and its clients. More than once activists have experienced sometimes subtle—and sometimes much less so—signals to butt out of policy involvement, especially with the legislature, but occasionally with the higher education policy structure, too, because of perceived conflicts in purpose with the "larger" interests of the college or university.

NUMBER 11: CONFLICTING MOTIVATIONS

Legislators may not be as interested in the specifics of change as the fact or perception of change as accomplishment in itself. Lobbyists talk of legislative aides who acknowledge that all their principal wants is a "boffo," something that stands out and looks good.

Whatever teacher educators may be tempted privately to think in such instances, what we need to remember is that policy makers of all stripes have career agendas, as indeed do teacher educators, and while theirs are different from ours, they are no less legitimate in their particular context. They have constituencies to which they are responding, as presumably do we. But their's are different agendas and different constituencies, just as legitimate as ours, and we need to understand and respect those differences if we are to be effective players.

NUMBER 12: DIVISIONS WITHIN THE PROFESSION

The serious divisions within teacher education—purposively, institutionally, professionally—weaken us in our dealings with policy-making bodies. When professional sectors speak with divided voices, the range of choice open to policy makers expands dramatically. When we cannot "get ourselves together" or, worse, when we actually fight with one another in the policy arena, we have only the illusion of involvement, for the operational effect of disunity among us is the certainty that decisions will be made by nonprofessionals on premises other than ours.

NUMBER 13: TEACHER EDUCATORS AS REACTIONARIES AND FOOT DRAGGERS

This observation is related to the one already made about treating expertise as vested interest. But it is different. (Pursuing vested interests, for example, can lead to the request for change as well as stasis.) All too often we are seen as reactionary, seeking only a return to times of quiet and inattention by others. Some who would make teacher education policy view, or at least talk as if they view, teacher educators as incompetent or contemptible. Though the perception be false, however, does not eliminate its impact on the policy process. Where it is present, it is deeply held and tends to be extremely resistant to head-on challenge.

NUMBER 14: YOGI BERRA WAS WRONG

The adoption of a policy or the passage of a statute should never be seen as the end of a policy process; it is only the beginning of a next round. In other words, it isn't over when it's over. That next round may be the tasks of regulation writing, the development of enabling procedures, or the implementation of the intended programs. Or it may be the beginning of an initiative aimed at seeking eventual reversal. Policy engagement must be seen, therefore, not as an episodic phenomenon but as a continuous commitment.

These observations shared with the TECSCU teacher education administrators are admittedly impressionistic and highly experiential, perhaps not terribly profound, and yet still important for teacher educators to comprehend. However, one way to look at these specifics in the aggregate plus the TECSCU request that they be addressed in the first place is the perceived need to increase the sophistication of teacher educators' involvement in the policy processes affecting us.

There was a second stimulus to this volume. After a twenty-two year absence from full-time teaching responsibilities owing to the assumption of a variety of administrative duties, in and out of the university, I sought to design a seminar on teacher education policy as my contribution to the offerings of a department many of whose graduate students ultimately assume teacher education responsibilities. While I had been living, working, and writing in the policy arena for over twenty years, shifting to a more exclusively scholarly and instructional role itself proved to be a learning experience.

Systematic examination of the policy literature pertaining to teacher education was, at first, disappointing, mainly because of the discovery of its scarce supply. A few important works existed (for example, Shulman and Sykes, 1983). Materials were available from research centers (for example, RAND's Center for the Study of the Teaching Profession or the Center for Policy Research in Education), a number of the major policy agencies (for example, the National Governors Association, the Southern Regional Education Board, or the Education Commission of the

States), or professional associations (for example, the National Education Association or the American Association of Colleges for Teacher Education). Journal sources, notably *Phi Delta Kappan* and the *Journal of Teacher Education*, contained a fair amount of material, and the national education press of record—the *Chronicle of Higher Education* and *Education Week*—offers considerable discussion of the specifics of emerging teacher education policy proposals. With the recent publication of *Handbook of Research on Teacher Education* (Houston, 1990) several useful chapters with some comprehensiveness bearing on teacher education policy concerns are newly available.

Examination of the materials available from this variety of sources showed that while many policy issues were treated and were subjected to a variety of different kinds of analysis (e.g., quantitative, philosophical, policy, historical, etc.), in very short supply were expositions and studies of policy development—stories, narratives, and cases that explored the how and why of policy development for teacher education as compared with the what (that is, the more or less formal analysis of the issues *per se*). This very imbalance is part of the problem faced by those who might wish to participate constructively in the development of teacher education policy—the issue orientation subtly reinforces the belief that rational analysis and action can be achieved, thus drawing attention away from the complex, idiosyncratic, personalized, context-bound, and sometimes seamy political realities which often govern. This volume aims to make a contribution toward meeting the need for narratives, stories, and cases illuminating realities of the policy processes for teacher education.

The planning for the volume followed a straight-forward path. Policy was defined as goals, criteria, standards, sanctions, and accepted procedures impinging on performance. Any policy arena has a particular set of topics which identifies its domain. Teacher education policy embraces stakeholders, actors, and agencies, and it follows the rules and norms of the agencies in which it originates or is applied.

Among the categories for teacher education policy may be found, for example:

Topics

State licensure standards (initial and continuing)
Degree and program approval

Supply and demand
Testing for licensure purposes
Professional certification
Curriculum sanctions in higher education institutions
Accreditation
Continuing education standards
Financial provisions for support of teacher education
Structural arrangements for policy (e.g., state boards; advisory commissions; legislatures; professional standards and practices boards; etc.)

Stakeholders

Society
Children
Parents
Education professionals of all kinds
Policy makers

Actors

The public
State and local education policy officials
State and federal legislators
Education professionals (teachers; administrators, state and local)
College/university personnel (professional education and other faculty;administrators)
Educational and policy research community
Professional organizations
Temporary systems (e.g., commissions, etc.)

Given this considerable diversity of topics, stakeholders, and actors and given the aim of increasing the awareness and sophistication of teacher educators in such matters, several parameters were set for the development of the volume. Yarger and Smith (1990) reference five distinct research methodologies commonly used in teacher education: narrative studies, case studies, surveys, correlational studies, and causal/experimental studies. Clearly, the substantive chapters of the volume fit into both the narrative and case study classifications, but as a group they range widely from historical treatments, to personalized narratives, to quite demanding and highly structured case studies, one of which even aims at assessment and interpretation in terms of theoretical propositions bearing on educational policy.

The variety of approaches is a direct consequence of the development strategy for the volume. Two considerations were central: attending to the credibility of the authors in the eyes of the teacher educator audience; and facilitating the preparation of the chapters in a reasonable period of time.

Accordingly, all the chapters presented herein (excepting only the one by Nona Prestine) were commissioned specifically for this volume. They were drafted by individuals who, in the main, participated directly in the events they describe and analyze. This has the effect of reducing substantially the scholarly "start-up" time. On the other hand, it risks objectivity as it is classically understood. Then again, commissioning authors who themselves have lived through or close to the events they consider promises to increase the credibility of the exposition and interpretation in the eyes of eventual audiences, primarily because it gives greater promise of preserving the perceived meaning of the unfolding events.

This, of course, speaks to an issue in behavioral and social inquiry that is ultimately unresolvable. Can objectivity ever be achieved save *within* the boundaries of a given cultural or dispositional paradigm or point of view? Conversely, can steps taken to serve the principle of objectivity have the effect of damaging or at least interfering with credibility and essential meaning? The best that can be hoped for is recognition of the problem and then action with that knowledge in mind. Accordingly, each author identified at least two persons equally involved or close to the case to undertake a formative critique. Authors were asked to present their cases in a nonpartisan (though not necessarily dispassionate) fashion. (Policy debates are "juicy" for those whose lives are affected by them; to deny that characteristic would have been a mistake.) In preparing their chapters, each author was asked to address common topics—significance; key actors and structures; motivations, purposes, and strategies; chronology; policy outcomes; and case study sources.

The chapters selected sought to represent a broad range of issues and arenas for teacher education policy. The chapters are grouped into seven that focus on state-level policy developments, two that focus on policy development at an institutional level,[4] and three that address national or regional policy developments.

Substantively, the largest set focuses on state-level policy developments. Richard Ishler addresses Texas SB 994 and its imposition of credit hour caps on teacher education programs.

David Colton and Barbara Simmons narrate New Mexico's different attempt to impose caps, in this instance on the amount of *subject matter* future teachers could be required to take.

Richard Mastain and Ralph Brott draw lessons from the last thirty years of legislative and administrative policy developments in California bearing on teacher credentialing. The importance of this experience can be seen in, among other things, the ups and downs of California's willingness to second-guess or trust the role of professionals with responsibility for defining and maintaining teacher credentialing standards.

Kenneth Carlson treats New Jersey's imposition of the alternate route to teacher certification, an object lesson in teacher education's vulnerability to an unfriendly policy blitz.

Ellis Joseph and James Biddle address the background for and then the pursuit of 1989 initiatives in Ohio to create an alternate route for teacher certification, on the one hand, and a uniform teacher education program for all institutions in the state, on the other. It is a story of a drift from collaborative, cooperative policy development within the larger professional community toward less responsive, more directive, and more political legislative processes.

Robert Barr describes and analyzes Oregon's experiences as it moved to master's-level professional certification, including a coda added after completion of the chapter to report the surprising demise of the OSU College of Education and the decimation of teacher education at the University of Oregon.

Finally, James Cooper and Philip Tate describe and explain Virginia's teacher education reforms of the mid-1980s, a rather different approach to the establishment of a less constrictive form of credit hour caps in teacher education.

Two chapters focus on institutional policy in higher education. Donald Anderson employs the catbird seat of his deanship of the Ohio State University's College of Education to narrate and reflect upon implementing curricular reform in connection with the Holmes Group initiative.

Nona Prestine presents and analyzes the University of Wisconsin's unsuccessful struggle with the Wisconsin Department of Public Instruction over the governance of teacher education programs.

Three chapters address policy activities in regional or national terms. Maynard Reynolds treats the passage and implementation of PL 94–142 as an instance of federal policy initiatives impacting teacher education.

Richard Wisniewski explores the Southern Regional Education Board's role as a disseminator of teacher education policy ideas during the 1980s.

My own chapter tells the story of the 1980 to 1986 redesign of the standards, processes, and structures of the National Council for Accreditation of Teacher Education.

The volume concludes with David Clark's cross-chapter analysis. In it he comments on the condition and future prospects for developments in teacher education policy as illuminated by the case studies.

PART I

STATE POLICY DEVELOPMENT

1

Richard E. Ishler

Teacher Education Policy:

The Texas Experience

Introduction/Backdrop

The history of education in Texas embodies reform dating back at least one hundred years. Reform, as used in this context, is defined as actions or intentions to build, support, improve, or change the educational opportunities offered in the public schools of Texas and in the way teachers who staff those schools are prepared and certified.

Reforms in education have not made Texas a trend setter for the nation. Instead, reforms in Texas have historically tended to reflect trends that have emerged in other states. Frederick Eby, writing on educational development in Texas sixty-five years ago, characterized it as follows:

> In no other state has the struggle of such diverse traditions and ideals been so prolonged and bitter. Many have wondered at the slow and fitful development of education in a state so large and wealthy. (1925, p. v)

It has only been during the last two decades that Texas has emerged as a state striving for excellence in education. Reform in the 1980s, however, may prove to be a game of catch up with other states because of the current decline in the Texas economy. Today's educational reforms may be better understood if viewed in the context of mandated reforms over the years.

The following are significant events and mandated reforms designed to improve Texas education:

1. The law of 1871 set up the most imperial system of education known to any American state. It was organized along military lines and assumed absolute authority over the training of children. A State Board of Education was provided, consisting of the superintendent of public

instruction, the governor, and the attorney general (Eby, 1925, p. 159).
2. In 1876 a new Texas constitution was enacted. Eby described the impact on education as follows:

> The article on education as finally adopted after so much wrangling was naturally a disappointing compromise which fell short of meeting the real needs of the times. In its intense hatred of the radical school system, the convention blindly wrecked the entire organization, destroying the features which were good with those which were bad...The new constitution abolished the Office of Public Instruction, together with all other supervisory functions. It eliminated compulsory attendance and all provision for districting of the counties. (1925, p. 170)

3. The School Law of 1884 was enacted by the Eighteenth Legislature in special session. This law began the gradual and incremental formation of the system of public education that exists today in Texas.
4. By 1900 such topics as the recurring ones of school funding, teacher education and performance, and curriculum mandates were very much on the agenda of the legislature.
5. In 1906 State Superintendent R. B. Cousins commented on the organization of the public education system in Texas, including higher education, as a "loose, crude, and wasteful patchwork rather than a system" (Eby, p. 8).
6. F. M. Bralley (1913) summarized education legislation of the Twenty-second Legislature. Notable was a teachers' certificate law "simplifying, unifying, and making more pedagogical the certification of teachers, whereby they are authorized to contract to teach in the public schools of Texas" (Eby, p. 15). Teaching certificates were to be issued by the State Superintendent's Office. Prior to this law, cities could issue certificates.
7. In 1920 the governor appointed a committee of "men and women especially interested in educational matters to make recommendations to him and to the Legislature as to the actions necessary to improve conditions in the crisis of school affairs" (Blanton, 1921, p. 10). As a result, the legislature, in special session, appropriated

$4 million to increase salaries of public school teachers and revised the laws for teacher certification.
8. By 1947 interest in bringing Texas up to national standards resulted in the formation of the Gilmer-Aiken Committee by the Fiftieth Legislature. This committee was to study means of overcoming educational inequalities in Texas. Several bills, emanating from this committee, were passed in the Fifty-first Legislative Session. These bills provided the organization and funding principles for public education in Texas which still exist today. Passing and implementing education reform legislation then was little different from today in the wide range of political maneuvering, influence peddling, and open hostilities of both proponents and opponents.
9. During the 1950s and 1960s several committees were formed to study education which resulted in legislated reforms. In 1958 a committee recommended changes involving the school program, teacher supply, school construction, and finance. The committee also made suggestions for recruiting and retaining teachers, in-service education, and higher teacher salaries. In 1965 the Fifty-ninth Legislature established a Governor's Committee on Public School Education which was charged with, among other things, developing a long-range plan that would enable Texas to emerge as a national leader in educational aspirations, commitment, and achievement.
10. In the early 1980s reform attention shifted to "reforming the curricula, student learning, meeting the unique needs of students, fostering responsible student behavior, preparing teachers to teach, promoting excellence in teaching, increasing operational effectiveness, and affecting state/federal relationships" (Governor's Advisory Committee on Education, 1980, p. v). The Governor's Advisory Committee recommended such things as essential skills in the curriculum and including specific recommendations for allocation of time in all subjects at each grade level. The committee also recommended that teacher education institutions cooperate more closely with school districts and that competency tests be required for entry into programs and for teacher certification. Also, the committee recommended a single set of institutional standards for colleges preparing teachers.

Legislation was passed that implemented most of these recommendations.

11. By 1983 the State Board of Education reported that legislation enabling the recommendations of the Governor's Advisory Committee had been passed and that Texas was high among the states in its response to *A Nation at Risk: The Imperative for Educational Reform*.
12. The Select Committee on Public Education was appointed by the governor in 1983 to recommend sweeping changes in the schools. The work and significance of this committee will be discussed later in this chapter, but suffice it to say here that its recommendations resulted in passage of House Bill 72, the most comprehensive and controversial educational reform legislation ever enacted.
13. In 1985, the Select Committee on Higher Education was appointed by the governor. The recommendations of this committee resulted in the passage of Senate Bill 994, legislation that dramatically changed the state's teacher education programs.

The history of educational reform in Texas is one of mandating changes rather than allowing for local and institutional initiatives. Recent educational reforms have attempted to create schools for the future but have curtailed the universities' ability to adequately prepare teachers to staff those schools.

SELECT COMMITTEE ON PUBLIC EDUCATION

The Select Committee on Public Education (SCOPE) was created during the closing hours of the legislative session in 1983 after Governor Mark White was unable to get the legislature to help him fulfill his commitment to improve teacher salaries made in the 1982 gubernatorial election. No one had put together a salary package that was acceptable to the lieutenant governor, Bill Hobby, the speaker of the house, Gib Lewis, and the business community. The speaker insisted that he would not support a tax increase to put money into salaries unless there was a complete, wide-scoped study of the education problems facing the state. In the waning days of the session the governor was being heavily criticized for not delivering on campaign promises. As an alternative and to take some positive action, the governor's office sent down a resolution calling for a study of education (Chance, 1986).

Even though the Select Committee was sometimes referred to as the "governor's committee," it was actually appointed jointly. The lieutenant governor chose five members, the speaker five, and the governor was given the authority to appoint five including the chairman. Three State Board of Education members were added and as the committee began its work, White, Hobby, and Lewis also became members of the committee.

The committee structure featured an Oversight Committee that also included the governor, the lieutenant governor, and the speaker, in addition to the state comptroller, the chairman of the State Board of Education and the committee chairman, Ross Perot. The key subcommittees were chaired by politicians on the committee: Senator Carl Parker, Senate Education Committee chairman headed the Finance Committee; Representative Bill Haley, House Education Committee chairman led the Teaching Profession Committee. In some cases these same people later served as chairs of the key committees of the legislature that approved the Omnibus Education Bill, House Bill 72, which was written to implement the committee's report. Several other politicians were on the committee: Representative Frank Madla, Senator Grant Jones, and House Ways and Means Committee chairman Representative Stan Schlueter. There were no teachers, principals or superintendents on the committee. It did include a few members who had served on school boards and several education committees or commissions. It also included a small number of people who had worked with or represented minority groups. Several members came from the business community. This was a high priority for Governor White. He believed it was necessary for the business community to consider support for education as directly related to the state's economic development.

The charge to the committee exceeded the original purpose for which the committee was initiated. It focused on four major areas:

1. Teacher excellence, competency, and compensation.
2. Distribution of financial resources among school districts.
3. A revenue package to pay for educational improvements.
4. Special programs and problems, including the children of undocumented and migrant workers, classroom discipline, and the educational demands of high technology.

The key decision in the Texas reform scenario was the appointment of H. Ross Perot as chairman of SCOPE. It came at a time when nationally the *Nation at Risk* dialogue was unfolding. In Texas the recommendations that came from what was commonly known as "the Perot committee" became the topic for discussions in every home. Perot attracted publicity and attention. He had become something of a legend with his "Wings of Eagles" adventure in Iran and an airlift to Vietnam. After resigning his position as a salesman at IBM and starting his own company, he had become one of the most influential business leaders in the country. He had also made over $2 billion. His success as an entrepreneur, his financial contributions to many community causes and projects, and his dynamic personality made him unique. He had previously chaired the former Republican governor's "War on Drugs" Committee. Even though some legislators were shocked to see a Republican appointed by a Democratic governor to chair the Select Committee on Public Education and even though all did not consider themselves his disciples, most admired him for his leadership abilities and his demonstrated commitment to public service (Chance, 1986).

Once appointed, Perot dedicated himself totally to the work of the committee. He identified all of the education groups active in Texas and made personal calls on them and spoke at their conferences. He visited with hundreds of teachers and many schools. He listened to everyone who had something to say about the ways education could be improved. Perot also hired William Alper of Sirota and Alper Associates, New York, to conduct a management survey of over forty school districts. He referred to this data many times as basic feedback on the conditions in Texas' public schools, particularly in the way leadership was perceived (Chance, 1986).

Prior to hearing testimony from experts, the committee traveled to all parts of the state to hear testimony from various community groups, professional organizations, and individual citizens. In one month it visited ten school districts. After this initial state-wide sampling of opinions, monthly public meetings of the total committee were held. These were major media events covered by television and held in places like the ballroom of the Westin Hotel in the Dallas Galleria. Several hundred people attended each of these sessions. Everyone on the committee usually showed up, including Governor White, Lieutenant Governor Hobby, and Speaker of the House Lewis. Many consultants came before the committee at these meetings including John Goodlad, Mortimer J. Adler, and Admiral Hyman Rickover. Every interest group had a chance to be heard, including the forty or so professional education associations.

In addition to the Oversight Committee, subcommittees were organized to work on different phases of the report. The subcommittees were: School Organization and Management; Finance; Educating the Child; The Teaching Profession; Legislative Action; and Public Relations. Each SCOPE member served on two subcommittees which met at least twice a month between the monthly meetings of the whole committee.

The publicity generated by the committee was extensive, mostly due to Perot's personality, reputation, and ability to turn a phrase. Perot's style in leading the committee was an important factor in determining its outcomes. As past experience had shown, when he undertook a project he went all out.

Perot's enemy in the school battle was school administration, particularly superintendents and school boards. Rather than being interested in school improvement he felt that too many boards and superintendents were satisfied with maintaining the status quo and that was the most dangerous position the schools could take in a world characterized by rapid change. He used the Sirota study and personal impressions based on his visits to schools to come to that conclusion. He described superintendents as a "good ol' boys" network, standing in line, holding hands, singing the status quo (Chance, 1986). He did not believe the State Board of Education would make necessary changes either. Therefore, he proposed that the State Board be appointed rather than elected. To Perot this was an essential recommendation that he would not change in the face of opposition by some of the members of SCOPE or even later on when it became a major issue in the legislative debate on House Bill 72.

Perot felt a great deal of empathy for teachers especially after observing and visiting with many of them in their work setting. He felt they worked hard, were underpaid, and were doing the most important of all jobs. On the other hand, incompetence couldn't be tolerated in teaching, he said, because teaching was so important (Chance, 1986).

Perot heard many teachers and other educators make negative comments about their own preparation to be a teacher. Because of this he felt teacher education must be of a low quality. Often he posed the question, "How can anything get such bad evaluations and be any good?" Many teachers who came before the committee during the months of deliberations, especially in the district hearings held throughout the state, said that the only thing worse than their preservice courses was the in-service training they were having to put up with in their current districts.

Perot was very concerned about certification requirements especially for people who, in mid-career, wanted to change their profession to teaching. He felt the lack of flexibility in meeting requirements was a plot designed by colleges of education to expand enrollments. He once stated that if teacher education was a paving job they would be calling it fraud and be putting people in prison. Perot, a believer in options and competition, supported the creation of alternative models for entry to the profession, thinking that such programs would force colleges of education to compete and therefore improve.

In March of 1984 the SCOPE subcommittees delivered their recommendations to the full committee. At the same time, Chairman Perot submitted his amendments. These dealt with: (1) the appointed State Board of Education; (2) career ladders for teachers; (3) teacher testing; (4) State Board of Education authority; (5) annual performance reports from school districts and colleges; (6) management and finance; (7) equalized and simplified allocation of state funds; (8) alternative means of teacher certification; (9) no special state financial support for vocational and distributive education; (10) annualized testing of all students with results to be made public in each district's local annual report; (11) placement of the University Interscholastic League under the supervision of the State Board of Education; and (12) a single-track curriculum.

All of these amendments replaced or revised the recommendations made by the subcommittees; they were simply Chairman Perot's amendments. By the time of the meeting, however, they were being recommended not only by Chairman Perot, but by Governor White, Lieutenant Governor Hobby, and Speaker Lewis. All were included in the final April, 1984, version of the report of the committee.

House Bill 72

The aspects of House Bill 72 (HB 72) which most directly affected teacher education were: (1) advanced academic training, (2) career ladder, and (3) alternative certification. Most of the other aspects of the bill, which was over one hundred pages long, dealt with schooling rather than teacher education. A few of the other recommendations did, indirectly, affect training programs, for example, the section dealing with school discipline required preservice and in-service teachers to take a course in classroom discipline.

The bill concentrated more on rules directed at getting tough with students than did the Select Committee report. The report placed a greater emphasis on child development training than appeared in the bill. House Bill 72 emphasized stricter class attendance, no-pass/no-play, and other elements which emphasized threat as the primary motivation for learning.

Anyone reading the press reports of the committee meetings would have thought that the committee was totally focused on interscholastic activities, particularly football. Actually the main focus of the Select Committee report and the testimony given before the committee was primarily on early childhood education. The recommendations on smaller class sizes in the early grades, preschool programs for four year olds in disadvantaged areas, and mandatory kindergartens were given high priority.

One Select Committee recommendation that did not appear in the bill called for all colleges of education to develop a partnership with a neighboring school district. The purpose of the partnership would be to operate a school in which new ideas in teaching, counseling, and administration could be demonstrated. Perot felt that this would be an ideal way for colleges of education to show knowledge and skill did exist that could improve practice. These proposed schools would not be laboratory schools located on campuses. Instead, they would be "real" schools located in real districts, like the professional development school concept now being advocated by the Holmes Group.

House Bill 72 was a complex piece of legislation. It included many good provisions. A major element of concern to Texas teachers was an increase in salary from a base of $11,200 to $15,200 and provision for a career ladder. Governor White had promised teachers a significant pay raise. This raise presumably allowed him to meet his responsibility. However, increases in salary were traded off for several qualifiers in the bill. In order to support the pay raise, smaller class sizes, and other expensive aspects of the bill, promises of productivity to tax payers were required. These consisted of quality control measures such as the testing of career teachers, the controversial uniform Texas Teacher Appraisal System, and a test to be taken by preservice students and out of staters seeking Texas certification. The test for all current teachers became a lightning rod issue which alienated teachers far more than the promise of greater pay attracted them.

The issues which drew the greatest and most ardent opposition were the teacher tests, no-pass/no-play, and the appointed state board. These issues pitted school personnel against each other, the state, and the Texas Education Agency. Also, these were the issues that contributed to Governor White's eventual loss in a close gubernatorial contest with Bill Clements in 1986.

Select Committee on Higher Education

In 1985 the Sixty-ninth Texas Legislature created, and Governor Mark White appointed, the Select Committee on Higher Education (SCOHE). Interestingly, the then chairperson of the Texas Higher Education Coordinating Board was named to head the SCOHE. The governor appointed himself to the SCOHE along with several key legislators including the lieutenant governor, speaker of the house, chairperson of the Senate Education Committee, and chairperson of the House Higher Education Committee. In addition, several prominent citizens and business leaders were appointed to the twenty-two-person SCOHE. A full-time paid executive director was employed to assist the SCOHE with its work.

The SCOHE met fifty times during its fifteen-month existence and made a comprehensive study of all issues and concerns related to higher education in Texas. Their work included a management audit of public higher education in Texas; three task forces to study the issues in depth and to develop appropriate recommendations; twenty-six meetings of the task forces; two hundred and thirty-five formal briefings; and sixty-four public testimony presentations. The recommendations of the SCOHE were presented to the Seventieth Texas Legislature; many of them resulted in new legislation affecting higher education in Texas.

Select Committee on Higher Education's Task Force on Quality and Access included in its charge a review of teacher education. This task force was chaired by Dr. Earl Lewis, chairperson of the Department of Urban Studies at Trinity University. He invited the Texas Association of Colleges for Teacher Education (TACTE) to provide his task force with position papers on the following topics:

1. What is the case for and against extended teacher education programs?
2. How does current funding of teacher education programs in Texas compare with funding for such programs in the ten largest states? What changes are needed in the funding formula in order to reflect the clinical/laboratory/field-based nature of state-of-the-art teacher education programs?
3. How can universities involve faculty members from across the campus in the development and delivery of teacher education programs? In what ways can universities collaborate with public schools to improve education for the boys and girls of Texas?
4. Should teacher education institutions have a responsibility to assist first-year teachers as they are inducted into the profession? If so, what are some successful models of induction-year programs and how are they funded?

Position papers were written by various members of the TACTE and submitted to the Task Force on Quality and Access. In addition, other relevant materials and information were sent to Dr. Lewis for use by the task force in arriving at its recommendations.

The president of TACTE offered the human resources of the organization to provide additional information or to assist Dr. Lewis' task force in any way as it developed its recommendations on teacher education to be presented to the full Select Committee on Higher Education. No additional input was sought by Dr. Lewis.

In late December 1986, the Task Force on Quality and Access presented its recommendations on teacher education to the Select Committee on Higher Education. Included was a recommendation that five years of postsecondary education be required to secure certification to do precollege teaching in Texas. After much debate by the SCOHE, this recommendation, along with several others, was deleted. Major revisions were made in a number of recommendations made by the Task Force on Quality and Access.

These recommendations served as the basis for the development of Senate Bill 994 which originated in the Senate Education Committee and was passed by the Seventieth Texas Legislature in April 1987. Senator Carl Parker, chairperson of the

Senate Education Committee, was also an active member of the Select Committee on Higher Education and the Task Force on Quality and Access.

SENATE BILL 994

In April 1987 the Seventieth Texas Legislature passed Senate Bill 994 which states, in part:

1. A person who, after September 1, 1991, applies for a teaching certificate for which the rules of the State Board of Education require a bachelor's degree must possess a bachelor's degree received with an academic major or interdisciplinary academic major including reading, other than education, which is related to the Texas school curriculum as defined in chapter 21.101 of the Education Code.
2. After September 1, 1991 no more than eighteen semester credit hours of education courses at the baccalaureate level may be required for the granting of a teaching certificate by the State Board of Education. Included in the hours needed for certification, the State Board of Education shall provide for a minimum number of semester credit hours of student teaching. The board may allow by rule additional credit hours for certification in bilingual education, English as a second language, early childhood education, or special education. (Texas, 1987, Section 1)

This piece of legislation includes several components, but in addition to the two above, two others are of particular interest because of their implications for teacher education policy. They are:

1. Graduates of teacher education programs or persons admitted to alternative certification programs shall be recommended for probationary teacher status for entry into an induction program for their probationary year.
2. The performance of graduates of teacher education programs on the state-mandated tests for graduation from a teacher education program and performance by teachers on the statewide appraisal system implemented in each school district shall be included in the deliberations by the State Board of Education in determin-

ing the accreditation status of each teacher education program. (Texas, 1987, Section 1)

Senate Bill 994 was ostensibly based on the recommendations of the Select Committee on Higher Education (SCOHE). Senator Carl Parker who introduced and secured passage of the bill was also an active member of the SCOHE. During the time Senate Bill 994 was under discussion in the Texas legislature, a new set of certification standards designed to improve teacher education programs was awaiting approval by the newly appointed State Board of Education. In his quest to gain passage of Senate Bill 994, Senator Parker disregarded the proposed tougher standards and, in fact, was openly critical of efforts by professional educators to reform teacher education. He perceived colleges of education to be of lower quality than other colleges and resistant to change. Parker did support some pedagogy in the program but he felt that teacher education students should major in academic subjects.

During the hearings by the Senate Education Committee, chaired by Senator Parker, TACTE and other professional organizations provided testimony in opposition to several aspects of Senate Bill 994. At one point, a member of the Senate Education Committee, apparently swayed by such testimony, offered an amendment that would have excluded students preparing to become elementary school teachers from the provisions of the legislation. A vote was taken on the amendment and it passed by a slight margin. However, Senator Parker would not allow the vote to stand and recessed the committee. Later when the committee reconvened, the amendment was withdrawn. One can only speculate on the lobbying efforts that occurred during that recess.

During the latter discussion stages of Senate Bill 994 pressure was felt by some university presidents. The presidents were in the midst of strong lobbying efforts to pass an omnibus higher education bill which would provide significant increases to the state institutions' budgets. They apparently learned that the efforts of their education deans to change Senate Bill 994 could be counterproductive and might place their larger goals in jeopardy. As a result, the deans of education in some of the largest universities were directed to stop fighting to change Senate Bill 994. At least one dean of education was instructed to draft a letter for his president's signature which supported Senate Bill 994.

Roles of State Agencies in Implementing Senate Bill 994

Now that Senate Bill 994 is law, two state agencies have responsibility for implementing its provisions.

Texas Higher Education Coordinating Board

Senate Bill 994 involves the Texas Higher Education Coordinating Board more directly in the control and administration of teacher education programs in state universities. This is because the Coordinating Board must approve all degree programs and academic majors even though the State Board of Education controls the certification programs. State institutions were informed by the Coordinating Board staff that they must make baccalaureate degree programs which lead to teacher certification available to their students. As a result, even the Texas Holmes Group state institutions will have to develop five-year or fifth-year extended models as alternatives to the required four-year programs. These requirements are based on the Coordinating Board staff interpretations of Senate Bill 994 and not on the language of the law itself. A careful reading of Senate Bill 994 leads one to the conclusion that the eighteen semester hour restriction on professional education courses prevails only for programs leading to a baccalaureate degree. However, members of the Coordinating Board staff base their interpretations on the intent of the law as envisioned by its chief architect, Senator Carl Parker.

Another unwritten but clear interpretation of the law by the Coordinating Board is that no baccalaureate degree program leading to teacher certification shall include more than 139 semester hours of credit. Interestingly, the Coordinating Board imposes no such limitations on other degree programs in state institutions.

The Coordinating Board adopted guidelines which eliminate all degrees involving a major emphasis in education. Even agriculture education, home economics education, and physical education majors are no longer permitted.

Revised teacher certification programs, which require Coordinating Board approval, must be provided within the requirements of an academic major and degree or within an interdisciplinary academic major. The academic or interdisciplinary major must be directly related to subjects taught in the public schools of Texas. Explicit requirements for interdisciplinary academic majors have been developed by the Coordinating Board. No course to be counted in the academic major or interdisciplinary academic major may include pedagogical content. For example, a course titled "Physical Education in the Elementary School" may not be used in the interdisciplinary academic major for prospective elementary school teachers.

Texas Education Agency

The State Board of Education has the responsibility for establishing standards for the accreditation of institutions of higher education offering teacher education programs and for the requirements for certification of all educational personnel. A legislatively created group called the Commission on Standards for the Teaching Profession applies the standards in considering institutional applications for approved teacher education programs. The commissioner of education, who is appointed by the State Board of Education, nominates individuals to serve as members of the Commission on Standards for the Teaching Profession to the state board for approval. Currently, the composition of the commission includes classroom teachers, administrators, support personnel, and representatives of higher education. The State Board of Education has approved new standards for the certification of teachers that incorporate the provisions of Senate Bill 994. Although the number of credit hours in pedagogy was reduced from thirty to eighteen for elementary teachers and from twenty-four to eighteen for secondary teachers, there was no reduction in pedagogical content from Texas Education Agency's 1984 standards to their 1987 standards. However, it should be noted that these standards are stated as minimum, and thus, institutions are limited by the State Board of Education to eighteen semester hours of education courses only if they prepare teachers at the baccalaureate level. The Coordinating Board requirement that institutions must make certification programs available at the baccalaureate level applies only to state universities, thus giving private institutions the flexibility of only offering extended programs if they elect to do so. This discrepancy in the interpretation of Senate Bill 994 by the Coordinating Board and the Texas Education Agency has resulted in confusion for the teacher education institutions.

As indicated earlier, House Bill 72 replaced the elected State Board of Education with an appointed one. The old elected State Board had approved a new set of standards for teacher certification and the accreditation of teacher education institutions in April 1984, just three months before it was abolished and replaced by the appointed board. The 1984 standards were placed on hold by the new State Board of Education so they could be reviewed and possibly revised in light of other reforms mandated by House Bill 72. This was the case even though all but one of the sixty-seven teacher education institutions had received approval for their programs by the Commission on Standards for the Teaching Profession. In Texas, however, the new teacher education programs are not official until acted upon by the State Board of Education. The commissioner of education then informed the institutions that they could continue to operate with the 1984 standards, standards approved earlier in 1972 or 1955, or within any combination of these sets of standards until the state board officially approved the new standards.

The 1984 standards, which had been seven years in the making, were not on the cutting edge but they included dramatic improvements over previous standards. Among other changes, they increased the number of professional education credit hours to a minimum of twenty-four for secondary teachers and thirty for elementary teachers. In addition, the 1984 standards called for six semester hours of reading and significant changes in the general education requirements for prospective teachers.

The State Board of Education was in the process of making final changes in the 1984 standards during the spring of 1987 when Senate Bill 994 was being considered in the legislature. Upon the recommendation of the Commission on Standards for the Teaching Profession, the chairperson of the State Board of Education requested that the legislature not pass Senate Bill 994 and instead allow the 1984 standards to be implemented. This request fell upon deaf ears and Senate Bill 994 became law. As a result, the State Board of Education incorporated the new provisions into the 1984 standards and they became the new 1987 standards. All institutions were then required to resubmit their programs for approval to be implemented in September 1989. This allows for all graduates to meet the new standards by September 1, 1991.

Education Agencies and State Associations

On both HB 72 and SB 994, education associations tried to influence the policy makers and the politicians. Each group had different targets and different priorities. Consequently, no forces combined in a way that was powerful enough to have a great impact. Once the decisions had been made by the politicians and the powers that be, the hearings had little impact on the committee reports or the legislation that implemented the reports.

In the case of HB 72, the state teacher associations and the school administrator groups operated separately from one another. In fact, the teacher lobby ended up in a split over support for the bill in the final days of debate.

Because of the pace at which SB 994 was created and passed through the legislature, the Texas Association of Colleges for Teacher Education came into the picture after most of the decisions had already been made. The state AACTE group has no effective mechanism for day-to-day monitoring of legislative activity. The Texas Holmes Group proposal, titled *A Plan for Quality Education*, was presented to Senator Parker, the Texas Education Agency, and the Texas Higher Education Coordinating Board. It emphasized the completion of an academic major and strong pedagogical preparation, including a supervised internship, in an integrated, sequential combined undergraduate and graduate program of extended teacher education preparation. Senator Parker viewed this and other proposals as an attempt to end-run Senate Bill 994.

Just as at the state level, due to the rapidity in which SB 994 was written and pushed through the legislature, at the national level, AACTE did not make an official response to the issues surrounding Senate Bill 994 until it had become law: Neither the state nor national AACTE had the mechanisms in place to respond to this political situation or the resources to design them. The National Council for Accreditation of Teacher Education (NCATE) considered the implications of the legislation after a member from another state had raised a series of issues regarding its implications nationwide. This dialogue is still in process.

The issue facing NCATE focused on whether or not a state legislature can prescribe the curriculum for a profession and, if so, what are the consequences for professional accreditation standards and procedures. Senate Bill 994 also raised the issue of a legislature's not only prescribing the curriculum, but, in the same piece of legislation, prescribing the tests and evaluation procedures used to evaluate the products of the mandated program and then holding the institutions accountable for the results.

Very few members of the state legislature or other professional groups paid attention to suggestions made by the teacher education arm of the profession either at the state or national level. Whatever influence they had was through the staff of key state agencies or legislators. When professional teacher education associations attempted to gain input directly through formal processes, they were perceived as being motivated by self-interest. The fact that NCATE was a voluntary agency and that it had previously approved some programs that were low quality did not escape the members of the Select Committee or the politicians.

In addition, public testimony from practitioners about the quality of teacher education was always in the background. For ten months the Perot committee had heard few positive comments about teacher education. The major source of information for the Select Committee on Higher Education was an outdated, Southern Regional Education Board (SREB) study (Galambos, 1985) critical of professional education. It did not consider the new program changes that had already been approved by the Commission on Standards for the Teaching Profession.

Furthermore, the SREB study was based on the faulty premise that the more courses a person takes in arts and sciences, the better prepared they are to teach. Instead of comparing the programs of teacher education students with the programs of students training in other professions, the study compared the education students' programs with those of students in liberal arts. If they took fewer courses with arts and science prefixes, it was considered a less worthy program.

Education programs were characterized as easier than other programs. The SREB study and the Select Committee completely disregarded a state study which showed that 70 percent of the sixty-three teacher preparation institutions had implemented higher GPA requirements in teacher education than the institutions' graduation requirements and 84 percent required higher requirements for certification than the institutions' graduation requirements. Due to NCATE and new state standards, most institutions had established higher matriculation requirements for entry into teacher education at the beginning of the junior year than the requirements for staying in the college of arts and sciences. This GPA requirement for entry to teacher education was based on courses taken in arts and science colleges, since Texas' teacher education majors took little or no coursework in education until after the sophomore year. The powers that be preferred to operate on the old "Mickey Mouse course" stereotype rather than examine the state study. That stance fit the political mood of the time.

Lessons Learned

There are many lessons to be learned by teacher educators from the Texas experience. Just a few are highlighted here. These lessons have wide implications. They are important not only for educators in Texas but also in the development of national education policies and practices.

1. *"How terrible is the past that awaits us"* says an old statement in Jewish folklore. Our current plight is due to our unwillingness to change teacher education while we had more control of the process and were not in crisis. Today the consequences of past inaction are coming home to roost, and not just in Texas.

   In 1961 the New Horizons Report of the National Commission on Teacher Education as Professional Standards, chaired by Margaret Lindsey, proposed five-year programs for all elementary and secondary teachers (Lindsey, 1961). This call has been repeated since that time, in ten-year cycles, including in *Educating a Profession* (Howsam, et al., 1986). It has received support and "approval in principle" by boards and the membership of professional organizations but no action has been taken. Many battles have ensued over small potatoes. Deans and faculties of AACTE institutions have fought to get arts and sciences to relinquish three more credit hours of "life space" (the proportion of program credit hours to the total for the degree) for undergraduate teacher education, as if that would bring about reform.

   While the knowledge base of teacher education has expanded, student teaching has become the way to justify teacher education. With side glances at specialty areas such as reading, special education, and bilingual and multicultural education, teacher education has continued to suffer from a "hardening of the categories." Like the famous bird who flies backward to see where he has been, we have charted our course from a rearview perspective. Seldom, if ever, have professional teacher educators flown positively toward the goals we seek via the route we should travel.

Now the rallying cry heard from every major national reform group is to eliminate undergraduate teacher education (Carnegie Commission in *A Nation Prepared*, 1986; National Governors' Association in *Time for Results*, 1989; and the Holmes Group, *Tomorrow's Teachers*, 1986).

It is clear that teacher education will never become more than a minor if it is relegated to compete for life space at the undergraduate level. If education courses are pitted against courses in the academic major, they will never win. Teacher educators would be wiser to recognize that these reports are not calling for the elimination of professional education or pedagogy. Instead, they are calling for an undergraduate baccalaureate degree with a major in a teaching field followed by an integrated professional graduate sequence. In other words, the lesson is to capture the fifth year for teacher education and develop integrated, sequential programs. This is not very different from the program proposed by Lindsey and Stratemeyer thirty years ago. In their model, students could enroll in the teacher education sequence beginning with the junior year and develop a preeducation program, followed by a three-year integrated sequence including a college-supervised internship.

Thirty years ago the most educated people in communities were teachers. Today it is expected that teachers have a baccalaureate degree to be as well educated as the generally educated public. It is not too difficult to read the landscape and recognize that even the reformers who believe in the necessity for pedagogical training realize the necessity for an academic major and a sound general education. Instead of fighting it, the teacher training arm should support it as the National Education Association and the American Federation of Teachers (AFT) have supported it for the past twenty years.

Continuing resistance to such change reinforces the analysis that teacher educators have been the albatross around the neck of the teaching profession. Most teacher education programs are the same today as they were twenty years ago except for a shift of the distribution of courses from foundational topics to student teaching. At least two reasons can be given for the lack of change: (1) self-interest in maintaining the status quo; and (2) too many teacher educators wouldn't know what to do with the extra time even if they had it. Too many have not stayed abreast with the knowledge base for teacher education which has exploded during the last twenty years (Reynolds, 1989).

2. *Education is a "many splintered" thing.* Every education association and agency provided testimony to the study committees and legislative hearings during the course of the debates on the legislation reported in this Texas case. Unfortunately, they did so as individual organizations and not as a unit. There was no one voice speaking for the education profession. In many cases professional associations were pitted against each other: administrators against teachers, English teachers against vocational educators, etc. The higher education community was silent on issues such as teacher salaries and career ladder and the teacher groups were silent on the teacher education legislation. Because the legislation was so comprehensive and contained so many pieces, each group fought for its own special priority. The politicians liked the splintering because they did not have to deal with the full power that a unified profession could have wielded.

The lack of comprehensive change in schools and teacher education institutions during the last thirty years has not been a result of our failure to conceptualize education adequately. On the contrary, the concepts and recommendations for improving teacher education have been in existence for a long, long time, but they have not moved from thought to action.

We have approached educational change as if it were a logical, educational process. This is the reason for the lack of action. Instead, we must proceed from the premise that changing schools and teacher education involves political, economic, and social reforms as well as educational reforms. Our strategies must connect with those dimensions of society and be powerful enough to have an impact on them. Unless we do that, educational policy making is a waste of time. Education is not simply influenced by politics, it *is* politics. Furthermore, to expect political decision making to be logical is illogical. We must understand and use political strategies to get attention and to have influence. We must reorganize our professional associations with this purpose in mind. Our state and national AACTE associations are not as effective as they might be if they were structured to be proactive in the political action arena. We have not looked at the mission of our professional organizations that way and have not invested the resources in them to equip them with the capacity to take on this role. Furthermore, we have not defined the roles of our executive directors and their staffs to accomplish this mission, especially as it relates to assisting state units to shape or influence impending legislation.

The above notwithstanding, the Texas deans of education must shoulder some of the blame for perceived inactivity on the part of AACTE. The executive director asked for official directions from the state unit two years ago, but apparently the organization cannot decide on a course of action because at this writing the state association has not made a decision regarding how or if AACTE can be helpful. In short, the Texas deans have been unable to create a common political strategy, solicit the support of the various Texas teacher and administrator organizations, and convince Senator Parker that the caps imposed on pedagogy by SB 994 are not educationally sound.

If the constituent groups represented in schools and universities were to conceive of themselves as members of the same profession, they would represent the largest work force in the country. The potential to touch all spheres and levels of influence is unequaled for such a coalition as a professional group, especially if it keeps its values straight. If it kept the focus clearly on the goal of developing caring, rigorous, innovative, quality schools for all of America's children and the design of professional programs and research development policies and procedures to foster them, it would represent power with a purpose.

If this new education coalition started moving in a long, wide line, in one direction, toward a targeted politician or policy maker, it would get action on its recommendations. This will not happen if the professional associations which represent teachers and teacher education remain splintered.

3. *The future of teacher education and the future of teaching are inextricably interlocked.* It is critical that new directions in teacher education be embedded in and consonant with equally innovative directions in school renewal. Major reform in one cannot occur without concurrent reform in the other. School and university professionals must be partners in simultaneous school/teacher-education reform. Unless we can make this connection between theory and practice we will not gain the support of classroom teachers.

Those of us who work in the training arm of this profession must accept a vivid truth: if the content of teacher education cannot be used in the workplace of the teacher then colleges of education will continue to be viewed as out-of-touch and obsolete.

Teachers are leaving the profession not only because they and their families cannot survive on their salaries but because the conditions to practice their *profession* do not exist widely.

Up to now, campus-based teacher educators have done little to help improve either the conditions in which school teachers work or the rewards teachers receive for their labors. In fact, the reverse is more than likely true. Some professors have made a living by criticizing the schools. College professors generally have not seen themselves in a common enterprise with elementary and secondary teachers; they certainly have not been their advocates in legislative halls.

It is no wonder that teacher organizations find little reason to testify in support of improved teacher education. Too often they see themselves as members of a culture different from that of the professional teacher educator. Teachers are controlled by a different set of rules, roles, expectations, and rewards. They have other items on their unfinished agenda. College professors are often viewed as teachers who escaped from the front lines to the ivory tower. Unless new models of teacher education such as professional development schools emerge, college teacher educators and school teachers will become even more separated and will be more likely to support a separate system of training, on-site in their own districts sanctioned by state agency alternative certification mechanisms. The apprentice model rather than the internship model may become the predominant pattern for training especially in urban areas.

If teacher education institutions do not want to be out in the cold, a high priority in college faculty meeting discussions must be given to developing partnerships with schools and teachers. After all, this should not be too hard—they are our graduates. The building of these partnerships should begin before the students graduate.

Instead of expecting arts and sciences faculties to defend us when we battle state legislatures, we should look to our constituent group, the teaching profession. We are the training and development arm of the teaching profession. The history of America and the history of professions demonstrates that no profession is any stronger than its development arm. We need to convey that message to the National Education Association and the American Federation of Teachers.

Also, we need to remind the faculties of colleges of education that the future of teacher education is inextricably interwoven with the future of teaching in the schools. Teacher education will improve in direct relationship to the improvement in the status of teachers in society. We will be able to improve teacher education if we reform the school, create the conditions for professional practice, pay teachers a decent salary commensurate with training, and develop other career-long incentives which will attract and retain the kind of teacher-scholars needed. Improve the status of teachers and we will change the funding formulas for teacher education. Use teacher education as an instrument to reform the school setting so that teachers are treated as professional decision makers instead of executors of someone else's orders and we will get the "necessary revolution" we need in teacher education.

It is my contention that every aspect of education, including teacher education, is affected by the public's view of the importance of teaching. The movement to empower teachers could be the movement that places colleges of education in an equally important position. At long last the public may have realized that the aspirations of America cannot rise any higher than the quality of America's teachers and the institutions which prepare them.

We must eliminate the barriers that separate schools from colleges and the barriers that separate educational associations at both the state and national level. The people who have the most to lose by not acting are members of colleges of education. In the current context of change, the most risky position is to try to maintain the status quo.

4. *Excellence cannot be created by fiat; reform through regulation does not work.* Top down rule making produces a straight jacket that is counterproductive for students and teachers. If reform is to take place, it must be focused on the interaction among the student, the teacher, and the curriculum. Any attempted reform that does not affect that interaction positively will not succeed.

McNeil (1987), in her article "The Politics of Texas School Reform," points out that the educational restructuring in Texas may provide an analytical forum for questioning links in other states between economic ills and expected educational remedies. She suggests that the Texas "top down" model for change is anachronistic and contradictory to the rhetoric of highly technological and inventive economic futures. Instead of producing entrepreneurs and people who can produce new uses for the new technology, it will produce just the opposite. Bureaucratic controls that come with state testing, uniform state-mandated appraisal systems, and standardized curriculum all limit risk taking, experimentation, visionary possibilities, and open-ended instructional purpose. The rigidity and controls embedded in Texas school regulations threaten to undermine even the very economic basis for education they are purported to advance. Taken seriously, the rhetoric of tying education to a restructuring of the economy would demand a serious level of creativity and a spirit of innovation not typical of reforms. The very idea of teaching as a profession is threatened to the extent that legislative reform limits the autonomy and flexibility of creative teachers. The extremes of the Texas model may serve one purpose: perhaps by the negative example of those policies that are most shortsighted and have the effect of deskilling teachers the most, Texas reinforces a graphic call for a reform that will ground teaching and learning in the needs of children.

McNeil's (1987) studies of the effects of top down, lock-step reform on magnet schools showed that centralized, minimum standards had the effect of raising the level of the worst teaching. In many schools, according to McNeil, they have had more effect on the upper level of quality (and on the morale of the best teachers) than on the raising of minimum standards. This kind of unintended consequence (and it is impossible to believe any of the reformers wanted these effects from their well-intended policies) must be addressed before other states, and especially the federal government, institutes minimum standards of content through a national student assessment program or national system for appraising teacher performance. The Texas scenario may enlighten other states if it brings to light the futility of trying to sacrifice professional decision making for the sake of ease in accounting. As McNeil says, "...education will be truly reformed when it can be a public good in its diversity, not in artificial uniformities" (McNeil, 1987, p. 215).

2

DAVID L. COLTON AND BARBARA M. SIMMONS

New Mexico:

Caps on Content

Education reform proposals in the 1980s emphasized the need for more teacher preparation in the arts and sciences. Whether this additional preparation was to be accomplished by deferring pedagogical training until after completion of an arts and sciences degree, or by placing caps on the hours of pedagogical study within an undergraduate program, or by requiring that teachers receive their degrees in arts and sciences, the message was the same: an arts and sciences major for teachers was essential to improved academic performance of American youth.

New Mexico's State Board of Education gave the matter a unique twist. Late in 1989 Albuquerque newspaper pundit Jim Arnholz mused upon items that had accumulated on his desk during an out-of-state vacation:

> Now what's this?
>
> The State Board of Education is sending a clear message to its two leading universities: If you people insist on having future teachers learn as much as possible about the subjects they will teach, we'll show you. We won't hire them.
>
> Do I have that right? The Board of Education says the University of New Mexico and New Mexico State exceed state standards, which leaves the Board of Education only one option: It won't certify teachers who know too much about the subject they teach.
>
> That has a certain appeal for me. I'm comfortable with it. I'm beginning to feel like I'm back home. (October 3, 1989)

Arnholz was referring to a recent flurry of newspaper articles reporting state officials' refusal to approve secondary teacher preparation programs in science, social studies, and language arts at the University of New Mexico (UNM) and New Mexico State University (NMSU), the state's two research universities. The refusal, the papers said, was based on the fact that the universities' proposed programs exceeded the board's credit hour cap on preparation in a teaching field.

This chapter reviews the circumstances leading to the state board's decision to cap training in teaching fields, the decision by UNM and NMSU to exceed the cap, the state's decision to insist upon adherence to it, and the eventual resolution of the issue. The story offers insights into the politics of teacher education and the conditions which make for effective and ineffective participation in those politics.

The Setting

Except in Albuquerque, Las Cruces, and Santa Fe, New Mexico's immense spaces are thinly populated. Schools are small and widely separated. The State Board of Education (SBE) has a preponderance of members from rural areas. Rural district problems dominate the board's agenda. One such problem, voiced with growing intensity as the decade of the 1980s began, focused on rural and small city district officials' reports of difficulty in obtaining sufficient numbers of multiply-licensed teachers, and the frequency with which it was necessary to obtain licensure waivers. The problem was attributed to teacher training programs.

Five public universities provide most of the teacher training in New Mexico. Three are regional master's-level institutions—Eastern (ENMU), Western (WNMU), and Highlands (NMHU). Two are comprehensive research universities—The University of New Mexico (UNM) in Albuquerque and New Mexico State University (NMSU) in Las Cruces. Because of their urban locales and student demographics, UNM and NMSU are particularly sensitive to the needs of large school districts, while ENMU, NMHU, and WNMU are more oriented to the needs of rural and small city schools. Moreover, in the two research universities the academic disciplines and the expectation of disciplinary mastery are more dominant than they are in the smaller regional institutions. These differing institutional orientations, coupled with the rural orientation of the state board and the State Department of Education (SDE), helped fuel the conflict which developed over teacher licensure and preparation during the period from 1985 to 1990.

As in most states, teacher preparation in New Mexico is a responsibility of the universities while teacher licensure is a responsibility of the State Board of Education. In 1966 the board adopted an "approved program" policy whereby institutions offering teacher preparation programs approved by the board became de facto licensing units. Under the policy, an institutional recommendation signifying completion of a board-approved program virtually assured issuance of a state license to teach. Thus, once the board approved a university teacher preparation program, the board's authority effectively ceased. The board's program approval decisions were based on the recommendations of a semi-autonomous Professional Standards Commission, created in 1977 as a response to legislative pressure to professionalize licensure. The system was flawed. Like most "good government" schemes designed to insulate licensing and hiring decisions from partisan and personal politics, the New Mexico licensure system became increasingly insensitive to bona fide personnel needs in the schools. Thus the Professional Standards Commission, created in response to one set of political concerns, inadvertently gave rise to another. Dismay was particularly apparent in the small rural schools. A Small Schools Task Force was created within the Professional Standards Commission to study the problem of training and licensing teachers for such settings, but the task force produced no solutions (Minutes, Professional Standards Commission, 1982–1984).

State Board of Education member Herb Walsh, from the sparsely populated Gallup-McKinley district, thought that the program approval system was the culprit. In 1982 he asked Alan Morgan, Assistant Superintendent for Instruction, and Jeanne Knight, Director of Elementary and Secondary Education, to prepare a comprehensive assessment of the program approval system. Their report, presented to the board in mid-1983, emphasized "inequities" in the implementation of the board's licensure standards: programs varied from institution to institution, and almost all institutions had requirements exceeding the board's. An appendix summarized concerns expressed in a survey of district personnel directors. During board discussions of the report, Walsh said "that the inequities...would continue to exist as long as the state board made no effort to retain its certification (licensure) authority" (SBE Minutes, August 22, 1983, pp. 12–18).

Most New Mexico college of education deans reacted indignantly, believing that Walsh, Morgan, and Knight sought to destroy the program approval system and the autonomy of the Professional Standards Commission. Rather than destroying the program approval system, the deans contended, the system should be streamlined. Late in 1983 the education deans at UNM and NMSU wrote to the commission urging it to simplify the system and give more attention to the differing needs of urban and rural districts (D. Byrne and D. Colton, November 17, 1983). The Professional Standards Commission did not respond.

Dissatisfaction grew. Much finger pointing occurred. Some blamed the Director of Licensure, claiming that he had been co-opted by the teacher training institutions and the Professional Standards Commission. Some blamed board members who appointed the commission and approved its recommendations. Some blamed the universities, and particularly the college of education deans who were said to exercise disproportionate influence on the commission.

Calls for reform intensified. In 1984 a Governor's Commission on Public Schools, which included the UNM education dean, recommended formation of a Task Force on Teacher Preparation and Licensing to address issues of quality among new teachers, the "fragmented and cumbersome" character of the licensing system, and the need to make special adaptations for small schools (Governor's Commission on Public Schools, 1984). However, the governor was increasingly unpopular, and his call evoked no response. In 1985 the legislature adopted several memorials requesting its standing Legislative Education Study Committee (LESC) to analyze teacher preparation and licensure in New Mexico. In addition, the legislature created a powerful School Reform Commission which was to devise a comprehensive school reform plan for the 1986 legislative session. The warning signal to the State Board of Education was clear: the legislature was seizing the school reform initiative.

Thus the stage was set. All agreed that the existing licensure system needed reform. The education deans at UNM and NMSU, the governor, the legislature, some state board members, and some State Department of Education officials were seeking change. The UNM and NMSU deans viewed themselves as advocates and leaders of teacher licensure reform, but they wrongly concluded that they would be integral participants in the licensure reform process. State board and department officials had a different strategy in mind (Professional Standards Commission Minutes, June 24, 1985).

THROWING DOWN THE GAUNTLET

The 1984 elections, heavily infused with school reform rhetoric, brought seven new members to the ten-member New

Mexico Board of Education. One of the hold-overs was Herb Walsh. As noted above, Walsh was convinced that the board should assert more control over teacher licensure. He had privately written to the universities to obtain descriptions of their approved programs and he had confirmed that many of them exceeded the licensure requirements adopted by the board. That upset him. It upset him that the Professional Standards Commission had endorsed and the board had approved these programs (D. Colton and H. Walsh, 1983–1985). In 1984 Walsh was the sole negative vote in a motion to approve NMSU teacher education programs in several fields; board minutes report that "Mr. Walsh...said he would vote against approval because the programs exceeded the requirement established by the state board" (SBE Minutes, March 1, 1984, p. 8). Thereafter, each university program approval action would evoke the same question from Walsh: did the university exceed board licensure credit hour requirements? (SBE Minutes, April 30, 1984, p. 15; September 27, 1984, p. 16). A Walsh strategy, the significance of which the deans would not grasp until far too late, was to reconstitute the commission; early in 1984 Walsh persuaded the board to adopt a motion making the terms of all members of the Professional Standards Commission expire in June, 1985 (SBE Minutes, April 30, 1984, pp. 15–16).

Until the 1984 elections, college of education deans viewed Walsh as a bit of a crank. However, his voice seemed a solitary one, and little attention was paid to it. That was unfortunate, for in January, 1985, the mostly new board elected hold-over Walsh as its president (SBE Minutes, January 14, 1985). In New Mexico the board presidency is a powerful position with respect to agenda formation. At his first board meeting as president, Walsh solicited testimony from numerous groups and individuals concerning their recommendations for priority items. Assistant Superintendent Morgan urged that attention be given to teacher preparation and licensure—a proposal echoed by many others who testified. The UNM dean, still anticipating a collaborative approach and speaking for the New Mexico Association of Colleges of Teacher Education (NMACTE), also called for licensure reform, noting that the board "had an excellent opportunity to encourage collaboration among elementary, secondary, and postsecondary institutions" (SBE Minutes, January 14, 1985, p. 24).

Walsh, Morgan, and Knight had a different game plan. A "white paper" was drafted within the Department for presentation at the March, 1985, board meeting. Morgan promised to involve NMACTE. But as the board meeting date approached, no "white paper" appeared. The UNM dean, also serving as NMACTE president, wrote to Morgan, reminding him of his promise to involve the education deans in the design of new approaches to teacher education and licensure and recalling a recent controversy over teacher testing: "Our recent history has made it painfully apparent that after-the-fact participation tends to be adversarial rather than cooperative" (D. Colton, March 12, 1985).

A few days later the deans received the "white paper." Its many proposals for reform of teacher preparation and licensure were mixed together with attacks on teacher educators and teacher education (Knight, 1985). NMACTE members were shocked and incensed—partly by their exclusion from the fashioning of such a comprehensive reform document, partly by the lack of time for input prior to the board meeting at which the paper was to be presented, partly by several recommendations which seemed to indicate a state takeover of teacher preparation, and partly by the view stated in the paper that teacher educators were resisting improvement rather than welcoming it.

At a meeting among Morgan, Walsh, and teacher educators three days before the board meeting, a heated discussion occurred (Professional Standards Commission Task Force, Minutes, March 25, 1985). Morgan agreed to tone down the document; however, the toning down involved style, not substance. The SDE had staked out its position: teacher preparation, licensure, and hiring were to be thoroughly reconfigured. The reform agenda was to be defined by the SDE with little participation from teacher educators.

The deans speculated upon the causes of their exclusion. Did the state officials in Santa Fe want to control teacher preparation and licensure in order to gain favor with their clients in rural district personnel offices? Were the Santa Fe people suspicious and jealous of university professors and administrators? Were ideological differences the source of the difficulty? Did they not understand that the way to promote change in colleges of education and colleges of arts and sciences was to secure participation at the outset? In retrospect, the deans attached insufficient weight to the regulatory orientation of Walsh and the department and to the top-down thrust of the entire first wave of school reform in the 1980s. The deans greatly underestimated the animosity which Walsh and others felt toward higher education and teacher educators in particular. Walsh wanted no part of discourse and accommodations; what he wanted was firmness and control executed by his board.

JUGGERNAUT

The Walsh-dominated board moved swiftly to implement its agenda. Just before the board's March 1985 meeting, the chief state school officer suddenly resigned. An interim chief was named, and Walsh took charge (SBE Minutes, March 28, 1985). He named Associate Superintendent Knight—a principal architect of the "white paper"—as chairperson of a Steering Committee for Teacher Preparation and Licensure (SBE Minutes, May 2, 1985, p. 2). From that post she would control agendas, appoint task forces, and select information for distribution. On the board, Walsh influenced votes. In previous years Walsh's voice was the only one favoring denial of program approval when a university program exceeded the hours included in the state's licensure regulations; however, by May 1985 he had enough votes to block the lame duck Professional Standards Commission's recommendation to approve three programs at NMHU (SBE Minutes, May 2, 1985). That institution, preoccupied with other problems, swiftly capitulated, lowering its requirements in order to fall within Walsh's ceiling (Professional Standards Commission Minutes, June 6, 1985).

In July, Morgan, who shared Walsh's small-school orientation, was appointed as chief state school officer (SBE Minutes, July 23, 1985). A week earlier the certification director, a proponent of the planned program approach to teacher preparation and licensure, had resigned his position, stating that he was "concerned that some individuals are pursuing these [teacher preparation and licensure] issues for publicity, power, and self-esteem," and criticizing "an individual's obsession to discontinue this process" [of program approval] (J. Pierce, March 17, 1985). It was widely assumed that the reference was to Walsh. A new certification director, sympathetic to the Walsh-Morgan-Knight orientation, promptly was chosen (SBE Minutes, July 23, 1985, p. 10). In August the rout of the old system was largely completed when the board completely reconstituted the Professional Standards Commission and greatly intensified board oversight of commission operations (SBE Minutes, August 23, 1985, p. 43). With the new cast of characters in place on the board, in the department, and on the commission, the education deans were shut out of the licensure reform process.

Favoring licensure reform, but denied an opportunity to participate in redesign activities, the deans turned to other forums, hoping that the SDE would deduce that it would be better to include the deans in the in-house dialogue than to have them free wheeling in other forums. The deans testified at Legislative Education Study Committee hearings and at hearings by the special interim Public School Reform Commission (NMACTE, 1985, 1986).

In these forums NMACTE representatives always expressed their support for licensure reform and always stated their hope that collaborative reform with the board would be possible. However, the deans were on delicate ground. Their testimony often was muted and ineffective. The deans could not object to reform, because they favored it. They could not mount a broad attack on the board or department for fear of triggering retaliation against existing and future contracts which the board controlled. They could not instigate legislative wrath against the state board and the department, because legislatively driven reforms might be worse than those of the board and department. Indeed, the most powerful senator in the state was publicly advocating abolition of colleges of education (Legislative Education Study Committee Hearing, May 26, 1986). His view was symptomatic of a deeper anti-teacher sentiment which would lead to legislative recision of teacher tenure in 1986. Moreover, the national media were railing against teacher preparation and colleges of teacher education. It was virtually impossible to neutralize suspicions that the deans sought to be included in the reform process merely to protect their institutions' interests—as board president Walsh contended they had been doing all along.

Nonetheless, NMACTE members continued to hope that they would be participants in the licensure reform process. A few hopeful signs materialized. When UNM's programs came up for board approval in mid-1985, Walsh pointed out that several of the programs exceeded SBE requirements, but the board voted to approve the UNM programs anyway (SBE Minutes, June 24, 1985). Sporadic lobbying of individual board members suggested that some members might be won over; for example, one of the board members who voted against Morgan's appointment as chief state school officer spoke out on the importance of including the colleges of education in the design phases of the new licensure and teacher preparation program (SBE Minutes, July 23, 1985, p. 9).

In late summer there was a mini-summit: Walsh, Morgan, Knight, the new certification director and the deans met to discuss their differences (NMACTE, August 28, 1985). Walsh's hostility toward NMACTE was palpable. The UNM and NMSU deans concluded that their participation in licensure reform was not acceptable to the board and SDE. The deans began to speak out against Walsh, depicting him as an advocate of lowered standards and of a return to the "bad old days" preceding the program approval system and the Professional Standards Commission. The UNM dean suggested that Walsh was seeking to establish an Orwellian regime in which minimum standards became ceilings (D. Colton, October, 17, 1985). Surreptitious voices—some of them from within the State Department of Education—cheered for the UNM and NMSU deans. However, the regional institutions, each with its own internal problems of enrollment and leadership, quietly removed themselves from the fray. The task of speaking out fell upon UNM and NMSU.

Meanwhile, Walsh and SDE personnel pressed ahead with the task of designing a new system of teacher preparation and licensure (J. Knight, July 8, 1985). In July, Knight issued a call for volunteers to serve on five task forces that were to consider changes in teacher preparation and licensure. Charges for the task forces were drawn up in a fashion which made it difficult for members to obtain a picture of the whole plan being designed by the department staff (J. Knight, September 16, 1985).

When the list of task force members was released in the fall, the form of the ultimate impasse between the board and UNM/NMSU could be discerned. Of the eighty task force members, not a single person was from arts and science faculties (SDE, Task Force Membership, 1985). To UNM and NMSU the omission seemed particularly ominous because both institutions had education deans who were committed to the view that improvement of teacher education required increased engagement with arts and sciences faculty members rather than exclusion of them.

However, the omission of arts and sciences faculty members ultimately provided a golden opportunity for the education deans. By focusing on the importance of arts and sciences involvement in teacher preparation, the deans could link themselves to the nationwide reform movement, avoid the charge that they were merely protecting their own institutional turf, and perhaps establish some credibility with faculty groups traditionally hostile toward teacher education. In November the UNM dean wrote a lengthy letter to Walsh and the board criticizing the absence of arts and sciences faculty members on the task forces and pointing out that "a reform commission which does not take the disciplines into account will not have much credibility." The rest of the letter contained numerous criticisms of the reform strategy (D. Colton, November 6, 1985). Walsh never responded. In January he was deposed as board president (SBE Minutes, January 29, 1986).

His successor was Catherine Smith, a tough-minded veteran elementary school principal from a rural district. Smith, unlike Walsh, was not opposed to the planned program concept. She saw it as a device for asserting board control over university teacher preparation programs (SBE Minutes, January 29, 1986).

However, Smith was not sympathetic to the idea of strengthened preparation in arts and sciences disciplines. She saw academic major requirements as interfering with the availability of teachers qualified to teach in multiple fields. She sought academic generalists—teachers who could be licensed in two or three teaching fields (SBE Minutes, October 2, 1986, p. 2). Moreover, the fields were to be broadly defined, e.g., science, language arts, social studies. Concentration in a single discipline such as chemistry or history was antithetical to that goal. Smith believed that twenty-four hours of study in a broad field was sufficient for an entry-level teacher. Thus it would be possible to complete the legislature's fifty-four–hour general studies requirement, a teacher education sequence of thirty hours, and twenty-four–hour endorsement programs in two or even three teaching fields. However, to attain this goal, universities would have to cap their education and arts and sciences requirements.

As Smith's agenda was coming into focus in early 1986, the national reform agenda was concentrating on arts and sciences mastery. The reports of the Holmes Group and the Carnegie Forum celebrated the central role of arts and sciences and the importance of teacher mastery of subject matter. These emphases paralleled the orientations of UNM and NMSU. Both joined the Holmes Group—further distancing themselves from the regional institutions. As the UNM and NMSU campuses embraced the Holmes Group emphasis on rigor in teacher preparation, the Smith view that twenty-four hours would prepare a teacher to teach all the sciences, or all the social sciences, or all the language arts brought incredulous responses at the two universities. Task force members had a ready explanation: they were being manipulated by department staff members oriented to the needs of small districts.

However, Smith was concerned about much more than the rural constituency of the board and the department. Smith and the board urgently sought to head off further legislative interference with board prerogatives—a desire shared by the deans and most school personnel (SBE Minutes, January 20, 1986, pp. 42–46). The legislature's adoption of the School Reform Commission's plan was a stinging defeat for the board and the State Department of Education, as was legislative approval of a referendum which would add five gubernatorially appointed members to the board (SBE Minutes, March 6, 1986, pp. 38-41; June 26, 1986, Appendix). All of this seemed to strengthen the resolve of President Smith, Superintendent Morgan, and Associate Superintendent Knight: speed was critical (SBE Minutes, March 6, 1986, pp. 24–25, 59).

Pleas from UNM and NMSU to become involved were interpreted as moves designed to delay and defeat licensure reform, and as invitations to legislative intervention. Thus the UNM and NMSU deans, with their persistent questions and complaints, came to be viewed as board adversaries.

By late 1985 the task forces, appointed during the Walsh era and guided by Knight, had turned in their recommendations to the department. In the ensuing months SDE staff members selected and merged elements from the reports and developed a whole new framework for teacher preparation and licensure. The system was competency-based rather than course-based, included a career ladder concept, emphasized broad teaching fields rather than narrow academic specializations, and permitted direct SDE licensure of teachers trained in other states. Much of the proposed new framework was welcomed by the education deans (SBE Minutes, April 10, 1986; May 1, 1986).

However, the design was flawed. At a hearing in which the new framework was first unveiled to the board, NMACTE's spokesperson expressed concern about "a built-in unexamined contradiction between credit-based and competency-based teacher training." He urged the board that more study should be undertaken as to how concepts of course counting and competency-based training could be merged (SBE Minutes, April 10, 1986, p. 17). The concern applied not only to pedagogical competencies already elaborated by the task forces but also to the competencies which would be developed by future task forces in each of the teaching fields.

The SDE proposed to resolve these difficult matters by fiat. Pedagogical competencies were to be taught within thirty hours. When the deans objected that an arbitrary limit was not equally applicable in elementary education, secondary education, and special education, discussions ensued, adjustment were made, and the issue of caps in the pedagogical area was resolved amicably.

However, the issue of caps in the teaching fields was another matter altogether. The task forces, it will be recalled, contained no representatives from the traditional arts and sciences disciplines. Thus, no voices of dissent were heard when the SDE staff proposed that content area endorsements could be issued upon completion of twenty-four hours in a teaching field, and when these teaching fields were defined not as single disciplines, but as broad fields (i.e., "Science," "Social Studies," "Language Arts") (SDE, "Proposed Licensure System Framework", April 11, 1986). NMACTE objected, and the hour limit in the teaching field was raised to thirty-six. But thirty-six hours would not be enough to settle the issue of caps on content.

JOINING FORCES

Serious discussions between arts and sciences and college of education faculty members about competencies and broad field specializations began when new SBE-appointed task forces were formed to specify competencies in the broad field endorsement areas of science, language arts, math, and social studies. Guidelines of national professional societies, such as the National Council of Teachers of English and the National Council of Teachers of Mathematics, were consulted. Task force members were given little time to formulate their recommendations and to consult with their colleagues. Members were told by chairs not to discuss the number of hours needed to meet the competencies.

The new Professional Standards Commission, charged with the task of implementing the board's framework, insisted that the competencies must be taught within the thirty-six credit hours allowed by the board. Faculty experts from the academic disciplines never were asked how many hours would be required to meet the competencies. An analogy used by many was that the competencies were created, then the "bucket" to hold the competencies was given to the individuals responsible for writing the academic programs. Except for individuals writing the math programs, arts and sciences personnel viewed the bucket of thirty-six hours as insufficient to permit both breadth and depth of study.

The three regional institutions in the state decided to accept the Professional Standards Commission caps on content; programs from these institutions promptly were approved by the commission. University of New Mexico and NMSU faculties met on their own campuses and attended commission subcommittee meetings to express their concern about the loss of academic majors in the sciences, social studies, and language arts. At the January, 1987, board meeting the arts and sciences dean of NMSU, speaking for himself and his counterpart at UNM, objected to the elimination of academic majors. The New Mexico State Federation of Teachers spokesperson also objected to the reduction in training requirements (SBE Minutes, January 1987, pp. 23–25). During the March 1987 meeting, the UNM Dean of Arts and Sciences told board members that UNM and NMSU were designing slightly modified majors in one area of science, social studies or language arts, with a distributive minor. He stated that in some cases the caps on hours would need to be exceeded slightly. He also strongly supported the Holmes Group recommendation for rigor in teacher education programs.

Involvement in Holmes Group activities strengthened the tie between UNM and NMSU. Information gained by arts and sciences and COE faculty members who attended Holmes Group conferences supported their belief that students needed both in-depth knowledge and broad field training before they could be competent entry-level teachers. On several occasions the NMSU arts and sciences dean spoke to Holmes Group audiences about the collaborative efforts of the two institutions.

In June the dispute between UNM/NMSU and the Professional Standards Commission became public. The front page of the *Albuquerque Journal* had a headline stating: "Teacher Training Plan Is Question of Degrees." Columnist Miller stated: "Efforts to revamp the New Mexico teacher certification system could water down standards as teachers are forced to become generalists in many subjects rather than experts in one or two." The importance of the National Board for Professional Teaching Standards was mentioned, and the UNM College of Education dean was quoted: "The SBE has reduced the expectations for teachers' mastery of subject matter. I think that's very much opposed to national trends which stress that teachers be the real masters of their subjects" (C. Miller, June 26, 1987).

The *Journal* article included a quotation from John Mitchell, president of the New Mexico Federation of Teachers (NMFT): "Watering down standards won't help our professional image." During the preceding months Mitchell, testifying at the same legislative forums as the NMACTE deans, had noted that his organization was concerned about many of the same issues as the deans. NMACTE and NMFT testimony on certification issues often was similar. Both groups were concerned about standards, and about representation on the task forces. In March, Mitchell had urged the SBE to demonstrate "intellectual integrity and courage" and to show that it "really cares about children" by raising the ceiling on training in the content areas (SBE Minutes, March 5, 1987, pp. 34–35).

In August the arts and sciences deans, college of education deans, and about twenty-five arts and sciences and college of education faculty from NMSU and UNM met together. The unprecedented meeting was indicative of the institutions' desire to work cooperatively with each other in order to improve teacher education. In a follow-up letter to Associate Superintendent Knight, who had attended the meeting, the four deans stated their understanding that the thirty-six–hour limitation could be exceeded if additional competencies were identified (D. Colton, T. Gale, B. Simmons, and H. Wildenthal, July 20, 1987).

At a second joint meeting of arts and sciences and COE faculty and administrators from UNM and NMSU a decision was made to design broad field minors and retain disciplinary majors, even if the thirty-six–hour limit was exceeded. For example, a student with a broad field science endorsement might select chemistry as a major focus, but would still take other science courses to complete the broad field minor.

At a third joint meeting of the four faculties and deans, the proposed endorsement programs from the two institutions were compared in order to assure that their deviations from the state standard were similar and hence would prevent giving the state an opportunity to split UNM and NMSU by approving one and not the other. Subsequently the deans met with Superintendent Morgan urging his support of the proposed programs. Morgan stated his desire to cooperate with UNM and NMSU; however, his support was not forthcoming.

In March, 1989, UNM and NMSU presented their programs to the Professional Standards Commission. Arts and sciences faculty members spoke forcefully in support of the programs. The math endorsements, which fell within the thirty-six–hour cap, were approved. Science, language arts, and social studies, which exceeded the thirty-six–hour cap, were not approved. The presenters suggested new competencies as the rationale for additional hours. However, the commission declared that the proposed new competencies were already included in the board's original list. When an arts and sciences faculty member asked if it was possible to write any additional competencies that would be accepted, the commission chair stated: "I can't think of any" (Professional Standards Commission Meeting, March 30, 1989).

After learning of the commission's decision, the university presidents at UNM and NMSU wrote a letter to President Smith asking for reconsideration of the decision to place ceilings on the language arts, science, and social studies broad field endorsements. President Smith responded with a letter asking UNM and NMSU to submit position papers for a public hearing scheduled for late September, 1989. The commission also would prepare a position paper. The UNM/NMSU paper stated that the commission should not reject programs in secondary science, social studies and language arts simply because the programs exceeded the state minimums. The point was made that most of the NMSU/UNM programs had satisfied the state credit hour requirements. Even in the three disputed programs, credit hour requirements would not greatly exceed state requirements—and in no case would they exceed normal bachelor's-level degree requirements. The paper argued for high standards and both depth and breadth of training in the content areas. The paper further stated that the dispute occurred because arts and sciences specialists were not included on the 1985–86 task forces which placed ceilings on subject matter preparation programs.

The commission's position paper (September 1, 1989) made three basic points: (1) the universities had not justified the additional hours in the three endorsement areas by providing additional competencies, (2) the universities had the flexibility within the framework to develop programs which would comply with state board regulations; and (3) there had been broad participation in the design of the new licensure system, with only UNM and NMSU finding it impossible to comply.

During the public hearing both sides mobilized speakers. The board recruited some small school administrators to testify on behalf of the board's new licensure system. The UNM/NMSU position was supported by a member of the National Board for Professional Teaching Standards, a key legislator, the state board member who formerly had been president of NMSU, principals, department chairpersons, and others. The general consensus among observers was that UNM and NMSU had presented the stronger case. After hearing all of the testimony, the commission decided to send the issue to the board for a decision at the October 1989 meeting.

Newspapers throughout the state documented the hearing with headlines—"Teachers Who Learn Too Much Can't Get Jobs" (P. Guthrie, September 27, 1989) and "State Weakening Teacher Standards, Educators Say" (P. Guthrie, September 28, 1989). The UNM arts and sciences dean said: "It's gone too far. We are not going to be a party to fraud...by lowering standards." The NMFT president stated: "In no other profession do they lower standards to meet supply and demand. Eventually it's going to get to the point that anyone who can breathe can teach in New Mexico."

An early October editorial, entitled "Education Sideshow," was particularly inflammatory. Editor Crawford stated: "New Mexico may have the only State Board of Education in the nation seeking to water down its requirements for teacher certification at a time when the national goal is education excellence." The solution offered in the editorial was:

> The state board should back down and certify the more rigorous UNM and NMSU programs—and if the smaller school districts want teachers with broader, but shallower, teaching certificates, they can hire from the graduates of state institutions which have brought their teaching curricula down to the state's less rigorous standard. (G. Crawford, October 2, 1989, p. A6)

Attention then turned to the October board meeting. The NMFT presented to the board more than one thousand teacher signatures on a petition requesting that the UNM and NMSU programs be approved. A handful of district administrators, mobilized by the board, presented their views. Evidently stung by the negative publicity in the preceding weeks, the board unanimously approved the UNM and NMSU programs. However, there was a contingency: the institutions must identify the competencies associated with in-depth knowledge of a discipline. Superintendent Morgan was encouraged to be flexible when negotiating the settlement of the impasse (SBE Minutes, October 12, 1989, p. 12).

After much deliberation, a joint statement on in-depth knowledge was forwarded to Morgan by the UNM and NMSU education deans in November. Competencies associated with in-depth knowledge were spelled out (D. Colton and B. Simmons, November 22, 1989). Morgan responded by accepting the six key competencies which were described in the COE deans' position paper. However, Morgan then asked for specification of the discrete courses in which these additional competencies would be mastered (A. Morgan, December 5, 1989). The UNM and NMSU arts and sciences deans responded to Morgan by stating that they too accepted the six statements, but they declined to relate specific courses to the six competencies (H. Wildenthal and T. Gale, personal communication, February 9, 1990). For a time it appeared that the impasse would continue. However, in early March, 1990, the arts and sciences deans received a letter from Superintendent Morgan stating that it was not necessary to link competencies to courses and congratulated UNM and NMSU on the approval of their endorsement programs (A. Morgan, March 1, 1990).

Discussion

The dispute between the New Mexico board and department, on one side, and UNM and NMSU on the other, was characterized by ill-defined issues, a changing cast of characters, a variety of venues, and consumption of inordinate quantities of emotional energy and scarce resources. Outwardly, the stakes were pitifully small: a few credit hours in a handful of undergraduate teacher preparation programs. How did it happen that state and university officials were willing to invest so much effort on behalf of such small stakes? Bystanders asked the same question: one legislator referred to the matter as "this incessant squabble" (J. P. Taylor, September 19, 1989), while the press referred to it as a "sideshow" (G. Crawford, October 2, 1989).

In fact, however, the dispute was symptomatic of underlying issues of some importance. The outward pettiness did not register the nature of these issues—as often seems to be the case in teacher education. Three issues were paramount.

The first was a classic urban-rural division. The board's dominant reference group was the rural areas and small schools; UNM and NMSU centered more on the large urban districts. When the board adopted a licensure system clearly designed to meet the needs of small secondary schools at the expense of large ones, i.e., to require the preparation of content generalists and to prohibit the preparation of disciplinary specialists, conflict was virtually inevitable. However, neither side wanted to depict the conflict as an urban-rural one. UNM and NMSU are statewide research universities committed to rural as well as urban education agendas; by the same token, the state board has urban as well as rural constituencies. Thus, rather than describing the conflict as urban-rural, different formulations of the issue were chosen, e.g. breadth versus depth, uniformity versus variation, compliance versus noncompliance. While these varying formulations served to deflect attention from the underlying urban-rural split, they also prolonged the dispute and confused observers.

A second underlying source of conflict was a struggle for control of teacher education. The school reform movement of the 1980s was highly critical of teacher education, which was deemed to be overgrown, lacking in quality, overbalanced toward pedagogical rather than academic training, and unresponsive to the needs of schools and the larger society. One reaction was for state officials to mandate change. New Jersey's alternative licensure plan, the imposition of caps on pedagogical training in states such as Texas and Virginia, and the New Mexico board's recapture of the Professional Standards Commission's control over teacher licensure and program approval functions were manifestations of "get tough" orientations toward teacher education. A second reaction was for teacher educators themselves to initiate reforms through agencies such as the Holmes Group, the National Council for the Accreditation of Teacher Education (NCATE), and the American Association of Colleges for Teacher Education (AACTE). NMSU and UNM perceived themselves to be part of the self-reform effort. Denied an opportunity for effective participation in the board's redesign effort and threatened with state nonapproval of programs which exceeded state standards, UNM and NMSU rebelled. Aspiring to excellence in teacher education, the institutions simply would not accept the ceilings which the state sought to impose upon arts and sciences preparation.

A final issue fueling the New Mexico dispute was a bona fide argument about the preferred design of teacher education programs. The board and department were committed to competency-based teacher education programs. The universities agreed that a competency orientation—and even a reasonable cap on professional preparation courses—could be helpful in revising and tightening college of education professional training programs; consequently, the universities readily accepted the competency requirements which the board set forth in the area of professional preparation. Initially, it did not occur to anyone that the state would try to impose a competency model on arts and sciences too. However, for the board and department, competencies became a virtual obsession. Everything was to be competency oriented. Pressed to meet its self-imposed deadlines, the board found itself adopting endless lists of competencies—some well conceived and some mere laundry lists—and then demanding that the teacher preparation institutions (a) fit these competencies into a predetermined number of credit hours, and (b) designate the courses in which each competency was taught. The education deans warned the board that by imposing these demands on arts and sciences there was a great risk of triggering a backlash which would disrupt Holmes Group–inspired efforts to nurture arts and sciences interest in teacher education. However, the warnings were treated as resistance. Not until the arts and sciences deans officially declined to prepare course-competency matrices did the SDE and SBE finally acknowledge their limited viewpoint.

In sum, the New Mexico dispute was not merely a "squabble," however much it appeared that way. The appearance masked real issues embedded in the surface dispute about a few credit hours.

Why did it take so long for the issue to be settled? Three considerations are important here. The first, already discussed, is that each side in the dispute deemed the stakes to be high. The UNM and NMSU deans decided it was better to prolong the dispute than lose. Here the deans had some tactical advantages. Professional Standards Commission and SDE personnel, pressed by the board's urgent desire to forestall legislative intervention, had neither the time nor the desire to engage the education deans in consultations about licensure proposals; however, the deans then invoked principles of consultation and openness, winning delays in timetables and thus providing time to gather public and campus support (a frustrating task among faculties befuddled by the mysteries of licensure and by past views that the state board should of course defer to the teacher preparation institutions). Moreover, when board president Smith embraced the program approval concept, thinking it would give additional board leverage over university programs, she inadvertently handed the deans a tactical tool: the board could not approve programs if the universities deferred submitting them or declined altogether. Ultimately, the state simply did not have the power to compel compliance—a problem which the board and SDE evidently failed to anticipate when education deans and arts and sciences personnel were excluded from the initial redesign work.

Second, third-party mechanisms for accommodation were notably absent. In New Mexico the State Board of Education, UNM, and NMSU are constitutional entities, coequal with one another. Throughout the dispute there were murmurings about constitutional prerogatives and about possible litigation (SBE Minutes, August 20, 1986, p. 12; D. Colton, June 13, 1985). However the universities eschewed efforts to seek solution in the legal arena, given the murkiness of the law, the imprecision of the issues, and doubts about institutional readiness to undertake legal action on this matter. Thus, the courts were ruled out as a mechanism for dispute resolution. The legislature was not deemed to be a suitable forum either; one of the points on which the board and the universities agreed was that legislative intervention was to be avoided if possible. The board's close monitoring of the Professional Standards Commission preempted that body's capacity to serve as a mediating group. Neither the business community, the governor, nor civic groups stepped forward to assist in resolving the conflict.

In the end it was the New Mexico Federation of Teachers which helped break the impasse. Seeing the dispute over licensure standards as an opportunity to speak out on a matter of professional significance, the NMFT orchestrated a media blitz and a teacher petition movement which hurt the board. Emphasis on the theme that the board was "lowering standards" helped bring about a resolution of the contest.

A third factor prolonging the impasse involved the dynamics of the issue itself. Over time, its faces and manifestations changed. Initially seen as a fight over the program approval concept, the focal point later became the integrity of the Professional Standards Commission, then the role and composition of the board's task forces, then the issues of minimum standards versus excellence, breadth versus depth, licensure versus preparation, and on and on. Unable to articulate the issues cleanly and permanently, it was difficult for either side to form alliances and to clarify public and professional opinion. Even insiders intimately involved in the dispute were greatly frustrated by its multiple and changing facets. Efforts to secure clarification of one piece, even if successful, merely served to deflect attention to another aspect of the dispute. All of this was greatly complicated by the changing cast of players on the board, in the department, and in the universities. The changing of personnel not only interfered with the establishment of linkages which might have been helpful in resolving the issue; it also meant that few actors were knowledgeable about the history of the dispute and about the intricacies of its development. In addition to the changing character of the issues and actors, the dispute moved from setting to setting—board, Professional Standards Commission, legislature, professional associations. Each setting had its own agendas and actors; both sides of the dispute had to invest time in estimating the purposes and consequences of moves from one forum to another.

The education deans at UNM and NMSU often wondered whether the immense investment of time, emotional energy, and organizational resources was worthwhile. In the end the dispute was settled satisfactorily, but there will be consequences both positive and negative. Personal and professional relationships between UNM/NMSU personnel and members of the SBE, SDE, and Professional Standards Commission were strained and ruptured. The dispute prompted a realignment of interests within and among teacher education institutions and their various constituencies. It forced teacher educators and others to be more articulate about their beliefs and expectations. The dispute destroyed the tenuous cohesion and effectiveness of the New Mexico Association of Colleges of Teacher Education, but it built strong ties between ostensible rivals UNM and NMSU. Forms and channels of communication between the State Board of Education and the universities were fundamentally altered, as were long-standing assumptions about mutuality of interests among the parties. It remains to be seen whether the settlement of the New Mexico licensure dispute will result in the preparation and licensure of better-prepared teachers for either rural or urban schools.

3

RICHARD K. MASTAIN AND RALPH BROTT

The California Commission on Teacher Credentialing:

Seeking the Ingredients for Change

California affords a rich thirty-year perspective from which to view teacher education policy development. The Fisher Act (1961) eliminated the undergraduate education major and required a fifth year of postgraduate training for elementary teachers (similar to secondary teachers). To become fully credentialed, teachers and administrators were required to have an academic major. Distrusting the state superintendent and state department employees as "educationists," the State Board of Education undertook writing the regulations itself, producing an extremely confusing and complex set of regulations.

Rather than making exceptions for the many minor credentialing problems, the state board started refashioning the regulations almost on a monthly basis. Some school districts suffered from chronic teacher shortages, prospective teachers could not get accurate information, teacher training institutions were uncertain of their requirements, and the distinction between academic and nonacademic practitioners had become confusing and divisive.

As early as 1965, the increasing state of confusion caught the attention of the legislature. The Assembly Education Committee created a subcommittee to study the problem, and named as its chair former teacher Leo Ryan, whose application for a credential in the late 1940s had been denied because he lacked a minor course requirement. As a result of his experience, Ryan wanted credential requirements that were clear and understandable and administered by an agency independent of the state department of Education.

In January, 1967, after a series of hearings, Ryan's committee report, labeling the credentialing bureaucracy a "red tape jungle" (Subcommittee on School Personnel and Teacher

Qualification, p. 8), claimed that there was no evidence of a teacher shortage except in districts with low pay and isolated working conditions, and noted that the credentialing regulations were of "immense complexity and instability."

Leo Ryan established himself as an independent leader in shaping educational policy. A new joint assembly/senate committee was empowered to study credentialing practices with Ryan as its chairman and Denis Doyle as its staff member. Over the next two and a half years, Ryan and Doyle's efforts culminated in 1970 in the passage of the Ryan Act.

THE RYAN ACT

The Ryan Act contained several innovations. It established an independent regulatory commission with fifteen members appointed by the governor and confirmed by the senate. That commission would be composed of practitioners, representatives from higher education, members representing the public, plus six nonvoting ex officio seats representing the state superintendents and California's five higher education entities. The concept was advanced to Assemblyman Ryan by James D. Koerner who worked on an advisory group that proposed a similar idea in Massachusetts. Koerner was extremely critical of teacher educators and state departments of education—groups that he considered academically inept and responsible for the poor quality of teachers (Koerner, 1963). Koerner conjectured that an independent commission balanced with academic scholars, practitioners, and the public members would keep credentialing out of the hands of the state department of education and teacher educators.

Ryan and Doyle embraced Koerner's ideas. When the Ryan Act passed, it contained provisions severely constraining teacher education programs. It restricted professional education courses to nine units and required that half of teacher preparation be spent in student teaching.[1] The Fisher Act's divisive academic major or minor requirements were dropped. Examinations would be imposed on all prospective teachers except those who had passed through a subject matter program approved by the newly formed Commission on Teacher Preparation and Licensing (CTPL). When he signed the Ryan Act on July 30, 1970, Governor Ronald Reagan proclaimed the law to be "one of the most fundamental and far-reaching breakthroughs in the history of California's public school system" (*San Francisco Chronicle*, p. 8).

A Difficult Beginning

Any new state agency can expect problems and challenges; one that has been separated from an existing state agency, against the agency's wishes, can expect a few extra headaches. Governor Reagan balanced the commission's membership with conservative partisans being rewarded for party favors and moderates who had some knowledge of credentialing. During the three-year implementation phase, the partisans held power. Open hostility was displayed towards teacher educators and lobbyists, information was scarce, and participation was limited; the staff was actually instructed to avoid the people interested in the commission's activities.

The drafters of the Ryan Act had aimed for a high degree of cooperation between the commission and the state board (which had veto power over the commission's regulations), but the state board resented the removal of credentialing from its authority. Moreover, soon after he was elected, state superintendent Wilson Riles announced that he intended to sponsor a bill to place the commission (with the members appointed by him) within the State Department of Education.

Perhaps the most severe problem for the commission in the beginning was funding. When it became independent, it had to support itself from credentialing fees, and there were not enough funds to support its ambitious legislative mandates.

Even with these forces working against the commission, its role gradually evolved. In mid-1973, a liberal/moderate faction took control of the commission. The abrasive first executive secretary, George Gustafson, was replaced by Peter LoPresti. In a dramatic reversal, LoPresti surrounded himself with administrators from the old State Department Bureau of Credentials, made information and staff freely available, became accommodating towards teacher training institutions and lobbyists, and attempted to establish lines of communication with the state superintendent and board. The hostility between the commission and observers gradually changed to an atmosphere of cooperation and a beginning of trust.

The Ryan Act had saddled the commission with some rather ambitious and difficult proposals. These included implementing an examinations system, setting standards for subject matter and professional training programs, and undertaking a study to determine what effective teaching demanded.

Development of an examination system posed many problems. Because money was not available, the commission had to use existing, less desirable examinations administered by the Education Testing Service (ETS). Compounding the situation, most of the examinations had been negotiated out of the Ryan Act. For example, out of concern for minority performance, the framers of the Ryan Act had allowed graduates of California institutions, whose curriculum would be approved by the commission, to be "waived" from taking an examination.

Equally contentious was the commission's authority to accredit (approve) professional training programs. Education schools and departments resented the commission having control over their curriculum. The first on-site program reviews were completed at four-year colleges during the 1974–75 school year. The commission had brought together a well-balanced and knowledgeable advisory committee that recommended process standards for a discrepancy model of program evaluation. Nevertheless, the commission's staff fell short in its written directions to the colleges and evaluators, and in giving training to team members (teachers, administrators, and college faculty). Because of disorganization and poor evaluations, these efforts hurt the commission's credibility at a time when it needed it most.

Some critics questioned a system that measured the degree to which the college's program met the commission's standards, but did not measure the quality of individual candidates. Early in its existence, therefore, the commission decided that if it was going to set teaching training standards, it must know the qualities of an effective teacher and incorporate those qualities in training programs. In 1972, it initiated the Beginning Teacher Evaluation Study (BTES), but the study shifted its concentration from how effective teachers teach to how successful students learn. As valuable as the study was in focusing on the learner's engagement in the classroom, it offered little to policy makers seeking to change credentialing requirements. For those who were looking for the commission to provide leadership, the inability of this long, well-publicized, expensive study to give clear policy direction was a severe disappointment.

Finally, clarification of the difference between the standards for Fisher and Ryan credentials also took a great deal of the commission's time and energy. Colleges had Fisher and Ryan programs in operation at the same time; candidates who started under Fisher regulations up until 1973 had until 1976 to complete their credential. This duality of standards created confusion and hostility through the 1973 to 1976 period. There were numerous complaints that the commission was cumbersome, impersonal, and inept.

CHANGES IN POLITICAL CLIMATE

In 1975, Democrat Jerry Brown was elected governor, bringing his anti-government and Spartan philosophy to Sacramento. In 1977 the property tax revolt brought California Proposition 13, effectively transferring most financial responsibilities for schools from local property-tax payers to the state. Policy-making authority rapidly followed. In 1978, in a movement that swept through most regulatory commissions in California, the public was given the majority membership.

During this period, the commission entered a new level of maturity and change. The need to establish credibility and provide leadership was becoming apparent. The agency started to do long-range planning, set goals, and establish an agenda.

Executive Secretary LoPresti had come to the commission in 1974, leading it through a rocky period. He made great progress in gaining credibility with the commission constituents, undertaking a process of self-study, and articulating a number of significant policy issues. LoPresti and the commission expounded a set of goals that included developing a way to assess individual teacher candidates, reevaluating the examinations system, finding the relationship between teachers' education and their classroom performance, assessing the usefulness of the life credentials, improving the program review process, better enforcing the disciplinary process, achieving financial stability, and defining the agency's leadership role.

In mid-1979, however, Robert Salley, a teacher with AFT affiliation, was elected chairman. Salley and others on the commission thought that LoPresti had not developed successful relations with the legislature, and felt that if the agency was going to be on the forefront of leadership and innovation, the agency needed a bold and innovative leader. LoPresti's accommodating style did not meet with the commission's new leadership vision, and in April, 1980, he tendered his resignation.

The commission hired John Brown, former executive director of the Midwest Teacher Corps Network and well connected to the powerful ways and means chairman, John Vasconcellos, who was among a group of legislators who were critical of the commission. There was hope that Brown could forge a stronger relationship with the legislature. Initially, Brown's attention was consumed by financial problems; with fewer applications for credentials, the self-supporting Commission was undergoing a financial crunch.

As early as 1977, however, policy makers had started to rethink the Ryan Act's major assumption—that rigorous examinations would weed out the unqualified. It appeared that this policy was not working with administrators; those who passed examinations were no better, and were perhaps worse, than those who underwent training programs. In 1979, the examinations option for the administrative credential was eliminated from the law, training programs became mandatory, and the commission undertook a study of administrator training. Following a study of 192 school principals, an advisory panel made recommendations that led to a requirement for a two-tier credential for administrators. The first tier would prepare candidates for entry-level positions such as principal. Training would have a practical orientation. After gaining employment, administrators would take advanced courses in the theoretical and broader aspects of administration.

The concept of the second tier posed questions regarding teaching credentials. Should traditional teacher training be followed by an internship or "residency"? What are the most effective ways to bring theory and practice together? What components of preparation should be placed with colleges and with schools? What is the most effective way to link preservice and in-service education?

By 1981, the commission was attempting to formulate a major reform proposal. A year before, it had established an internal subcommittee to study the values and content of the fifth year of postgraduate professional training required of all teachers. The Committee came to advocate a two-tier credential that would involve three to five years of postgraduate training which included education courses, student teaching, and an extended supervised internship. This two-tier proposal presented major obstacles related to turf issues. Preservice preparation was the commission's turf and in-service education was the state department's area. Cooperation would be required between the commission and the state department and between universities and school districts, institutions that often had widely disparate priorities and values. The proposal was immediately criticized by teacher educators who were threatened by a potential loss of their "authority."

Commission Chairman Salley expressed frustration with the glacial pace of the proceedings. At the February, 1981, meeting, Vice-Chairman David Levering wrote his colleagues of the "considerable difficulty in sorting out the tangles of this particular issue" and proposed four hypotheses to guide the body. These were that: (1) the undergraduate years should be devoted exclusively to subject matter; (2) preservice and in-service education should be linked; (3) teacher training should be extended over two or three years beyond graduation; and (4) there is a need to overcome the problems associated with education's fragmented governance structure.

In the summer, 1981, the commission appointed two distinguished panels, a National Panel and a California Panel, to review the commission's accomplishments and make recommendations for the future. The panels recommended that an initial credential be issued upon the completion of teacher training, that beginning teachers be given support, and that the issue of a permanent credential be based on the assessment of teaching performance after two years of teaching. All teachers would be required to take a basic skills test, preservice and in-service functions should be linked, periodic professional growth would be required, internship-type programs would be initiated, and there would be recognition for excellent teaching.

In September, 1981, Assembly Education Committee chair, Gary Hart, visited the commission and told them that he was going to sponsor legislation for a basic skills examination. In his bill, Hart proposed that the State Department of Education develop the examination but that the commission be in charge of its administration, expressing hope that the commission and State Department of Education could put aside their long-standing differences and work together. Hart questioned whether an independent commission could administer credentialing better than the department. Later that fall, Hart's bill was enacted, requiring all applicants for a teaching or administrative credential to pass the California Basic Educational Skills Test (CBEST).

By the end of 1981, the commission's staff had prepared five "concept papers" undergirding its legislative reform proposal. Basically, they proposed the two-step teaching credential; however, the second tier had been influenced by heavy lobbying by teacher educators to require an additional twenty-four units of an individualized program at a college. The concept papers also proposed eliminating the life credential and imposing periodic professional growth requirements, higher standards for emergency credentials, and reexamining the practice of using examinations to measure subject matter competence.

In the meantime, Assemblyman Hart had formed a task force to investigate the commission and its activities. In a strange twist of events, the task force (which included commission chair Salley) accepted many of the commission's reform ideas, and Assemblyman Hart agreed to carry the commission's reform bill. In March, Hart introduced a bill which contained most of the ideas outlined in the concept papers. Almost immediately, Hart was under heavy pressure from the powerful California Teachers Association (CTA) to remove the provision that would eliminate the life credential. Hart felt that he could not move the bill against the CTA's opposition and modified the provision.

After passing through the Assembly Education Committee in June, Hart reinserted the provision to eliminate the life credential back in the bill. Both Hart and the commission had underestimated the CTA's influence. Hart's bill died in the Senate Education Committee on a five to three vote.[2]

Both vast and minor changes occurred in California education politics during 1983. Conservative George Deukmejian was inaugurated governor and outspoken Bill Honig became State Superintendent of Public Instruction. *A Nation at Risk* was published, and in a flurry of reports and criticism, education moved higher on the state's political agenda. A minor change was made in the name of the licensing agency; it became the Commission on Teacher Credentialing (CTC).

Accommodating higher education and the California Teachers Association, the commission's 1983 legislative reform package was more timid. For a full credential, teachers would be required to take thirty units of pedagogy. The advanced credential would require a combination of "systematic staff development" and college courses equivalent to twenty-four units. Rather than eliminating life credentials, the new bill stated that the advanced credentials would require 150 hours of in-service to be renewed every five years. Renewal would be linked to successful performance and professional development.

The commission's own reform bill was submerged by the major reform bills. Democrats were seeking a one billion dollar increase in educational funding; however, Governor Deukmejian wanted fundamental reforms in exchange. Now-Senator Hart and Assemblywoman Teresa Hughes, chairs of the legislature's respective education committees, eventually combined their bills into the landmark Hughes-Hart Education Reform Act (SB 813). As negotiations were taking place, Assemblywoman Marian Bergeson persuaded Governor Deukmejian to insist that the proposals be included to eliminate life credentials and impose professional growth requirements. With little effort on its own, significant parts of the commission's reform package were enacted.

During the fall of 1983, however, there were rumblings in the legislature. Because of the lack of success in getting its two reform bills passed, several legislators considered the commission ineffective and often remarked that it was not providing leadership. After the passage of SB 813, the Assembly Education Committee turned its attention to credentialing. An internal policy paper was written outlining the various governance structures for credentialing and the advantages and disadvantages of each. In almost all the alternatives, credentialing would be more closely bound to the state department and superintendent. Freshman Republican Assemblyman Charles Bader was concerned about credentialing's fragmented governance structure and separation of responsibilities of preservice education under the commission and in-service education under the state board and state department.

In 1984, Assemblywoman Bergeson carried the commission's reform bill for the second time. Very similar to the previous reform bill, it also proposed eliminating the unit limit on pedagogy. But Assemblyman Bader's concerns had been relayed to Superintendent Honig, who persuaded Bader to introduce a bill to place the commission in the State Department of Education. Suddenly, the commission's attention was taken up with fighting the "Bader Bill" rather than lobbying for their reform legislation.

To resolve the impasse, a joint meeting was arranged between the Assembly's Education and Ways and Means Committees to hear both Bader's and Bergeson's bills at the same time. After a day-long hearing in July, the committees did not move either bill; two weeks before, Senator Hart, Assemblywoman Hughes, and Superintendent Honig had announced their sponsorship of a blue ribbon commission to study ways to improve the teaching profession. The legislature was not going to take any action until it heard from the prestigious California Commission on the Teaching Profession eventually to be known as the Commons Commission (named after its chair, former state board member Dorman Commons).

1985 brought a marked leadership change for the commission. The AFT members who had led the commission for five years were gone. Administrator Alice Petrossian and university professor Mary Jane Pearson vied in an open contest for chair, with Petrossian winning in an eight to five vote in May.

Those who supported Petrossian knew that she would lead an effort to replace Executive Secretary John Brown. In some ways, Brown had been his own worst enemy. His shows of independence had made a poor impression on legislators and Sacramento professionals. Even though he hired some outstanding staff members from higher education institutions, he had given the impression that he was unsympathetic to the problems of higher education and failed to build credibility among its representatives. He was unable to form coalitions that people trusted or to effectively communicate with those who held the ingredients for change. Dr. Brown resigned in late June 1985. Licensing Coordinator Richard Mastain was asked to assume the duties of executive secretary, first on an acting basis and then permanently.

This was a low period for the commission. Assemblyman Bader had reintroduced his bill to place credentialing back in the state department. Petrossian wrote a letter to the governor's staff urging that the governor take a position opposing the bill, but it had little effect. The assembly passed the bill on a fifty-one to twelve vote, and the governor declared himself neutral on the bill. Bader's bill appeared to have a full head of steam. However, resistance was building.

A loosely organized group called the Friends of the Commission started to lobby the Senate Education Committee. Seven hundred credential analysts in the field, former commissioners, people who had served on program review teams, and commission observers wrote letters, called upon their legislators, attended committee hearings, and spoke out against the bill. Prominent among those who lobbied were the members of the Credential Counselors and Analysts of California (CCAC), who provide information to prospective teachers in California's seventy teacher preparing institutions, fifty-eight county offices, and some large school districts. In 1980, when the 600-page *Credential Handbook* was created, members of CCAC embraced the document as their "bible." Crucial to the dissemination, utilization, and continual updating of the *Credential Handbook,* they had formed an effective working relationship with the commission's licensing branch.

Legislators started to listen. Sound evidence was given that the terms "red tape jungle," "immensely complex and instable," and "lacking consistent information" were not terms that applied to the licensing branch in 1985. The licensing staff had built understanding and established credibility, and it paid dividends at a crucial time.

The Friends of the Commission argued that some major policy issues should be settled before the bill moved out of the Senate Education Committee. The key policy question was whether credentialing could be more effectively administered under the policy umbrella of the state superintendent and board or under a broadly based independent commission. Moreover, the legislators were told that they should wait for the recommendations of the Commons Commission before taking action. The Bader bill was held up in the Senate Education Committee. This was a crucial turning point for the commission; it was learning to lobby effectively.

Early in November, 1985, the Commons Commission report called for vast changes in the way schools were managed and the way teachers were trained. In schools, teachers would be given more authority. Teacher training was to be deregulated. The commission was to be replaced by a Teaching Standards Board with broader authority and a teacher majority. The Teaching Standards Board would concentrate on policy; teacher discipline would be under the authority of a separate autonomous body. The report called for the fifth year of teacher training to become more rigorous, with in-depth assessment of subject matter and pedagogy. It recommended that beginning teachers undergo a one-year internship with a reduced load and the help of a mentor. Permanent credentials would be based on a performance assessment conducted by peers, administrators and college faculty, and a "state examination."

Two days later, the Commons Commission report was discussed at a senate interim hearing. Assemblyman Bader continued to be disturbed by the report's recommendation to continue the separation of preservice teacher training and in-service professional development under two policy umbrellas. Without a vote on the Teaching Standards Board, the state superintendent would be the "odd man out" (Senate Education Committee, 1985). Bader was pleased that the report recommended eliminating the commission and program review, but was disturbed by the establishment of a new, more powerful Teaching Standards Board.

Going against the Commons Commission report, of which he was a sponsor, state superintendent Bill Honig spoke in favor of the Bader bill. Honig made it clear that he wanted credentialing under his authority. Honig was alone. Almost every other organization or agency spoke against placing credentialing back into the State Department of Education. Bader's proposal died.

In the meantime, a new climate was developing on the commission. A politically savvy and aggressive chair and a consensus-seeking executive secretary, Alice Petrossian and Richard Mastain were developing into a dynamic team. The new chair shared Armenian heritage with Governor Deukmejian; able to see and talk with him at cultural functions, an important political relationship was being forged. Hoping to develop a working relationship, Petrossian and Mastain invited legislators to commission meetings to discuss policy issues. Assemblyman Bader was one of the first to be asked. Other legislators were honored at banquets for the important work they had done to improve teacher education or the status of teachers. The commission's newsletter was published in a more polished format on a monthly basis. Informal discussions with various representatives who attended meetings were initiated to allow closer work with special interest groups and to build consensus for the commission's legislative proposals.

In January, 1986, Senators Hart and Bergeson introduced companion bills based on the recommendation of the Commons Commission. Generally, Hart's bill dealt with school site reform and Bergeson's bill dealt with credentialing reform. Bergeson's bill proposed the separate Teaching Standards Board and Enforcement Board envisioned by the Commons Commission.

The commission was determined to preserve itself as an agency and to preserve as much of its reform agenda as possible. On the other hand, the Commons Commission reformers wanted a new agency with a new agenda. Senator Bergeson wanted to bring the two parties together. Negotiations at the staff level were intense.

The most difficult issue was the composition of the proposed Teaching Standards Board. For individuals and organizations in Sacramento, the symbolism of having seats on a regulatory board or commission is crucial. In the bill's final form in June, the board consisted of fifteen voting members—six teachers, one administrator, one other certified person, one member from higher education, one school board member, four public members, and the state superintendent. If the administrator was included, certificated members or school people held the majority.

Bergeson's bill had passed the Senate Education Committee in April, but it received a major blow a month later—the Department of Finance's opposition. The department claimed that the bill did not provide for a revenue source for the additional $127 million per year that would be required for the "residency" support program (an 80 percent workload for new teachers, the help of a mentor, and being evaluated by peer teachers). Moreover, the department questioned whether it was essential to abolish the commission to accomplish the bill's reforms. In the meantime, both Hart's and Bergeson's bills had become "bottled up" in the Senate Appropriations Committee because of CTA's strenuous objection to many of the Hart bill's proposals for school sites—especially the peer review process.

Meanwhile, the commission exerted constant pressure on now-Senator Bergeson to modify her bill regarding the composition of the commission. Mastain's July testimony failed to make an impression, and the bill passed out of committee. However, the bill was running into difficulty. When it reached the assembly floor, Bergeson's Democratic colleagues voted the bill down.

During this period, the commission was gaining respect and stature. Its strategy of engaging in coalition building with politicians and constituent organizations, becoming an adept negotiator, and overcoming some of its bureaucratic and financial problems was starting to pay off. With the raises in credential fees, along with other incomes, the commission was able to staff and undertake many of the improvements that were sorely needed. Personnel changes strengthened the staff. The commission moved to more modern quarters, installed data processing equipment, and continued to meet the objectives established in its comprehensive 1985 work plan. As a result of its improved performance and image, many people no longer saw the need to replace the commission with a new Teaching Standards Board.

By the end of 1986, the commission decided to push its own reform agenda. Using many of the provisions of Bergeson's previous reform bill as the foundation, the commission persuaded Senator Bergeson to introduce a new bill for the commission in the 1987 session.

In January, 1987, Senator Bergeson introduced the commission's credentialing legislation. She made it clear that the contentious issue regarding the composition of the fifteen-member policy-making body settled upon in the previous session would not be negotiable. By mid-March, the commission's bill had passed out of the Senate Education Committee on a unanimous vote and went on to the Senate Appropriations Committee where it was once again held up by the committee's chair, Senator Presley. Because Senator Bergeson did not come out in support of, nor vote for, Presley's own education omnibus bill, Presley would not allow Bergeson's bill to move out of committee. As the deadline passed in June, 1987, SB 148 failed to move.

Senator Bergeson was optimistic that the bill would move in the 1988 session. The governor's office was taking an interest in the reform bill. Commission chair Petrossian and Mastain had convinced the governor's new education assistant, Peter Mehas, of the merits of a beginning teacher support and assessment system, and he offered to help them get their proposals through the legislature and governor's office.

Shortly thereafter, Governor Deukmejian signaled that he would openly support Bergeson's SB 148 and would consider support for a pilot project for a beginning teacher support and assessment system. Petrossian and Mastain started to solicit support for the concept so that a full-fledged support and assessment system could be enacted with the Bergeson bill, a system Mastain hoped would utilize various modes of evaluation (written exams, the interpretation of video vignettes, oral interviews, observation of classroom performance, and other viable means of judging future teaching success) to provide a composite summary of an individual's subject matter and general knowledge, level of basic skills, and ability to perform in a classroom.

By January, 1988, the commission's agenda had a full head of steam. In his State of the State Address, Governor Deukmejian announced that he was allocating $1.1 million to the commission and $1.9 million to the State Department of Education to study alternative models of beginning teacher support and assessment. The California Teacher Assessment Project proposal was immediately incorporated into a number of credentialing bills, including Bergeson's. With this level of support, Bergeson's bill easily passed out of Senate Appropriations in late January, and three days later, the senate passed SB 148 in a thirty-eight to zero vote.

With the governor's support, SB 148 began to get serious interest group attention. Some teacher educators expressed concern for a plan that would lessen higher education's hold on teacher education by implementing a beginning support and assessment system. Objections by the Department of Finance led the governor's office to request that Bergeson remove the provisions that would obligate the state to implement a costly support and assessment system before the results of the pilot studies were known.

At its May meeting, the state board took an "oppose unless amended" stand on SB 148. It objected to removal of the state board's authority to "review and approve" the commission's regulations and its ability to "waive" credentialing status. The state board appealed to the governor to oppose the provision.

The University of California retained its long-standing opposition to program review as an infringement of university autonomy.

Because of Assemblyman Bader's objections, SB 148 had been held in the Assembly Education Committee. However, towards the end of June, Petrossian, Mastain, and the commission's staff lobbied the members heavily and rallied the interest groups. At the bill's hearing, most major interest groups and agencies spoke in favor of SB 148. Assemblyman Bader asked a number of pointed questions, but his opposition seemed to have little effect on the committee. The bill passed out of the Assembly Education Committee on a twelve to two vote and went on to the Assembly Ways and Means Committee for it to deal with the financial issues. On cost grounds, the Department of Finance opposed the bill, and it was placed on the committee's "suspense file."

In the meantime, the commission and Senator Bergeson were attempting to get the governor to intervene on their behalf. Three issues were submitted to the governor for his decision: (1) the Department of Finance's opposition to a permanent support and assessment system; (2) Assemblyman Bader's recommendation that program review be terminated; and (3) an appeal by the state board that they retain review authority over the commission's regulations. The governor was unwilling to go against the Department of Finance's recommendation. He had no opinion about program review and expressed hope that Senator

Bergeson and Assemblyman Bader could reach an agreement. On the third issue, the governor felt that the commission's regulations should not be subject to approval by the state board.

Governor Deukmejian's decision to support the piloting of a support and assessment system led to a more phased-in implementation over time. In late August, with the piloting of a support and assessment system and without the opposition of the Department of Finance, SB 148 passed out of Assembly Ways and Means on a twenty-two to one vote, and several days later passed the full assembly on a sixty-five to one vote. The senate voted to concur on the assembly amendments, and the bill went on to the governor. Without the assurance of a permanent assessment system, Assemblyman Bader's argument that program review be replaced was severely weakened. Without either assessment or program review, teacher preparation programs would be without any accountability whatsoever. Moreover, to initiate a permanent support and assessment system would require subsequent legislation—another battle—perhaps years away. The issue could be taken up then.

On September 26, 1988, Governor Deukmejian signed the Bergeson Act into law to take effect on January 1, 1989. The governor reappointed five members of the commission (including Alice Petrossian) whose terms would have expired in November. This kept the commission at full strength until it was reconstituted on July 1, 1989.

Seeking the Ingredients for Change

By studying the characteristics associated with change in the Fisher, Ryan, and Bergeson reforms, a framework can be formulated that categorized shifts in four political attributes—politics, power, values, and institutional choice. The three successful reforms since World War II were accompanied by shifts in all four of these political attributes, and the reforms contained the ingredients for change. They were brought about by the pressures and circumstances that make it possible for change to take place.

Shifts in Politics

Arthur M. Schlesinger, Senior (1963), and Junior (1986), claim that the United States alternates between liberal and conservative values in regular, self-generating thirty-year cycles. While credential reforms are neither self-generating nor have regular cycles, the concept can be expanded to categorize ingredients for change. In the successful credentialing reforms since World War II, several political ingredients have always been present. Listed under this heading are several political attributes that appear to have been present in credential reforms.

1. *There have always been shifts in conservative and liberal thinking.* In the Fisher Reform, there was a conservative shift in politics. The reaction to Sputnik in 1957 brought about a national demand for more academic and rigorous schooling. In the Ryan Reform, there was a liberal shift in politics. An independent regulatory commission was created to replace the Bureau of Credentials in the state department of Education. The Bergeson Act was characterized by a conservative shift.

2. *Prestigious commissions or committees are essential for successful reforms.* The significant recommendations of these prestigious commissions have most often found their way into legislation. In the Fisher Reform, almost every recommendation by the Citizen's Advisory Committee was eventually enacted into legislation. In the Ryan Reform, the legislature's Joint Committee on Teacher Credentialing Practices led by Leo Ryan was instrumental in getting the legislation through the legislature. The Commons Commission recommendations and the legislative proposals of the Commission on Teacher Credentialing were the basis for the legislation that eventually led to the Bergeson Act.

3. *In each reform, the governor has played a significant role.* In the Fisher Reform, Governor Pat Brown made credential reform one of his top priorities. He envisioned that improving teacher quality would be the top issue for his reelection campaign for governor. Governor Ronald Reagan vetoed Assemblyman Ryan's first bill and appointed his own advisory commission to address the issue. After Ryan's bill was modified to meet the wishes of the advisory committee, Reagan eventually signed the Ryan Act. Bergeson's bill kept getting bogged down in committees until Governor Deukmejian came out in support of the bill, provided funds for pilot assessment and support studies, and applied pressure to get the bill out of the legislature.

4. *Successful reforms are led by key people who are crucial in enacting the reform.* In the Fisher Reform, Senator Fisher himself was the key player. In the Ryan Reform, Assemblyman Ryan and his staff person, Denis Doyle, were the key players. In contrast, the Bergeson Act had a host of individuals who affected the legislation. Those who had a major impact were legislators Berge-

son, Hart, Hughes, and Bader. Throughout the 1980s, the leading legislative figure in credential reform was Senator Bergeson, who carried most of the commission's and Commons Commission's legislative proposals on credentialing. She was also influential in having several credential reforms included in SB 813.

The politics of promoting the legislation fell to several people, primarily Senator Bergeson, commission chair Alice Petrossian, Executive Secretary Richard Mastain, and Governor Assistant Peter Mehas. Governor Deukmejian's first education advisor, William Cunningham, was unsympathetic to the commission and wanted credentialing placed back into the hands of the state department, but Mehas was almost the opposite. Alice Petrossian fostered a warm working relationship with Mehas and gained his support; and ultimately they persuaded Governor Deukmejian to support Bergeson's bill.[3]

5. Reform notions often have long gestation periods. Some solutions can be present for over fifty years before being noticed, gaining acceptance, overcoming obstacles, and being implemented. Notions of eliminating the life credential, imposing renewal requirements, and tying credentialing to teaching performance were first proposed in the 1920s. Giving teachers greater control of credentialing to gain status was proposed in the years immediately following World War II. It was not until the 1980s that these notions were taken seriously.

Shifts in Power

Educational reforms are also brought about by cyclic shifts in political power (Kirst, 1984).

1. There has been a gradual shift in credentialing power from the state to the profession. In the 1950s, the professional standards movement advocated replacing state certification with professional licensure. At the time, that movement had little appeal either to policy makers or teachers. However, over the past thirty years many professional standards notions evolved, gained recognition and have been implemented.

In the Fisher Reform, power shifted from the State Department of Education and teacher educators to the legislature and the state board. In the Ryan Reform, power shifted from the state board, department, and superintendent to a commission with broad representation. The Bergeson Reform reduced the higher education and public representatives, broadened the commission's policy-making authority, and gave school people a majority on the commission. Symbolically, it can be argued that teaching is becoming more professional with school people in charge of the commission. This is very different from the public majority (seven public members and two school members) of the previous Commission. The state superintendent gained a voting seat; however, the state board lost its ability to reject the commission's regulations.

2. *Credentialing authority has become increasingly diverse.* Before the Fisher Act, the state superintendent made most of the important policy decisions. With the passage of the Fisher Act, credentialing authority was assumed by the state board. That authority passed to the commission with the passage of the Ryan Act.

A number of interest groups followed the commission's activities since its beginning in 1971, especially the California Teachers Association, the California Federation of Teachers, and teacher training institutions. However, since the passage of Proposition 13 in 1977, which shifted the majority of school funding to the state, the number of interest groups has increased dramatically. Education has come to consume such a large portion of the state's budget that departments, agencies, the legislature, and even the governor maintain education specialists, and they all endeavor to influence policy. The various branches of higher education, large school districts, and the unions have increased their lobbying presence, not only with the legislature but also with the agencies that might affect their affairs.

In the Bergeson Reform, a large number of organizations were involved. Major players were the California Teachers Association, California Federation of Teachers, United Teachers of Los Angeles, California School boards Association, Association of California School Administrators, University of California, California State University, California State PTA, Los Angeles and San Diego school districts, and the California Council for the Education of Teachers. Government departments and agencies involved were the commission, State Department of Education, Department of Finance, and the Governor's Office. Teacher training and credentialing policy making has become a very diverse undertaking.

Shifts in Values

Reforms are also products of both symbolic and real competing values in our society. Educational problems are struggles over value conflicts where there are no solutions, only trade offs (Cuban, 1990).

1. Reforms are driven by broad changes in opinion and preference outside of education. Successful reforms are preceded and accompanied by broad changes in public opinion. In the three successful reforms since World War II, there have been broad shifts in opinion. Sputnik in 1957, distrust of teacher educators in the 1960s, and international economic competition in the 1980s were all forces that originated from outside education. Credential and other kinds of educational reforms are neither self-sufficient nor independent in nature, but reliant on the politics, pressures, and events in the larger political arena. Credential reforms result from large-scale dissatisfaction with teacher quality, demands for a better system, and a willingness to try something new.

2. As credentialing policies fail, more effective policies are formulated. In the Fisher Reform, the undergraduate education major was eliminated and an academic major required for a standard credential. Values shifted away from a progressive education system to one that emphasized academics; policy makers thought the quality of teachers would be improved by requiring an academic major. In the Ryan Reform, values shifted from a system of assessing teachers on the basis of counting courses and units to one based on standardized examinations and passing through approved programs of preparation. In the Bergeson Reform, policy makers addressed the issues of how teachers actually learn their craft and how they need to be supported in the beginning years. If the Bergeson Act is fully implemented, teachers will be issued a credential after passing a set of composite examinations (possibly standardized, written, oral, video, etc.) and passing a direct assessment of teaching performance. Beginning teachers would work with a mentor and have released time to further their professional development during their induction period.

Shifts in Institutional Choice

Reforms can also be explained within the context of institutional choice. To formulate substantive policies, an effective choice between decision makers or institutions is required.

1. Dissatisfaction and distrust appear to be a driving force behind credential reforms. Dissatisfaction and distrust stand out as essential ingredients in credential reforms. In the Fisher Reform, there was large-scale dissatisfaction with schools in general, and teacher educators in particular. There was distrust of the education community to implement the reform, and the state board assumed the task. In turn, dissatisfaction with the state board's ability to write and administer credentialing regulations led to the Ryan Reform. Again, distrust of teacher educators as well as with the state superintendent, board, and department led to the creation of an independent commission. In the 1980s, dissatisfaction with schools and the quality of teachers reemerged. Distrust of an agency governed by a cross section of teachers, faculty members, and public representatives resulted in a changed composition in which teachers were given a larger voice. At the same time, distrust of higher education led to plans being made to give schools and teachers a larger role in the training of teachers.

2. *If teachers are to be trained well, schools must be involved.* Most teachers are currently trained and credentialed in a system based on what policy makers think teachers ought to know rather than one based upon how they learn to teach. Almost all teachers agree that the most important part of their training is teaching. As with many other professions, experience is the best teacher. It often takes up to five years for a teacher to become fully competent and effective in the classroom.

On the other hand, most teacher training and credentialing policies concentrate on what teachers ought to know and be able to do. By specifying the content and experiences that potential teachers must undergo, policy makers hope that generic preparation courses and a student teacher experience will prepare individuals for the full responsibility of the classroom.

By ignoring the way teachers learn, and by imposing notions of what they think teachers ought to know, policy makers have invited disaster. It is difficult to ignore the evidence that up to one-half of beginning teachers are leaving the profession within five years. Equally difficult to ignore is that where support and assessment systems have been implemented, the attrition rates have been cut up to one-half.

In the Bergeson Reform, although there was little change in the institution for making policy, there was a significant shift in thinking for the choice of institutions to implement policy. If fully implemented, the Bergeson Act will transfer a significant portion of teacher training responsibility to schools; hopefully there will be a close collaboration between schools and colleges.

3. For a credentialing agency to be effective, trust is essential. Because the commission was able to improve its performance and image and learned how to engage in coalition politics, it remained the policy-making institution of choice. It gained trust. A new Teaching Standards Board could have been easily established, but that would have a been symbolic change in name. Credentialing could have been placed back in the state department; however, there was distrust of Superintendent Honig by the legislature and Governor Deukmejian.

One key element in the restoration process included the opening up of lines of communication within the agency and without—in fact, to almost anybody who was willing to listen. This was a staff function but also a commission aim as well. Under the leadership of its chairs the commission became known as a state agency that listened to its constituents.

A second element was the quality of the analytic work done by commission staff. The research and studies on professional growth, subject matter preparation of elementary teachers, validation of examinations, rules of professional conduct, standards for elementary and secondary teacher education programs, assignment of personnel, and the support and assessment of beginning teachers were done in ways that, over time, gained the agency both attention and trust.

A third element has been the performance of the Committee of Credentials. As the discipline arm of the commission, it developed a reputation as the most effective professional practices (revocation, suspension, reprimands) unit in the United States; annually 35 to 40 percent of all disciplinary actions taken through the United States against educators have been taken by this committee alone.

A last element was good constituent service, especially in connection with the licensing responsibility itself—twice-annual updating of the credential handbook, annual workshops, and daily service to applicants.

Over the last thirty years, a large number of reforms have moved California's credentialing system from a model based primarily on the completion of college courses to one based upon assessing individual competence. In a rough, uncertain and uneasy policy development, power shifted from the state superintendent, state board, and State Department of Education to the legislature and an independent commission. As politicians made efforts to improve the quality of teachers, credentialing became politicized, and almost all of the reforms have been brought by forces outside of education.

Credentialing in California has changed drastically. Now, its policies are primarily formulated by people who work in schools. Eventually, credentials will be issued on one's ability to teach after undergoing an internship supervised by a mentor. In addition, academic competence will be assessed by comprehensive examinations. By having teachers who have been screened both by academic and teaching ability, teaching will move closer to becoming a profession.

4

KEN CARLSON

New Jersey's Alternate Route

ANNOUNCEMENT AND REACTION

In September 1983, New Jersey Governor Tom Kean and Education Commissioner Saul Cooperman announced that teachers should no longer have to be prepared through college education programs. People who wanted to be teachers should have an "alternate route."

The alternate route which Kean and Cooperman proposed was:

1. Possess a bachelor's degree with at least a minor in the subject to be taught, with any liberal arts minor being acceptable for elementary and special education teachers.
2. Pass a test of content mastery in the subject to be taught or a general knowledge test for elementary and special education teaching.[1]
3. Complete a provisional year as a regularly salaried teacher. The provisional year would be preceded by a five-day orientation to the school and to all the important information about teaching (Cooperman, Webb, and Klagholz, 1983).

This proposal was offensive to the education professors in New Jersey for two reasons. First, they were excluded, both in the development stage (of which they had been kept unaware[2]) and in the implementation stage. Second, the proposal said that a prospective teacher could pick up all the essential professional knowledge in a few days.

The New Jersey branches of the American Federation of Teachers and the National Education Association also found the proposal offensive. Governor Kean and Commissioner Cooperman had said that the professional knowledge base for teaching was sparse enough to be acquired in a few days. Their implication that teaching was not a very professional career did not bode well for improvements in the status of the profession. However, at the same time that he seemed to be denigrating the teaching profession, Governor Kean did get an increase in the starting salary for teachers to $18,500.

Political Maneuvers

The opposing forces in the alternate route debate became Kean and Cooperman versus education professors and teacher unions. Kean and Cooperman were well known individuals; the professors and unions were amorphous assemblages. Kean and Cooperman were new on the state scene and fresh with promise; the professors and unions had been around forever. Kean and Cooperman embodied hope for something better; the professors and unions were cast as opponents of reform. Kean and Cooperman said they had only the public interest in mind; the professors and unions had an obvious self-interest at stake as well. Kean and Cooperman had a case which could be presented in simple terms; the professors and unions had to show that those terms were simplistic, but there was no simple way to do it. Kean and Cooperman had the public impulse to change that had been quickened by the National Commission on Excellence in Education; the professors and unions had journal critiques of *A Nation at Risk*.

Commissioner Cooperman went throughout New Jersey making the case for the alternate route. He used a three-word mantra: competition, economical, reform. The alternate route would be competition for the college education programs. Competition would cause everyone to try harder and do better. The alternate route would be much more economical than the college programs because it would be much less prolonged. It would attract people into teaching by putting them on the payroll immediately instead of charging them tuition and making them take numerous education courses of dubious value. This would also make it less costly for the state. And the alternate route would reform New Jersey's emergency certification procedure by insuring that even teachers hired on an emergency basis got some formal preparation. All of these arguments are found in Cooperman's (1983) testimony to the state legislature.

The education professors replied that the alternate route would be far too fast and easy, but they had difficulty demonstrating the necessity for something longer and harder. Their claim to higher-quality programs was countered by Cooperman's claim to higher-quality entrants. The commissioner touted the outstanding people who were waiting to get into the alternate route and made no mention of the ones who were less than outstanding. Moreover, the professors had to contend with research which showed that students in college education programs had low Scholastic Achievement Test scores compared to students in other college programs (Weaver, 1979). That the research results were false for many of the New Jersey college programs was a message that did not change the general perception.

The debate was carried on in the media, with each side trying to get coverage of its position. New Jersey's largest circulation newspaper, the *Newark Star-Ledger*, had backed Tom Kean for governor and was friendly to his administration. In May of 1983, several months before the announcement of the alternate route proposal, the *Star-Ledger* carried a Sunday front-page story, with photos, of an accomplished young woman who wanted to be a teacher but had no intention of subjecting herself to the required education courses. The story was sympathetic to her and did not suggest that any of the required education courses might be justified (Braun, May 29, 1983, p. 39).

After the alternate route proposal was made public, the *Star-Ledger* regularly gave front-page coverage to Cooperman's pronouncements on it. The education editor of the paper, in his twice-weekly editorial column, shifted between support for the alternate route and attacks on the college education programs.

The professors and unions had been caught off guard and put on the defensive by the governor and commissioner, but they had access to the state legislature, one of whose members was an education professor. The New Jersey Education Association (an NEA affiliate) was the largest union in the state, and it had money plus votes. With this political power, it could command the attention of the legislature on any issue. Soon committees of the legislature were drafting bills that would scuttle the alternate route. As it turned out, no bills on the alternate route were brought to a vote in the legislature because the governor promised to veto them and the commissioner promised to appoint expert committees to refine the proposal.

For the next three months, and before the expert committees were convened, there were sporadic announcements that another prominent person or organization had decided to endorse the idea of an alternate route. The chancellor of higher education for New Jersey, the New Jersey School Boards Association, and the New Jersey Principals and Supervisors Association all got on board. The organizational endorsements were made by the leadership and it was never known how much these reflected member sentiment, but member grumbling was heard. In the case of the state School Boards Association, officers complained that the executive director had not consulted with them before he committed the organization. With the Principals and Supervisors Association, two of its county chapters announced opposition to the endorsement. Press coverage of the demurrers was imperceptible.

The chancellor's endorsement was given an interesting interpretation in a letter written much later by Commissioner Cooperman. The chancellor had angered Cooperman, who then accused the chancellor of endorsing the alternate route because he wanted to reduce the size of college education programs and capture faculty lines for the liberal arts programs (Cooperman, September 20, 1984) The chancellor's staff then acknowledged that cutting back on the faculty lines in the college education programs had been a goal of the chancellor (Braun, October 2, 1984).

This may have been one of the reasons that college presidents began weighing in with their endorsements. The presidents had an additional inducement. They knew that Cooperman intended to create an Academy for the Advancement of Teaching and Management, and it was expected that the academy would be based at a college. (The academy was established eventually and is still operating—at a noncollege site.) The president of Rutgers, the State University of New Jersey, may have had a third inducement. He announced his support of the alternate route at a morning press conference (Braun, January 13, 1984), and that afternoon Governor Kean announced a special $3 million appropriation to upgrade the training facilities for Rutgers' football team (Remington, 1984). There was a lot of joking among education deans about this coincidence, with one wag going so far as to suggest that Rutgers should have held out for a nuclear reactor.

The most prominent person to endorse New Jersey's alternate route proposal was the president of the United States. In a speech on December 9, 1983, Ronald Reagan said:

> In New Jersey, Governor Tom Kean has a proposal that deserves wide support. Under his plan, the New Jersey Board of Education would allow successful mathematicians, scien-

tists, linguists, and journalists to pass a competency test in their subjects, then go into the classroom as paid teaching interns. If they performed well, they would be issued permanent teaching certificates. ("President Praises State Licensing Plan," 1983)

The most legally significant endorsement came from the State Board of Education. A few days after Reagan's endorsement, the state board ruled that New Jersey would have an alternate route to teaching, details to be worked out later.

Two Expert Committees

The first of Cooperman's expert committees was chaired by Ernest Boyer, president of the Carnegie Foundation for the Advancement of Teaching, and came to be known as the Boyer Panel. Other members of the panel were David Berliner, an educational psychologist at the University of Arizona; Frank Brown, dean of education at the University of North Carolina; Edgar Epps, Marshall Field Professor of Urban Education at the University of Chicago; C. Emily Feistritzer, director of the National Center for Education Information; Jay Gottlieb, an educational psychologist at New York University; Lawrence Lezotte of the administration and curriculum department at Michigan State University; Archie Lapointe, executive director of the National Assessment Office at Educational Testing Service; Kathryn Maddox, director of the Multi-Institutional Teacher Education Center for the Kanawha County (West Virginia) Schools; and Barak Rosenshine, an educational psychologist at the University of Illinois.

Cooperman's main charge to the Boyer Panel was to answer the question: What is essential for beginning teachers to know about the profession? Since none of the panelists was a teaching field specialist, for example, a science educator, the panel was predicted to recommend a generic knowledge base, and it did. It recommended that a beginning teacher know about curriculum development, teaching strategies, materials selection, human development, assessment of pupils, classroom management, and the sociology of schooling. These recommendations were the result of a two-day meeting and were contained in a fourteen-page report (Boyer, 1984). The Boyer "topics" were adopted by Cooperman as the mandatory topics for all teacher education programs in New Jersey.

Before the Boyer Panel report was issued, some New Jersey education deans met with Boyer at the annual conference of the American Association of Colleges for Teacher Education. The meeting was arranged by David Imig of the AACTE. (The AACTE had earlier given $5,000 to the New Jersey education deans to assist them in exposing and combating weaknesses in the alternate route.) The deans were worried that the Boyer panelists were being co-opted by Tom Kean and Saul Cooperman, and would have their names invoked in support of the alternate route in whatever form it finally took. Cooperman did extract from the panelists a promise that they would not comment on the final product, and their silence was construed as tacit support.[3]

The second of Cooperman's expert committees was composed entirely of New Jerseyans. It was chaired by the Tenafly schools superintendent, Harry Jaroslaw, and became known as the Jaroslaw Commission.[4] Its charge was to decide how the Boyer topics could be taught to beginning teachers in the alternate route program.

The New Jersey Association of Colleges for Teacher Education—the education deans' group—was not invited to designate a representative to the Jaroslaw Commission. Twelve of the twenty-one commission members had already endorsed the alternate route proposal. Other commission members were laypeople whose questions indicated that they were not conversant with the issues. They asked what the education curricula of the colleges included and how this differed from the Boyer topics, seemingly unaware that the colleges had subject-specific teacher training and the Boyer topics ignored the need for such specificity.

The Jaroslaw Commission concluded that the Boyer topics could not be communicated adequately to people in the alternate route in the five days which Commissioner Cooperman had allotted in his original proposal. They recommended that this be increased to twenty days before the provisional teaching year began, and be followed by a seminar taken during the year. The Jaroslaw Commission went on to say that the thirty college credits in the subject to be taught could be waived for someone who had "five years of full-time work experience in a professional level job related to the subject to be taught" (Jaroslaw, 1984, p. 5). The commission agreed with Cooperman that alternate route programs could be operated by local school districts without college involvement.

At this point the union opposition to the alternate route began to dissolve. The state AFT president, Marco Lacatena, and his NEA counterpart, Edithe Fulton, had both served on the Jaroslaw Commission. Lacatena issued a dissenting report. Fulton did not, and she voted to have the majority report transmitted to Commissioner Cooperman. Lacatena suspected that the state NEA was positioning itself to make a claim on the academic seminar that alternate route teachers might have to take during their provisional year. The New Jersey Education Association has an institute for the training of in-service teachers, and the solvency of the institute would be strengthened if NJEA could conduct the seminar for the alternate route teachers. At any rate, Lacatena stepped up his opposition to the alternate route while Fulton ceased to be heard from.

CHALLENGES TO THE COLLEGE PROGRAMS

The college teacher certification programs in New Jersey are under the control of the state education commissioner. At the same time that Cooperman's alternate route proposal was being refined through his expert committee arrangement, he set about to alter the college programs.

Cooperman and the chancellor of higher education issued a joint ruling that if an educational foundations course, for example, educational psychology, were taught by an education professor, the professor's vita had to be submitted for review by the New Jersey Departments of Education and Higher Education. If the educational psychology course were taught by someone in a psychology department, no review was needed (Cooperman and Hollander, December 30, 1983). The discriminatory nature of this demand caused the American Association of University Professors (AAUP) at Rutgers to protest, and Rutgers' president indicated that he would not comply with the demand. The demand was then changed so that the education professor's vita did not have to be submitted, but instead the professor had to acquire a joint appointment in the counterpart liberal arts department or else have the course cross listed with that department (Cooperman and Hollander, March 9, 1984). This gave liberal arts departments veto power over faculty and courses offered in the educational foundations area. The president of Rutgers agreed to go along with the new demand, and the AAUP remained silent.

Cooperman and the chancellor also reinterpreted the requirements of the college certification programs. These requirements had been promulgated in 1982 under the previous commissioner. They called for sixty credits of general education, thirty credits in a liberal arts major, eighteen credits in the behavioral and social foundations of teaching, and thirty credits in professional education. (The distinction between the last two categories has been elusive and problematic.) Cooperman and the chancellor insisted that the sixty credits of general education and the thirty-credit liberal arts major were absolute minima, but the rest of the credits could be reduced without objection so long as the reduction resulted in an addition to the two liberal arts categories. Prospective teachers would be required to take an irreducible minimum of liberal arts credits but not education credits.

In addition to the credit hour requirements for its college certification programs, New Jersey has requirements governing the admission and continuation of students, the prestudent teaching field experiences, student teaching, and testing. To check compliance with all these requirements, Cooperman issued forms which every college program had to complete. The completed forms were given to a group of out-of-state reviewers. College program officials then met with the reviewers to explain what was on the forms.

Given the number of requirements which had to be satisfied and the interpretational nuances that could be placed on many of these, it was quite possible that a college program would be found wanting in some area. The front page of *The Newark Star-Ledger* confirmed this with a headline that read "Teacher Training Fails State Test," and with a subheading that said "21 of 26 Colleges Facing Major Cutback in Programs" (Braun, May 29, 1984). The story could have come only from Cooperman's state education department. It discredited the college programs, thereby making the emerging alternate route look more desirable. The story also discredited education professors, who had been the most informed critics of the alternate route. The subsequent acknowledgment by the state education department that many of the college program "failures" had been minor technical—and easily corrected—violations lacked the sensationalism of the original report (Braun, May 31, 1984, p. 1).

Lacatena's Initiatives

With the education professors discredited and demoralized by Cooperman's regulatory assault, and with the NJEA lying low, the major opponent to the alternate route became Marco Lacatena of the AFT. Lacatena and the AFT published a newsprint booklet which was distributed to 2500 members of the Association of Teacher Educators, 735 institutional representatives to the American Association of Colleges for Teacher Education, 455 education reporters, the members of the Boyer Panel and Jaroslaw Commission, 619 New Jersey school boards and 510 superintendents, the members of the state legislature, New Jersey's college presidents and faculties, and the members of the State Boards of Education and Higher Education. The booklet contained an overview of events, the text of the Boyer Panel and Jaroslaw Commission reports, reprints of newspaper articles, and letters.

The person who was most activated by the Lacatena booklet was Hendrik Gideonse, then the education dean at the University of Cincinnati. He wrote critiques of the Boyer Panel and Jaroslaw Commission reports. Then he came to New Jersey and testified before the State Board of Education.

Gideonse's testimony had to be revised at the last moment. The hearings were scheduled to be on the Jaroslaw report, with the first hearing on June 28, 1984. On June 6, Cooperman issued a 102-page set of proposed changes in the New Jersey Education Code, including changes in the college programs and a detailed specification of how the alternate route would be operated. Two weeks later, Cooperman issued a 111-page revised set of changes, so that this became the last minute focus of the hearings.

The last-minute changes, and the voluminousness with which they were presented, made it difficult for members of the State Board of Education to keep up with events. This was the group that would make the final decision, but the issues had become blurred in a welter of technical detail.

To refocus and dramatize the issues, Lacatena persuaded the education deans to hold a conference. This took place in mid-July, and attracted as speakers J. Myron Atkin, dean of education at Stanford; Robert Egbert, chair of the National Commission for Excellence in Teacher Education; and Albert Shanker, president of the American Federation of Teachers. Penelope Earley of the AACTE was the key person in lining up these speakers.

All three speakers expressed their dismay with New Jersey's alternate route to teacher certification. However, the conference was not well attended, and only one member of the Jaroslaw Commission showed up to defend the commission's report. Other members of the commission who had agreed to speak withdrew after checking with the state education department. Press coverage of the conference was low. Most depressing of all for those who hoped that the conference would turn events around was the message brought by two state legislators. One of these was the education professor who had been railing against the alternate route proposal for almost a year. The legislators informed the audience that they, too, had finally been persuaded to change their minds. They said that their concerns about the alternate route had been allayed by promises made to them by Cooperman's staff. They left the deans' conference and hurried to the state capitol where a press conference had been arranged for them to announce their new position.

The Alternate Route and Its Aftermath

On September 5, 1984, the New Jersey State Board of Education unanimously adopted the alternate route to teacher certification. On table 1 are the requirements of the alternate route, as finally adopted, contrasted with the state-mandated requirements for the college certification programs.

TABLE 1

College Programs	Alternate Route
1. Sixty cr. of general education, to include arts, humanities, math, science, social science, and technology.	1. Bachelor's but no general education specification.
2. Demonstrated proficiency in English and math.	2. Nothing.
3. Minimum grade point average of 2.5 (A=4).	3. Nothing.
4. A major of at least thirty cr. in the subject to be taught (any liberal arts major for elementary and early childhood teaching).	4. Thirty cr. in subject to be taught.
5. Extensive and progressively developed field work from sophomore through senior year.	5. Twenty-day practicum.
6. In a comprehensive field, a distribution of coursework	6. Nothing.

TABLE 1 *(continued)*

College Programs	Alternate Route
(e.g., in social studies, courses in world history, American history, political science, economics, geography, and sociology or cultural anthropology).	
7. College cr. coursework in curriculum, student development and learning, the classroom and the school, and physiology and hygiene to a maximum of thirty cr.	7. Two hundred hours of instruction in these areas.
8. College cr. coursework in methods of teaching particular subjects, e.g., techniques of social studies instruction.	8. Nothing.
9. Comprehensive test of subject mastery.	9. Comprehensive test of subject mastery.
10. Full semester of student teaching without pay.	10. One-year internship at full pay.

Each year, Commissioner Cooperman presented a progress report on the alternate route. According to the 1989 report, the program is endorsed by the National Governors Association, the Council of Chief State School Officers, and President Bush's Education Summit (New Jersey State Department of Education, 1989). By March 1991, more than 7,500 applications to the program had been received, with 1,884 applicants being hired as provisional teachers (New Jersey State Department of Education, 1991). Praise in these reports is to the effect that the alternate route teachers score higher on the National Teacher Examination subject tests and general knowledge test than do students in the college education programs. And teachers in the alternate route are not as likely to drop out of teaching in their first year as are teachers who have come through the college programs.

Cooperman's press releases on the alternate route have received favorable treatment in New Jersey's newspapers and in the *New York Times* (see, for example, Braun, November 16, 1986, and November 19, 1989; Carmody, 1989; "New Jersey, in Five Years, Solves Teacher Shortage," 1989; and Saul, 1986). Cooperman himself has promoted the alternate route through articles in national journals (for example, Cooperman and Klagholz, 1985).

Critical reaction has been muted from the education professors in New Jersey. This may be explained by the fact that enrollment in the college certification programs has increased in recent years due to the national focus on education, and thus the preparation of teachers in New Jersey has not become a zero-sum game. Cooperman's alternate route is attracting more applicants annually, but so are the college programs. Another probable reason for the relative quiescence is that some of the colleges have acquired a role in the alternate route. The academic seminar (two hundred hours of instruction) which alternate route teachers must take is now offered under college auspices. College faculty also claim that they jeopardized state approval of their own programs if they spoke out against Cooperman's program.

Those who continue to examine the alternate route critically have several concerns about it. One concern is that the agency which created and operates the alternate route is also the agency that evaluates it. The state education department evaluates its own program. That constitutes a conflict of interest, and the conflict is compounded by the fact that the state education department also evaluates the college programs.

This situation has produced some questionable comparisons. For example, it is said that the people in the alternate route score higher on the National Teacher Exam than the people in the college programs. However, the test results are controlled by the state education department, and it can decide whom to count as being in the alternate route. After the first year's count, when the names of the people allegedly in the college programs were released, college education officials complained that many of the people listed as being in their programs were unknown to them. Even if the numbers are assumed to be correct, their significance is not obvious. For example, in June 1990 the state issued a comparison of the NTE scores of alternate route applicants and college program students (Annual Report on Certification Testing, 1990). For some of the NTE tests, the difference in the average score between the two groups is only a few points. If one group has an average score of 629 and the other 624, is that significant either statistically or predictively? Or is it only significant politically?

The state also says that alternate route teachers are more likely to finish out their first year than are college-prepared teachers. The alternate route teachers have to complete their first, or provisional, year in order to get certified, whereas the college-prepared teachers start with that goal already achieved. This motivational difference between the two groups is absent from the state's discussion.

A second area of concern is with the kinds of schools that hire alternate route teachers. More than a quarter (554 of 1,884) of the alternate route teachers have been in nonpublic schools (New Jersey State Department of Education, 1991, p.4). After their provisional year and certification, they can apply for public school positions, and many do. That raises the question of whether private school teaching is appropriate for public school certification. If these teachers remain in nonpublic schools, a question arises for taxpayers whether public money should be used for the training of nonpublic school teachers.

Of greater concern is the fact that alternate route teachers are used so extensively to staff urban schools. Of the 1330 public school teachers in the alternate route, about a third (488) are accounted for by four urban districts: Newark, Camden, East Orange, and Paterson (New Jersey State Department of Education, 1991, pp. 14-21). Commissioner Cooperman frequently complained about the quality of the teaching in New Jersey's urban schools. Indeed, this complaint was part of his justification for creating the alternate route. Now these schools are the major training sites for alternate route teachers, and the Paterson schools have been taken over by the state because of their general ineffectiveness.

Related to the concern about the quality of the on-site training that alternate route teachers receive is the quantity. A 1989 survey of alternate route teachers reveals that 79 percent of them assumed full responsibility for their classes on day one (Smith, 1990). This is permitted if the alternate route teacher has "teaching experience," a term that is not defined. Urban schools, which in New Jersey are relatively underfunded, may not have the luxury of paying a full salary to an alternate route teacher who begins with part-time work.

Regardless of their prior "teaching experience," alternate route teachers are supposed to be supervised on a regular schedule. The amount of supervision actually received is far below that specified in the state's requirements, and for which the alternate route teachers themselves must pay. For their first four weeks on the job, alternate route teachers are supervised for only 15 percent of the time specified by the state (Smith, 1990, p. 5). These survey findings are of the same order and magnitude as those that were gathered by the New Jersey Education Association in the first year of the alternate route (NJEA, 1986). It is widely known, and has been since the first year, that a key component of the alternate route program—supervision—is well below the amount prescribed. This is not mentioned in the state's annual progress reports.

Again, poor schools may lack the personnel to provide the specified amount of supervision, but it is precisely these schools that are most dependent on alternate route teachers. Effective state monitoring of this is almost impossible because of the way the system is designed. From 1985 to 1991, 246 public school districts and 323 nonpublic schools had alternate route teachers (New Jersey State Department of Education, 1991, p. 5). The sheer number of schools involved each year augurs against field inspection. Even so, the New Jersey Education Association and an independent researcher were both able to find evidence of wholesale disregard of the supervision requirements. The Council for Basic Education, in its examination of the alternate route program, got a sufficient sense of this situation to recommend that "the state monitor the school support teams more closely, and that districts be required to provide resources for schools hiring provisional candidates so that those schools can, in turn, provide adequate support for the provisional teachers" (Gray and Lynn, 1988, p. 16).

The academic seminar which alternate route teachers take is another area of concern. The Boyer Panel recommended, and logistics dictate, that the instruction in this seminar be generic. If there are twelve alternate route teachers in one location in New Jersey, and if these teachers are scattered among grade levels and subject fields, it is infeasible to have anything but generic instruction. Problems peculiar to mathematics teaching or science teaching or elementary school teaching are ignored in the focus on teaching in general. The state even recommends that this instruction be carried out by an "education generalist" (New Jersey State Department of Education, 1985). Grade- and subject-specific instruction are thus left to supervisors at the teaching site. Even if the supervision were occurring, it would have to be by people who have kept abreast of developments in their teaching specialties to be effective. There are now hundreds of public schools and hundreds of nonpublic schools with alternate route teachers, and no evidence whatsoever that the supervision which is not occurring would be good if it were occurring. In his 1983 legislative testimony, Cooperman repeatedly expressed concern about the quality of supervision for practice teachers in the college programs (pp. 27, 37).

Added to this is the problem of when the academic seminar is held. Eighty hours of it are supposed to take place before the alternate route teacher begins the provisional teaching year, with the remaining 120 hours taken in evening or weekend sessions. However, more than half of the alternate route teachers are hired at the beginning of the school year or after the year has already begun, so they have no academic preparation when they start (New Jersey State Department of Education, 1991, p. 3).

Again, schools that depend on alternate route teachers often do so because they still have staff vacancies at the onset of the school year. These tend to be the poorest schools. The alternate route teachers in these schools not only have difficult teaching situations and a lack of supervision, but they must complete the full two hundred hours of the academic seminar during the school year. This may explain the finding of the New Jersey Principals and Supervisors Association. The PSA surveyed the principals who had alternate route teachers in their schools. Forty-five percent of them reported that there was too much stress on the alternate route teachers and too little preparation time ("Confidential PSA Survey," 1986). One of the alternate route teachers in an urban school reports that he had to commute an hour each way to the site of the academic seminar, which consisted of the regular teacher preparation courses offered by that college and all the attendant requirements. He found this to be extremely burdensome and to detract from the time he had to prepare for his own teaching (Harris, 1990).

An accommodation that has been made to this situation is that the state no longer cares if the academic seminar has any pupil performance requirements. The alternate route teachers must demonstrate attendance at the seminar, but nothing more is expected, and in some of the seminars nothing more is realized, according to the director of the alternate route seminars conducted by Trenton State College (Smith, October 20, 1990).

C. Emily Feistritzer, director of the National Center for Education Information, has said that New Jersey (along with Connecticut and Texas) has the best designed alternate route of the thirty-three states with such routes ("More Alternative Paths," 1990). It should be noted that Feistritzer was one of the Boyer panelists and thus had a hand in designing New Jersey's route. At any rate, if New Jersey's truly is among the best alternate routes in the nation, the other states have a long way to go.

An Uncertain Future

New Jersey's alternate route has suddenly become endangered, at least in its present form. In January 1990, Republican Tom Kean was succeeded as governor by Democrat Jim Florio. Soon thereafter Saul Cooperman became aware that the Florio administration was considering other people for the commissioner's job, and he announced his resignation, effective in June. Following upon Cooperman's resignation, the chancellor of higher education announced that he, too, would be leaving by the summer. The ranking officials who had made the alternate route a reality, and who evinced considerable antipathy to schools of education have gone.

In the meantime, there has arisen a fresh skepticism about alternate routes to teaching, and about New Jersey's route in particular. In December 1989, Arthur Wise, director of the RAND Corporation's Center for the Study of the Teaching Profession, challenged the idea of allowing amateurs to teach. He was responding to remarks Cooperman made at a conference on alternate routes sponsored by the U.S. Department of Education ("Alternate Certification for Teachers Is Examined," 1989). The RAND Corporation had earlier completed a study of alternate routes and found that those like New Jersey's, which entail the least preparation and supervision, are the least well rated by the recruits (Darling-Hammond, Hudson, and Kirby, 1989).

The departure of Kean and Cooperman may embolden people who claim to know of horror stories in the alternate route to go public with their evidence. The stories fall into two major categories: those by school officials about alternate route candidates who were so emotionally unsuited to teaching in today's schools that they had to be released during the school year, and those by alternate route candidates about the total lack of supervision they received. The latter category has been quantified by Smith's study, cited above, in which the identities of the respondents remain confidential. The former category is one about which the New Brunswick schools superintendent has been willing to speak. His district has a sizable minority student population and hired a minority candidate in the alternate route. The person turned out to be a poor teacher who responded badly to constructive supervision and eventually abandoned his teaching role to organize a sit-in of minority students. The superintendent refused to continue this person into a second year and banned him from school premises. There followed a year of inquiries from the state education commissioner, the governor, New Jersey's two U.S. senators, and civil rights organizations, all the while the individual at issue was acquiring and being fired from other jobs (Larkin, 1990). None of this was noted in the commissioner's annual report on the alternate route.

There may, however, be a reluctance to throw the infant alternate route out with the bathwater. It has become a mechanism for staffing urban schools, and if it is abandoned, something else will have to be found. To Cooperman's credit, the alternate route has brought some very capable and mature people into teaching, including many from minority groups. It is unreasonable to expect such people to forgo an income and pay tuition and undergo full-time protracted study toward a teaching certificate. Between what Cooperman demanded of these people and what might be ideal in a resource-rich world, there is a lot of ground on which to fashion a compromise. The compromise should be worked out by all the major players to avoid the unnecessary wrangling which Cooperman provoked when he excluded teacher educators.

Conclusions

Education became highly politicized during the 1980's. Governors vied to be known as education governors. Shifting education to the political realm, that is, to the arena of professional politicians, meant debasing its substance with public relations ploys and slogans. Oversimplifications abounded during the start-up period for the alternate route. On the other hand, this politicization of education did catch the public's interest and made teaching seem like an important career to people who had not thought so before. A lot of these people have become teachers.

The alternate route struggle in New Jersey is also a lesson in the uses of power. The governor had the power to punish and reward. The punishment might be the withholding of a potential reward. Rutgers, the state university, underwent enormous growth during the Kean administration. For the president of Rutgers, the prospect of this growth could well have made his endorsement of the alternate route seem like a wise tradeoff. That the president was not that enamored of the alternate route became known later when he sent a confidential letter to Cooperman warning that the alternate route was a "grave mistake" (Bloustein, 1984).

The governor and the commissioner were consistent newsmakers, so they could command press attention whenever they wanted it. Moreover, by favoring certain reporters with leaks, they could guarantee a degree of press support for their actions. Their opponents, the education professors and teacher unions, were not as reliable newsmakers. They were offering the status quo, which was not news, or else they were reacting to the initiatives of the governor and commissioner, in which case their reactions would be quoted at the end of articles about the governor and commissioner.

Another conclusion that was made obvious by events is that education professors have few allies. Their liberal arts colleagues would not rally to their defense even against the meretriciousness of the original alternate route proposal. Education school bashing is so time honored a pastime in academia that it is almost a reflex action among people who pride themselves for objectivity.

Thus, the college certification programs were easy targets. Everyone knew that these were supposed to be of low quality, and that perception was impossible to overcome. It may even have been heightened by the anger with which the education professoriate responded to Cooperman's animadversions, as though they were protesting too much.

The end result has been not just the establishment of an alternative to the college programs but a weakening of these programs to make them more similar to the alternate route. Generic teacher education is all the state now expects of the college programs, and programs that are struggling for resources no longer have state support in maintaining subject-specific teacher preparation.

5

Ellis A. Joseph and James Biddle

Teacher Education in Ohio, 1960 to 1990:

Strong Paradigm; Emerging Anomalies

Atomistic Beginnings

In the early 1960s, Ohio emerged from a period when one could become a teacher by undertaking a two-year college or university preparation program; upon completion of the program one was designated a "cadet" teacher. During April, 1966, the Ohio Department of Education decided to utilize funds made available under Title V of the Elementary and Secondary Education Act on a project having as its aim the upgrading of student teaching.

The project was labeled the Findlay Conference (Metz, 1967). (The conference actually included five colleges: Findlay, Ohio Northern, Heidelberg, Defiance, and Bluffton colleges, all located in northwestern Ohio). Topics for discussion at the conference grew out of questions presented in advance by 209 educators who subsequently attended. Questions were also posed by Dr. L. O. Andrews of the Ohio State University, known in those days as "Mr. Student Teaching." Student teaching was considered the "heart" of teacher preparation by the committee preparing for the conference. Agreement on the central importance of student teaching was held by all those involved: teacher educators, cooperating teachers, principals, and superintendents.

Unlike currently used modes of inquiry at major conferences, the Findlay Conference employed the strategy of presenting the energetic rhetoric of that period's most towering figure in the area of field experience, Dr. L. O. Andrews. Andrews used common sense and logic to focus upon personal, logistic, and structural concerns which heightened participants' awareness of the conditions that were thought to make student teaching a successful component of teacher education. The conference was completely devoid of empirical studies and of what today is associated with rigor in examining student teaching. The relationship between prerequisite studies as the knowledge base for student teaching received no mention. References were made to James B. Conant (1963) and to Margaret Lindsey (1961) who suggested the crucial need to obtain more knowledge about the problems and weaknesses related to the area of student teaching. Indeed, participants at the Findlay Conference shared Conant's and Lindsey's focus on student teaching by developing a problem statement for themselves: "Among the many controversies about the professional education of teachers there is one area on which authorities in the field agree. This area of agreement is student teaching" (Metz, 1967, p. 13). Congruence was achieved between the problem statement and Conference conclusions. Developing state standards for student teaching programs was among the most important suggestions for future conferences.

In May, 1966, the Ohio Department of Education arranged the Granville Conference whose purpose was to assess the amount and kind of need for assistance in the upgrading of college supervisors of student teaching (Greene, 1967). A strategic intent emerged from the conference: namely, to use Title V (Elementary and Secondary Education Act) funds for upgrading supervisors of student teaching. While the Findlay Conference was slanted toward student teaching in rural settings, the Granville Conference placed some emphasis upon the inner city. Again, a charismatic rhetorician, Dr. Paul Briggs, superintendent of Cleveland schools, was called upon to deliver the keynote address. After citing statistic after statistic on abject conditions in Cleveland (e.g., 5,000 children in the Hough area have never seen Lake Erie), Briggs concluded colleges and universities were not prepared to train teachers for urban teaching because education professors had not spent the necessary time in central city schools. Further, Briggs concluded future teachers should be placed in urban situations for at least three to six months in order to understand the problems of urban education.

Despite the content of Briggs's address, conference participants proceeded with conventional topics, achieving little direct relationship between those topics and urban education. They dutifully considered how much student teaching and related experiences should count for one semester hour of credit, the relationship of college supervisors to the principal and school supervisors, the role of the college supervisor in evaluation of student teaching, minimum state standards for student teaching, and so on. Again, these issues were treated descriptively and with logic and common sense. There was no evidence that empirical findings and knowledge bases provided a foundation for participants' deliberations.

EMERGENCE OF A STRONG PARADIGM

The Conference on Teacher Education Targets (known as the Targets Conference) held in May, 1967, greatly broadened the scope of topics related to teacher preparation. At a time when Ohio was deliberating on the implications of a teacher shortage, Superintendent of Public Instruction Dr. Martin Essex (1967) courageously called for an adequate supply of suitably prepared teachers, for a differentiation of teaching duties, and for a greater reward and a greater status for the superior practitioner. Essex's call is in direct contrast to Ohio's current mood: that is, cheapening teacher preparation by legislating a short-cut three-week preparation track amidst no teacher shortage. Essex launched a process of thinking that eventually resulted in Ohio's exemplary redesign of teacher education, which became known as the 1974 standards.

The Targets Conference was a forum for consideration of: problems and issues related to the approval of institutions for teacher preparation, subject matter preparation and certification, and the nature of professional preparation. Student teaching took its place as one topic amongst many rather than being the primary focus of the conference, as it was in previous conferences.

In the process it employed, the Targets Conference achieved a rather complete forum of collaboration. College presidents, school administrators, teacher educators, and the Ohio Education Association were all involved. Such collaboration was a forerunner of structuring the 1974 standards which involved all the stakeholders in teacher education.

Building upon the Targets Conference, the Ohio Department of Education entered into a contract with the Educational Research Council of America in order to conduct a systematic and purposeful investigation of teacher education in Ohio. The investigation was called the Teacher Education Assessment Project (TEAP) (Blankenship and Marquit, 1970), and the 506-page report was concluded in 1970. TEAP surveyed the current status of teacher education in Ohio, identified improved approaches and structures for teacher education, and proposed new ways of conducting teacher education. Once these assessments were made, planning could begin for restructuring teacher education. While the TEAP was occurring, the Ohio Department of Education and the University of Toledo cooperated in developing a competency-based teacher education model for elementary teacher education. Both the TEAP and Toledo efforts stressed accountability, an emphasis which was to appear later in a position paper developed by education deans in relation to Ohio's developing 1974 standards (popularly known as "Redesign").

Teacher Education Redesign, an effort which culminated in the 1974 standards, may have been the most massive collaborative effort ever undertaken to create new standards for teacher education. Over three thousand persons were involved in one hundred meetings held in the fall and winter of 1973. Eight representative councils worked in behalf of major educational organizations. Regional meetings were held involving citizens, school board members, college and university faculty, teachers, administrators, students preparing to be teachers, and PTA representatives. An overall representative advisory committee was involved in distilling conclusions which led to the new standards adopted by the State Board of Education in 1974.

These standards, at the time, were regarded as the most stringent and perhaps the most revolutionary in the nation. A total of three hundred hours of field and clinical experiences prior to student teaching were required of all students preparing to teach. These experiences, which were to begin in the first year of higher education and be continuous in following years, were to be in urban and suburban and/or rural settings. All students were to be prepared to teach reading. Faculty/student ratios were set at one to fourteen. Education professors would be required to have taught successfully for three years in elementary and secondary schools. Students were to become proficient in diagnosing and prescribing for learning problems. The teacher education program was to be characterized by sequence and pattern. Each program and each course were to elaborate knowledge, skills, attitudes, and values. Most important of all, state funding for all institutions was to be forthcoming in order to help them implement new standards. Annual appropriations for this purpose now total approximately $12,800,000 (State Board of Education of Ohio, 1989).

These standards were accompanied by a most rigorous and meticulous system of on-site evaluations. In addition, each president of each institution had to verify before examiners that appropriations for implementing new standards were actually spent for that purpose as contrasted to being used to replace funds already in regular budgets. This was accomplished despite strenuous objections of college and university presidents and provosts. Ohio's state university education deans issued *Ohio Teacher Education: A Position Paper* (1973) which called attention to the fact that the Ohio General Assembly and the Ohio Board of Regents were implementing a subsidy classification for teacher education which was approximately $500 per teacher education student lower than the support of students enrolled in home economics, agriculture, social work, nursing, dental hygiene, and so on. In fact, teacher education students were not classified as "professional" for purposes of subsidy, while the aforementioned students were so classified.

G. Robert Bowers, an assistant superintendent of public instruction at the time the 1974 standards were in the process of gaining approval, displayed brilliant political acumen and exceptional conciliatory skills in inducing a variety of special interests to endorse stronger and funded standards. The teaching profession was persuaded to go along with massive increases in field experiences without funding. The objections of presidents and provosts to receiving funds which they did not control was overcome. The legislature was persuaded to provide subsidies for teacher education in *both* state and private higher education institutions. Funds flowing to teacher education institutions were to come through the Ohio Department of Education and not through the Ohio Board of Regents, an entity responsible for administering all other subsidies.

ANOMALIES

In 1985 the State Board of Education appointed a Teacher Education and Certification Standards Revision Committee to consider needed revisions in teacher education and certification standards. Admirable collaborative efforts continued in this, the latest effort to revise standards (State Board of Education of Ohio, 1989). A total of 499 small-group sessions involving over 8,300 persons were held amidst promise of producing some creative advances in teacher education. However, few, if any, creative advances occurred. Instead, anomalies began to appear. These were principally due to the pragmatic fact that no increased funding would be forthcoming even though new and expensive standards would be mandated in 1987. Support for individuals in entry-level positions was mandated but not funded. A major position paper on career ladders was ignored. The issue of depth and breadth in general education was sidestepped. The "life space" of the undergraduate curriculum was not considered even though the proposed standards placed unbearable and unrealistic strains upon a four-year program. Special education was inadvertently omitted from professional sequence requirements for all students. The temporary certificate loophole was not addressed. Standards for graduate work were made more rigorous without funding. Less professional preparation was required of secondary teachers than for elementary teachers.

On the positive side, academic preparation was increased, and a state examination for certification was mandated. Also, 122 classroom teachers participated in critiquing programs for approval. Permanent certificates were abolished.

The response of teacher education institutions to the anomalies in the 1987 standards was in stark contrast to their vigorous action during the 1974 standards approval process. In 1974, colleges and universities made it quite clear they would not implement new standards without proper funding. When it appeared, for a time, that the 1974 standards would be mandated without funding, George E. Dickson, the powerful and influential long-time dean of the College of Education at the University of Toledo, made a motion directing the officers of the Ohio Association of Colleges for Teacher Education to confront the state superintendent of public instruction to inform him that standards would not be implemented without funding. In addition, a formal letter was sent to the state's chief school officer informing him of the collective will of colleges and universities on the matter of funding. Even when funding was secured through House Bill 191, the Ohio Department of Education made moves to use much of the appropriation for bureaucratic purposes. Heads of teacher education institutions, using the Ohio Association of Colleges for Teacher Education as their mechanism, demanded the creation of an advisory committee to advise the Ohio Department of Education that most of the appropriation should be awarded to colleges and universities for the implementation of the new standards. The heads prevailed (Earley and Imig, 1979).

Unfortunately, by 1987 the leadership style in colleges of education had changed dramatically. Heads of teacher education, who used to meet regularly and take cohesive, strong positions, seldom could muster a full complement of attendees at important meetings. During the 1970s, many Ohio deans and heads of teacher education were exemplars of stability and achievement on their respective campuses and on state and national levels. However, retirements and a growing unwillingness of faculties to support deans who had identified a terrain of struggle resulted in frequent changes in weak deanships. The high turnover of deans was a major factor in the transition from assertive state leadership to a more acquiescent style of management.

In many ways the unique and extraordinary funding which accompanied the 1974 standards created a kind of bond between colleges and universities and the Ohio Department of Education. Institutions of higher education were grateful for the Ohio Department of Education's success in securing funding for teacher education. Quite naturally, the Ohio Department of Education expected loyalty from the colleges and universities when issues with potential conflict arose. Colleges were continually reminded, particularly from 1987 on, of the source of their funding for teacher education standards. These reminders by the Ohio Department of Education diffused debates on many positions held by colleges and universities which were contrary to state department views. Issues such as a proposed professional standards board and anomalies in the 1987 standards became especially divisive. By April, 1989, a serious rupture in Ohio Department of Education higher education relations became apparent to all when the department supported House Bill 212, which was an "alternative" certification measure originally proposing to create teachers with but three weeks training.

This rupture, while a surprise to some, was inevitable. The decline in vision, strength, and leadership of the deans and heads of teacher education in educational policy issues created a professional vacuum soon filled by critics of professional teacher education. During the process to revise the 1974 teacher education standards in 1985, a strong lobbying effort was mounted to establish a "New Jersey–type" alternative certification program. Led by State Board of Education member, Ms. Pat Smith, and Ohio Board of Regents Vice-Chancellor for Academic and Special Programs, Elaine Hairston (now chancellor), the platform was advanced that subject matter knowledge is both a necessary and sufficient condition for teaching.

However, a majority of the members of the Ohio Teacher Education and Certification Advisory Commission, as well as a majority of the appropriate subcommittee from the State Board of Education, voted that neither a professional nor even a pragmatic case for such a program had been made. It was noted that innovative and flexible teacher education programs consistent with the emerging knowledge base were encouraged in the current standards.

By 1988, the handwriting on the wall should have been clear to all—but most were not looking. Governor Richard Celeste's State of the State Address stressed the need for "...an education challenge program that will bring out the best in our students, our teachers, and all our citizens as we move into the 1990s." On February 2, 1988, his press secretary released Celeste's announcement of the appointment of the Education 2000 Commission. The governor said, "I have asked this commission to recommend bold steps Ohio can take to become a leader in education by the year 2000." The twenty-member commission was composed of educators, community leaders, legislators, and concerned citizens, but not one teacher educator. Pat Smith, who by this time was president of the State Board of Education, was a member.

Not unexpectedly, the commission recommended the establishment of "...an alternative certification method, based on the New Jersey model" (Ohio's Education 2000 Commission, p. 13). The rationale for the recommendation was that "...capable people who want to change from another career into a teaching career can do so with a minimum of interruption to their earning power." The relationship between minimal interruption of earning power and student achievement must have been self-evident to the commission because neither empirical nor conceptual considerations were supplied to support the recommendations.

While it is not possible to document all the behind-the-scene activity focused on alternate routes during this time, several strong assumptions can be made. Of the seven legislative members of the Education 2000 Commission, both Senate President Stanley Aronoff and Senate Education Committee Chairman Cooper Snyder became proponents of alternate routes. Senate Bill 140, introduced by Aronoff and Snyder and passed in April 1989, contained Ohio's legislation establishing an Internship Certificate, another name for an alternate route to certification.

Representative Randall Gardner played the critical role of marketer and lightning rod in the "by-pass" debate. In August of 1988, Rep. Gardner had the opportunity to meet with Governor Thomas Kean of New Jersey. According to Gardner, "One of Gov. Kean's notable achievements has been his Alternate Teacher Certification Program, which began attracting new quality people to the teaching profession" (Gardner, 1989b, p. 1). With Gardner, Aronoff, and Snyder embracing this concept, Gardner was chosen to introduce the Internship Certificate legislation in House Bill 212 (this same bill would reappear several weeks later as a part of Senate Bill 140, introduced by Aronoff and Snyder and passed in April, 1989). In his sponsor testimony, Gardner stated that "...we cannot ignore that 23 states are now implementing alternate route programs and 12 more are considering such changes in their certification standards" (Gardner, 1989b, p. 1). The parade was forming and Ohio was not represented.

The involvement of the Ohio Department of Education baffled the teacher education community. However, events defy the assumption of either coincidence or neutrality. While the Education 2000 Commission was writing its report and Gardner was meeting with Kean, the department was preparing a draft, dated August 5, 1988, entitled "Alternate Certification Routes Background Information." From at least this time on, the department became an active player in the quest for an alternate route. In a letter to deans and chairs of teacher education, dated March 14, 1989, Rep. Gardner stated that

> ...the Ohio Department of Education has been working closely with me as we strive to develop the finest alternative certification program in the nation. The Ohio Department of Education has demonstrated in the past, and in consultation on the drafting of House Bill 212, a willingness to consider innovative teacher preparation programs. The department's involvement and advice in the writing of the bill's language was invaluable.

Rep. Gardner, a staff member from Sen. Aronoff's office, and other "interested" parties worked on alternative certification legislation from September to December, 1988. (Pat Smith, as a member of the Education 2000 Commission and president of the State Board of Education, remained a key figure; but the involvement of the state board itself remains unclear). By December, enough work was done on the legislation and key legislators that William Phillis, Assistant Superintendent of Public Instruction responsible for all legislative interactions, informed Superintendent Franklin Walter that an alternate route bill would be passed in this session of the general assembly. Whether the department hierarchy supported alternate routes out of political expediency or professional principle cannot be determined; regardless, the department supported and legitimized the bill.

In late January, 1989, after the legislation had been written, the Ohio Department of Education announced that it was in the process of "exploring additional options for the preparation and certification of individuals who hold baccalaureate degrees and desire certification" (Gardner, 1989b, p. 4). Furthermore, it was preparing to review the "policies, practices and results of alternative certification programs in other states." As far as can be determined, no dean or head of teacher education in Ohio knew anything about the alternate route legislation until January 30, 1989. The first time anyone from the department officially informed the teacher education community was on February 15, 1989. Assistant Superintendent G. Robert Bowers, in his monthly meeting with the State University Education Deans, informed the deans that an alternate route bill had been introduced in the house on February 7. Dr. Bowers tried to persuade the deans that: (1) passage was inevitable; (2) opposition would be perceived as self-serving, hence counter-productive; and (3) opposing the bill on "professional principle," i.e., not being willing to tinker with a bad bill, would be political suicide. Keeping the deans quiet and passive seemed to be the goal of his presentation. The department, the deans were told, was doing everything it could to make the bill as palatable as possible.

The next two months were characterized by dizzying activity. Proponents had the edge because any opposition would confront "a done deal on a fast track." House Bill 212 was introduced on February 7, with sponsor testimony presented on February 28. On March 15 Senate Bill 140 was introduced; one of its sections was a verbatim HB 212. At the time, opponents were confused about the strategy behind having the same bill introduced in both the house and senate. Two months later it was learned that HB 212 was a diversion; SB 140 was to have been the vehicle from the beginning. The discovery of this strategy was one of the few serendipitous events of this affair. During a day of working the halls of the State

House and meeting with legislators, a key legislator mistook one of the authors of this study for the dean who supported HB 212. The author pursued the "proponents" plans; in less than fifteen minutes, the legislator laid out the entire strategy of the alternate route. Indeed, this case study could not have been written without knowledge of that strategy which brought all the disparate pieces together.

Meanwhile, opponents of the by-pass certification being proposed had to fight time, the political machine, and of course themselves. The leaders of the opposition were in hourly contact at times; six to eight phone calls and faxed materials per day per person was not uncommon. After hearing about HB 212 on February 15, the thirteen state university education deans on March 2 drafted a position statement (with one dean opposing and one abstaining) declaring opposition to the bill because of its incompatibility with the foundational principles and beliefs of the profession; HB 212 was seen as a by-pass leading in another direction, not an alternative route to the same destination. Political naivete and impotence did not result in paralysis. Four or five of the key opponents attended legislative hearings, haunted the halls of the State House, and met two or three times per week.

During the same period, the Ohio Association of Private Colleges for Teacher Education and the Ohio Federation of Teachers decided not to publicly oppose the legislation, but to work to try to make the bill as tolerable as possible. Indeed, organized public opposition to the bill was minimal. The Ohio Education Association and the state university education deans were the only education organizations working to defeat rather than amend the bill.

As a side light to the alternate route debate, SB 140 had another surprise for teacher education. Section 9 of the bill called for a "new uniform curriculum and specific admission and student evaluation standards to be used in the education of teachers." The development of such a curriculum was placed with the Ohio Board of Regents (OBR); upon repeated questioning, the regents personnel insisted they had no idea who originated Sec. 9 of SB 140—they knew nothing about it. Elaine Hairston, testifying before the Senate Education Committee on April 6, pledged that OBR would cooperate with the intent of Sec. 9. She suggested amended language that called for "a new curricular approach that uniformly creates conditions for the highest possible level of education for creating outstanding prospective Ohio teachers and a means of evaluating its success in achieving this goal" (Hairston, 1989, p. 4). Section 9 was removed in the final bill, but not from the agenda.

Minimalism in teacher education requirements, it seems, appeals to presidents and provosts as well as legislators. Ohio's Inter-University Council, an organization representing state institutions, and the legislative agents from each university, were fully informed about both the alternate route legislation and the uniform curriculum section. The presidents and provosts chose not to oppose alternate routes; it was an open question about their reaction to the uniform curriculum. Informed sources indicate that they probably would have opposed it, but not in order to protect colleges of education—they were primarily concerned about the precedent of such intervention by the legislature and the Ohio Board of Regents and its potential impact on other professional schools.

As the legislative hearings for HB 212 and SB 140 continued, the state university education deans testified against both the alternate route and the uniform curriculum. Representative Gardner brought in the director of teacher education from New Jersey to testify. She, one state dean, and by this time the president of the Ohio Federation of Teachers represented the education establishment case for alternate routes. Even though Gardner met with all three witnesses, presumably to coordinate the testimonies, the "outside expert" was wrong on several points. She praised Gardner for the "open and participatory manner in which HB 212 was drafted" and she stated that she understood that "almost all of Ohio's educational organizations supported HB 212" (Schechter, 1989).

After this trio of praise, the chair of the State University Education Deans, James Biddle, presented opposition to the bill. Representative Gardner expressed that he was "offended and hurt" by the state university education deans' position, "after he'd worked so long and hard on the bill" (Gardner, 1989). After questions implying the ineffectiveness of teacher education, the chairman of the education committee asked, "Don't you [teacher educators] have any friends?" (Bara, 1989). Good question.

Hendrik Gideonse presented cogent testimony against both the alternate route and uniform curriculum provisions; Don Anderson, Dean, College of Education at the Ohio State University, brought an MAT student who testified both to her unpreparedness to have taught under the proposed internship certificate and her chagrin to think that her children might have such an unprepared teacher as she would have been; sessions with legislators and lobbyists were held almost daily; and the Ohio Teacher Education and Certification Advisory Commission, as well as the Ohio Association of Colleges for Teacher Education (OACTE), passed resolutions opposing alternate routes. In other words, the opposition mounted an active and diverse attack but succeeded only in toning down a few of the worst provisions—the bill would pass easily and quickly.

While much more of the political nitty gritty could be added, the role of teacher educators in general is perhaps the most instructive. Concerned about the apathy of teacher educators to the preceding litany of events, three active teacher educators wrote a manifesto entitled "Teacher Education in Ohio: Chaos and Complexity" and presented it to the Assembly of chief Institutional Representatives of OACTE (the heads of forty-eight institutions in Ohio approved to offer education programs) on April 19. The following paragraph captures the theme and spirit of the paper:

> Seizing the professional initiative is, perhaps, the major innovative challenge we face. Teacher educators have traditionally taken their leadership from other sources, contenting ourselves to negotiate within the parameters established by others. What is now known in our field dictates a new assertive stance on our part that may be uncomfortable to some of us, belated in the eyes of others outside of our limited teacher education circles, and threatening to the perceived interests of some. (Biddle, Gideonse, and Joseph, 1989, p. 4)

The overall reaction in the discussion groups which followed was cool; the general response was that we shouldn't overreact, burn bridges, or initiate substantive changes. Most of the deans and heads of teacher education were basically content to follow wherever the state department was leading.

OACTE's spring conference followed and the next two days were a case study in themselves. During the "hall sessions," the tone and tenor of those who only the previous day had been cool to the manifesto began to change. Concerns on the direction of teacher education in Ohio and the role of the state department in these changes were acknowledged and actions which only yesterday had seemed a bit extreme were now more plausible! Apparently, breaking the barrier of openly discussing subjects considered taboo by the state department (as well as testifying against a bill after being warned not to) had an overnight cathartic effect. During the remainder of this conference and for the next year, the issues of governance (and an autonomous professional standards and practices board controlled by teachers) were to weave in and out of almost every meeting of teacher educators.

After the passage of SB 140, the OACTE created a Governmental Relations Committee composed of representatives from public and private institutions. The committee declared its strategic intent to be the preservation of the integrity of teacher education through concerted action with the only politically powerful entity committed to what most teacher educators believe to be a credible knowledge base. That entity in Ohio is the Ohio Education Association (OEA), one of the most effective and powerful lobbying groups in the state.

After many joint planning sessions with the hierarchy of the Ohio Education Association, the Governmental Relations Committee organized a conference involving all deans and heads of teacher education to explore the many threats to the profession. Participants at the conference decided to back OEA's desire to create a professional standards board dominated by teachers. Despite vigorous opposition from the Ohio Department of Education, HB 779, a bill to create a seventeen-member professional standards board (with a membership of nine teachers and four teacher educators) was introduced in March, 1990. Deans and heads of teacher education believe the bill, if passed, will ultimately be a safeguard against know-nothing insults to teacher education emanating from bureaucracies, legislators, and advisory boards. The supportive positions for HB 779 taken by deans and heads is a drastic change from positions taken a few years ago when a similar bill was attempted. A new era of cooperation between the organized teaching profession and teacher educators is emerging. In addition, Jan Kettlewell, dean of the School of Education and Allied Professions at Miami (Ohio) University, and Marilyn Cross, president of the Ohio Education Association, are collaborating to form a Congress of Education Organizations (CEO). The congress is to consist of the major education organizations in Ohio. One purpose of the CEO is to educate Ohio professional organizations about the professionalism and the integrity which should characterize teacher education. In Ohio it was ironic that state affiliates of the national organizations which are constituent members of

NCATE (school board associations, administrator associations, school psychologists, etc.) refused to combat efforts to bypass teacher education programs. Perhaps CEO stands a chance to achieve congruence between national organization and state organization platforms.

IMPLICATIONS FOR THE FUTURE

During the five-month period when alternate routes to teacher certification moved from nonissue to reality in Ohio, teacher educators had the opportunity to see educational policy making in its raw form as well as to experience the clash of academic and political cultures. In the attempt to understand the rush of events, questions typical of the professorship were constantly asked: How could *they*...? Why are *they* doing...? Why aren't *they*...? Why weren't *we*...?

In other words, teacher educators spent an inordinate amount of time and energy trying to recreate the political world after their own *modus operandi*: they seemed confident that a rational-professional basis for political action was somewhere beneath their rhetoric and actions. In the desperate search to discover an interpretative framework to make sense of the Ohio General Assembly's initiative and the Department of Education's collaboration, they seemed to believe that the discovery of motives and purposes would make all things rational. However, it soon became apparent that political functionaries try to cover more than uncover; i.e., real motives, true purposes, and actual rationales remain under the table. The puzzlement of the professor, then, is often met by the protective paternalism of the politician.

Another jolt to the professional mind came with the realization that in the political arena, particulars often precede the plan. Rather than some overarching scheme determining particular actions, there are as many, if not more, plans formed by organizing disparate particulars as they unfold—politicians play the cards they are dealt.

AREAS OF CLASH

In the relatively short but intense involvement in the political arena, seven areas of potential culture clash emerged.

Pace

While the political process is often methodical and plodding, it can also move with inordinate speed. Politicians, contrary to popular opinion, can keep secrets! The "background" phase of legislation can be as public or as private as the parties wish. If advance work is done (behind closed doors) with the major inside players on a piece of legislation, and if the intent is to minimize external opposition, the timing of the introduction and hearings on a bill can be such that organized opposition is effectively curtailed. For example, by the time teacher educators heard about alternate route legislation, the process toward final enactment was so tightly scheduled that they could scarcely marshall enough information and participants to mount any concerted challenge. Not being able to drop everything and engage in a fray within the timelines determined by one's opponents is almost a guarantee of defeat.

Trust

Legislators, like attorneys, have a practice that baffles many teacher educators—they can attack one another in a hearing room with a vehemence one degree below a street brawl and afterwards walk over to the corner hangout like long-lost friends. Politicians know the rules of the game and they know each other's agenda; but they also know their mutual agenda. Underneath much of the partisan rhetoric is a commonality born of a practicing pragmatism which unites more than it divides. Moreover, politicians can trust each other to be "good" politicians (i.e., to do what is needed to be re-elected), and they respect each other's abilities in that arena.

While these aspects of the political culture are not unknowable, they are neither widely understood by nonparticipants nor sufficiently respected by academicians. The "good-ol' boys and girls" network has been remarkably resilient; the campus culture will not win in this culture clash.

Time

A corollary to the pace of the political culture is its time intensity; to be a player, one must be willing to devote an extended period of time positioning oneself, earning some trust and respect, and getting to know the other players. Because of the primacy of the oral tradition, one must be around to talk (or more importantly, listen). For many academicians, those hours seem to be wasted; perhaps this is one of the most difficult of culture clashes. It is commonly held that lobbyists need eight to ten years of "hard work" before they reach peak effectiveness.

Large corporations generally acknowledge that their CEO's do not earn their salary 98 percent of the time. Indeed, many corporations maintain that the CEO is there to make one or two major decisions a month—if that often. The political culture, at least the culture of the lobbyists, likewise focuses on big events rather than daily routines; how much time is involved is rarely an issue. Being seen, involved, helpful, and influential require time and availability on a political schedule, not an academic calendar.

Serendipity

Perhaps the twist on "chance favors the prepared mind" is "luck falls on those present." Being at the right place at the right moment is an experience which has changed most of us. Spending time, adapting to the rhythms, and developing trust and respect increase the opportunities for the serendipities. Again, given the oral traditions of the legislature, overhearing casual remarks or being mistaken for a proponent and being told the entire policy strategy are events of the political culture.

Leadership

To read the reports about education in general and teacher education in particular, and to listen to elected officials, one gains the unmistakable impression that change is coming. To listen to teacher educators, on the other hand, one gets the equally unmistakable impression that "this too shall pass." With remarkably few exceptions, teacher educators have voted with their feet that continuity will win out over change.

Furthermore, of those teacher educators believing that change is inevitable, the majority seem devoted almost exclusively to their own institution's reaction to such change. Conspicuously absent in the national and even state debates over educational policy are teacher educators; apparently, leadership to teacher educators seems to be confined to managing on-campus struggles, rather than proposing policy issues and initiatives affecting the profession. Indeed, our collective inability to unite as a profession has taken us beyond fragmentation to the brink of solipsism. The rallying cry that "if we don't hang together we shall hang separately" is deemed to be alarmist and reactionary; and so it may be, but it also may be accurate!

Evidencing primarily a survival mentality, many teacher education administrators manage rather than lead; our instincts seem to lean toward defending and reacting instead of initiating and leading. It is always a cause for celebration when deans and heads of teacher education collaborate on state or national policy issues; unfortunately, even these occasions are often in reaction to impending externally initiated events. The culture of campus survival and issue reaction certainly seems to clash with the political culture of educational policy making.

Polish or Substance

Legislators, for a wide variety of reasons, believe that the "reforms" of the 1980s have failed. Furthermore, they attribute much of this failure to the education community's vested interests in retaining the substance of the status quo while adopting only the trappings of reform; "polishing the brass on a sinking ship" is a refrain heard frequently in the halls of state houses. Educators in general are painted as protectors of turf rather than promoters of learning. Adopting the "bottom-line" mentality, legislators claim that all of the "hard data" points to the inability of the education community to deliver increased student achievement or to reform itself.

Reacting to pressure from business and industry, media, and voters, legislators have mounted their white horses and are charging into the fray. Bills are flowing, tests are being mandated, alternate routes are being mapped out. Given their preconceptions of teacher educators, one can imagine legislators' reaction when educators claim that such mandates are wrong-headed, boilerplate, "boffo," and lacking any research justification! Without a basis of trust and respect, legislators have no reason to listen to teacher educators.

Program

Policy makers are increasingly treating education as an entity—i.e., they are looking less at elementary, secondary, and higher education as separate units and more at the overlaps, "articulation," and interrelationships. In particular, they view colleges of education as a means to improved student learning in grades K-12. In other words, their view is that if teacher education efforts don't produce increased performance from K-12 students, then teacher education is either ineffective or unnecessary—or both. What else do "by-pass" certification routes mean? Again, the operational disunity of educational organizations may guarantee that we hang separately.

From the mid-1960s to the early 1970s, Ohio's teacher education and certification standards made the quantum leap from a "warm-body" stage which required only two years of college or university preparation to the stage which required professional knowledge reflecting current research and scholarship. During that time, the collaborative efforts of state department officials and deans and heads of teacher education provided outstanding vision and leadership. However, as institutions struggled to implement new standards, deans and heads tended to drift toward administration and away from leadership; the state department became focused more on processes and procedures than on products. The tyranny of the urgent turned vision to looking and leadership into management.

When *A Nation at Risk* pressed against teacher education in Ohio in the mid-1980s, the downside momentum from the previous rigorous endeavors militated against substantive reform and resulted in hurried and unreflective cosmetic adaptations. Instead of going on the offensive to declare that many of the called-for "reforms" were already in the 1974 standards, state department officials allowed themselves to be blown about by the current winds of change. The 1980s ended, then, with slogans, political mandates, bureaucratic maneuverings, and a foreboding of a return to a repackaged "warm-body" condition now requiring four rather than two years of college or university courses.

A small but active group of deans and heads of teacher education and leaders from other educational organizations remains committed to building coalitions dedicated to genuine collaboration and substantive change. It remains to be seen whether the maturing experiences of the 1970s and 1980s will be marshalled toward the goal of creating a true profession for the 1990s.

6

ROBERT D. BARR

Turmoil in Teacher Education in Oregon

The term 'reform' fails to adequately capture the intense struggle that has occurred around teacher education during recent years in Oregon. Like the old adage regarding the making of sausage and legislation, it has not been a pretty process to observe. The reform effort has gone on for almost ten years, and it is still far from over.

Almost everyone who is anyone has been involved in teacher education reform: two governors, though in relatively minor roles; the speaker of the Oregon House of Representatives and the president of the Oregon Senate; two chancellors of higher education, one fired and one hired, though both wrestled with teacher education as one of their most persistent problem areas; and, of course, deans of education, the Oregon Education Association leadership and staff, influential politicians, teachers and school administrators, professors, university presidents, and concerned citizens. The reforms have included everything from an inter-institutional merger, program elimination, funding issues, a teacher warranty program, a mentor program for beginning teachers, teacher testing, higher admission standards, a four-year, five-year, and fifth-year controversy, output measures, and assessing preservice teachers on the basis of their ability to foster effective student learning. The process has featured a number of statewide surveys of teachers and administrators, a few pieces of legislation, new policies by state boards and commissions, and if not "smoke-filled rooms," at least behind-closed-doors intimidation, deal cutting, and plea bargaining.

What makes the controversy surrounding teacher education so complex is the fact that the issues have not been neatly drawn. Almost everyone disagrees with some aspect of the reforms. It is hard to find anyone who is pleased with the current outcomes, and there are few, outside education faculties, ready to end the process.

Given the continuing turmoil over teacher education, it is surprising that Oregonians generally believe they have the finest schools in America. They are vainly proud of the fact that with one of the largest percentage of high school students taking the Scholastic Aptitude Test, the state is consistently ranked second only to New Hampshire in reported scores. Yet there has been growing concern regarding the fact that with Oregon's rather homogeneous school population, approximately 30 percent of school-age youth drop out of school. Similar concerns have focused on the international competitiveness of our public school youth, especially in the areas of math and science. There has also been a feeling, at least among educators, of confidence regarding teacher education programs. Recent surveys of beginning teachers and their employers indicate that educators are reasonably confident in the teacher education programs in Oregon.

Lacking any widespread sentiment within the profession for significantly improving teacher education, the initiative for reform came from the general population and a few key individuals. The speaker of the Oregon House of Representatives, Vera Katz, was a member of the Carnegie Commission on Education and the Economy and she returned to the state from her work with Carnegie intent upon implementing the commission's recommendations. The deans of education of the state's two research universities, the University of Oregon (U of O) and Oregon State University (OSU), both championed five-year teacher education programs and were charter members of the Holmes Group. Another strong personality involved in teacher education reform was an executive director of the Teacher Standards and Practices Commission (TSPC). And two chancellors of higher education worked hard, not only to raise college entrance requirements, but also to improve the quality of teacher education. Most teachers, school administrators, and teacher education faculty were not happy with what they considered to be a "top down" reform effort.

GOVERNANCE OF TEACHER EDUCATION

Oregon is rather unique in the governance of teacher education. The TSPC reports directly to the Oregon Legislature. The commission is independent of the Oregon State Board of Education (with authority for K–12 and community college education) and the State Board of Higher Education (with authority over four-year and graduate institutions in the Oregon State

System of Higher Education [OSSHE]). The Teacher Standards and Practices Commission has administrative rule-making authority regarding the development of licensure standards, authority to enforce the standards by levying fines, censuring teachers and administrators, and authority to revoke and suspend licenses. Until recently the commission did not simply establish minimum standards, but through an approved program approach the commission established the exact requirements for certification. The commission is composed of a seventeen-member board with commissioners appointed by the governor and approved by the Oregon senate. The commission is dominated by teachers who are often influenced by the Oregon Education Association (OEA). Only two of the designated seats on the commission represent institutions of higher education.

What complicates the Oregon situation is the fact that the Oregon State Board of Higher Education also has responsibility for establishing policies regarding teacher education and related issues involving higher education. Because the responsibility for governing teacher education in Oregon has been delegated to these two boards, legislators appear to have been reluctant to intrude into teacher education issues. During the last eight years, the legislature has passed only one piece of legislation that directly affects preservice teacher education.

FACTORS LEADING TO REFORM IN OREGON

Reform of teacher education in Oregon was stimulated by a number of different, though interrelated, issues.

1. Follow-up Evaluation

Beginning in 1984, there were a number of surveys and follow-up evaluations of Oregon teachers and administrators to gain insights into their attitudes toward their teacher preparation programs (Oregon Educational Coordinating Committee, 1984; Citizens Advisory Committee, 1986; OSSHE, 1985, 1988). Even though critics of teacher education found the results of the surveys to be surprisingly bland, only 10 percent of the teachers surveyed felt they had experienced a truly excellent teacher education program. One survey found that 90 percent of the teachers felt that their education professors should be required to spend at least one academic quarter every several years as a full-time teacher. Even the OSSHE follow-up evaluations of graduates reported a high level of discrepancy between teaching competencies that teachers reported as being important and the adequacy of their teacher education program in helping them achieve these competencies.

And while these surveys reported mixed results and certainly better support for teacher education programs than is typically found in other state and national surveys, decision makers in the state of Oregon used these surveys to verify their negative opinions about teacher education and to serve as a rationale for reform.

2. State and National Reports

A number of key documents and reports provided the "reform architecture" for Oregon's teacher education reform. One was the report of the Carnegie Commission on Education and the Economy, but not so much for the influence of the report on educators in Oregon, as the impact of the speaker of the Oregon House of Representatives who served on the commission.

A far less influential report was made by the Holmes Group which called for moving teacher education to the fifth-year. While it was widely believed that the Holmes Group was instrumental in bringing change to Oregon teacher education, it was in fact all but inconsequential. After gaining national attention for the recommendation for moving teacher education to the fifth-year, the Holmes Group moved on to less controversial topics, leaving the Oregon deans to struggle alone to reform teacher education. The deans of education at the University of Oregon and Oregon State University both were disappointed with the Holmes Group's lack of interest in developments in Oregon and with the majority of the charter membership of the group who seemed to have little interest in the fifth-year concept. To the Oregon deans, the Holmes Group seemed to be little more than an exclusive, and indeed, expensive club with little interest in fifth-year programs.

While certainly influenced by external reports and national developments, the focus for reform in Oregon came from a number of in-state reports, recommendations, and strategic plans (Oregon Educational Coordinating Committee, 1984; Myton, 1985; Citizens Advisory Committee, 1986; OSSHE, 1983). And while there was a remarkable degree of agreement between these various reports and recommendations, there was no single clear-cut reform agenda. All of these reports focused on the quality of students in teacher education programs, accountability, certification programs, and academic preparation, and most focused on moving teacher education to the graduate level. It should also be noted that the OEA was not involved directly in any of these sets of recommendations.

3. Concern for Cost, Quality, and Accountability

Like so much of the rest of the country, in the 1980s Oregon saw a growing concern for the quality of teachers being prepared there. Oregonians were also concerned with the cost of teacher education. One of the oldest controversies in Oregon centers on the fact that teacher education is available in all fifteen public and independent colleges and universities, including six campuses of the OSSHE. This concern ultimately led to the merger of education programs at OSU and Western Oregon State College (WOSC), located only twenty miles apart (Barr, 1985). The merger involved significant budget reductions on both campuses, the elimination of some duplicated programs, and the appointment of a single dean. Even though the merger was championed as a bold, effective response by the Oregon Legislature, the merger never worked up to its potential and was later ended in 1989.

During the 1980s, every major committee, commission, and report called for replacing the approved program approach to teacher certification, which defined program requirements in minute specificity, with some new system that would allow for diversity and innovation in higher education. The key to this freedom was to be accountability. While teacher education programs would have greater flexibility in preparing teachers, a set of common "outcome measures" would be developed and used statewide to insure teacher quality. This search for outcome measures focused initially on basic skills and subject matter tests and a more careful supervised first year of teaching where school districts would be required to provide the final evaluation of the teacher's effectiveness. The Teacher Standards and Practices Commission and others even explored the use of a new one-year "initial certification" for this first year of teaching.

The merged OSU/WOSC School of Education, where more than half of all new teachers in Oregon were prepared, responded to this interest for outcome measures with a program that was widely reported as a bold innovation. The OSU/WOSC School of Education became the first major school of education in America to announce in 1985 a Beginning Teacher Warranty Program that, in effect, guaranteed their graduates (Barr, 1987). Perhaps because of the criticism of teacher education programs and the general belief that teacher education programs were largely ineffective, the Warranty Program received wide popular acclaim.

Work on the Warranty Program led a few Oregon scholars to begin exploring a more systematic approach to predicting teacher education effectiveness (Schalock and Barr, 1986). Research on this issue led eventually to TSPC emphasizing output measures rather than the traditional approved program approach. In addition to acquiring test scores on basic skills and subject matter content, TSPC required that students who were recommended for certification would have to provide evidence in the form of "work samples" of their ability—not just to plan lessons and interact effectively with students and teachers, but to effectively foster student learning (Schalock and Myton, 1988). Students were not only to plan lessons and teach those lessons, they would be required to assess the degree to which their students achieved the stated goals of their lessons. While this program component is now in the developmental stage and will be field tested during the coming year, this approach represents one of the most dramatic new directions for change in teacher education to occur in the state and probably in America.

4. Teacher Education as a Political Issue

Teacher education emerged in the 1980s in Oregon as it did in other areas of the country as a "hot" political issue. Improving the preparation of teachers was an issue with which few could disagree. It was an issue that attracted support from many teachers, citizens, and newspaper editors, and as it was proposed in Oregon, it did not cost any additional tax money. Neither TSPC, the legislature or the OSSHE ever allocated or recommended the allocation of additional funds to reform preservice teacher education. The most that occurred was for the State Board of Higher Education to promise to hold the budgets of education programs "harmless" during the reform. And, given the relatively small size and political powerlessness of teacher education faculties even within academia, it was an issue easy to impose externally. Unlike the reform of public education where the organized teacher and administrative groups were forces in the political arena and the issues were complicated, teacher education reform was a rather simple, straightforward issue with little or no opposition.

Controversies Over Teacher Education

The major battles for teacher education reform in Oregon centered on whether teacher education should remain an undergraduate program, become exclusively a graduate program (a fifth-year program), or encompass both undergraduate and graduate components in an extended program lasting five years.

Maintaining and Improving Four-Year Teacher Education Programs

While TSPC and the OEA were not always in agreement regarding reform of teacher education, there was agreement between the two groups that teacher education should not be eliminated at the undergraduate level. They were both willing to consider the development of a one-year fifth-year program as an alternative to the traditional undergraduate program, but neither was willing to eliminate four-year programs. Throughout the 1980s, representatives of the OEA continually maintained that teacher salaries were too low to require students to spend an extra year in college. The OEA also maintained that increasing the salaries for a beginning teacher with a fifth-year program was not justified. If new money was to be invested in teachers, the OEA felt the money should not go to inexperienced teachers. Administrators in rural areas and the membership of the Oregon Small Schools Association likewise objected to any change in teacher education that eliminated the four-year program, claiming they would not be able to afford the more expensive five- or fifth-year teacher education graduates. Oregon Education Association membership never took a position on the reform of teacher education and the testimony of the rank and file of teachers at public hearings was mixed. During the 1980s, at least one OEA president appeared before the State Board of Higher Education to support the five-year program, but the executive secretary and chief lobbyist for the OEA continued to oppose the elimination of the undergraduate teacher education program.

During the mid-1980s, TSPC initiated a number of changes in certification standards designed to strengthen teacher education in Oregon. The commissioners had come to largely disregard grade point averages as any reasonable indication of student abilities. The inconsistencies of standards for grades between institutions and between academic units, grade inflation in general, and the special problem of grade inflation in teacher education programs led the commissioners to question the value of grade point averages. No matter the ability level or background, if students could gain admission to a teacher education program, their GPA tended to improve significantly. The commission began demanding some type of objective, consistent evidence of student's abilities; standardized tests provided the security they sought.

The TSPC ultimately responded to concerns regarding the abilities of teachers by requiring passing scores on the California Basic Educational Skills Test. The OSSHE reacted to this new requirement by making the CBEST a requirement for admission to teacher education programs. Later, TSPC likewise demanded objective data regarding subject matter knowledge of teacher education graduates, requiring passing scores on the appropriate National Teacher Examination Specialty Tests.

Leadership of OEA was never particularly pleased with these teacher tests, but since they were required only of people entering the profession or for teachers seeking to add new certification in school counseling and administration, the organization did not forcibly object to the new requirements. The TSPC also developed a carefully regulated alternative certification program for identified areas of teacher shortage.

The testing requirement for certification has been a very controversial issue in Oregon. Approximately 20 percent of the people in California and Oregon fail at least one section of the CBEST during the first attempt. The exam also excludes large numbers of minority students. The current governor of Oregon has appointed a minority teacher task force to explore why there are so few minority teachers in Oregon. There has been continuing pressure to find different and better alternatives to basic skill testing. Yet teacher educators now tend to admit that the basic skill testing program has improved the quality of students entering teacher education programs.

Five-Year Programs

As early as 1985, the deans of OSU and U of O appeared before the Oregon Legislature recommending that teacher education be extended to include a fifth-year. In the early 1980s, the University of Oregon developed a long-range plan that included a five-year program. As the years passed and the growing interest in teacher education occurred, these two deans encouraged the chancellor of higher education to be more pro-active regarding teacher education. It was evident to them that if the OSSHE did not reform teacher education, it would be reformed for them either by TSPC, the legislature, or both.

In one meeting between the speaker of the house, the chancellor, and the OSU dean of education, the speaker insisted that the state system take significant action regarding teacher education, especially if higher education wanted their budget funded adequately. After the meeting, then chancellor, William E. Davis, playing on the old saying, "Let's do it to them before they do it to us," chuckled, "Well, we better do it to ourselves before they do it to us" (Davis, 1985).

Through the mid-1980s, education faculties were extremely slow to respond to the growing external demands for reform. Teacher educators initially resisted basic skill testing and continued to resist content testing. They are still largely divided regarding the value of moving teacher education to the graduate level. Faculty from some campuses have testified against the OSSHE in legislative hearings and even placed copies of basic skills tests in reserved reading rooms for their students to review. Without external pressure and new certification standards, education faculty would likely have changed little during the 1980s.

The OSSHE eventually developed policies that created an extended five-year teacher education program that was to be initiated in 1990. The policies:

1. Required an undergraduate academic major in an area that related closely to the desired teaching field.
2. Phased out all undergraduate majors in education and replaced them with a prerequisite undergraduate education minor.
3. Moved teacher education to the graduate level.
4. Raised admission requirements to a 3.0 GPA.
5. Enriched the content of teacher education.

Since the fifth-year was to include a substantial student teaching component, the master's degree would not necessarily be earned at the end of the fifth-year. Only two of the OSSHE institutions are currently planning to award a master's degree at the end of the fifth-year. All other institutions plan to award the master's at the end of an additional term of work, hopefully after a year of teaching.

The OSSHE five-year program was based upon the fact that increasing numbers of college graduates were returning as post-baccalaureates to pursue teaching careers. With large numbers of returning women and individuals involved in career changes, approximately half of all teacher education students were post-baccalaureates by the late 1980s. These post-baccalaureates tended to be strong students. Some were coming from careers in engineering, law, and even dentistry. Some of the most significant criticisms of teacher education came from these post-baccalaureates who were required to pursue teacher education as part of an undergraduate program.

With a growing research-based body of knowledge, there was too little time in an undergraduate program to provide all the areas that contemporary teachers tended to need. Program graduates identified a number of areas of program deficits including computer literacy and technology, classroom management, special education, and too little field experience (OSSHE, 1985). Also, many undergraduates were taking five years to finish the baccalaureate degree. As a result of these developments, the OSSHE concluded that there was no way to include all the things that teachers needed to know in either an undergraduate program or a one-year graduate program. The state system established policies that created extended teacher education programs that encompassed both an undergraduate and a graduate component.

And, with increased attention to graduate-level teacher education by the Carnegie Commission and the Holmes Group, the OSSHE announced the new policy and held seven public hearings throughout the state. The hearings drew mixed reviews from teachers and school administrators as well as education faculty members from higher education. The Oregon State System of Higher Education nonetheless adopted the policy and announced that the new extended programs would be implemented no later than the summer of 1990.

Fifth-Year Programs

As early as 1986, the interim education legislative committee of the Oregon Legislature had recommended that schools of education should develop the option of a one-year graduate-level teacher program including a strong emphasis in field-based training and culminating in a master's degree (Citizens Advisory Committee, 1986). The committee report stated that the OSSHE five-year concept had been reviewed, but the committee chose to recommend that teacher education be limited solely to a nine-to-twelve-month graduate program. The interim committee was primarily interested in reducing the amount of education coursework that they felt was not particularly challenging or productive by limiting teacher education to a single year of "rigorous graduate study." The committee felt that this action would attract a new "talent pool" in teaching—people who were interested in teaching but who were not willing to endure undergraduate education courses.

It is important to note that the interim committee saw the fifth-year program as only one option for teacher education. The report sanctioned the continuation of undergraduate four-year teacher education programs. The TSPC quickly moved to establish the recommendations of the interim legislative committee as new certification standards. By doing so, they placed themselves in conflict with the new policies of the OSSHE and intruded into areas that were felt to be the exclusive domain of higher education. The new TSPC certification standards included several highly volatile requirements (TSPC, 1987):

1. The standards prohibited any undergraduate education prerequisites for the fifth-year. This rendered in a single stroke the end of the OSSHE extended five-year programs and the undergraduate prerequisite education minor that was being planned.
2. The standards almost doubled the amount of time required for student teaching, expanding the undergraduate eight-week program to a fifteen-week graduate program. This represented more than a single full quarter of the fifth-year program currently being designed. This made it even more difficult for higher education to award a master's degree at the end of the fifth-year.
3. The standards also specified that students would earn all university requirements for both basic and standard certification during the fifth-year. This would mean that once a teacher completed the fifth-year, they would never be required to return to a university campus again.
4. The standards also stated that students who finished a fifth-year program could earn a master's degree with no more than nine hours of additional graduate coursework.

Many academicians in higher education tended to support the prohibition of any undergraduate education prerequisites, but took strong issue with the commission efforts, as they saw it, to establish requirements for graduate degrees—a responsibility that they believed was clearly the prerogative of the State Board of Higher Education and the faculty governance at the various institutions. It was also viewed as an intense issue of academic freedom.

This issue ultimately led to a request for an opinion from the Oregon attorney general. Unfortunately, the opinion proved to be less than clear-cut. The opinion indicated that TSPC did, in fact, have some indirect responsibility to establish requirements for degrees that related to teacher education. The commission was finally to reverse itself on this issue, but only through political pressure by key legislators. In one stormy interim legislative committee session, an influential Oregon senator directed the executive director of the commission to "back off" this issue or suffer legislative action that the commission would not like. Lacking any similar support for the undergraduate education prerequisite minor, education faculty found that teacher education in their state had been limited to a nine-to-twelve-month graduate program. And since the OSSHE had eliminated all undergraduate education majors, the only teacher education option would be at the graduate level. The issue, however, was far from over.

While developing new standards for the fifth-year teacher education programs, TSPC did not eliminate the standards for undergraduate teacher education. This left independent institutions the choice of deciding which approach to teacher education they would like to pursue. Most believed that eventually all of Oregon would embrace the graduate-level teacher education concept, but such was not to be.

Diversified Teacher Education

The OEA had tended to be less than enthusiastic regarding graduate-level certification programs. In spite of their concerns and the mixed reviews from the OSSHE public hearings, one president of OEA testified in general support of the OSSHE five-year program. In 1989, that support came to an end with the OEA responding with an unexpected counter move.

Even though the OEA never took an official position against the five-year program, the primary lobbyist for the OEA, John Danielson, worked with legislators to submit a bill (House Bill 3038) that would require any institution of higher education that offered teacher certification to offer a four-year certification program. The bill did not exclude five-year programs, but required that a four-year program be available on every campus. This meant that the OSSHE would have to eliminate the fifth-year program or have both five- and four-year programs available on all campuses.

With a chorus of criticism leveled at higher education, the Oregon House of Representatives responded to the power of OEA and passed HB 3038 by a resounding majority. Only after the bill reached the Senate Education Committee did momentum slow. No one was really sure whether the bill was a reflection of an OEA position or simply the personal position of the OEA executive director and lobbyist. The word was out that HB 3038 was an OEA "hammer" to be held over the OSSHE and to insure that the association would have its way. Ultimately, in negotiations with the chair of the Senate Education Committee, the OEA lobbyist, and the new chancellor of higher education, Tom Bartlett, a compromise was struck. The bill would be amended to require that the OSSHE would offer a "diversified" system of teacher education, including both undergraduate and graduate programs. The legislation also led to a softening of TSPC standards regarding undergraduate prerequisites for fifth-year teacher education programs.

Currently, the OSSHE is developing an array of teacher education programs. The University of Oregon and OSU are both offering only graduate teacher education programs, WOSC is offering only an undergraduate program, and the rest of the state system is offering some combination of four-year and fifth-year programs (OSSHE, 1989). At this time, OSU is the only campus developing five-year programs, but U of O is likely to expand its fifth-year program to include an undergraduate component. Only two institutions will offer a master's degree at the end of the fifth-year: OSU will award a new Master of Arts in Teaching degree; Eastern Oregon State College will award a Master's in Teacher Education. For now, most of the education faculties seem depleted and are reluctant to do much additional planning and development until their programs are implemented.

With the exception of OSU, all of the new fifth-year programs will be initiated during the summer of 1990. Oregon State University and the new four-year programs will start some time during 1991. Even at this point, reform and revision of teacher education are not over. Some are criticizing the new programs as appearing to be the "same old programs" simply moved to the graduate level. There is also criticism leveled again at the education faculties who continue to be characterized as "divorced from the reality" of the contemporary classroom. Since most of the fifth-year programs are approximately fifty to sixty quarter hours in length, critics are reminding higher education that even engineers can earn a master's degree in sixty hours of graduate work. On the other hand, academic faculty members are uneasy about awarding graduate credit for the fifteen-week required field experience. The controversy goes on.

REFORMED TEACHER EDUCATION

The good news after a decade of turmoil is that teacher education has been significantly improved. The programs have been developed over a three-to-five-year period with widespread participation by public school teachers and administrators, and professors from academic areas. Some educational faculties have visited teacher education programs throughout the United States to learn more about current developments. At some of the campuses, teacher education has become truly a campus-wide concern with widespread faculty involvement. With the exception of one campus, all new teachers will now enter the classroom with academic majors. Western Oregon State College not only returned to exclusively undergraduate programs, but reinstated the major in education. Even their students will have a second major in interdisciplinary studies. Requiring an academic major will not have great impact at the secondary level where students typically earned academic majors. It will have a major impact on the preparation of elementary teachers who often have few academic courses at the upper division. At OSU, undergraduate students interested in elementary education will major in one of three academic areas, liberal studies, general science, or human development and family studies. In addition, elementary students will also complete a preprofessional core of required academic studies prior to the MAT.

For the first time, teacher education will have imposed enrollment caps and will be involved in a highly selective admissions process. Admission requirements have also been strengthened. All graduate programs will require a 3.0 GPA, passage of a basic skills exam, passage of the National Teacher Examination Specialty Test, supervised experience working with children or youth, specified academic coursework, and a baccalaureate degree in an academic area. This will mean a truly outstanding student body for teacher education. All new teacher education programs will have an expanded fifteen-week practicum in schools with required portfolios of "work samples" that document the student's abilities to effectively foster student learning in their classroom. The content of teacher education has been upgraded and enriched with research-based knowledge, and emphasis on at-risk youth, multicultural education, special education, and technology education.

For the graduate programs teacher education has been planned as a professional school year, much like law school, pharmacy school, or veterinary medicine school. Students will complete a year-long, intensive program full time in professional education working with cohorts of faculty, teachers, and peers. Great effort will be focused on strengthening the professionalism of teacher education graduates. Some programs will complement practica in schools with assigned activities in business and industry. Two elementary programs seem especially innovative. The University of Oregon program has elementary students assigned to a school for an entire year. Oregon State University is proposing a new MAT degree that will likewise assign elementary students to a school for a year. The OSU program will place teams of five students per school rather than assign a student to a particular teacher. More important, the OSU program will place student teams only in schools that are significantly involved in major restructuring efforts. The student teams will join these faculty and share decision making, conduct in-depth case studies, and participate in major research and development program. University faculty will serve as resident scholars in the schools.

The down side of the reform is the wide array of different teacher education programs that will be available in Oregon. With the one exception of WOSC (whose faculty worked actively to reinstate the undergraduate program), the campuses where a five-year program had been planned seemed to have been reluctant to design a second new undergraduate program. The strain on resources for those campuses having two programs will likewise be great. For school personnel directors, it will be challenging to sort out new teachers from a confusing set of programs. Some new teachers will have completed five-year programs, others fifth-year. Some will have a master's degree at the end of the fifth-year, others will not. Some will have a BS/BA degree in an academic area, others will not. And the reform effort is far from over. Educators were recently surprised when TSPC temporarily suspended the rule requiring satisfactory scores on the California Basic Skills Test. In spite of the controversy that had surrounded the CBEST requirement, there was no indication that the commission was considering changing the rule. In an unexpected move, several commission members (representatives of OEA), alerted to the fact that four veteran commissioners were absent, proposed the rule suspension which ultimately passed after a heated debate with a vote of nine to four (with four commissioners absent). This action suspended the rule for 180 days and allows anyone who has been unable to gain certification because of the CBEST an opportunity now to do so. The current executive director of TSPC, David Myton, believes it would be irresponsible for the commission to reinstate the CBEST requirement after permitting so many to gain certification during the suspension. The commission will make a final decision on the issue following a public hearing in July.

Meanwhile, the OSSHE, which uses the CBEST as a requirement for admission to teacher education, is now scrambling to determine whether or not to change its policy. The education deans of OSSHE have agreed that some type of basic skill testing is essential, but they are searching for other standardized test alternatives and other assessment options.

There is also speculation that OEA may well return to the legislature in 1991 and seek to require four-year programs at all of the OSSHE campuses. There is also some speculation that OEA might ultimately work to eliminate fifth-year teacher education programs. Only time will tell. There is a real possibility that after a decade of turmoil, teacher education may ultimately return to the place where the effort began.

Other problems are emerging. Higher education has traditionally paid cooperating public school teachers approximately $120 to supervise student teachers. The cooperating teacher also receives reduced tuition rates at the university. Now, two influential school districts, Springfield and Eugene, are demanding over $1,000 for student teacher supervision, plus a number of other items. The OSSHE is currently exploring a legislative package and attempting to gain the support of OEA, the School Administrator's Association, and the School board Association for the package. The two school districts have stated that unless their demands are met, they will accept no more student teachers. Such a development would create a crisis in teacher education that would likely spread to other school districts.

Lessons from the Reform Effort

Ten years of reform effort have left most teacher educators all but exhausted and demoralized. The years have helped to identify important lessons regarding teacher education reform.

Powerlessness of Teacher Educators

Given the divided governing authority over teacher education in Oregon and the political power of the Oregon Education Association, teacher educators have been at the mercy of external groups. But, looking back over a decade, it is evident that education faculties could have been more influential in their destiny.

Education faculties have failed to use effective public relations to improve their situations. The OSU Warranty Program and the OSU/WOSC merger were classic exceptions to this situation. By their indifference or inability to develop effective public relations or marketing efforts, teacher educators have permitted a kind of traditional mythology to grow up about bad teacher education programs. Many of the most negative perceptions of teacher educations are often based upon experiences that have occurred a decade or more ago. Yet teacher educators have been unable to change these long-time perceptions. Teacher educators have also failed to use their research and evaluation skills to document their successes, identify problems and improve their programs. Inevitably, in almost every major controversy in Oregon, decisions have been based on data obtained by groups outside of higher education, because of higher education's unwillingness to undertake its own studies. It is evident that teacher education faculty must become more intimately involved in the policy controversies of their day and provide research and advice based upon strong, accurate data.

Consensus Building

None of the groups in Oregon involved in teacher education reform have worked well at consensus building. Rather than attempt to work together to achieve agreed upon objectives, the various groups have tended to war with one another. This can be explained to some degree by the scattered and overlapping nature of the Oregon system of boards and commissions. As a decade of reform is now ending, leadership from the Governor's office is seeking to bring all of the various groups associated with teacher education together to establish a consensus agenda (Office of Education Policy and Planning, 1990). Of all of the efforts of the past ten years, this effort seems to hold the greatest merit. Clearly, with teacher education in a relatively weak political position, the advantage of consensus building seems evident.

Individual Leadership

It is evident that key individuals, especially individuals in positions of power, can have great impact on the nature and direction of change. Individuals with clearly defined goals proved to be extremely influential over time. Groups and individuals with less clear-cut ideas regarding future direction constantly found themselves in reactionary positions. During the past ten years, the Speaker of the House of Representatives made specific demands on the Chancellor of Higher Education and was determined to have her way, even without passing legislation. On at least one occasion, a dean of education witnessed the "closed-door" sessions with the Speaker of the House at which big-ticket legislative programs could be held hostage until one powerful legislator had her way. A strong lobbyist representing the Oregon Education Association pushed his piece of legislation through the Oregon House of Representatives and changed in a single stroke the direction of teacher reform in Oregon. Individual deans have been able to influence the Chancellor of Higher Education and the executive director of TSPC to reflect their positions in their deliberations and actions. In several instances, "eleventh hour" phone calls led to the development of policy revisions just before they were implemented. This occurred both with TSPC and the Oregon State System of Higher Education.

Conclusion

A review of ten years of development in teacher education in Oregon presents an alarming picture. Most of the events and actions of the past decade seem to verify a clear erosion of authority and responsibility of teacher educators in the state of Oregon. Some in the state now believe that with teacher testing, academic degrees, and with the State Department of Education being funded by the legislature to provide support for beginning teacher mentor programs and professional development, there is little or no need for teacher education programs in higher education. At least one influential educator in the Oregon Department of Education has indicated that the state still needs a "teacher academy" and an "administrator academy" where practicing teachers and administrators can participate in a more significant training role. Once these academies are in place, it is claimed, there will be even less need for higher education to prepare educators.

Whether this prediction is an accurate forecast of the future, it is clearly evident that higher education must take teacher education as seriously as it has the professional programs of law, medicine, pharmacy, and veterinary medicine. Not only must strong new teacher education programs be initiated, but these programs must build strong pride and confidence in their graduates. These programs must also be funded at a level that is consistent with other professional programs in higher education.

Teacher education in Oregon is at a turning point. It can develop powerful, professional programs at the graduate level, or it can continue to lose authority to practitioners in the field and the legislators who seem so eager to fight their battles.

In some ways, the future of teacher education in Oregon is in the balance. In the decade ahead, it seems essential to the integrity of higher education that education faculties become intimately and intensely involved in research and evaluation of programs and issues that relate directly to the policy decisions of the day. They must carefully accelerate the effectiveness of their programs. They must graduate teachers who report strong positive attitudes about their teacher education program. If not, higher education responsibilities will surely continue to erode and perhaps even disappear. It seems, as it always has been, that our future is clearly in our own hands.

Addendum

In February, 1991, six months after the draft of this chapter was completed, the Oregon State System of Higher Education received recommendations for dramatic budget reductions and accompanying program actions from the presidents of Oregon's seven state colleges and universities. The cuts followed the passage of a property tax limitation initiative similar to the California Proposition 13 two decades ago. For teacher education in Oregon, the property tax limitation may prove disastrous, for it is obvious that the colleges, schools and departments of education are one of the primary targets of the proposed cuts. The University of Oregon has proposed closing the Department of Curriculum and Instruction in their college of education and eliminating all teacher education programs, leaving only the departments of School Administration, Special Education, and Counseling. At Oregon State University, the president has proposed that the College of Education be closed altogether. A small group of education faculty would become a department in the College of Home Economics. This means that the OSU College of Education with over fifty faculty members and a budget of over $3,000,000 will be reduced to approximately thirteen faculty members and a budget of approximately $900,000. Over thirty tenure-track education faculty members will lose their positions. A number of education faculty members will become part of other colleges on the OSU campus. Oregon State University plans to use the remaining faculty in education to continue their new, but very small, Master of Arts in Teaching program.

If implemented these recommendations would largely eliminate teacher education from the state's two major research universities and turn teacher education over to the three regional colleges and the state's urban campus, Portland State University. Some graduate programs eliminated at the University of Oregon may well be moved to Portland State University. The chancellor of the Oregon State System of Higher Education has stated that Portland State University, located in the state's major population area, will become home to the state's major education program in Oregon. Although OSU will continue its fifth-year MAT program, the majority of new teachers will be prepared in the more traditional four-year undergraduate programs. The rationale for these program elimination recommendations has been based on the fact that teacher education is duplicated on six OSSHE campuses and on the basis of a perceived oversupply of teachers. (The same rationale led to recommendations to eliminate the Colleges of Health and Human Performance at both the University of Oregon and Portland State University.) The presidents of both OSU and U of O refused to make across-the-board cuts that would weaken all the university's programs. Instead, they chose to focus their budget cuts primarily on duplicated programs, and unfortunately that focussed largely on education programs. What is perhaps most distressing is the fact that both the University of Oregon and Oregon State University have education programs that are nationally recognized.

While alumni groups and professional associations are currently lobbying the chancellor's office and the State Board of Higher Education, there is a clear message that even if funds are reinstated by the legislature at some later date, education programs will not be reopened. School districts in Oregon have been informed that they will have to rely more heavily on teachers prepared out of state.

Thus ends a decade of turmoil in teacher education in Oregon. After years of reform efforts, it now seems that teacher education improvements will not only be largely erased but significant institutional retrenchment has occurred. Only small fifth-year programs at Oregon State University and Portland State University will likely survive. It is difficult to imagine the future of teacher education in the state of Oregon without major programs at the two research universities. Oregon State University may well be the only land grant university in America that will be without a college of education.

7

JAMES M. COOPER AND PHILIP M. TATE

Restructuring Teacher Education in the Old Dominion

As this volume bears witness, during the 1980s policy makers in many states turned their attention to reforming teacher education and to improving the teaching profession. They often bypassed established patterns of decision making in their zeal to set things right and, in many cases, the expertise of teacher educators was ignored. The Commonwealth of Virginia experienced similar changes in the usual patterns of policy making. In Virginia, persistent and committed state officials, discouraged by what they perceived as a lack of attention to their pleas for reform, decided to take matters into their own hands. They led two new, powerful groups, the Governor's Commission on Excellence in Education and the Ad Hoc Committee on Teacher Education, to demand the restructuring of every certification program in the commonwealth's teacher education institutions. In less than four years they managed to gain important political support and to develop and implement a set of new guidelines for teacher education that, no matter how distasteful or controversial for teacher education institutions, was impossible to ignore. The reform of teacher education in Virginia centered on three key requirements: restructuring teacher preparation programs from the ground up; requiring arts and sciences majors for prospective teachers; and limiting professional education courses to eighteen semester hours.

In this chapter we examine the policy-making process for reform in Virginia in several ways. First, we describe the events that set the stage for the unprecedented new requirements. Next, we describe the policy-making process that led to the restructuring. Then we attempt a deeper analysis in order to answer questions such as: What was the impetus for this sweeping reform? How did the limit on professional education courses come to be set at eighteen hours? Why was the teacher education community so powerless? Why did the change process seem to move so quickly and so smoothly, despite the protests of teacher educators?

To determine how these proposals became regulations, we examined state documents covering the period 1981–1989 and interviewed ten key informants about their roles in and their impressions of the policy process. The informants were high-level officials associated with the Department of Education, the State Council of Higher Education, the Virginia Education Association, and teacher education institutions, as well as decision makers on the Board of Education and State Council of Higher Education. Our research efforts were enhanced by the inside information gained by one of the authors as a participant in the policy-making process described in this case study and by the knowledge obtained by the other author as a researcher of similar cases in other states.

TEACHER EDUCATION IN VIRGINIA BEFORE RESTRUCTURING

Governance

Virginia has operated on an approved program basis for teacher certification since 1968. At the time of the restructuring process, thirty-five colleges and universities had been approved to offer teacher education programs. Each was on a five-year review cycle that required preparing an institutional self-study report; submitting the report to the Virginia Department of Education; and hosting an on-site visit by an external committee representing higher education faculty and administration, local school teachers and administrators, Department of Education personnel, and others. The programs were evaluated according to the standards of the Virginia Board of Education (BOE), the State Council of Higher Education, and the Southern Association of Colleges and Schools.

Individual certification could be obtained by graduating from an approved program in Virginia or in a state that had agreed to certificate reciprocity with Virginia. Other applicants were evaluated by transcript analysis according to regulations established by the Virginia Department of Education. Exceptions were available for those seeking certification in vocational education and for alternative certification. The alternate route was designed for prospective secondary teachers who held a baccalaureate degree in an appropriate field. The candidate had to have a written promise of a teaching job and within two years had to take at least nine semester hours of education courses that addressed seven competency areas. Initial certification resulted in a two-year, nonrenewable provisional certificate. After two years of satisfactory service, including making up all deficiencies, a five-year, renewable Collegiate Professional Certificate was issued (Virginia State Department of Education, 1986). All prospective Virginia teachers have been required to complete the Beginning Teacher Assistance Program (described below) since 1985 and to tally above the cutoff scores on the National Teacher Examinations (NTE) since 1986.

Virginia's Teacher Education Advisory Board is composed of members representing teachers, local administrators, and teacher educators. This committee, appointed by the Board of Education, was created in the early 1980s. The Teacher Education Advisory Board advised BOE on matters pertaining to certification and teacher education. In addition to participating in and reviewing five-year review reports, members also discussed policies relating to improving the teaching profession. The Teacher Education Advisory Board usually seconded the recommendations of its staff and the board's recommendations were usually approved without modifications by BOE. The pattern of governance of teacher education in Virginia before 1986 was a common one: the authority was vested in the Board of Education, but the majority of the decision making was handled by the deans and department chairs, Department of Education staff, and the Teacher Education Advisory Board.

Related Issues

Even though our chapter focuses on the forced restructuring of teacher education in Virginia, this particular reform can best be understood by placing it in the context of other recent actions involving policies for teacher education and the teaching profession.

Pay incentives for teachers. Charles S. Robb led successful efforts to raise teachers' salaries significantly during his term as governor (1982 to 1986). His successor, Governor Gerald L. Baliles, continued to ask for and to get more money for teachers and committed the Commonwealth to raise teachers' salaries at least to the national average—a modest goal, since Virginia ranks about tenth in per capita income. However, a recent budget crunch has caused the postponement of these plans.

Beginning Teacher Assistance Program (BTAP). Initiated in July, 1985, BTAP required beginning teachers to demonstrate a set of fourteen competencies in the classroom before qualifying for the renewable Collegiate Professional Certificate. Experienced, trained educators served as observers and collected data. If the standards were not met, teachers received assistance from BTAP supervisors (McNergney, Medley, and Caldwell, 1988). State financial woes, revealed in 1990, have led to the termination of the BTAP program.

Professional Standards and Practices board. For years the Virginia Education Association (VEA), the state affiliate of the National Education Association, has worked to motivate the General Assembly of Virginia to create a professional standards board. In 1989 a compromise was reached with BOE and with legislators which would strengthen the powers of the Teacher Education Advisory Board (composed of members representing teachers, administrators, and teacher educators). The new plan calls for more teacher representation, a narrower focus (no authority over the teaching profession outside of certification and program approval), and increased reviewing and recommending powers.

Commonwealth Center for the Education of Teachers. In 1988 the State Council of Higher Education funded seven centers for excellence in research, including a center for the study of teacher education. The Commonwealth Center for the Education of Teachers was established as a joint endeavor by the University of Virginia and James Madison University. Its mission is to promote research on teacher education curriculum and policies and to improve teacher education programs in Virginia through a League of Innovative Programs.

Task Force on Improving Teaching as a Profession. In October, 1989, the BOE created a task force to advise them on how to make teaching a more attractive profession in Virginia. The Task Force included members of organizations representing teachers, administrators, higher education, local school boards, local governments, and business. Among the topics it addressed were: equity in teachers' salaries; working conditions; collaborative school-based management; teacher evaluations at the local level; differentiated pay; and recruitment of minority and male teachers.

COMMISSION ON EXCELLENCE IN EDUCATION

In the early 1980s, concern over the state of teacher education in Virginia grew as it became clear to state officials that most teacher education institutions were not going to reform their programs voluntarily. A study of teacher preparation made by the State Council of Higher Education of Virginia (SCHEV) in 1981 (SCHEV, 1981) showed that the standards for acceptance into teacher preparation programs were unacceptably low. This report was generally ignored by the teacher education community, as were the urgings for reform sent by SCHEV members, BOE members, and key staff to both boards.

In December, 1984, a new impetus for reform appeared. In its report, *Toward a New Dominion: Choices for Virginians*, Governor Charles S. Robb's Commission on Virginia's Future placed a heavy emphasis on the improvement of education as a key to the state's well-being. Among the topics addressed were several teacher policy issues such as teacher pay, preservice and in-service teacher education, teacher certification, and the use of new technologies in classrooms. Specifically, *Toward a New Dominion* recommended that teacher salaries should be raised above the national average, that the state should place a high priority on in-service training, and that "the curricula in Virginia's schools of education should be changed to place emphasis on instruction in the subjects a new teacher will teach, coupled with some instruction designed to sharpen classroom techniques" (Governor's Commission on Virginia's Future, 1984, p. 20).

Another incentive for change was added in the mid-1980s when several respected higher education institutions restructured their teacher education programs. The University of Virginia switched to a five-year, integrated bachelor's degree/master's degree plan (Moore, 1985), Virginia Commonwealth University began planning to offer five-year programs in many of its certification areas, and other institutions were considering changes. The time was ripe for reform.

On March 26, 1986, Governor Gerald L. Baliles convened the Governor's Commission on Excellence in Education, charging it to recommend specific actions to make Virginia one of the nation's top states in the quality of education it offers. The sixteen-member commission included state legislators, members of SCHEV, and all nine members of the BOE. Several committees were formed to divide up the work of the commission. Four of the commission members were assigned to the Committee on Teachers and Teaching. They were assisted and advised by several high-ranking staff from the BOE and SCHEV. Beginning in April, this group listened to testimony from invited speakers with national reputations as experts on education and educational policy. Other witnesses included selected Virginia teachers and students, deans of education, and Department of Education staff. The committee members read several national reports and summaries of reports. They agreed with the Carnegie report that prospective teachers need better-structured field experiences and stronger backgrounds in the academic disciplines (Committee on Teachers and Teaching, 1986).

On October 28, 1986, the full commission presented its report, *Excellence in Education: A Plan for Virginia's Future*, to the governor (Governor's Commission on Excellence in Education, 1986). The commission members and staff divided the recommendations into groups, according to their focus. Nine of the thirty-six recommendations were deemed to be related to teacher education. The three proposals that led to teacher education reform—requiring an arts and sciences degree, limiting education courses to eighteen hours, and forcing the restructuring of teacher education programs—were considered to be parts of a whole and will be dealt with in that fashion later in this discussion. Since the educational policy makers saw the other six recommendations as part of the teacher education and teaching profession package, it is important to understand their purposes and their outcomes.

Field Experiences

Although no separate recommendation was developed at this time regarding longer and improved field experiences, the commission report did mention this aspect of reform, and the policy makers and staff members involved in the restructuring effort from the beginning considered it a key piece of the final plan.

Forgivable Loans

In the mid-1980s, in an effort to encourage able college students to consider teaching in critical shortage areas, BOE recommended and the general assembly created a special loan program that allowed debts to be forgiven in exchange for teaching in Virginia. Originally designed for mathematics, science, foreign language, and special education teachers, the pool was expanded after the commission report to include minority students in any teaching area and students who planned to teach in rural areas.

School Administrator Training

The commission report contained two recommendations calling for principals to be trained to be better instructional leaders and teacher evaluators. The same committee that carried out the commission's recommendations for reform in teacher education later implemented plans to restructure the education of school administrators.

Recertification

The commission recommended that the five-year recertification process be revised in order to move away from a college credit orientation. The new procedures, implemented in 1990, installed a point system which allows both university credit and staff development experiences to be counted toward recertification and gave the responsibility for decision making to local school divisions.

Required Graduate Degree for Teachers

The commission, reacting to the fact that only about 30 percent of Virginia's teachers held master's degrees, decided that all teachers should eventually obtain graduate degrees. The Commonwealth Center for the Education of Teachers and the Center for Public Service at the University of Virginia were asked to examine this issue. Their report, presented in September, 1988, recommended against requiring a graduate degree for all teachers because of the expense to the state and to the teachers, but did suggest creating incentives for qualified teachers to earn master's degrees (McNergney et al., 1988). The study appears to have ended this policy recommendation.

Graduate Professional Education Centers

The commission recommended the establishment of graduate professional education centers at selected state-supported universities to provide programs on a regional basis. This recommendation seems to have fallen between the cracks in its passage from BOE to SCHEV. No action has been taken, and it is unclear whether anyone intends to bring the subject up again.

AD HOC COMMITTEE ON TEACHER EDUCATION

Reconfirmation of Recommendations

Soon after receiving the report of the commission, Governor Baliles strongly endorsed the proposed changes in teacher education and asked BOE and SCHEV members to take the actions they felt were necessary and prudent to further the cause of educational reform in Virginia (personal communication, December 8, 1986). Board of Education Chairman W. L. Lemmon responded by appointing BOE members to five groups to deal with the various recommendations of the commission (personal communication, January 5, 1987). Three new Ad Hoc Committees (teacher education, the program for four year olds, and special education) were added to two standing committees (Curriculum, Instruction, and Professional Relations and Administration, Assessment, and Finance). Lemmon made it clear that he thought that the BOE committees had the authority to revise any part of any of the commission recommendations, including the deadlines.

Three BOE members were assigned to the Ad Hoc Committee on Teacher Education to act on the nine teacher education recommendations. By the third meeting, the Ad Hoc Committee had officially added three members of SCHEV. This unusual collaboration was supported by a legal opinion of the commonwealth's assistant attorney general. She pointed out that SCHEV has two important roles: it is the coordinating agency for public higher education in Virginia and it is the approving agency for all postsecondary academic degree-granting institutions operating in Virginia. By state code SCHEV is required to cooperate with BOE "in matters of interest to both the public school and the state supported institutions of higher education, particularly in connection with coordination of the college admission requirements and teacher training programs with the public school program" (J. W. Murphy, May 5, 1987, p. 3).

At the first meeting, on March, 6, 1987, invitations were sent to schools of education, division superintendents, and various professional organizations to attend a hearing on April 21 on the nine teacher education recommendations. Although a number of concerns were expressed by the organizational representatives, the chairman of the Ad Hoc Committee later summed up the testimony as being generally favorable for each of the nine recommendations with the exceptions of the ones concerning the liberal arts major and the eighteen-hour limitation on education courses. The Committee decided to consider the first three recommendations (arts and sciences degree, eighteen-hour limit, and restructuring) as belonging to one package, and agreed that this package should be implemented as soon as feasible.

On May 21, 1987, the Teacher Education Advisory Board presented its recommendations to the Ad Hoc Committee to permit prospective teachers in fields where the content does not correspond to an arts and sciences discipline (music, business education, speech pathology, industrial arts, etc.) to major in an appropriate area, and to exempt elementary, middle, and special education programs from the eighteen-hour limit on education courses. The Ad Hoc Committee agreed to some exceptions in the liberal arts degree requirement (at this point in time for health and physical education students and most vocational education students), but continued to support the abolition of the education major for elementary and special education students and reconfirmed its intention to limit professional education coursework to eighteen hours for all prospective teachers. A significant alteration occurred when the exemption of field experiences from this cap was clarified and communicated to the deans. By this action the Ad Hoc Committee confirmed the intentions of the commission's Committee on Teachers and Teaching to encourage more and better field placements and insured that credit hours for field experiences were not dropped from programs to meet the eighteen-hour limit.

In June, 1987, the first of several letters were sent to the presidents and governing boards of all institutions of higher education in Virginia, informing them of the expectations of the Ad Hoc Committee and giving a timetable for compliance. January 4, 1988, was set as the deadline for submission of the institutions' internally approved plans for restructuring their teacher education programs. With staff assistance, nine general guidelines were developed as a proposed framework for the restructuring (Ad Hoc Committee on Teacher Education, 1987).

Reactions and Restructuring

Teacher educators were unhappy with the forced reform (Olson, 1988). On August 10, 1987, a meeting was held by the Ad Hoc Committee to which were invited the deans or directors of schools or departments of education. Also in attendance were the Superintendent of Public Instruction and the Director of the State Council of Higher Education. The purpose of the meeting was to share with the deans and directors the plans for restructuring and to solicit feedback regarding the nine guidelines. In general, the teacher educators appeared angry and frustrated. In particular, they resisted the arts and sciences degree requirement for elementary and special education and other specialty areas, the eighteen-hour cap on professional education courses, and the January 4 deadline. Many of the deans believed that such a short timeframe would insure that only tinkering would occur, rather than a comprehensive restructuring.

At its next meeting (August 19, 1987) the Ad Hoc Committee responded by designating January 4, 1988, as the deadline for submission of a conceptual plan for restructuring; the full, comprehensive proposal would not be due until May 4, 1988. On the other hand, the committee was less flexible about the guidelines, approving them with few modifications. One major alteration allowed the exemption of graduate programs of initial preparation. It should be noted that the University of Virginia had already abandoned the undergraduate education major, except in physical education, and had instituted new programs requiring an undergraduate degree in the arts and sciences and a master's degree in education. The guidelines asked that teacher education institutions: consult reform reports, research, arts and sciences colleagues, and school teachers; address competencies in general studies, professional studies, field experiences, and appropriate disciplines; develop programs to attract minority and academically talented students; provide for comprehensive monitoring and evaluation of students and programs; remain within the limits of the eighteen-hour cap (excepting field experiences); and require an arts and sciences major. On September 9 and 10, 1987, deans and academic vice-presidents again met with the Ad Hoc Committee and asked, to no avail, for a further extension (Cox, 1987).

Thirty-seven teacher education institutions met the January 1, 1988, deadline for submitting conceptual plans; this number included all of the former schools, colleges, and departments of education in Virginia and two new institutions. According to the plans, a few certification programs had been dropped, and there were proposals for several new certification areas. Later that month the first of several progress reports was sent to Governor Baliles. For the next four months the Ad Hoc Committee members and the staff met with the deans and institution presidents about the specifics of the individual proposals for restructuring. Although they said they were willing to be reasonable, members of the Ad Hoc Committee stressed their commitment to the eighteen-hour limit on education courses, the requirement of an arts and sciences degree, and the need for restructuring.

Restructuring Teacher Education in the Old Dominion 143

The May 4, 1988, deadline for presenting the comprehensive plans for restructuring was met by all thirty-seven institutions. This date was only eighteen months after the release of the Commission on Excellence in Education report, fourteen months after the first meeting of the Ad Hoc Committee on Teacher Education, and eight months after the announcement of the guidelines for restructuring. The plans were reviewed by panels of national experts on May 23-25. The general institutional plans were examined by former United States Secretary of Education Terrell Bell and three staff members from the Southern Regional Education board (SREB). National external review panels, one for each of nine certification areas, commented on the adequacy of the specific subject area programs. The proposals were also reviewed by Department of Education staff. After the review reports were compiled, the Ad Hoc Committee members and/or staff met with the deans and academic vice-presidents from each of the teacher education institutions to share their concerns about the weaknesses of the proposals. All thirty-seven institutions were asked to address these concerns in their plans.

On August 17, 1988, BOE, meeting jointly with SCHEV, approved one restructuring plan, denied two, and gave preliminary approval to the other thirty-four. Over the next ten months the members of the Ad Hoc Committee and staff again held numerous private meetings with the deans, offering advice on how to revise the plans (Ad Hoc Committee on Teacher Education, 1987-1988). James W. Dyke, Jr., chairman of the Ad Hoc Committee and BOE member, was particularly active in this phase of the negotiations.

Although most schools grudgingly agreed to attempt to meet the expectations of the Ad Hoc Committee, several quietly but emphatically fought to preserve their own conceptions of restructuring until it became obvious that they were isolated. In particular, the deans of education in two large state universities persisted in presenting plans that called for education degrees in several programs. Members of the Ad Hoc Committee personally met with the presidents and governing board members of the two institutions to push for compliance with the guideline. Outflanked, the deans submitted revised plans that eliminated the education degrees.

Another controversy began in November, 1988, when the Association of Colleges and Schools of Education in State Universities and Land Grant Colleges and Affiliated Private Universities (known as ACSESULGC/APU or "the Land Grant Deans") became aware of Virginia's cap on professional education coursework. The Land Grant Deans passed a resolution condemning the action of the legislature in Texas which had limited the number of credit hours in education to eighteen. They agreed to work within their states for the revocation of certification reciprocity agreements with Texas. An identical resolution calling for sanctions against Virginia institutions was also passed with the support of two deans from Virginia (ACSESULGC/APU, 1988). Considerable concern was evoked when copies of the resolution reached Virginia state officials. Members of the Ad Hoc Committee, the Director of the State Council of Higher Education, and the Superintendent of Public Instruction in Virginia lobbied for repeal of the Virginia resolution. They succeeded in persuading the presidents of ACSESULGC/APU institutions in Virginia to repudiate the action of the Land Grant Deans. They explained to an ACSESULGC/APU committee that the commonwealth's eighteen-hour cap differed from the one in Texas in that Virginia's regulations exempted field experiences and graduate programs of initial teacher preparation. The deans, who continued to assert that setting a maximum as a limit was poor policy, were nonetheless persuaded that their resolution might indiscriminately harm programs which met the standards of almost every board and commission report. As a result, the Land Grant Deans dropped any intention of working for the revocation of reciprocity agreements with Virginia in the spring of 1989. The Texas resolution was not rescinded.

During the winter and spring of 1989, the schools, colleges, and departments of education in Virginia revised their plans for restructuring and presented them to the Ad Hoc Committee. The revised plans were approved a few at a time. All of the teacher education institutions met the May 5 deadline for the presentation of final plans. The Ad Hoc Committee met a final time on June 22, 1989, and approved the last of the thirty-seven restructured programs (Ad Hoc Committee on Teacher Education, 1988–1989).

Results of Restructuring

The Ad Hoc Committee reported that several institutions moved to five-year and graduate programs, especially in special education, since graduate programs were exempted from the eighteen-hour cap. Many others met the arts and sciences degree requirement by designing new interdisciplinary majors for prospective elementary and special education teachers. Eventually, all of the certification areas in vocational education were allowed to keep their education degree programs. Health and physical education programs also remained in education schools, but their content was beefed up. Secondary education programs were basically unaffected by the arts and sciences degree requirement and the limitation on professional education courses, especially since field experiences were not counted in the eighteen semester hours. In fact, some institutions actually increased the total number of education credits for prospective secondary teachers. About one-third of the thirty-seven institutions gained approval for exceptions to the professional coursework limit, mostly for elementary and special education programs. These plans required from twenty-one to twenty-seven semester hours in education credits in addition to credit hours allotted to field experiences. Exceptions for programs at other institutions were not granted because their rationales were not deemed sufficiently clear and convincing.

Before they disbanded in June, 1989, the Ad Hoc Committee members made several decisions that were designed to keep the reform process on track. They set July 1, 1990, as the deadline for the implementation of the restructured programs, which means that the new plans will have totally replaced the existing teacher education programs by June, 1994. They designated the members of the Administration, Assessment, and Finance Committee of the Board of Education as their successors. All decisions and reports about teacher education are to be routed to this committee. They asked that Department of Education staff conduct a "mini-visit" to each of the thirty-seven teacher education institutions and that they report to the Administration, Assessment, and Finance Committee in June, 1990, as to how conscientiously the universities and colleges are following their own plans (Ad Hoc Committee on Teacher Education, 1989, June 22). Finally, they made it very clear, at least to the staff, that any changes in the new programs would have to be approved by BOE, not the staff serving the Ad Hoc Committee.

ANALYSIS

The historical account of the policy-making process given above leaves many unanswered questions. We will attempt to deal with many of them by taking three passes at the material. First, we will examine the causes of the reform efforts as they relate to the original recommendations of the Commission on Excellence in Education. Second, we will look at the relative power of the actors, especially as it relates to the activities of the Ad Hoc Committee on Teacher Education. Third, we will comment on the unique attributes of the change process in Virginia, with the goal of teasing out lessons for teacher educators and educational policy makers.

Causes

Each of the nine Commission on Excellence in Education recommendations relating to teacher education was given a rationale by its creators. For example, the forgivable loans and financial incentives for teachers were designed to attract and keep good teachers in the classrooms. The two recommendations for better graduate training for administrators recognized that the principalship demands strong leaders who must be prepared, selected, compensated, and recertified according to higher standards. The recommendations on revising recertification regulations, requiring a graduate degree for teachers, and developing graduate professional education centers all spoke to the need of teachers to continue to update their educational qualifications in a changing world. The recommendations for the arts and sciences degree, the eighteen-hour cap, and the restructuring of programs were justified as responses to similar needs for improved preparation of teachers. However, the actual impetus for the restructuring process for teacher education had deeper historical roots.

Our interviews with members of the BOE, SCHEV, and Department of Education and SCHEV staff, most of whom were also members of or advisors to the Commission on Excellence in Education and/or the Ad Hoc Committee, showed that officials had been displeased with the state of teacher education in Virginia for some time before the reform efforts began. Subtle and overt messages had been sent to teacher education institutions, they said, that business as usual was not good enough. They could tell that their pleas were falling on deaf ears by reading the predictable program approval review reports passed on by the Teacher Education Advisory Board. A growing determination to make wholesale changes was facilitated by the support and encouragement of the governor during the deliberations of the Commission on Excellence in Education. Members of the commission's Committee on Teachers and Teaching reported that since they were ready to demand the restructuring of teacher education, the discussions centered on how radical the reforms were to be and what regulatory mechanisms could achieve the desired results. Early ideas about abolishing teacher education divisions in institutions of higher education were replaced by the notion of limiting education classes (Committee on Teachers and Teaching, 1986, April 23). The decision makers were influenced strongly by the testimony of five teachers, the report of the Carnegie Forum, and scare stories of enormous numbers of hours wasted in education courses (in some cases, over sixty semester hours).

The specification of eighteen hours came about after members of the Committee on Teachers and Teaching discovered from staff and from transcript studies that typical secondary education programs ran about eighteen semester hours (twelve hours of professional education courses and six hours of student teaching), leaving students time for an academic major and a good background in general studies. Members of the Committee on Teachers and Teaching and the Ad Hoc Committee on Teacher Education felt that preparation for elementary and special education teachers should be redesigned to fit the secondary model. By excluding field experiences from the eighteen-hour limit, they allowed the elementary and special education programs a little flexibility and protected credit hours set aside for field experiences from being replaced by hours for professional education courses. By excluding graduate programs of initial preparation, they ratified the recent changes made by the University of Virginia and Virginia Commonwealth University. These two exceptions differentiate the Virginia cap from the eighteen-hour limit in Texas and may have prevented the kind of public outcry that characterized the situation in the Lone Star State. In any case, it is clear that from the beginning educational policy makers in Virginia were determined to make drastic changes in the education of elementary school and special education teachers. The radical concept of a maximum as a limit fit in well with their plans.

Teacher educators admitted that they were slow to react to calls for reform—they felt that "if it ain't broke, don't fix it." Representatives of teacher education groups and teachers' organizations thought that political expediency, rather than desires for educational improvement, weighed heavily in the decision to focus on restructuring teacher education (Duncan, et al., 1989). After the commission recommendations were clustered and prioritized, they said, teacher education became an easy target because it offered opportunities for quick and cheap action, for publicity reporting the willingness of the state to take tough stands on educational issues, and for the punishment of a weak opponent.

Actors

A key feature of the reform movement in teacher education in Virginia is the relative powerlessness of the teacher education community. In order to explain this loss of control, it is necessary to take a more detailed look at each category of participants in the policy-making process.

Teacher educators. Before reform, schools of education could usually count on the program approval process and specific certification regulations to legitimize their designs for teacher education programs. They were represented on the Teacher Education Advisory Board, which was the accepted venue for discussing teacher education issues and for reviewing reports on teacher preparation programs. Deans could deal directly and discreetly with Department of Education staff to resolve any problems.

This seemingly stable system was shattered by the events following the report of the Commission on Excellence in Education. Because the teacher education community was not expecting such a swift and relentless follow-through to the recommendations, they did not begin to react as a group until the proposals were already accepted by the policy makers as policy guidelines rather than as ideals. When they did act, teacher educators found themselves somewhat divided. Some liberal arts colleges welcomed the recommendations, and several universities, including Virginia Commonwealth University and the University of Virginia, had already restructured their teacher preparation curricula. As a result, strong critics found it difficult to make the case that the Virginia Association of Colleges for Teacher Education or the general teacher education community was united against the reforms. It probably would not have made any difference if teacher educators had made strong, concerted efforts to sidetrack the call for restructuring; educational policy makers had already decided to utilize the occasion of the commission investigation as a starting point for irrecoverable change.

Teachers. Officials of the VEA also felt left out of the policy-making process. Their representatives on the Teacher Education Advisory Board, like the teacher educators, were neither consulted in the early stages nor included in the development of regulations. Because many other commission recommendations and other possible policy actions were of more importance to the general teaching profession, VEA also got a late start in protesting the destruction of the status quo in teacher education and was not able to muster resources to fight restructuring. This lack of wholehearted participation, replicated by administrators' groups as well, meant that the teacher educators were even more isolated in their attempts to be heard. An interesting irony is that VEA felt completely ignored, although the members of the commission's Committee on Teachers and Teaching were in agreement that it was the testimony of a small group of teachers that produced the most powerful and most memorable images of time wasted in education courses. This can be explained by noting that the five teachers who testified to the Committee on Teachers and Teaching were not representative of the teaching profession in Virginia nor of the VEA. It is very likely, however, that they did represent the true feelings of many of Virginia's teachers rather than the official position of the VEA.

Staff. In the former system, the staff of the Virginia Department of Education had considerable discretionary power in the regulation of teacher education programs. With the advent of reform, two basic changes in the status of teacher education officials occurred. First, there was a contemporaneous change in personnel in the Teacher Education Division. This meant that the Department of Education staff members, as well as the SCHEV staff, did not have the experience and expertise of the long-time specialists in teacher education policy. The new staff also shared the objectives of the Ad Hoc Committee and sensed a need for reform in teacher education. Second, and most importantly, the Ad Hoc Committee and BOE made it very clear that BOE, and not the staff, was to become the party primarily responsible for the quality of teacher education in the commonwealth.

Board of Education and State Council of Higher Education. The Board of Education had possessed the authority to reform teacher education all along, but chose not to make unwelcome decisions about individual programs because of the political threat of negative reactions from protective legislators. However, when the opportunity for comprehensive reform arose, BOE members jumped at the chance to make far-reaching changes. The unusually close collaboration of BOE and SCHEV members gave the Ad Hoc Committee an aura of authority that allowed them to do just about anything they pleased. Several of these officials were particularly adamant that change had to occur and that the number of education courses had to be limited. They were not only unafraid about taking an unpopular stand, but were also willing to put in the long hours of work required to monitor the reform process. Members of the Ad Hoc Committee attended meeting after meeting with university officials and state education agency staff. Their persistence allowed them to develop the expertise needed to deal with teacher educators and placed them in a position to monitor the day-to-day progress of the restructuring.

Governor. Governor Baliles executed a master stroke of policy administration by appointing all of the BOE members and many of the SCHEV members to his Commission on Excellence in Education. As the representatives of the public in matters of educational policy, these officials were likely to know what needed fixing and what remedies might be practical. Moreover, they already possessed the authority to mandate much of the reform agenda in a timely and appropriate manner. Since the governor appoints and reappoints BOE and SCHEV members, he might expect that they would pay special attention to his interests. Governor Baliles and his secretary of education, Donald J. Findley, helped insure the success of several of the projects, including the restructuring of teacher education, by publicly supporting them and their architects. It is important to note that although prominent members of the General Assembly of Virginia were appointed to the Commission on Excellence in Education, they had little impact as commission members and as legislators in directing Virginia's educational reform efforts.

Change Process

In a bold and swift stroke, the Ad Hoc Committee on Teacher Education completely wiped out all certification regulations. This was meant to encourage creativity by allowing teacher preparation institutions to start from scratch, using their own ideas as well as research and collective wisdom to build brave, new programs. However, many teacher education institutions interpreted this offer of an opportunity as an imposition, preferring to focus on the limitations of the guidelines instead of the possibilities for improvement. Why, if the former insiders were so unhappy, did the change process seem to move so smoothly and so quickly? (In Texas and other states, proposals for similar reforms have certainly been challenged much more publicly. See Richard Ishler's chapter in this volume.) The answer is that state officials made astute political moves that preempted any sustained, concerted, or effective opposition.

Governor Baliles appointed people to the Commission on Excellence in Education who were not only knowledgeable about the issues but were, by virtue of appointments to BOE and SCHEV, in a position to follow through with binding policies. The governor allowed BOE and SCHEV to make their own judgments about the practicality of the recommendations; but, he also knew that they would have a vested interest in pushing for regulations based on proposals that they had themselves authored. Governor Baliles's support for teacher education reform lent legitimacy to the change process. This made it difficult for teacher educators to denounce the recommendations publicly.

By choosing to oversee personally the restructuring of teacher education, the Ad Hoc Committee members emphasized the importance of the task. Anticipated claims that the expertise of teacher educators was being ignored were preempted in at least three ways. First, members of the Ad Hoc Committee educated themselves to the point that teacher educators could not say that these officials were ignorant of the issues involved, at least not without sounding like sour grapes. Second, each individual plan for restructuring was developed by the teacher educators themselves (subject, of course, to the restrictions of the guidelines) in concert with their arts and sciences colleagues, their presidents and academic officers, and local school teachers. This tactic insured that institutional contexts were taken into consideration. Third, by utilizing an extensive review system consisting of national and state experts, no one could claim publicly that the broader teacher education community had been bypassed.

The members of the Ad Hoc Committee further avoided open conflict by setting a good example. We have already described how their dedication led them to adopt a hands-on approach to policy making and to participate in the reform process from start to finish. Because they had determined for themselves that their solutions were the best, they were able to fight off the attempts to dilute the restructuring proposals. This persistence explains why the radical intentions of the commission passed unchanged through the policy-making process.

Although their intentions and public stance remained unchanged, members of the Ad Hoc Committee allowed some adjustments in the details of the final plans for restructuring. Exceptions to the arts and sciences degree requirement were made for programs in vocational education and in health and physical education. Field experiences and graduate courses were exempted from the eighteen-hour limit by presenting clear and convincing rationales for exceptions. All of this means that critics of the reforms could not say that officials were inflexible. One might assume that the Ad Hoc Committee was being duplicitous by appearing intransigent in public and then by making concessions behind the curtain. Ad Hoc Committee members said that they dealt with each case individually and reasonably, as is right and proper when dealing with the complexities of educational institutions, and that they never compromised on the key issues.

Other factors contributed to the relative lack of overt conflict. In a cool and effective display of power politics, the Ad Hoc Committee circumvented the deans by convincing the presidents of the necessity of change. Some teacher educators remain convinced that the SCHEV members on the Ad Hoc Committee represented a powerful threat of retaliation that the presidents could not ignore. By the same token, the deans and department chairs could not afford to burn their bridges behind them by making a dramatic last stand, thereby antagonizing the BOE. The University of Virginia and a few other state-supported institutions had already restructured their teacher education programs in ways that came close to fitting the intentions of the policy makers. Therefore, deans in the other schools of education could not claim that what was being asked of them was impossible, nor could they count on the support of the deans who had already led their institutions through a restructuring process.

It may also be that those affected by teacher education reform in Virginia were by nature not the sort of people who would raise a public fuss but were instead people who prefer to work quietly behind the scenes. We doubt that this is the case. The masterful political moves of the governor and the members of BOE and of SCHEV thoroughly gagged the critics. If they had spoken out, they would have sounded like spoiled children whining over lost candy, or, at best, like isolated ivory tower professors who were trying to protect their turf.

Our portrayal of the reform of teacher education in Virginia stresses the political aspects of educational reform. Other observers would agree that educational change is political in nature (Corwin, 1973; Cuban, 1988; Deal, 1984; Evetts, 1973; House, 1974; Kirst and Walker, 1971; Ravitch, 1983) and that change in teacher education shares this tendency toward politicization (Corrigan, 1985; Drummond and Andrews, 1980; Gideonse, 1984; Roth, 1981; Smith, 1980). A reexamination of the interview reports and government documents showed us that this is the correct interpretation for this case. Civic values were important only at the beginning of the policy-making process; once the preliminary decisions had been made, the resultant policy process had a distinctly political flavor. This does not mean that values other than political ones were ignored or forgotten; on the contrary, the educational policy makers were convinced that they were on a quest that would lead to the improvement of education for the state's children. There was no indication of the kind of wheeling and dealing one might expect from dirty politics, where ambition and greed are the motivating factors. However, the tactics of legitimization and preemption employed by the main participants are textbook examples of political maneuverings.

Besides the appeal to higher values, another possible justification for educational change in a case such as this one might be that the research recommends it. Clearly, research played little or no part in the establishment of new guidelines for teacher education. We are confident that political solutions took precedence over any research reporting on the nature of good teaching, good teachers, or effective teacher preparation.

It is too early to tell whether or not the reform will be universal and lasting. Since every teacher education program in Virginia has been restructured, and since many of the same educational policy makers are still around to insure that the restructuring process continues (for example, Ad Hoc Committee chairman, James W. Dyke, is now Secretary of Education in Virginia), we think that this is one of those unusual cases of educational change where reform became institutionalized quickly. Department of Education staff have said that some institutions are backsliding—asking staff for exceptions, making only cosmetic changes, and so forth. However, the interest and determination of the powerful educational policy makers should offset any attempts to water down the restructured programs.

Reform in teacher education programs is one thing; reform of the state's governance structure is another. Yet, we see evidence of changes in the patterns of control as well. The regular oversight of teacher education policy seems to have shifted to the BOE. The Department of Education staff has realized that its role has changed from activist to advisor. Although the Teacher Education Advisory Board is scheduled to become more powerful, it must report to an activist BOE. The narrowed range of the Teacher Education Advisory Board was demonstrated by the establishment of a separate Task Force on Improving Teaching as a Profession. These instances of alterations in the power structure for teacher education in Virginia lead us to suggest that the authority of the former insiders has been circumscribed by an active, hands-on BOE, and that this modified configuration may not be temporary. (See Walker, 1990, for a contrasting view of the early results.)

Several tasks remain to be completed. The Teacher Education Advisory Board and the state staff are writing new program approval and licensure standards scheduled for adoption in 1992. These proposed standards will be based on the nine guidelines for restructuring and NCATE standards. Institutions seeking NCATE approval will have joint visits by an NCATE Board of Examiners team and a state team. Non-NCATE institutions will be visited by a state team using the NCATE standards and a few state standards relevant to program approval.

Five-year reciprocal agreements are being negotiated with other states. At this time it does not appear that teachers holding teaching licenses in states with whom Virginia has established reciprocity will be required to pick up extra arts and sciences courses in order to satisfy the requirement of a college major outside of education. Thus, the restructured guidelines will affect only graduates of Virginia institutions, not those graduating from approved programs in states with whom Virginia has reciprocity agreements. These out-of-state graduates will be required to pass the NTE at the same level as graduates of Virginia institutions.

Lessons Learned

For Educational Policy Makers

Viewed through the eyes of an educational policy maker, the reform of teacher education in Virginia would be seen as a success. Recalcitrant educationists were forced to develop new, streamlined programs. The financial and political costs were minimal. This success was the result of two major strategies. First, a consistent cast of authoritative players was maintained throughout the process. The survival of policy innovations has been enhanced, so far, by assuring that the same leading actors have been involved at every stage of policy making—initiation, regulation, implementation, and maintenance. Second, special efforts were made to thwart serious challenges to the most radical proposals. Policymakers required the participation of the affected institutions; they allowed public discussion of proposals, even though they seemed committed to their original intentions; they were flexible in dealing with individual cases while maintaining a clear, tough public posture; they worked hard to become instant experts; and they avoided failure by asking the possible.

Lessons for Teacher Educators

Many teacher educators have viewed the forced restructuring with alarm. They now realize that teacher education is an easy political target. They must remember that policies are not based on research and that policy making is not primarily a rational process. A few forceful impressions are more likely to influence policy makers than thousands of pages of expert advice. Teacher educators should also realize that it is not business as usual in the teacher education policy arena. The recent changes in teacher education should be seen as part of a broader reform of the teaching profession and, in many states, part of a broader educational reform movement. In this new, expanded policy environment, a group's chances of success are heavily dependent upon its ability to enlarge its pool of political support. Therefore, teacher educators in every state should work to strengthen their ties to teachers' organizations and other educational interest groups. Teacher educators and their new allies must react quickly to calls for reform, not by fighting losing battles against powerful opponents, but by developing their own mechanisms for accountability and by preserving continuity in purpose. They will have to prove themselves accountable to the public and its representatives before regaining control of the preparation of teachers.

PART II
HIGHER EDUCATION INSTITUTIONS

8

Nona A. Prestine

The Struggle for Control of Teacher Education:

The University of Wisconsin-Madison

In response to the report of the National Commission on Excellence in Education (1983) and the numerous reports that followed it, hundreds of pieces of legislation and administrative rules and regulations have been passed by state legislatures to rectify perceived inadequacies in the education system and to promote educational quality. This "first wave" of reform, as it has become known, emphasized the legislating and mandating of controls by state level authorities over educational programs (Hawley, 1988: Kirst, 1988; Passow, 1988) and has varied considerably from state to state. These legislative initiatives addressed numerous educational concerns (McLaughlin, et al., 1985) with one predominant area of activity being that of teacher preparation. Although reform of teacher education has been examined from a variety of perspectives (Corrigan, 1985; Guthrie, 1983; Hammond, 1986; Howey and Zimpher, 1986; Murray, 1986; Roth, 1985; Schuck, 1985; Soltis, 1987), one perspective that has been largely ignored is that of governance issues between institutions with teacher preparation programs and state-level authorities. This perspective, which looks at such regulation as a fundamental issue between higher education institutions and external authorities, involves questions of who decides and who decides what in the governance of academic program and policy.

This study examines such a governance conflict between the University of Wisconsin-Madison and the Wisconsin Department of Public Instruction over the question of who has the decision-making authority over the content of the teacher education program. Like many other public land grant institutions, the University of Wisconsin-Madison (UW-Madison) has a broad grant of statutory authority over academic, organizational, and governance matters. "The faculty of each institution...shall be vested with the responsibility for the immediate governance of such institution and...shall have the primary responsibility for academic and educational activities..." (Wisconsin, 1990, 36.09 [4]). On the other hand, the Department of Public Instruction and the state superintendent are delegated power and authority to oversee and maintain the public education system, including the licensing of teachers, in part by prescribing "standards and procedures for the approval of teacher preparatory programs leading to certification or licensure" (Wisconsin, 1966, 115.28 [7]).

Historically, UW-Madison has epitomized the concept of strong faculty participation in institutional governance (Millett, 1978). This is reflective of the university's history, tradition, and mission (Curti and Carstensen, 1949). "Faculty involvement in decision-making has become so ingrained in the operation of UW-Madison that the term 'faculty governance' is often used in place of the broader concept of 'shared governance'" (University of Wisconsin-Madison, 1978, p. 28). The umbrella of such university-wide faculty governance shelters even stronger enclaves of faculty control of academic program and policy in the numerous schools and colleges under its auspices.

Correspondingly, the School of Education of UW-Madison has jealously guarded the role and prerogative of faculty control over academic curriculum. In the 1960s an exacerbated conflict with the National Council for Accreditation of Teacher Education (NCATE) over such authority resulted in the university's withdrawal from that organization. One of the primary objections raised by Madison was that NCATE was an external organization attempting to dictate curriculum and other internal policy matters to the School of Education (Elam, 1963; Stiles, 1963; Travelstead, 1963; Wiggins, 1964). As the then dean of UW-Madison School of Education noted, it was the duty of the university administrator to "see that the powers of accrediting bodies and certifying boards are kept within proper limits-that they are not allowed to become harmfully dictatorial forces robbing his university of its autonomy and needlessly depriving its faculty of its essential right to keep its academic house in order" (Elam, 1963, p. 157).

From the early 1970s onward, however, the school's attention was drawn to what it perceived as increasing interference by the Department of Public Instruction (DPI) in the teacher preparation program. As reported by the School of Education in the self-analysis report for North Central Association review:

> The substantial increase in control of programs exercised by the state's Department of Public Instruction is currently causing concern.... DPI is now seemingly attempting to dictate academic program content in a manner which would usurp the traditional place of faculty in designing instruction programs and courses.... (1978, p. 117)

This had been an on-going issue between several teacher preparation institutions, including UW-Madison, and the DPI. The institutions' complaint was that DPI was applying program approval standards unfairly and unevenly from one teacher preparation program to another. It was felt that the "standards of attainment" phrase from Wisconsin Statute 115.28 (7) was being used as an "open notebook" to indulge the idiosyncrasies and predilections of individual DPI review teams. Some departments and programs were being held to what they believed was unrealistic and far too strict accountability, whereas similar departments and programs in other institutions were given only the most cursory of evaluations.

The university gained support for its position from the chair of the state legislature's Assembly Education Committee, who proposed a bill limiting DPI's authority to impose rules and regulations that have not gone through the legislative process on schools of education. A substantially amended version of the bill eventually passed and became Chapter 28, Laws of 1979. The School of Education believed the issue was settled and interpreted the law as specifically limiting both the powers of the state superintendent (Wis. Stat. 115.28 [7]) and the general authority to promulgate rules in an area exempted from rule making by the legislature, that is, academic programs of higher education institutions (Wis. Stat. 227.01 [11] [f.]). That this was a totally inaccurate interpretation would be evidenced by later events.

In the early 1980s, with the national concern that erupted over the quality of public education in general, and the criticism leveled at teachers and the institutions responsible for preparing teachers specifically, the conflict between the DPI and the university rekindled with the department's announcement of its intention to promulgate new program approval rules. The salient issue was not whether the teacher education program needed to be changed, but the larger governance question of who was to determine the content of the change and who ultimately had authority over the content of the teacher preparation program. It pitted the authority of a state agency charged with the responsibility of certifying teachers for the public schools of the state against the authority of another state agency, the university, delegated with the responsibility for its academic programs and procedures.

The primary objection of the university to the proposed DPI program approval rules are best summarized in a memorandum circulated from the dean of the UW-Madison School of Education to UW System deans of education and vice-chancellors of academic affairs. Although six areas of concern were noted, "the governance issue is primary" (Palmer, 1985, p. 1). The intrusive nature of the proposed rules into the governance structure was expecially onerous. In addressing this issue, the dean noted that the proposed rules would remove several levels of university authority by specifying aspects of each institution's administrative structure. This would give DPI "the right to review salaries, workload, tenure, insurance, sabbatical leaves, retirement, and other policies...." Also, the department would be able to "define program and course content in a wide variety of fields and departments." In effect, this meant that DPI would be empowered to review syllabi from any course in any department taken by a student in the teacher education program and to decide whether that course was acceptable or not, thus substituting the expertise of the DPI staff for the expertise of the faculty. As the dean noted, it was one thing to require a given number of credit hours for completion of an academic major or minor; it was something quite different to specify content of the courses taken. Moreover, the recomendations for statewide requirements-that is, GPA for students seeking admission to the teacher education program and exit text scores-would remove from individual faculties the power to determine appropriate levels of academic performance.

Returning to the governance issue once more in closing, the dean noted,

> We believe that faculty-initiated changes will continue to produce positive results, not the imposition of rules from the outside. What is the evidence that increased regulation is needed or that program conformity is desirable?... Is this primarily a political document or an academic one? The document has been written, it seems safe to assume, in a very sweeping fashion, in the expectation that there will be objections and that a compromise will be reached giving the DPI most of what it wants. If that occurs, it will confirm the power of DPI to regulate the internal affairs of another state agency, and

we can expect more regulation later from the DPI and other state agencies with interest in programs in other schools and colleges. (Palmer, 1985, p. 4)

In 1986, with the passage of a set of administrative rules and regulations, commonly cited as PI 4, the Department of Public Instruction asserted and imposed its authority over the school of education's academic program. The PI 4 standards are specific administrative rules under which the colleges and universities in Wisconsin receive approval to train teachers for licensure in the state. Included in these standards are mandated courses in pedagogy as well as in specific academic majors and minors, prescribed course content, admission standards, and graduation or exit requirements. The passage of these administrative rules marked the climax of a long and bitter battle between the state education agency and the School of Education at the University of Wisconsin-Madison and provided a focal point and context for analyzing a major governance struggle.

SIGNIFICANCE OF THE STUDY

In recent years, institutional autonomy and the decision-making authority implied in shared participation in governance over academic programs have come under increasing attack from external groups seeking redistributions of power and pressing for authority over the internal functionings of institutions of high education (Baldridge, 1983; Corson, 1975; Epstein, 1974; Mason, 1982). The uniqueness and diversity that has characterized the American system of higher education for so long seems endangered by the forces of centralization and unification, especially at the state level (Clark, 1971b, 1976; Nickerson and Stampen, 1978; Shotzberger, 1972). The Carnegie Commission on Higher Education in 1973 reported, "External authorities are exercising more and more authority over higher education.... The greatest shift of power in recent years has taken place not inside the campus, but in the transfer of authority from the campus to outside agencies" (p.1). Although such "transfer of authority" to external agencies may have its historic roots in financial funding contingencies (Dressel, 1980; Nickerson and Stampen, 1978), it seems to be branching now in the new direction of direct program control. This eroding of internal decision-making authority over academic programs has been noted widely (Baldridge, 1975;

Berdahl, 1978; Bok, 1982; Clark, 1976; Corson, 1975; Kerr, 1972; Nickerson and Stampen, 1978; Shotzberger, 1972). Yet there is paucity of data that describe or document the actual loss of decision-making authority over academic programs to an external agency. Consequently, "the thick descriptions" necessary for understanding the complex nature of the variables, forces, and processes involved in such a shift of governance authority are noticeably lacking. These types of data are critical to building descriptions, explanations, and, eventually, substantive theories of governance and the external change process in higher education.

This chapter focuses specifically on how one external agency was able to successfully expropriate the decision-making authority over an academic program from the internal control of the faculty. Although limited to one university and one external state agency, the findings are likely to be applicable at least in part to governance conflicts between other higher education institutions and external agencies who share similar relationships. It is imperative to understand how this happened and under what variable conditions if an assessment is to be made of its meaning in the context of the governance of higher education.

Research Problem and Procedures

The major objective of this study was to examine the constituent variables and forces that determined the course of the struggle between the University of Wisconsin-Madison and Department of Public Instruction for the control of the teacher education program. Because this study approaches the conflict from a governance perspective, the level of analysis is focused on the university.

The objective was to analyze the process from the university's perspective in terms of what happened and why. A case-study approach was employed to provide a holistic mode of inquiry that would be consonant with and responsive to an exploration of the relationship and interactions between the organization and its environment or context (Patton, 1980; Yin 1981a, 1981b). This method allowed the discovery of the processes of events and context characteristics that shed light on the issue involved. As noted by Rist, addressing the general question of "'What's going on here?' is at once disarmingly simple and incredibly complex" (1982, p. 440).

Case Selection

The selection of UW-Madison as the focus of this case study was determined by two major factors: the purpose of the research and the interest of the researcher (Guba and Lincoln, 1985; Merriam, 1985).

Although there are twelve cluster campuses in the University of Wisconsin System, as well as another eighteen independent colleges in the state with teacher preparation programs—all affected by the same issue—the uniqueness of the Madison campus determined its selection. Such a choice was warranted because the overall goal of the research was to examine how and why a shift in governance occurred, and an exemplary instance was needed to fully document the process (Yin, 1984).

Along with the extraordinary tradition of faculty governance in academic matters, Madison is the recognized flagship of the state's university system, or as one respondent phrased it, "the jewel in the crown." Its prestige and renown as a world-class research university accord it a status and power different from the other universities and colleges in the state. It was the sum of these very qualities that also make it a lightning rod for the governance conflict.

Methodology

In general, data collection consisted of an application of two sets of interviews, in-depth and focused, with principal participants involved in this issue; examination of several forms of documentary and archival evidence; and observation of general School of Education meetings and School of Education Program Committee meetings.

The set of thirty-five open-ended depth interviews included the key actors and representatives of relevant stakeholders and interest groups involved in this issue. University of Wisconsin-Madison administrators, deans and professors, and Department of Public Instruction officials, were interviewed along with state legislators, system administrators, representatives of cluster campuses and independent colleges, DPI Task Force members, and interest group representatives. Starting from an initial list of eleven key respondents, the researcher either was referred by these individuals to other relevant sources or had these other sources emerge from the on-going data analysis process. Each of these interviews lasted between one and two hours, and four lasted more than three hours. These interviews were conducted over a nine-month period (September, 1987, to May, 1988), and most took place in the respondents' offices or places of employment. Six prestudy interviews with key actors were conducted in November, 1986, and contributed to the focus and clarification of parameters of this study.

The second set of interviews, which involved a more focused method, commenced while preliminary analysis of the first set of depth interviews continued (Rist, 1982; Owens, 1982). The focused interviews were with respondents more indirectly associated with the conflict; there were also specific follow-ups with the key respondents that were of a much shorter duration, lasting less than one hour.

A rich variety of documentary and archival evidence was also available for data collection. Because the records of state agencies are considered public, access was gained to files, legal opinions, and internal memoranda of the University Committee, the School of Education, and the DPI. Document analysis was also used with record of the DPI Task Force meetings and reports, the report of the University System Task Force, the legislative hearings and analysis, testimony given on the proposed rules, and newspaper accounts of the issue.

Because most of the direct confrontations had concluded by the time this research was started, data from observation were least revealing. However, attendance at School of Education Program Committee meetings from September, 1987, to May, 1988, and observation of a general meeting of the School of Education in December, 1986, did allow for some intuitive feel of faculty reaction to the promulgated rules.

The data collection procedures used, the length of time for data collection on-site, and use of multiple sources of evidence contributed to an understanding of the issues, familiarity and rapport with the key participants, and a knowledge of the interactions and history of the relations between the university and the Department of Public Instruction (Guba and Lincoln, 1985; Owens, 1982). To obtain the necessary hard data, it was necessary to gather evidence and verify information from all sources, thereby reinforcing interview information with written testimony, archival records, or another interview. In this manner, potential problems of construct validity were addressed because multiple sources of evidence essentially provide multiple measures of the same phenomenon (Rist, 1982).

Data Analysis

To organize the data in some systematic manner and assist in making judgments about the meaning and importance of the lines of inquiry, the researcher decided upon a thematic strategy of data analysis. This thematic approach emphasizes the clustering and presentation of material by key themes found in the study (Rist, 1982). Three broad sets of conceptualizations or themes emerged from the data: (a) statements, accounts, and documents associated with internal institutional variables; (b) statements, accounts, and documents concerned with external environmental forces; and (c) data reflective of the process of the conflict. These themes are reflective of the nature of the research question guiding the inquiry and of the sources available for data collection. It is important to note that this thematic framework emerged after the prestudy interviews and completion of the initial eleven key respondent interviews. Data were then further analyzed in searching for regularities and patterns within each of the themes or topics. These became the "coding categories" (Bogdan and Biklen, 1982, p. 156) used as a means of further sorting the collected data.

FINDINGS

Internal Variables

Organizational saga. One of the most potent internal variables identified was the overwhelming belief of UW-Madison in the role of faculty governance and the inviolability of the statutory grant of authority to the faculty over its academic programs. Some respondents called this control over programs academic freedom. Some called it faculty governance. Others referred to it as institutional autonomy. Regardless of the label, all referred to the same emotionally laden phenomenon. "The Madison argument has always been academic freedom. It's their institution; they should have full rein over its content." "Historically, Madison has had lots of autonomy to do whatever they wanted." "They believe that it is their God-given domain to decide on these matters; that the program belongs to them by academic freedom rights."

This belief has evolved into an organizational saga (Clark, 1971a, 1983). The trappings of traditional faculty independence and perceived statutorily granted invulnerability delayed and fragmented any serious efforts to organize or coordinate opposition. Respondents on both sides of the issue agreed that no one took DPI's initiatives seriously at first. The School of Education believed that its legal position, based on its interpretation of previously cited statutory changes in 1979, was unassailable even though university counsel was never contacted to corroborate such beliefs. "I think our understanding of the legislation was hope more than anything else." "It was [an Associate Dean's] refusal to believe that the state superintendent could impose rules. The advice was based on wishful thinking." "They [the School of Education] knew it was coming, and they buried their heads in the sand." In effect, the School of Education heard what it wanted to hear and believed what it wanted to believe. As Clark pointed out, a saga can "produce a striking distortion, with the organization becoming the only reality, the outside world illusion" (1983, p. 374). From the inception of the DPI's Task Force on Teaching and Teacher Education in 1982 until the publication of the proposed rules in the fall of 1985, the school held stubbornly to an indefensible and inaccurate legal position.

If the final realization of the seriousness and determination of the DPI's initiative came as a shock to the School of Education in the fall of 1985, it shook the College of Letters and Science (L & S) to its very core as awareness dawned that the rules contained in Subchapter V covered the academic majors and minors of teacher education students. Although professional schools have learned to live with varying amounts of regulation, the College of Letters and Science at UW-Madison has been somewhat of an icon of professional autonomy and academic independence. As one dean stated, "Nobody tells L & S what to do." The organizational saga of faculty governance and academic freedom achieves its highest degree of credence and practice in the College of Letters and Science, and it is this culture that dominates the university as a whole. The L & S faculty's reaction progressed from initial disbelief and denial to eventual indignation and outrage. This quickly involved the Faculty Senate ("The Faculty Senate opposes this intrusion into the responsibilities for determination of educational policy and curriculum...") and its executive arm, the university committee, ("We view these rules...as an unwarranted intrusion upon both our rights and our responsibilities...") in the general fracas. Yet, little could be accomplished by that late date.

Insularity and isolation. A factor closely allied to institutional saga was the cultural norm of isolationist behavior that promoted a sense of superiority, power, and differentness. A relative intransigence and resistance to suggestions not internally generated was noted by several respondents. "We've had a history of telling people to get lost, of being unfriendly." "There is an overall institutional resistance to the environment. There has always been a resistance to external demands and an unwillingness to respond." Although this behavior sought to insulate the system from those who would chip away at its foundation and lessen its distinctive status, it also had the unintended consequence of isolating the university from potential supports.

The insularity extended to the university's relationships with the other system campuses. Influenced by different perspectives, traditions, and histories, the differences were between Madison and everyone else. ("Madison is different. They see themselves as different and they are.") Of primary importance were historical differences involving the institutional role of the teacher education program. Nine of the eleven cluster campuses are former teacher preparation institutions or normal schools. Thus the teacher education program lies more at the heart and assumes a different importance at these institutions. This also affects these institutions' relationships with the Department of Public Instruction. "The role of teacher education at the other institutions is more important than it is here. So independence from DPI is also harder for them."

Differences in and of themselves are not necessarily detrimental. But the insularity generated by Madison's efforts to maintain its "different" status has caused the university's relationships with the other system campuses often to devolve into acrimonious and divisive wrangling. "It's not unheard of for other campuses to say, 'if Madison does it, we'll do the opposite.' There's not a lot of love lost between us." "There's a history of animosity toward this campus...and resentment...and envy for everything from our faculty governance to salary schedule." The culture that reinforced efforts to maintain Madison's insularity and integrity did so at the expense of possible support available from the other campuses. "When the gun was at our throats, there was no support from the rest of the System."

Pluralistic Nature of the School of Education. The pluralistic nature of the School of Education at UW-Madison was identified as one of the important structural variables. Under the operant form of organization, all faculty members who help prepare future teachers are automatically members of the School of Education. Technically, the faculty of the School of Education includes every professor who has even one teacher education student in his or her classes.

Whether this particular structure leads to closer ties between teacher education and the liberal arts strand of the university is a point not to be debated here. In the case under study, such diffuse and variegated membership makes coordination of effort difficult, if not impossible. Consensus opinion on the issue among just the seven departments formally within the School of Education was never reached, let alone with or among the College of Letters and Science departments or individual faculty. Several respondents commented on the difficulty of getting the school's faculty together and of communicating. "It's so hard to get the School of Education faculty together for anything. They don't communicate. Hardly anyone attends the meetings." "They (L & S faculty) never came to the School of Education faculty meetings until it got personal."

Large numbers of L & S faculty were either not aware of the impending DPI rules or simply did not pay any attention to them until they were nearly a *fait accompli.* An eleventh-hour attempt to head off the impending promulgation of the rules was made in November, 1985, with the department chairs asked to comment on the rules as they applied to their academic area. The wide range of responses reflected both the manic speed at which events were moving, as well as poor communication. Some departments found nothing objectionable in the proposed rules. "There doesn't seem to be much concern with the overall thrust of the recommendations." Others were bewildered by them: "We should observe that the language is in some instances confusing and so it is difficult for us to understand exactly what the authors of this section intend." Others raised rancorous objections: "We strongly question the advisability of a detailed specification by DPI of course requirements, gradepoint average and evaluation procedures." "Not a single member saw merit in the DPI draft...." One department completely misread the rules, thought they were proposed for the K–12 sector, and heartily endorsed them.

Decentralizaton. Closely related to the pluralistic nature of the School of Education is the decentralized structure of the university. The conflict with the DPI called for some measured, managed, consensus response, but the university was simply unable to respond in an appropriate manner. Several respondents faulted the decentralized sturcture. "As far as decentralization in responding to outside challenges, it's a bad structure." "With political issues, the governance structure can't deal with them." "It's too decentralized. The fundamental breakdown was an inadequate organizational structure."

In this particular case, decentralization combined with entrenched principles of faculty governance offered an especially potent combination. Information frequently did not get out to the faculty in a timely manner. Faculties did not make a timely response. Meetings were called, then cancelled. Decision by committee was a slow, tedious process and sometimes not done in the manner it should have been. As a former associate dean commented,

> The problem is we depend on the faculty for so much. They don't take this job as seriously as they should. It becomes crisis management. This whole issue had been in the winds for three years, and it hits like a bomb. When you ask for faculty participation, and they want to play a role in governance, there is a responsibility and obligation that goes along with this. If they don't hold up their end, they better not complain.

Such a system also has the effect of virtually hamstringing any efforts of administrators to provide strong leadership or make authoritative decisions. "Deans don't exercise early leadership. Deans look bad if faculty grumble, so they don't make decisions." The decentralized system allowed no clear positions of authority for those who endeavored to speak with a coordinated, unified voice for the university. As several respondents noted, if a dean attempts to exercise real leadership, that person "won't be dean for very long. There is always a part of the faculty that doesn't agree." The underlying principles of academic freedom in a decentralized system allow for and even encourage individual viewpoints and actions. This was manifested in a single department within the School of Education that had one professor serving as the Chair of the UW-System Task Force, another serving as project director of the DPI's Task Force, and a third on leave of absence to serve as deputy state superintendent.

The decentralized structure that hindered a unified response was especially detrimental to the university when it presented its case at the legislative hearings in December, 1985. Opposition testimony from the university came from individual professors or deans. None represented a consensus position. "The thing the legislature found so annoying was that no one speaks for the faculty as a group. The legislators kept getting different messages. They begin to wonder why they can't get their act together." In fact, the decentralized structure and underlying culture of the university made it difficult, if not impossible, for faculty to do so.

External Variables

Public Mood. The promulgation of the PI 4 rules came during what arguably might be considered one of the most turbulent periods of educational scrutiny and crisis in our nation's history. Heralded by *A Nation at Risk* (National Commission on Excellence in Education, 1983) and followed by a blitzkrieg of national media exposure, the perceived educational crisis was couched in terms of no less than a national emergency. Much as when education had borne the country's indignation and fear over the Russians' successful Sputnik launching, so now it became the "whipping boy" for the huge foreign trade deficit and fear for the economic security of the nation. If schools were producing an inadequate product, then the teachers must be at fault, and, by implication, the institutions that prepare teachers. Unlike the massive dose of federal monies poured into education in the late 1950s, the "Reagonomics" of the 1980s would look to the individual states for remedy. State legislatures, university study groups, distinguished educational leaders, and a host of self-proclaimed educational "experts" produced a plethora of recommended remedies and reforms. Thus, the impetus for change clearly originated in the environment. As one respondent stated, "If the public had perceived teachers as well prepared, this issue wouldn't have come up."

The general mood of the public demanded directive, assertive action. As had happened in other times of national crisis, people generally were more willing to tolerate the extension of power by central authorities than under more normal circumstances (Wallenfeldt, 1983). The primary imperative became to rectify the situation by whatever means necessary. As a state legislator noted, "it's a sign of the times. The call for university autonomy is secondary to the call for standards."

With its statutory responsibility for licensure of teachers in the state, the DPI was in a position to be especially sensitive to the mood of the environment in regard to the preparation of teachers. Heightened public concerns provided, if nothing else, a propitious moment for the promulgation of rules that had been under development for several years. It was, as the state superintendent noted, "a moment in the history of teacher education" to be captured and used, and was neither wasted nor squandered by the department.

Coalition of Interest Groups. The Department of Public Instruction was not the only external force in the environment that was sensitive to the prevailing mood and that wished to see change in the teacher education program. An extremely successful and powerful coalition of groups was brought in and joined with the department's efforts. Politically and morally, the most powerful of these groups was the Wisconsin Education Association Council (WEAC). From a political perspective, WEAC is one of the strongest legislative lobbyist groups in the state. As the representative of the teacher practitioners in the field, WEAC support lends a certain moral sanction to educational issues.

Although philosophically committed to raising teacher preparation standards, other motivations also prompted WEAC's unqualified support for the proposed rules. For years the union had felt shut out of the universities, especially UW-Madison. "There's been a long history of strained relationship between us and the university. They're arrogant, they're elitist, and they don't listen to anybody. Now they're going to have to listen." The proposed reforms of the PI 4 rules promised increased control, albeit through DPI, over teacher education programs. At a deeper level, much of this antagonism can be explained by differing perspectives of the two organizations over collective bargaining and unionization issues. Several respondents felt this to be a significant factor. "WEAC was probably so anti-University because the union notion has always fallen flat on this campus."

Along with WEAC, a well-rounded field of interest groups was recruited by the department. School board association members, district administrators, principals, teachers, business and industry leaders, labor and higher education representatives served on the Superintendent's Task Force on Teaching and Teacher Education. The task force's primary importance derived from its successful attempt to coalesce these highly influential interest groups into one body working under DPI's direction on a common venture—that of improving teaching and teacher education. Recruits became zealots. This is more than adequately documented in the numerous public statements, the volume of correspondence to state legislators, and the testimony offered at the legislative hearing by these groups and their representative members in support of the proposed rules.

Role of the State Superintendent. The key external variable, however, was the position of the state superintendent and the person occupying the position. Legally, the power to regulate and mandate changes by rule promulgation had been statutorily granted to the state superintendent and the Department of Public Instruction since 1979. It was the decision of the newly elected superintendent in 1981 to use such authority. Until this time, the DPI relied on guidelines, as they had done in the past, but no rules had been promulgated through the legislative process.

There was admittedly an underestimation of the political acumen, aggressiveness, and savvy of the new superintendent. As he stated, "The truth of the matter is that while others slept, we were toiling upward in the night. They didn't think we could do it and deliver a product of this scope." Guided by a clear vision and firm determination, the superintendent was not to be deterred from his chosen course. Also, as a former Wisconsin state legislator, the superintendent was not unfamiliar with playing political hardball to achieve his ends. ("We slam dunked it in the Assembly Committee.")

Moreover, in Wisconsin, the elected state superintendent also becomes one of two exofficio members of the Board of Regents of the University of Wisconsin System. The dual-role positions offer a potentially powerful combination. Although the power and opportunity to use such power have always rested in the dual positions, much is dependent upon the person who occupies the dual-role positions. Partisan feelings still run high on this issue, and so objectivity may be questionable, but there was virtual unanimity among the university's supporters that such power was abused and that a conflict of interest existed. ("Most important was his smooth political machine and his position on the Regents. He forced the top administration to compromise with him on this. He used his Regents position.") Most of these respondents felt that the superintendent had used his position as a regent to bully and intimidate system campuses as well as system administration into staying out of the conflict.

Supporters of the DPI and the superintendent see this in different terms. Although most agreed that the superintendent made use of his regent position, they saw this in a much less sinister and nefarious context. "He's the most activist Superintendent in this century. Others just came and sat on the Board of Regents. He's not like that." Only one respondent completely denied any conflict of interest, calling such allegation "a red herring."

Process

Proactive and reactive roles. The entire course of the conflict can be seen as casting the Department of Public Instruction in a proactive role and the University of Wisconsin-Madison in a reactive role. By choosing first to ignore, disregard, and underestimate the prevailing public mood and the very serious intentions of the Department of Public Instruction, the School of Education placed itself at a disadvantage from which it never recovered. Allies and possible supporters were never recruited; alternative proposals were not developed. The school's preeminent argument, at least until the fall of 1985, was a legal one, based on an inaccurate interpretation of the statutory changes in Chapter 28, Laws of 1979.

The department anticipated and read the mood of environment in mobilizing external support for their position. The DPI's Task Force on Teaching and Teacher Education is a prime example of such intiative. As the state superintendent noted, "We brought in a very representative group and had it chaired by a higher ed person.... The point is that, if objectively reviewed, the structure of the study and its end product is a classic example of public policy development." The Task Force held state-wide public hearings on proposed recommendations for the first half of 1983 and submitted a final draft in December, 1983.

In November, 1983, the university belatedly made an effort in this area by forming its own task force on teacher education. This task force included twelve representatives from system institutions and was chaired by a former executive vice-president of the UW System. In October, 1984, this task force issued their final report entitled *Benchmarks of Excellence* (University of Wisconsin System Teacher Education Task Force, 1984).

A comparison of the two reports revealed that the main point of divergence is over the governance issue. In an introductory note, the chair of the task force acknowledged that the full control of teacher education programs "does not reside with the faculties of our institutions." Considerable influence is wielded by other relevant groups; however, "primary responsibility for academic programs and degree requirements rests with the faculties of each institution...." The *Benchmarks* document recommended changes in teacher education, some of which closely paralleled those made in the DPI report and are so referenced, but it placed responsibility for such program changes firmly under the control of the schools of education and their respective faculties. It was the key phrases—"to be determined by the faculty" (p. 9), "the faculty review" (p. 10), "responsibility of the faculty" (p. 10), "the faculty responsible for course" (p. 11)—that touched the heart of the matter.

The timing of *Benchmarks* (1984) proved detrimental to its reception and frittered away much of its potential impact. Published nearly a year after the DPI Task Force report, it had the appearance of a hurried institutional response to a situation quickly slipping out of the control of the university. In fact, by the time the system task force was finally formed, not only had the university lost the initiative, but the tenor of the times had changed. Mandating, ordering, and legislating were the new order of the day. ("The [*Benchmarks*] report was too collegial in tone for the times.... A year earlier [it] might have been effective.") By this time, few outside the university had much patience with the niceties and subtleties of collegial debate, compromise, and consensus building.

Political Maneuvers. With authority over the teacher preparation program contested, both sides moved to bolster their respective positions, although in markedly different ways. The DPI moved to control what they believed they could control. The department refined, negotiated, and concentrated its efforts on those elements over which it had clear authority, thus dispersing university and systemwide resistance into isolated pockets. Early versions of PI 4 had provisions, for example, requiring institutionwide written policies pertaining to such items as salary schedules and faculty teaching load. As an internal DPI legal counsel memo pointed out, the broad scope of such items had little relationship to ensuring quality teacher education programs and exceeded the department's rule-making authority (Teel, 1985). Each of these rules was amended to be limited specifically to teacher education faculty exactly as DPI counsel had suggested.

The DPI used its authority over teacher preparation to gain de facto control over L & S, for which they do not have authority for direct control, by linking those courses to the teacher preparatory program. Although many university respondents were outraged by this, there was little that could be done. "This campus was prepared to tell the DPI to go fly a kite if only one other campus like UW-Milwaukee would have agreed to go along with us. But no one did.... So with no one else to support us, it was easy for him to attack Madison." The department reinforced its position by offering the provision that no one had to follow these rules. The state superintendent could establish standards for an approved program of study leading to certification for a teaching license but could not eliminate or revoke any program. In that happy course of events, a student could be admitted to the university and the school of education, complete his or her coursework along with a major and minor, and end up not certified to teach. In the words of one DPI official, "You can have your academic freedom, except we won't license them."

On the other hand, the university pinned its hopes on legislative contacts and allies in the Assembly Education Committee to "carry the day for them." Such hopes and expectations proved ill-founded and fruitless. In November, 1985, the University Committee arranged for a "discussion" of the proposed PI 4 rules with state legislators and DPI officials. While providing a forum for the university to vent its grievances and concerns, several respondents noted that the meeting deteriorated into little more than a debate and verbal sparring match between the university and DPI officials before a bewildered and dismayed audience of legislators. ("It was a bomb...a bad idea.")

Both preceding and following this meeting, the same DPI officials met with representatives of interest groups supportive of the department's position. These were neither isolated nor coincidental occurrences. The department, mainly through the efforts of the deputy state superintendent, was maintaining almost weekly contacts with legislators and interest groups and had been doing so for months. If the university fumbled politically, the department did not.

SUMMARY AND CONCLUSION

Analysis of the data indicated that four internal variables (the role of the organizational saga, the isolation and insularity of the university, the pluralistic nature of the membership of the

School of Education, and the effect of decentralization on university response) and three external forces (the prevailing general public mood, the formation of a successful coalition of external interest groups, and the role of the state superintendent) determined the course and outcome of the governance conflict between UW-Madison and the Department of Public Instruction. In addition, the data indicate that the interactive and interrelated nature of these factors was of greatest importance. No attempt was made to assess the degree of importance associated with each of the factors; cumulative effect was critical in this study. The important point is that, within the parameters of this research, the outcome of this governance conflict represented a substantial loss of control over academic programs and policy for the university. "Control exists when an order can be given to do or not to do some certain thing with penalties attached for noncompliance" (Carnegie Commission on Higher Education, 1973, p. 18). Although the conflict was not Armageddon, neither was it a tempest in a teapot. Yet, accurate assessment of the overall significance of this governance conflict cannot be made in the immediacy of its wake. Such assessment must await future analysis.

Beyond this, data point to the conclusion that institutional virtues can become vices and that the distinguishing hallmarks of the university can undermine efforts to defeat external threats. This conclusion is supported throughout the data. The reasons why UW-Madison chose the disastrous course it did are embedded in its internal variables. The themes of the organizational saga, decentralization, and isolation weave in and out of any such explanation. "In Madison this culture is firmly embedded...the institutional culture here carries this independence to an art form...." Much the same words and sentiments were expressed by nearly all University respondents. Such precepts are part of the litany of the faithful, the true believers, and as such they are as appealing and alluring as the idea of Madison as "the jewel in the crown." However, when invoked against intrusions of powerful environmental forces, such incantations have lost their power.

As Easton (1965) noted, it is the beliefs upon which a system is built that suffuse it with a sense of legitimacy. In examining the legitimacy of the belief system of the university, its organizational saga, data suggest that the concepts of institutional autonomy and faculty governance, at least in the area of teacher education, no longer carry the legitimizing force among the general public they once possessed. "Very few Regents understand faculty governance or care about it. We may have reached a point nationally that the public doesn't accept this any more." "I have great respect for faculty governance in appropriate areas, but...education is too important to be entrusted to the professoriate." Like ideas of divine right or noblesse oblige, these concepts may have become anachronisms, no longer relevant or meaningful, and mere relics and artifacts of a bygone era. As one state legislator noted, "Society has become more activist. The sacred nature of the university isn't what it used to be."

Justly or unjustly, politically adept handling of public accountability issues carries greater force than do counterarguments of faculty governance and institutional autonomy.

> Politicians in Washington, as well as in the state capitals, press for a more unified higher education establishment that will speak with a single voice rather than make claims at cross purposes.... [They] step forward with commands that are to be applied to every college and university...and always in the name of a good deed, a grievance that needs redressing, or an inequity that needs to be adjusted. (Clark, 1976, p. 35)

Data suggest that the university can not afford its "splendid isolation" (Moran, 1972, p. 12) from the political realities of its environment. A state legislator noted that "the university didn't see it coming." This conclusion is supported and echoed throughout the data. Also, the defensive posture assumed by the university seems no longer a viable option in such governance conflicts. As a UW system vice-president noted, "They [education deans] must be more politically astute, instead of waging a defensive battle. This is necessary or we will keep getting beaten about the head and shoulders."

IMPLICATIONS

The overall evidence from the data indicates the importance of institutional culture and structure in interpreting and responding to the external environment. The reluctance to look beyond the boundaries of the campus and to deal effectively with political realities hindered response in this governance conflict. Until this hard reality is faced and overcome, prospects of similar scenarios being repeated seem likely. Unfortunately, such a change does not seem imminent. As one administrator in the School of Education commented, "We don't have time in the dean's office to politically network and participate. We don't have the time, resources or energy." The evidence of this research seems to suggest that this must change.

With a reactive position no longer tenable, the university must learn to speak with one voice and make its case to the larger public and regenerate the supports it has available through deliberate, concerted, and coordinated actions. Implicit in the entire conflict was an undercurrent of lack of trust and confidence in the university's ability to prepare its students competently. (The whole basis for the DPI's case was that the faculty aren't doing the job.) Accountability to the public and the representatives of the public must be a high priority of the university if it is to continue to maintain influence and control over its own programs and policy. The university cannot afford to become, or even to be perceived as being an elitist, closed system, responsive in its actions or inactions to none except itself. The future may hold even greater potential for external agency actions, cloaked in accountability terms, that will further erode University autonomy and faculty authority over academic programs and policy.

Historically UW-Madison has succeeded best when it has been politically astute and offered its most valuable commodity–ideas. Both of these elements were absent in the conflict with the Department of Public Instruction. Although organizational culture and structure and adminstrative mishandling contributed to the defeat, mechanisms exist within the university for coping with such external challenges. However, they must be used in an effective and timely manner.

The intent of this research was to examine a specific conflict to gain an understanding or what happened in the context of the governance of higher education. The idiosyncratic nature of many of the important elements of this study makes the generalizability and replicability of its findings questionable. It was, perhaps, truly *sui generis*, and the findings and implications should not be pushed beyond their obvious limitations. As Kennedy (1979) suggested, those who wish to will make their own applications. Other qualitative studies focusing on governance issues between higher education institutions and external agencies are needed to gain a fuller understanding of the meaning of such conflicts for higher education.

9

Donald P. Anderson

Implementing the Holmes Agenda:
An Institutional Perspective

Late in the spring of 1984 and shortly after being named dean of the Ohio State University (OSU) College of Education, I was invited to join the "Wingspread Group" and, further, to serve as group coordinator in the Midwest region. There was little information about the group except for grapevine rumors. In fact, at the winter meeting of the Association of Colleges and Schools of Education in State Universities and Land Grant Colleges and Affiliated Private Universities, some concern was expressed about "the small group of self-selected deans who were working on teacher education reform." My decision to join this group greatly influenced the chain of events that followed on the OSU campus.

Within this report is a review of the work, the progress, and the frustrations that have taken place in the six years since that initial invitation. Included is an analysis of the formal decision to join the Holmes Group and the implementation of the decision. Special attention is given to the process, the actors involved, the problem areas requiring policy decisions, and the progress to date. The case study which follows is based largely on my experience as an actor in the process. The major sources of data include records of meetings with colleagues in the college and across the university.

The Decision to Join the Holmes Group

A number of events on the OSU Columbus campus during the 1985–86 academic year had great impact on the college's decision to join the Holmes Group. To understand this impact, it is important to provide some pertinent background information on the OSU College of Education.

The college's faculty is comprised of approximately one hundred sixty-five persons in tenure-track positions. They come from very diverse backgrounds. In recent years, an increasing number of the faculty have become involved in non-school programming, e.g. business and industry training, exercise science, and adult education. Roughly 70 percent of the faculty engage in work that is predominantly related to K–12 schooling.

Additionally, some of the teacher education programs are not administratively located within the College of Education. Music education and art education, for example, are located within the College of the Arts, agriculture education is located in the College of Agriculture, and home economics education is in the College of Human Ecology. Ohio's State Department of Education, however, views the College of Education as the organization responsible for recommending teacher certification for the university. Therefore, teacher education programs inside and outside of the college are under the control of the college senate and the dean.

The college also has a strong tradition of faculty governance with college policy-making authority vested in a college senate. The senate is comprised of faculty representatives from the college's departments, faculty representatives from the teacher education programs housed outside the college, and student representatives from the undergraduate and graduate student bodies.

The events that affected the college's decision to join the Holmes Group included: (1) the initiation of a new undergraduate curriculum, (2) my participation in the Wingspread Group, (3) the changing role of the college senate, (4) the turnover of OSU provosts, and (5) the developing interest by the university president in the Holmes Group initiatives.

Undergraduate curriculum reform was initiated to modify the general education component. The timing of this reform movement affected the college faculty's decision to commit to Holmes membership. For the past twenty years, the university's basic educational requirements have been comprised of approximately one year of study in a series of courses touching the arts, humanities, mathematics, sciences, and social sciences. Students could select a few courses from an ever-expanding list from each of the areas. There was limited logic to the programming, and the requirements added up to a series of unrelated course experiences. Student selection of courses was often determined more by classroom location, time of day, or other criteria not conducive to a good general or liberal education. When the president initiated a curriculum review, the intent was to provide a better general studies program to all OSU undergraduate students.

To give leadership to this major curriculum review, the president appointed a faculty member from the College of Education. The fact that a highly regarded professor from the college was chosen was noteworthy since most of the courses in the general/liberal studies curriculum were taught by faculty members in one of the five liberal arts colleges on campus. Clearly, this major university program initiative turned out to be complementary of what was to become the first goal of the Holmes Group, that of making teacher education programs more intellectually sound.

Another key factor in making the decision to join the Holmes Group was related to my participation in the Wingspread Group, later to be renamed the Holmes Group. Following my decision to work with this group and to serve as coordinator of the Midwest region, I participated in a number of meetings beginning in the summer of 1984 and extending through 1985. While not playing a central role in drafting the *Tomorrow's Teachers* (Holmes Group, 1986) document, I had early access to information about the work of the group and progress on the document. The fact that this information was shared informally with colleagues put the OSU education faculty at an advantage when the invitation to join the Holmes Group was officially forwarded to the university.

The changing role of the college senate also contributed to the decision to join the Holmes Group. While potentially a powerful body, the senate had been stumbling for some time. It had fallen into a trap of dealing only with mundane issues, spending excessive amounts of time on new course proposals and matters of similar magnitude. The senate members were ready to "flex their muscles."

The decision to affiliate with the Holmes Group was one of the most significant decisions to face the college in years. After much debate, the senate decided it had the authority and responsibility to make the decision on behalf of the total faculty. Meanwhile, a few faculty members (especially those who felt strongly that the college should join the Holmes Group) did not trust the senate with this decision. They lobbied for a collegewide vote. Ultimately, the senate won, and the decision process was underway.

Early in 1986 when the invitations to join the Holmes

Group were extended to the chief academic officers in the universities, an acting provost had just been named at OSU. She was formerly the dean of the College of Home Economics, and her background was in teacher education. She also was very committed to the direction outlined in *Tomorrow's Teachers*. Her appointment and timely support became the fourth event that directly contributed to the college's decision to join the Holmes Group.

The fifth and final major contributing factor to the college's decision making was the OSU president's interest in the program. At roughly the same time that the previously highlighted events were occurring, the president began mentioning the college in many of his presentations to university constituents. Clearly, the direction of the Holmes Group supported his views that all students needed a solid background in general and liberal studies. The president, a graduate of a professional school, began to talk about the "great College of Education at OSU." He often cited the leadership we were giving to teacher education reform in the state and across the nation.

During the four months that the college senate deliberated on the decision, the faculty met seven times. Normally, the college faculty convenes two or three times in a year. One of the most significant and best-attended meetings was one which the president attended. His support for the concept had not diminished. He suggested in his presentation that professional fields such as nursing and business might very well follow the lead of education in building a professional curriculum upon a solid liberal arts background. During the question and answer period that followed, the question was raised about the probability of securing new resources to implement such a program. The president, an experienced administrator and a professor of finance, indicated that no promise of continuing funds could be made at that time because of the uncertainty of future funding for the university. He also noted that a university president's tenure is often uncertain, and he might not be here when we were ready to implement the new programs. He did, however, identify and underscore what has become the most serious financial problem we face: the running of two programs simultaneously—phasing out the old, four-year undergraduate programs and phasing in the new master's-level teacher education programs at the same time. We have an obligation to continue to provide four year programs to all students in the pipeline. At the same time, we will begin to build our masters level programs. He assured the faculty that the university would provide some short-term funding to relieve this problem.

After everything the president had been saying publicly about the "great College of Education," followed by his presentation to the faculty, a number of faculty members were concerned about the consequence of not affiliating with the Holmes Group, especially the negative impact of such a decision on the president's perception of the college. Just as a number of institutions joined the Holmes Group because of the negative consequence of not joining—even though there may not have been commitment to making the program changes called for in the Holmes agenda—some of our college faculty were willing to go along for the same reason.

The decision to affiliate came to a senate vote at the end of spring quarter, 1986. Prior to that vote, a great deal of analysis and review was conducted. In addition to reviewing the document *Tomorrow's Teachers*, a few faculty members developed summaries and analyses of the document that they shared with the entire faculty.

As noted earlier, seven faculty meetings were held prior to the senate's vote. The last of these was an all-day meeting during which faculty members were given an opportunity to discuss the issues in small groups and to make statements to the total group. Additionally, members of the dean's staff and college senators visited the offices of the Ohio professional associations for teachers, administrators, and school board members, and distributed copies of *Tomorrow's Teachers*. Members of these associations were invited to present their views of the Holmes agenda. These groups included the Ohio Education Association, the Buckeye Association of School Administrators, the Ohio School Boards Association, and the elementary and secondary principals associations. Two key experts, Lee Shulman and Arthur Wise, also were invited to campus to share their perceptions and perspectives on teacher education reform.

Many faculty members predicted that when the senate voted to affiliate with the Holmes Group the vote to join would be positive, but very close. Sixteen senators were eligible to vote; the result was thirteen to three in favor of joining. The three negative votes came from teacher education faculty in physical education, special education, and music education. The physical education and special education teacher education faculty members had recently redesigned their undergraduate curricula. Because of a similar preparation philosophy, the two program areas had worked together in this program design and implementation. The new programs were working exceedingly well and were among the best of all of the teacher education programs in the college. Further, there was concern among the faculty in these two program areas about what an appropriate liberal arts preparation might be in their respective areas. The third negative vote came from a music educator who was representing the music education and art education program areas, both housed in the college of the arts. While the art education area was very supportive, the music education area and other music education programs in the Midwest region were opposed to the move. Their major concern was the possible reduction of music courses in the curriculum of music education students if a "Holmes program" was implemented. The extensive deliberations followed by the surprisingly high positive vote of the senate positioned the college to be one of the front runners among Holmes members in terms of program implementation.

Implementing the Decision—Key Actors

The important role the university president played in the decision has already been identified. The acting provost played a key role in the spring of 1985, when the college received over $50,000 in planning funds to begin deliberations. Another $25,000 in planning funds was received in 1987–88 and in 1988–89. These funds were distributed to program areas in and outside the college to begin their planning. During the first year, no specific product was demanded by the college. Our investment resulted in less-than-hoped-for results. During the next two years, proposals were called for and the resources were targeted.

A group of faculty members who played a low-key role in the early deliberations were from the mathematics and science teacher education areas. For a number of years, students with bachelor's degrees had come to the college seeking teacher education certification. In most cases, programs were designed for the individuals, and the students followed a slightly modified undergraduate teacher education program. In mathematics and science, however, the numbers got so large by the mid-1970s, that cohort groups were established to accommodate them. Students in these groups took some undergraduate coursework, but their pedagogy and field experiences were especially designed for the group and carried graduate credit.

Implementing the Holmes Agenda 187

The programs were very successful in serving the needs of persons who previously had worked as engineers or in science or mathematics careers. The students were more mature and generally more committed to a career in education. Most of the graduates stayed in teaching longer than the graduates of the traditional undergraduate program. The experiences in science and mathematics education provided some assurance that such programs would attract high-caliber students and that the graduates would be employable.

Other university administrators were key actors, too. The provost and the president asked me to make presentations to the Council of Deans, the OSU Board of Trustees, and to the President's Cabinet. The Council of Deans is comprised of the eighteen deans on the main campus, the four regional campus deans, and the director of libraries. The deans who give leadership to the five liberal arts colleges on the main campus and the four regional campus deans were the most interested in follow-up meetings. Beginning in 1986–87, the liberal arts college deans asked to meet with college representatives two or three times each year.

The university general education curriculum review mentioned earlier has continued a key role in OSU's Holmes implementation. The resulting new program of study will be implemented in 1990–91. Instead of one year's study, all new undergraduates entering the university in the autumn of 1990 will receive a general/liberal education that will comprise approximately half of their undergraduate programs. The addition of a data analysis course, three writing courses, and a foreign language requirement for all students is accompanied by a number of other changes in the undergraduate curriculum, most of which are taught in the five liberal arts colleges. The deans of these colleges have been most interested and supportive of the Holmes movement. Their interest has facilitated the work of the college's secondary teacher education programs in redefining appropriate major fields of study for students who might seek admittance to our new graduate-level teacher education programs. We made it clear from the beginning, however, that we would select students from liberal arts colleges across the country and not restrict admission to those who had graduated from the OSU liberal arts colleges. Discussions have been held with a few prestigious private liberal arts colleges in the state and a few predominately black undergraduate colleges with the possible result of developing relationships wherein their graduates might gain early admission to the graduate teacher training programs in the college.

Another group of key actors were the deans of the four regional campuses. These campuses were created in the late sixties to fulfill a commitment made by a former Ohio governor who assured all Ohio residents that they would not be more than fifty miles from a state university or one of its regional campuses. Five of the thirteen state universities in Ohio have regional campuses. The four communities that shared in the cost of building the OSU regional campuses were assured that they would have four-year elementary teacher education programs. While there was a surplus of elementary teachers at the time, the communities forced the creation of these programs at all four locations. These programs have been embraced by the regional campus deans and have become very strong over the years. Further, they represent a substantial portion of the income for each of the campuses. Since they are the only "upper division" baccalaureate programs on the regional campuses, they are supported at a considerably higher state subsidy rate than the typical "lower division" programs on these campuses.

The provost established a task force comprised of a number of his staff and representatives of the regional campuses, elementary education faculty on the Columbus campus, and college administrators to deal with regional campus/Holmes program issues. One alternative was to drop all elementary education on the regional campuses, an option that might have bankrupted the campuses. Another more attractive alternative called for development of a four-year "preelementary education" program to be offered on each regional campus. Unlike a traditional liberal arts degree with a major and minor configuration, this degree will be a general studies degree with areas of concentration centering on the content required of an elementary teacher. Following completion of that degree, students will complete most of their master's teacher education work on the regional campus with at least one quarter's study on the main campus. Prior to agreeing on that alternative, the regional campus faculty members, most of whom work in the arts and sciences, were very opposed to the Holmes affiliation. They were concerned that, if the elementary education programs were phased out on the regional campuses, enrollments would decline, and regional campus resources would decrease. In sum, they were fearful that their jobs were in jeopardy.

Because of the problems in creating an appropriate entry-level degree for elementary teachers on the Columbus campus, the regional campus solution will be used on the Columbus campus as well. Students in the preelementary education degree option will do most of their work in the arts and sciences, but will be advised by College of Education counselors.

As noted earlier, agriculture education, art education, home economics education, and music education reside in colleges other than the College of Education. Faculty members in these areas and their respective college administrators have been working closely with College of Education faculty and decision-making bodies in implementing the decision. Another example of potential impact on arts and sciences faculty can be found in the OSU School of Music. The music education program enrolls many students who are not proficient enough (or do not wish) to major in one of the music performance areas. As in the case of the regional campus faculty members, some of the School of Music faculty continue to be very much concerned about terminating the undergraduate music education degree because of a potential decrease in enrollment and the possible negative impact on their employment. As can be evidenced, progress towards implementing the new Holmes programs is proceeding at a slower rate in the program areas housed outside of the College of Education.

The elementary education faculty has played and continues to play a most significant role in implementing the new teacher education programs. Most of the elementary education faculty members were lukewarm in their support of post-baccalaureate teacher education programs. Among other things, they were most sensitive to the possible deficiencies in subject matter content that some liberal arts majors might have when choosing to work in the elementary schools. Many of the liberal arts graduates applying for admission, for example, had insufficient backgrounds in science and mathematics.

In the autumn quarter of the 1986–87 academic year, however, the faculty admitted thirty students to an experimental post-baccalaureate teacher education program in elementary education. While many of the students did have deficiencies in subject matter content that had to be made up, this group of students had a substantial impact on the elementary education faculty and, ultimately, the entire teacher education faculty. The students who went through the program in a cohort group were much more mature than the traditional undergraduates. They brought a different set of background experiences. Some had worked for a few years in another career. Some were parents. They had higher expectations for both the campus- and field-based components of the program. As this group of students "touched" the regular faculty in course experiences during that year, the elementary education faculty became the most outspoken advocates for pursuing the Holmes agenda. In 1987–88, a second group of thirty was chosen from more than two hundred seventy applicants. The faculty continue to enroll thirty students per year into this program as they downsize the undergraduate program. The elementary education program area was the first to redesign its professional program and prepare the documentation for review by college and university decision-making bodies.

Area school teachers and administrators also have much at stake in this reform effort. The Ohio State University has a rather unique exchange of services agreement with area schools dating back to the early 1940s. In exchange for college student experience in the schools, the university provides fee script. This fee script goes to the district, not directly to the person providing the service to the college student. In every case, the distribution of the fee script to teachers is part of teacher contracts negotiated with the Board of Education. For every thirty-five hours of college student contact time in a school district, the district receives fee script worth one graduate hour of instruction. The school systems compete with one another to provide service to the College of Education. Some have even provided transportation for college students to and from the field sites. With the possible elimination of the undergraduate program and the resulting reduction in the number of teachers prepared, the school system representatives continue to be very apprehensive about the amount of fee script that will be available. A number of meetings have been scheduled during the past few years with area school superintendents and presidents of the local teacher associations to keep them apprised of progress in implementing the new teacher education programs.

Implementing the Decision—The Process

If someone had suggested in the spring of 1986 how long it would take to implement the Holmes agenda on the OSU campus, I would have thought that person to be the ultimate pessimist. Obviously, I was overly optimistic and very naive about political and other realities of such a major shift in programming in a bureaucratic organization like the Ohio State University.

One of the first steps taken was to eliminate a ten-year-old standing committee of the senate, the Undergraduate Professional Education Committee. This committee was created to focus attention on an area of our mission that clearly had not been given high priority by most college faculty members. After deciding to join the Holmes Group, the senate abolished this group and created the Teacher Education Advisory Committee (TEAC), a body charged with advising the dean and the senate on policy decisions affecting teacher education. Members of the committee include program heads of all the teacher education units on campus plus the heads of units that provide some of the teacher education foundation work to students across program areas. This group, together with the college Executive Committee, has played a key role in moving the program effort along.

One of the first recommendations of TEAC was that we employ a faculty member on a part-time basis to be the "Holmes coordinator." The Teacher Education Advisory Committee felt that having a faculty member committed to the reform movement and working with college and department administrators was essential to the success of the effort. The Holmes coordinator has worked half-time for the past three years in this role and has played an important linking role to the faculty in program development.

Two issues, one respecting program prototype and the other addressing finance, have consumed massive amounts of time from the Associate Dean for Academic Programs. Since we are dealing with graduate-level preparation programs, the OSU Graduate School plays a key role in our efforts. The graduate school is comprised of graduate departments, most of which are the same as the traditional departments in the university. Besides the five education graduate departments (each having a graduate committee reporting directly to the graduate school), four graduate departments outside the college are involved. They embrace programs in agriculture education, art education, home economics education, and music education.

After a few conversations with representatives from the college, the graduate school dean appointed a task force chaired by the College of Education Associate Dean for Academic Programs and comprised of a graduate school associate dean and the nine graduate committee chairpersons. Their task was to create a prototype Master of Education proposal that would give some direction to each of the program areas as they developed their specific proposals. This prototype dealt with admission standards, common themes or elements of the curriculum, length of the programs, special project requirements, examinations and other exit criteria. It was assumed that if this proposal was approved by the graduate school, it would facilitate individual program approvals.

Developing that prototype was very time consuming, but became one of the most important steps in program development. These graduate committee chairpersons had no history of working together on such a task. In fact, there is a long history of considerable autonomy in teacher education program development in the college and a disdain for core courses in the curricula. After some painful compromises, the prototype was developed and approved by the graduate school council.

The second issue had to do with finances. From the beginning, there were no illusions that there would be large increases in the college's resource base. Other than receiving additional support when the old and the new programs are running concurrently, we assumed that we would operate within roughly the same resource base. The university is part of a state system with an enrollment-driven subsidy model. The subsidy formula takes into consideration the level of the students enrolled. Because the subsidy for master's-level students is approximately twice as high as for upper division undergraduate students, the assumption was made that we could reduce enrollments substantially without taking a reduction in resources when moving to the new programs.

While the university does not allocate resources based on enrollments alone, a relationship exists between the two. The provost's office has developed a new computer simulation model based on the very complex state subsidy model. Every new program proposed in the university will be reviewed by using this financial impact model. The magnitude of program change associated with moving to post-baccalaureate teacher education programs and the impact this move has on the arts and sciences colleges resulted in much attention being given to this kind of financial modeling. The College of Education was the first academic unit on campus to propose a major change in programming, and as a result, the college served as a guinea pig for testing this system.

A related financial and programmatic issue facing the university involves the movement of most of the professional colleges towards selective admissions. Following the implementation of selective admissions to undergraduate programs in education almost twenty years ago, the health science professional colleges, together with other large colleges such as business and engineering, have moved towards selective admissions.

Such a move has two significant impacts on the university, especially on the liberal arts colleges. First, the number of students arts and sciences must teach and advise increases, and second, the arts and sciences colleges become the dumping grounds for those students who are not admitted to one of the other degree-granting colleges. All freshman students entering OSU enroll in the university college and then transfer to a degree-granting college at the end of one year. Anyone maintaining a 2.0 grade point average can stay in the university and move into one of the liberal arts major areas if not admitted to a college approved for selective admissions. As the competition for admission into the professional schools becomes more intense and as enrollments subsequently increase, some pattern of managing enrollments becomes essential.

The three large professional colleges, education, business, and engineering, submitted plans for enrollment management within the past three years. Even though the College of Education was planning to phase out many of its undergraduate programs, a base level of support had to be determined. Clearly, no other college in the university has been subject to as much workload and financial resource study as the College of Education over these past three years. Once approved, the college's enrollment management plan called for a minimum and maximum number of students in each program area and provided a starting point for dealing with downsizing the undergraduate programs and increasing the size of the graduate programs. Thousands of hours were spent on this analysis, again in part because of the guinea pig nature of the College of Education in this arena. It is important to note the analysis did not result from efforts to penalize the college, but was a precursor of analyses to be done in all units across the campus.

The Midwest Holmes region played a substantial role in motivating and supporting program development in the college. The Midwest region is comprised of nineteen universities, eighteen public and one private. The public universities range considerably in size, but most have relatively large teacher education programs and a history of commitment to teacher education. The Midwest region has provided a format for exchanging ideas and sharing program development efforts among faculty in like-minded institutions. To a lesser extent, the four Holmes members in Ohio have worked together in this regard. The national Holmes Group provided the stimulus for reform. Without this stimulation, very little teacher education program review and reform would have taken place at OSU. Very few faculty members, however, have been impacted directly by the national Holmes Group program efforts, and as a result, the nature of the curricula that have developed to date have not been affected significantly by these efforts.

Where Are We Now?

Most of the problems encountered were anticipated. The issue of resources looms heavily as we face increasing graduate enrollments at the same time as we are serving undergraduate students already in the pipeline. Currently, there are two program areas with Holmes program proposals being reviewed by the graduate school and other university decision bodies. They are elementary education and mathematics education. When approved in the spring of 1990, letters were mailed to all counselors of Ohio high schools and other out-of-state high schools that send large numbers of students to the university. These letters were intended to alert current high school juniors that they should not plan to enroll at OSU in the autumn of 1991 if they want to complete a teacher education program in four years in any one of these areas. We hope that most of the other teacher education areas will have programs approved by the spring of 1991, and we will admit no new freshmen to four-year programs after the autumn of 1992.

What does that mean? For one thing, it means that we will carry very large loads for five or six years until we have cleared the system of undergraduate teacher education students. While there have been changes in key university administrative positions, we are optimistic that additional resources will be forthcoming to deal with this problem.

By design, we waited until the Holmes document on professional development schools was close to publication before we moved ahead with the creation of this most important element of the Holmes agenda. A Professional Development Schools Policy Advisory Committee comprised of school administrators, teacher association heads, and college faculty members was formed early in 1990 to begin to give direction to this activity.

Important issues to be addressed include details related to the clinical appointments for the field-based faculty, requirements for appointments, general descriptions of responsibilities, and issues of remuneration. There will be considerable competition on the part of school systems to become involved in the creation of professional development schools. Policies to govern selection of sites and funding the sites will be among the major issues to be faced.

Additionally, a number of graduate students are currently employed to work in the college undergraduate programs. These persons cannot play the same role in working with graduate students. Simply to transfer those graduate student support funds to field or clinical faculty would leave a major shortfall in the support of graduate students and would cause great damage to doctoral-level programs. This issue is being attended to, in part, by increasing the outside-funded research and development projects in the college.

The current exchange of services agreement that has served the college, the university, and the school systems well for over forty years may be in jeopardy. At the very least, the agreement which is currently renegotiated annually will be due for major revision. Establishing a reasonable level of parity between the key actors in the teacher education program—the education faculty, the arts and sciences faculty, school teachers, school administrators and board members—will require major, careful, and extensive deliberation. The university reward system which has shifted more and more towards emphasis on scholarly productivity may call for a two-tiered system of reward and support for the campus-based faculty who spend most of their time in the field. The medical colleges on campus have such a system in place.

Meanwhile, legislation was passed by the Ohio General Assembly in 1989 to allow for alternative routes to certification for those persons holding baccalaureate degrees. Some private higher education institutions in the state are gearing up to prepare teachers with the minimal requirements set forth in the legislation. Their actions might deter large numbers of those persons from enrolling in the more intense experiences required in our programs. Currently, there are rumors that the state legislature will impose caps on enrollment and require institutions to offer teacher education programs at the undergraduate level, as is the case in Texas. Any of these actions might reduce enrollments in the programs we have established. To let the customer or employer determine the product (graduate) is shortsighted. We will have to "sell" our graduates to employers based on product differentiation. We are confident that persons graduating from programs such as ours will be prepared to perform differently and better in tomorrow's schools than graduates of traditional or "alternative certification" programs (Seider, 1990).

Another unresolved issue relates to the preparation of school administrators, counselors, and other professionals whose traditional route to these positions has been through teaching. Counselor and administrator preparation faculty are just beginning to recognize the implications for working with this new kind of teacher and for the preparation programs for these persons.

Finally, there were a number of surprises that we encountered in beginning this reform effort. First, a number of administrators and faculty members from across the university assumed that moving to Holmes programming would mean that our students would not take all or most of their coursework in the College of Education, as is the case in other undergraduate professional colleges, but rather would do their work in the arts and sciences. These persons did not realize that our secondary education students already complete majors in the arts and sciences as well as complete the undergraduate general/liberal arts studies. Further, our students in elementary education, vocational and technology education, health and physical education complete significant parts of their study outside the College of Education.

Even more than expected, many persons were concerned about protecting their turf. Many faculty members from the college and across the university and area school personnel accept the premise that a teacher needs to have a good grounding in liberal studies. As indicated earlier, the regional campus arts and sciences faculty members supported this concept of a strong general/liberal arts component and a major concentration in the liberal arts in the undergraduate preparation of teachers, but they backed away from that position rapidly when they felt their own department might be downsized as a result. Brudel and Schussler (1990) in an analysis of a number of organizations, provide an interesting, but not surprising, set of findings regarding the "death" of many new organizations. Persons in new organizations have to learn new roles and tasks; new roles have to be invented; new social transactions are called for; and stable links to persons outside the organization need to be established. This does not come easily. The same reluctance was true of the nonteacher education faculty in the School of Music. The local elementary and secondary school administrators and teacher leaders are generally very supportive of the concept and excited about the creation of professional development schools, but are concerned about losing exchange of service credit generated by large numbers of undergraduate teacher education candidates.

There is still some apprehension within the college about what this move will do to the number of applicants to respective programs. Some faculty members have not been as successful as others in generating external funding to support doctoral-level students and feel some pressure to behave in ways different from before.

What is fascinating is that elementary education is taking the lead at OSU. On many campuses, elementary education is the area that is lagging behind the secondary areas. Because this is the college's largest program, it has done much to move the others forward. The elementary education faculty members, because of their early start, have been most influential in all of our redesign efforts, even to the point of marketing the graduates. Early adopters of any change in technology normally increase their power and centrality following the change (Burkhardt and Brass, 1990). Likewise, areas such as physical education and health education have moved ahead. As indicated earlier, the undergraduate physical education teacher education program was among the best in the college, and the faculty initially took a strong position in opposition to abandoning their four-year programs. Faculty members in that area have taken the initiative to maintain their leadership position by developing Holmes programs.

Epilogue

While the process employed to make the decision to join the Holmes Group was long and deliberate, few, including myself, realized the complexities of making this dramatic program change. These complexities resulted, in part, from the interrelatedness of elements and actors involved in the process. Besides forcing major curricular change on some faculty members who were not too interested in the preservice preparation of teachers, the process involved university academic and fiscal program officers, the graduate school, graduate studies committees, program areas both inside and outside the college, college governance bodies, arts and sciences administrators, and faculty members, local school administrators and teachers, as well as teacher union and administration organization representatives.

While some might say that we have made a mistake because of the problems we have faced and the enormous energies that were required to get where we are today, it has had a dramatic and positive impact on the college. The college has been living on a first-class reputation grounded in the work of Boyd Bode, Edgar Dale, Ralph Tyler, and other giants in the field who worked here in the OSU College of Education, and that reputation has been maintained by graduate-level activity. The undergraduate teacher education programs were given a low priority by everyone across the campus, including many of the college faculty members. The attention that "Holmes" has brought to the college in the university has pushed the college's teacher education efforts into the limelight. Conger (1990) presents some persuasive points related to the problems and pitfalls of attempting to change a vision before its time; the time was right at Ohio State University to change the vision of teacher education.

The process has been painstakingly slow, but there is real evidence of progress. Hindsight would have it that we should have been more attentive to organizational change and planning models such as those advanced by Ackoff (1970) and others. We are re-examining the role of faculty members, of graduate teaching and research associates, of department chairpersons, and college administrators. We are working harder than ever to generate research and development funding to support graduate students and to bring fresh new ideas to the college. We have a better focus on our international programs, again with the idea of learning from experiences in our work in foreign countries and with international students and not simply providing services.

Clearly, we have been living for the past few years in a world of change—within the college, in the university, and especially, in our relationships with the professionals we prepare and serve and the state agencies. The quality of services provided by the teachers we prepare in the future will be worth the investment.

PART III
REGIONAL AND NATIONAL INFLUENCES

10

MAYNARD C. REYNOLDS ⎯⎯⎯⎯⎯⎯⎯⎯⎯⎯⎯⎯

A Case Study in Teacher Education:
PL 94–142

"It's only slightly off shore for all of us"; so spoke an attorney for a Southern California school district in 1971. He referred to the consent decree of a federal district court in Pennsylvania in which it was declared that children who were mentally retarded had a right to education, that the preferred school placement for them was in regular schools and classes (with special classes next preferred) and that parents should be involved in planning school programs for each child. The decree, based on the Fourteenth Amendment—the equal protection provision—of the U.S. Constitution, was legally binding only in schools of the Eastern Federal Court District of Pennsylvania, but it was considered highly persuasive across the nation (*Pennsylvania Association for Retarded Children [PARC]* v. *Commonwealth*, 1971).

For decades American policy makers had talked about education for *all* children, but did not fully mean it. In 1948, for example, there was the important statement *Education for All American Youth* issued by the Educational Policies Commission, which hardly mentioned handicapped students. It remained for parents of handicapped children, even into the 1950s and 1960s, to create their own classes, often housed in rented space "above the dime store" or in the basement of the American Legion hall, for children regarded as "trainable" retarded, for many children with cerebral palsy, and for others who were "not toilet trained" or for other reasons excluded from the schools. Tens of thousands of children were still isolated in residential institutions into the latter half of the twentieth century in America.

But the exclusionary policies and practices crumbled rapidly following the PARC decree and the *Mills* v. *Board of Education* (1972) decision, which came only a year after PARC and spread the right to education principle to children with a broad range of handicapping conditions. Many states had made important progress in serving handicapped students in the schools in the immediate post–World War II decades. Waves of so-called mandatory special education laws referring to handicapped children then regarded as educable were passed by state legislatures. In some states, collateral provisions were made for specialized teacher preparation as well. For example, in California, the San Francisco State University was enabled to establish a strong program in specialized teacher preparation in the late 1940s; in Illinois, a comparable development in the same period occurred at the Normal State University.

Leadership in policy setting shifted strongly to the federal level in the 1970s and specifically to the Congress in 1975, with passage of PL 94–142, the Education for All Handicapped Children Act. Then President Ford signed the bill, but expressed well-founded doubts about the likelihood of full funding for its implementation. Described by Dean Corrigan as "the most important piece of educational legislation in this country's history" (1978, p. 10), PL 94–142 brought together the principles and policies expressed in federal court decisions of the early 1970s and added the full force of law and some new resources (money and staff) for implementation. Officially, the law went into effect in fall, 1977.

This chapter focusses mainly on the period of the 1970s in which PL 94-142 emerged, telling briefly about some of the precursors of the law and about problems and early steps in implementation, and with a final, brief update to issues of the 1990s. Although much of special education is controlled at state and local levels, the main emphasis here will be on federal policies and developments. That is because of the strongly emerging federal presence and leadership in the time segment being considered, but also because of the limited scope and purpose for the case studies comprising this book. The primary focus of the chapter is on teacher education as it was influenced by special education policies of this truly remarkable period. The chapter was prepared after review of some dozens of documents reflecting the development of teacher education in special education since about 1970, and on the basis of discussions with some of the principal figures involved in this field of work.

The Law and Implications for Teacher Education

Briefly, PL 94–142 included these provisions relating directly to children, parents, and schools: (a) a "right to education" or "zero-reject" principle applied to all handicapped children of school age;[1] (b) special education and related services must be free (no financial charge to parents); (c) instruction must be appropriate for each student as represented in a written, individualized educational plan (the IEP); (d) school placements are required to be made in accord with the principle of the "least restrictive environment" (handicapped children should be placed with nonhandicapped children in general schools and classes whenever such integrated situations can be made to be appropriate); (e) parents have a right to participate in planning school programs for their children; (f) due process principles must apply in major school decisions, including the right of parents to have full access to information held in the schools about their children and to make appeals to higher educational authorities (and ultimately to the courts) when they disagree with local decisions about education of their child.

PL 94–142 also included very important provisions relating to teacher education, specifically a mandate for:

> (A) the development and implementation of a comprehensive system of personnel development which shall include... detailed procedures to assure that all personnel necessary to carry out the purposes of this Act are appropriately and adequately prepared and trained and effective procedures for acquiring and disseminating...significant information derived from educational research, demonstration and similar projects [are developed], and (B) adopting, where appropriate, promising educational practices and materials developed through such projects. (20 USC 1413 [a] 3)

This language of the law proposes an unprecedented federal role in systematizing the preparation of personnel to operate the schools. Emphasis is given to quality as well as to quantity of personnel. Thomas Gilhool, attorney for the plaintiff in the PARC case, noted that federal court precedent has clearly established "that in the presence of important matters [like education]...the obligation is not to share the state of the practice, but to use the state of the art" (1982, p. 19). In another context Gilhool extended the responsibilities to teacher educators:

> ...in a real sense teacher educators are the custodians, if not the progenitors, of the state of the art. That is their role in this profession. In a legal sense, a juridical sense, we have long passed the point in these United States where colleges of education are one thing and public schooling another.... The

set of relationships between schools of education and the public schools is such now that teacher educators, as much as the state education authorities and the local education authorities, must consider themselves bound by this duty to use effectively the state of the art. (Gilhool, 1982, p. 23)

The American Association of Colleges for Teacher Education, representing the vast majority of our nation's colleges and universities offering teacher education programs, expressed formally its commitment to the mandate of PL 94–142 and to the "quest for quality" in meeting the needs of all individual pupils, including those with special needs (AACTE, 1978).

The Problems and the Challenge

So far, the case of PL 94–142 has been presented as a nicely positive, almost linear, story of extending educational opportunities to handicapped students. No doubt this story is positive, technically and morally, but that sees the situation with only half an eye. Saying that all handicapped students had a right to go to school—even regular schools—was easy, but making sure that the schools were able to deliver high-quality programs in response to that right involved enormous technical problems and difficult-to-achieve attitudinal shifts.

A very large question concerned the ability and willingness of school leaders to restructure programs, to employ thoroughly prepared teachers, and to provide the kinds of environment and supports that teachers would need to implement PL 94–142. Robert Howsam, former dean of education at the University of Houston, put the fundamental problem of quality programming this way:

> There is every reason to believe that schools were not designed to handle the whole range of educational problems in regular classrooms, even when special services are added. In consequence, both regular students and those with handicapping conditions lose out. Role, load and stress problems are created for teachers and morale problems are introduced. At the same time the public is given more legitimate reasons for "raging" at these institutions or defecting from the system.... Effective schools demand strong teachers working in situations where the conditions for learning and teaching are favorable. Our school systems have never come close to meeting such conditions.... (1983, p. 90)

These are some of the more specific problems associated with implementation of PL 94–142:

- Present rights. Legal rights are present rights; they can be demanded immediately. In no way were the schools and teacher-preparing institutions prepared in 1977 to deliver fully on the promises of PL 94–142. The policies were far ahead of educational practices, as shown, for example, in enormous waiting lists that developed just for psychological exams of children in some big cities. Compared with the local schools, the colleges and universities were one big extra step removed from the mandates of PL 94–142; it would take time to make changes in teacher education.
- Distribution. The law proposed that first claims for special education and related services should be made in the local school of each handicapped child. That calls, for example, for a teacher of braille in the rural areas of Montana as well as in the big city. The schools and colleges were poorly prepared to meet the distribution problem. For many years large multistate sections of the nation have lacked teacher preparation programs in certain specialties. For example, to the west of Illinois, no preparation program for teachers of children who are blind had existed for years in the northern tier of states all the way to the Pacific coast. Even if such a program had been in operation, there is no assurance that the trainees could be delivered efficiently and predictably to the school districts where most needed, including rural areas. The distribution problem has been serious.
- Authority. The law proposed a federal leadership in designing and implementing a "comprehensive system for personnel development" (CSPD). That would impact state governments, schools, and institutions of higher education in unprecedented ways. Would colleges yield to a system that made them subcontractors in a broad state and national system of specialized teacher preparation? Did PL 94–142 somehow endow the U.S. Department of Education and the states with authority to control teacher education? Authority has been a problem. Just to achieve a degree of "voluntary" cooperation would be difficult enough.
- Equity. Under PL 94–142, one could not provide special education programs and related teacher education in only the most promising situations; efforts would be required in less-promising environments as well. Handi-

capped children in even the least promising environments had rights equal to all others. Awarding government project grants, for example, on a competitive basis judging quality would not suffice. Helping the rich get richer is easy; helping the poor is a special challenge. How should equity and quality standards be met in teacher preparation situations where ideas, leadership, and resources were inadequate?

- Knowledge Base. Did special educators have enough well-confirmed knowledge and skill to deliver special education to all handicapped students, including even those with the most severe handicaps? Was the problem only one of dissemination? The answers are mostly no and no. Tested knowledge and demonstrated skill were beginning to emerge for teaching severely handicapped students in local schools in such places as Madison, Wisconsin (Brown, Nietupski, and Hamre-Nietupski, 1976), but such knowledge was far from complete and secure and certainly not broadly disseminated.

  The major national professional organization of special educators, the Council for Exceptional Children, had indicated its readiness to proceed into an era in which all children had a right to education by its policies as adopted in 1971 (Council for Exceptional Children, 1971). The first sentence of that policy declaration was: "Education is the right of all children" (p. 1). But this expression by the profession was more an indication of readiness to engage and struggle through an emerging aspect of its work than of secure and present knowledge about how to solve the problems in any precise way.

- Regular Education. PL 94–142 proposed that regular or general schools, classes, and teachers should become able to serve most handicapped students, thereby reducing referral rates to special education or—at least—enhancing their utility in collaborative approaches in meeting special needs. The mandate to create a comprehensive system of personnel development was directed to *all* educators. Though assigned mainly to special educators for administration and leadership, this requirement penetrated into every quarter of preparation programs for teachers, school administrators, school psychologists, and others employed in the schools. Special educators, operating out of their historically separate stations in the schools, colleges, and governmental bureaucracies were expected now to renegotiate their relations with general educators and to help lead the way toward more integrated and accommodative general school programs. Was this realistic? Were attitudes, resources, and ideas all ready and amenable to the proposed new direction? Highly doubtful!

- Numbers of Teachers. In congressional hearings leading to PL 94–142 it was proposed and apparently quite widely accepted that there were about eight million handicapped children in the nation and that large numbers of added special teachers would be required to teach them. In the late 1960s Gallagher (1968) estimated that less than half of handicapped children were getting the services they needed. The number of special teachers employed did expand for about three years after passage of PL 94–142, but slowed down beginning in 1980 (SRI, 1982). In 1977, the number of special education teachers employed was about 250,000 (Siantz and Moore, 1977), which then increased to just under 300,000 a decade later—a significant increase but far smaller than might have been expected if the "eight million" estimated number of handicapped children had been realized.[2] By 1981–82, about 4.25 million students between the ages of three and twenty-one were being served under the provisions of PL 94–142 (and the related provisions of PL 89-313) and by 1986–87 that number had increased to 4.4 million. The demands for special teachers just to replace those leaving the field tends to be high because of relatively high "burn-out" rates for special teachers, especially among those serving emotionally disturbed students, and the high attrition rate among young and new teachers. Though data about needs were never very clear or dependable, it seemed clear in 1975 that substantial numbers of added special education teachers would be required and that added capacity to prepare them was needed.

CONTEXT FOR THE NEW POLICIES

Before proceeding to a review and discussion of steps taken to implement PL 94–142, it may help to review some elements of context. What was it like in teacher education in the 1970s?

The 1970s was a period of declining demand for general

education teachers. The school-age population of the nation was in decline and significant numbers of teachers in many communities, especially the younger and newly hireds, were losing their jobs. Correspondingly, most teacher education programs were in retrenchment. In such a period, one might hope that there would be time and energy for major improvements in teacher education. Writing in 1975, B. O. Smith, a leader in teacher education, said, "Teacher training institutions have never before been in a period so favorable to improvement of their programs." He went on to stress that teacher education "must focus upon the preparation of teachers to work with the great body of children who have problems in learning. This will turn teacher training right side up and require the inclusion of skills and concepts now almost completely neglected" (p. 104).

By 1980, Smith's views had become less optimistic:

> Let's face it. Colleges of pedagogy will in all probability never overhaul their programs if each college is to do it alone. There are too many hurdles, too much disparity among institutions, too much institutional jealousy, too much divisiveness and lethargy among faculties, too much fear, and too much ineptness in the leadership. (Smith, 1980, p. 90)

The retrenchments appeared to cause more insecurity and turf-protection, and less creativity in teacher education programs than was desired.

During the 1960s and 1970s the Bureau of Education for the Handicapped (BEH) offered financial supports to hundreds of colleges and universities for the preparation of special education teachers. About four hundred fifty projects were supported in 1973–74 (NASDSE, 1973), and more than seven hundred such projects were funded in the fiscal year 1978–79 (J. Smith, 1979). It is not likely that BEH grants supplied more than a minor share of funding for college training programs, but they were significant in influencing priorities and provided important marginal resources for program improvements. In the earliest days of federal training grants, beginning in the late 1950s, funds were provided for support of advanced graduate students in training for leadership positions. Gradually such students moved into important leadership positions in the colleges and universities and in government offices. The directory of special education teacher preparation programs funded by BEH in the 1960s and 1970s served virtually as a "Queen's list," or sign of accreditation. Not that BEH intended expressly to be an accrediting agency; indeed, BEH assisted, through grants, the strengthening of the normal voluntary accrediting procedures and agencies. Through time BEH training grants were narrowed to specific and limited priority areas such as preparation of teachers of severely handicapped children and teachers for preschool education, leaving colleges on their own to prepare teachers in most categories.

In the same period (1960s and 1970s) the Congress began using "earmarks" on federal funds to assure that handicapped students were served in certain special programs. For example, a 15 percent earmark was placed on Title III funds (under the Elementary and Secondary Education Act) to assure that projects for innovation in education gave attention to handicapped students. A similar action was taken in vocational education. The "earmark" procedure did not redirect funds to special educators; to the contrary, it required action by general school administrators to make arrangements in their programs to be inclusive of students with handicaps.

The Education Professions Development Act (PL 90-35 of 1967) resulted in the creation of a new Bureau for Education Professions Development (BEPD) to be responsible for coordination of a variety of programs for preparation of teachers and other school personnel. Most BEPD programs related to equity concerns. The Teacher Corps program, for example, focused on the preparation of teachers for urban schools. By agreement between James Gallagher and Don Davies, heads of BEH and BEPD, respectively, programs under the Education Professions Development Act (EPDA) were not directed to personnel who worked directly and exclusively with handicapped children, but rather a minimum of 15 percent of EPDA funds was dedicated to the support of preparation for regular education personnel, including regular teachers, counselors, technology specialists, administrators, and teacher aides who would help in meeting needs of handicapped students. It was agreed that BEH would continue its important and central role in support of preparation for the main body of special education personnel. The BEPD role would be important but adjunctive and experimental. The result was a variety of somewhat new models for collaboration between regular and special education teachers (Deno, 1972). This was the period of rapid development for so-called resource room teachers who would serve handicapped students for limited periods of time during the school day when they were released from regular classes and sent to so-called resource rooms.

Even before the passage of PL 94–142, BEH also gave leadership to changing modes of special education delivery. In early 1975 Edwin Martin, who had become head of BEH, led the way in creating the Dean's Grant Projects (DGP). Actually, the DGP was constructed on a base of earlier work by a "network" (the Network for Alternatives in Undergraduate Teacher Education) of deans of education led from offices in the state Universities of Nebraska and North Dakota (Gideonse, 1978). The mission of the Dean's Grant Projects, which eventually reached 240 institutions of higher education, was to support the reformation of preparation programs for regular teachers so that the teachers would be better prepared to contribute to programs for education of handicapped children. These projects represented a concern expressed by Martin (1974) about the excessively dichotomous conceptualization and practices in the preparation of regular and special education personnel.

The Dean's Grant Projects clearly succeeded in making teacher educators aware of the important new policies expressed in Public Law 94–142. In many colleges the cooperation of teacher educators across departments was enhanced and beginning steps in curriculum revisions were taken. At first, the curriculum change tended to be quite superficial, for example, just introducing new laws and policies and providing introductory knowledge overviews on categories of handicapped students. Later, it appeared that more fundamental changes in the curriculum were considered. The story of these changes is told in two books, one edited by Grosenick and Reynolds (1978) and the other by Sharp (1982).

Also started by the BEH before passage of PL 94–142 was a set of projects for in-service preparation of general education teachers. In 1977, BEH supported 170 projects for that purpose. A project on comprehensive manpower planning was started in 1974 and, eventually, this became an important part of the response of the U.S. Office of Education to the comprehensive systems for personnel development provision of PL 94–142 (Schofer, 1978).

In these several ways much of the longer-term response to PL 94–142 was anticipated even before 1975. The main principles eventually expressed in PL 94–142 were recognized as "only slightly off shore for all of us" by leaders in government and in professional circles, and much was underway before the law was passed. But with the passage of the law, efforts were increased, federal resources were pressed into new areas of high priority, many expectations became formal requirements of law, and monitoring for compliance with the law began.

Quite apart from the specifics of teacher preparation, several other developments of the 1970s need to be understood as part of the context for PL 94–142, such as:

- Deinstitutionalization. In 1967, state institutions for persons who were mentally retarded had a population just under 200,000. By 1987, that was cut by more than half to 95,000 (White, et al., 1988). The rate of institutionalization for children dropped very sharply in this period, resulting in rate increases in the numbers of severely handicapped children presented to local day schools for their education. This trend was supported in the 1980s by the Medicaid Waiver policy which made it possible, under certain conditions, for states and local governments to use Medicaid resources in support of community placements for disabled persons rather than to use residential institutions.
- Normalization. Policies represented in PL 94–142 were developed in the context of a strong turn toward *normalization* as an overarching policy concerning persons with disabilities. This involves a downgrading of practices leading to homogeneity or congregating people with similar disability conditions in special conclaves. Instead, placements are preferred, to the maximum extent feasible, in normal or ordinary environments and in naturally occurring numbers and proportions. Normalization also causes the offering of experiences to disabled persons (in education, living arrangements, employment, social life, etc.) like those available to nondisabled persons to the maximum extent possible, adding special supports as necessary.
- Parents. This was also a period in which the rights of parents to serve as advocates for their own children were made explicit. Even in schools, where teachers had been assumed to operate in loco parentis (in the place of parents in matters of schooling), parents were demanding and obtaining a right to participate deeply in planning educational programs in general and specifically for their own children. This requires the preparation of parents to assume these relatively "new" functions and the creation of new forums in which parents and educators could

meet for evaluation and planning. With the passage of PL 94–142, this expanded role of parents became a *right* on which the schools were required to provide delivery. A variety of special resources to help in the preparation of parents was created, often operated by the parents themselves, and sometimes through leadership of professional organizations and schools.
- Minority concerns. PL 94–142 emerged in a period of great concern for the rights of minority children and families. Indeed, the *Brown v. Board of Education* decision of 1954 which declared racial segregation of schools to be inherently inequitable and unconstitutional provides an important precedent for court and legislative decisions relating to disabled persons. However, a concern developed that special education programs might actually be used as an indirect way of segregating pupils on the basis of race, ethnic origin, or sex. Gallagher (1968) had noted that one census tract in an inner-city environment comprising but 5 percent of the city's population had contributed 33.3 percent of the city's enrollment in special education programs. Beery (1972) reports that by 1968 we had about 32,000 special classes for "retarded" pupils in the U.S. and that between 60 percent and 80 percent of the pupils in such classes were members of ethnic minorities. In an important report by a special panel of the National Academy of Science, it was found that even into the 1980s the rate of placement for black children in classes for "retarded" children was three times higher than for children of white families (Heller, Holtzman, and Messick, 1982). The great push for expansion of special education programs had come largely from white, middle-class parents, but the growth of special education was greatest in areas serving disadvantaged minority populations. The results were not always welcomed and appreciated. A rash of court decisions decrying these disproportional rates of placement for minority pupils in programs carrying negative labels was part of the scene as PL 94–142 emerged as public policy (see, for example, *Larry P. v Riles*, 1972).
- Professionalization of Teaching. In the period of the 1960s and 1970s researchers began to produce, essentially for the first time, a dependable knowledge base for teaching. It produced evidence of clear cause-and-effect

relations between specific aspects of teacher education and student outcomes (Gage and Giaconia, 1981). This began to provide part of the basis for the professionalization of teaching. The pressures deriving from the "least restrictive environment" principle added force to concerns that all teachers have thorough, modern, "state of the art" preparation, including elements relating to education for handicapped students. On the other hand, it has been observed that proposals to professionalize teachers have sometimes omitted consideration of the needs of exceptional pupils. Pugach (1988) argues that the separateness of special education, in both the schools and in the colleges, may have created an artificial narrowness in conceptualizing the professional responsibilities of general classroom teachers. A much noted practical problem has been the limited amount of academic space/time for professional elements of teacher education available within four-year baccalaureate-level programs. A number of colleges moved toward "extended" (more than four-year) programs of teacher preparation. The drive toward professionalization of teaching appears to be growing even as we enter the 1990s, but with some uncertainty and debate about how much can and should be done in common across special and regular education.

Problem Solving

In this section attention will be given to a few especially notable efforts made to implement PL 94–142 in its teacher education aspects. Hedric Smith (1988) describes procurement policies of the U.S. Navy in these terms: "Get the ship hull in the water and then we'll fix it later." Experience was something like that in the case of PL 94–142. As a policy move, PL 94–142 was very big, cumbersome, and not fully designed when launched. Although many problems associated with PL 94–142 had been anticipated and important early plans and progress made, a lot of trimming was left for the period after "the hull" was afloat.

Technical Assistance Systems

One strategy used was that of technical assistance (TA) systems, created outside of government offices and intended to create networks of assistance in various project areas. Early in the operations of the BEPD a set of Leadership Training Institutes (LTI) was established to help transfer information among and to offer assistance to projects in various domains. One such LTI was in special education. BEH also supported a variety of TA systems, including:

- Cooperative Manpower Planning Project, headed at the University of Missouri by Richard Schofer
- National Inservice Network, headed at the Indiana University by Leonard Burrello
- National Support Systems Project for Dean's Grant Projects, headed at the University of Minnesota by Maynard Reynolds
- Dissemin/Action, headed by Judith Smith, of Falls Church, Virginia
- Evaluation Training Consortium, headed at the Western Michigan University by Robert Brinkerhoff
- The Technical Assistance Development System (TADS) serving demonstration preschool interventions programs for handicapped children, at University of North Carolina, headed by Talbert Black.

In each case the TA system developed a talent bank for use in assisting client organizations. Often this involved brokerage functions to deliver information and advice to local projects, the conduct of conferences, development and dissemination of publications, and many similar functions. Technical assistance systems were "set aside" from decisions about funding and concentrated on qualitative development and improvement of projects.

It is difficult to be sure how effective the TA systems were. The LTIs sponsored by the BEDP were given passing marks in a general evaluation made by Ahman, Loomis, and Kelley (1971). They found it "very clear" that project directors wanted "more of the same"—especially help on internal evaluation, project planning and management, in-service training for staff, and "collecting and synthesizing information in the field and developing theory in that field" (p. 112).

It seems very likely that the TADS operation has been very helpful in developing and testing ideas for programs relating to early education of handicapped students. The fact that TADS operated long before the big surge in early education for handicapped children undoubtedly helped put into place a talent bank and many ideas that have been useful in its burgeoning field.

Similarly, the work of the National Support Systems Project (NSSP), working in support of Dean's Grant Projects, managed to draw from projects ideas for the kinds of changes in preparation programs for regular teachers that are necessary. The ten "clusters of capability" specified by NSSP after discussions with literally hundreds of Dean's Grant Project staff members were as follows:

1. Curriculum—All teachers should study curriculum principles, and guides from preschool through secondary levels. This study should include practice in designing and modifying curriculum for individual needs.
2. Teaching Basic Skills—The preparation of all teachers should include competency in teaching basic skills. These include literacy, life maintenance, and personal development.
3. Class Management—All teachers should be able to manage groups and individuals in classrooms in ways that enhance instructional efficiency, reduce rates of disorderliness and disruptions, and provide a model for humane interactions among members of a community.
4. Professional Consultation and Communications—All teachers should master effective consultation and other forms of communication with other professionals and parents.
5. Parent-Teacher Relationships—All teachers should have skills and sensitivity in dealing with parents and families of handicapped students.
6. Student-Student Relationships—All teachers should be able to manage the classroom social environment in ways that include cooperative groups, peer and cross-age tutoring, and other approaches to the building of mutual understanding and helpfulness among students—including those who are handicapped.
7. Exceptional Conditions—All teachers should have preparation in understanding exceptional children and in school roles and procedures for the specialists who help to serve them.
8. Referral—All teachers need to learn how to refer students for special help, including how to make observations that support their reasons for referral.
9. Individualized Teaching—All teachers should be competent in assessment of the student's educational needs and in adapting instruction to the individual.
10. Professional Values—All teachers should learn to value individual students, their needs, and rights.

With the delineations of these knowledge and skill domains, many projects seemed to be helped. Supportive materials were developed and distributed widely. Evaluations showed positive response to this effort by faculty in the many colleges having Dean's Grants (Gazvoda, 1981).

Technical assistance systems provide an important means by which supports may be offered to training projects and systems in relatively undeveloped places. Perhaps the strong training centers need little TA, but they may be in position to be helpful to others. But it helps if there is a definite arrangement for brokering a relationship with colleges and schools having fewer resources and more needs. It appears to be very difficult for government staff to perform functions in funding and monitoring and also to offer direct technical assistance to projects. Government staff cadres tend to be small and limited in the range of their expertise. Local project staff also appear to have difficulty relating directly and honestly with government staff, because they are concerned about losing funds or credibility. Thus, an externalized TA agency has several important advantages; but they can be realized only through much hard work and shared views—among all parties involved—on what the goals and procedures of the TA system should be.

It is of interest to consider why the broad array of technical assistance centers (the LTIs) created under EPDA were discontinued in the early 1970s. Why did teacher educators not rally in support of the LTIs and the broader aspects of EPDA programs that were so centered on teacher education? A first answer is that the EPDA law was "taken off the books." Some legislators associated EPDA with the Nixon administration which was experiencing great difficulties at the time. Some teacher educators appeared to believe that too much of the EPDA resources went to schools rather than to colleges. In any case, support of EPDA by deans of education and the educators was far less than universal and enthusiastic. It was also a period in which a broader effort for educational "renewal" was attempted, only to fail for lack of broad support. Perhaps the question to be considered is why so many federal initiatives in education have disappeared.

Freight Train Technique

One of the areas showing the most remarkable advances following enactment of PL 94–142 was education for severely and profoundly handicapped students. That seems due to the imperatives of the law and the quite remarkable leadership shown by BEH staff in providing funds for programs of teacher preparation in this area. But, another positive aspect has been the way that a number of key teacher educators linked themselves together to make the cause for education of severely and profoundly (S/P) handicapped students. Lou Brown and Ed Sontag of Wisconsin, Wayne Sailor of San Francisco, and others first demonstrated that they knew how to conduct programs for S/P children and that teachers could be prepared for the programs. Then, with all their strengths, they linked themselves together, as in a string of cars of a freight train, and travelled wherever policy could be influenced—in courts, schools, and legislative halls. Luanna Voeltz, Paul Wehman, Robert Bruininks, Charlie Lakin, and many others joined the parade. The Association for Persons with Severe Handicaps (TASH) grew out of these early efforts; and today this field of work presents as able a group of young professionals and as fresh a set of positive developments as one can imagine. It shows what a relatively small group of well-informed, strong, and committed people can achieve—by "freight train technique."

Conclusion

This is a still incomplete story of a large vessel, already in the water, leaking here and there, and needing much further trim work. But, in the main, it is a positive story of good technical, attitudinal, and moral progress in teacher education.

Campbell (1969) noted several decades ago that to secure legislative support it was often necessary for professionals to advance ideas for programs as though they were certain to be successful, even if the evidence for optimism was limited. Along with other Americans, educators appear to believe that the needed solutions to problems can be invented after we get the money to get going and "get the hull in the water." So it was, in many ways, with Public Law 94–142. Campbell coined the phrase "reforms as experiments" for his idea and presented it positively, recognizing that usually it is essential to confront large and complex problems with less than perfect knowledge. It is hoped, however, that one will—to the maximum extent feasible—evaluate carefully as new steps are taken.

Evaluation has been a very large stumbling block. Despite all the rhetoric about evaluation and accountability for "outcomes" in education it is clear that we do not yet know how to evaluate progress in complex domains, especially in the outcome or "product" sense, and so we often proceed with incomplete and unsure knowledge about the effectiveness of programs. Perhaps it is true that all evaluation is process evaluation. What is a product to one stakeholder is but process to another. We can do relatively well on the process side, describing what we do and counting the rates at which it gets accomplished or problems diminish. That is mainly simple and descriptive, but perhaps it is about the best we can do at present levels of expertise.

When education is a right, it is the duty of educators to deliver on that right. With enactment of PL 94–142, we came to the end of a long journey in education in one important sense—it was declared that literally *all* children had a right to education, including even those who are most inconvenient and difficult to teach. But the situation has been made very complex by the policy of "least restrictive environment." Setting disabled pupils aside in separate groups has been declared to be less acceptable as an administrative arrangement than more inclusive or mainstream arrangements in regular schools and classes. In effect, educators have been asked to extend themselves to make the regular schools more powerful in service to students with exceptional needs. That requires close working relationships between regular and special educators, in the schools and in teacher education programs. At the moment there is raging debate about the so-called "regular education initiative" (REI), the view that stronger efforts in behalf of disabled students are needed in regular schools and in regular teacher education, with support by special educators (Davis and McCaul, 1988; Reynolds, Wang, and Walberg, 1987; Will, 1986). More leadership by regular educators is needed. The REI debate will continue.

This brief excursion is concluded in an optimistic spirit. Several lessons have been learned. Ideas for the future exist:

1. Special education programs and related teacher education cannot improve in a fundamental way except through close working ties with the remainder of education. There are continuing difficulties here, as shown in the fact that special education has received very little attention in recent efforts to restructure the schools (Boyer, 1983; Goodlad, 1984; National Commission on Excellence in Education, 1983; Sizer, 1984). As the numbers of narrowly framed categorical school pro-

grams has increased, a serious degree of disjointedness and inefficiency has developed in the schools; and a comparable disjointedness (separation, lack of coordination) has occurred in teacher preparation programs. In some colleges the "regular" and "special" teacher preparation programs are on almost totally separate tracks. It is time for repair. Above all else, this will require leadership by general school and college leaders.

2. Major changes/improvements in special education (and perhaps kindred categorical programs) will occur only if we are willing to consider seriously the redirection of money. With the Medicaid Waiver system and its changes in patterns of dollar flow, remarkable experiments became possible in the nonschool programs for disabled persons. Extraordinary progress has been made in deinstitutionalization and in development of community resources for disabled persons. A recent estimate suggests that about $18 billion are now delivered as categorical supports to special education annually in the United States (Moore, et al., 1988). There is good reason for many people to protect that money from new channels; but new patterns of finance must be opened, carefully to be sure, if we are to make further progress. Perhaps a system of waivers of rules and regulations can be tried in which schools with strong leadership and ideas can be approved to experiment with new approaches to serve handicapped children without financial disincentives (Reynolds, Wang, and Walberg, 1987).

3. More efforts need to be made in prevention of disabilities among children. To an extent this will be achieved through the further development of early education programs; but new modes of service are needed at the school-age level as well. It is unforgivable, for example, that schools should wait for big "discrepancies" to develop between expectations and achievements of children (those labeled as learning disabled) before introducing intensive special education. Interventions in such cases must begin at first signs of difficulty and not wait until problems are severe and perhaps intractible.

4. We need to devise means of recruiting more teachers for specialized preparation from indigenous populations in rural and inner-city environments and from the minority communities. It seems unlikely that needs will be met in communities now lacking quality special education programs by present methods of recruitment, preparation, and placement of teachers. We must work with more people who know intimately the situation of rural schools, for example, and who are committed to careers in the further development of special education in such "special" environments.

5. We need to become much clearer than in the past about the numbers of teachers and other specialists needed in special education programs. Progress is being made, yet there is too much uncertainty about turnover rates, burn-out rates, rates of new program growth and like matters, all influencing demands for teachers. Perhaps it will, and even should, remain difficult to get a tight bureaucratic management of a system for personnel development. At extreme, the CSPD could become a disputed and resented kind of top down or "sovietized" system. On the other hand, if data on needs for teachers and other personnel are dependable and valid, a kind of accountability "to the facts" becomes almost automatically a feature of the planning by all stakeholders and participants in teacher education programs.

6. Special educators should join in all progressive efforts for qualitative improvements in teacher education. There are strong efforts underway now (in the 1990s), such as the Holmes Group movement, which should draw the interest and active support of teacher educators in special education; and the approach should be a flexible one, showing willingness to enter new designs for dealing with individual differences among children.

7. We should see efforts for further development of programs under policies enunciated in PL 94–142 as "experiments" and try very hard to build a solid and cumulating knowledge base for dealing with individual differences (and exceptionality) as we go. This will not be easy, because special education as a field lacks a

reliable taxonomy for assembling knowledge. The field does not produce in quality or quantity its own researchers; instead it tends to borrow them, too often on short-term bases, from psychology and other disciplines. Here is another reason for special education to join fully the large community of educators, including the active researchers.

8. In teacher education the fields of special and regular education should seek to travel together for most of the way in preparation programs. There is no separate knowledge base for teaching reading, arithmetic, or other subjects to handicapped v. nonhandicapped students. Students in the special categories such as learning disability and mildly mentally retarded often require more instruction and more highly structured teaching than do other students, but not a different kind of instruction. Thus, there are reasons to avoid the separations in programs that have developed in the colleges as well as in the schools and to integrate programs with all of their strengths to serve all students. The content for integrated programs can be found in the emerging literature on "effective" instruction and schools and in the practices discovered through intensive work with pupils who have needed extra help.

Our society launched a large and unwieldy ship in teacher education upon the educational waters in 1975 in the case of PL 94–142. The struggle to repair the leaks and finish the trim is difficult and continuing; there is no time for dry dock relief. It is an interesting, worthy, challenging, and continuing journey in quite heavy seas.

11

RICHARD WISNIEWSKI

The Southern Regional Education Board and Teacher Education Policy

Partly because of the leadership of several "education" governors, the southeastern states received considerable attention over the past decade, a period that history may characterize as an era of educational reform. The Southern Regional Education Board (SREB) has been a major contributor to educational policy in this region.

This chapter reviews SREB contributions to the debate on teacher education. It does not critically examine its many recommendations since the literature is replete with discourse about such issues. The purpose here is to outline one policy agency's recommendations for the preparation of teachers, and to suggest how little is known about how policies are forged. Primarily descriptive in nature, the chapter touches on the sociology of knowledge, its production, dissemination, and utilization.

A Brief History

The Southern Regional Education Board was conceived in 1948 at a special meeting of the Southern Governors' Conference. It came into formal being in 1949 when the first six of sixteen legislatures ratified a compact for cooperation in higher education. The Southern Regional Education Board's inaugural meeting took place on June 11, 1949. The process was not without controversy. Meharry Medical College in Tennessee was at the core of the debate. In their history of SREB's first ten years, Sugg and Jones (1960) write:

> The Southern Governors' Conference was accused of wishing primarily to preserve Meharry Medical College as a segregated institution for Negroes—a sort of Siberia of medical education to which Negroes applying to white medical schools might be sent—and of hoping that similar arrangements might be made in other fields. Such hopes were undoubtedly current

among some proponents of the Compact, and several Southern newspapers published these views and in some instances adopted them editorially. The other, academic and educational as opposed to political, potentials of the Compact were largely ignored. (pp. 18-19)

At issue was whether the proposed compact would serve to create regional facilities or if it would provide services to its member states. The issue was resolved in favor of the services concept:

> Thus the idea of "regional services" was officially introduced into the new program to supplement and, as things have worked out during the first decade, to replace the idea of regional institutions, although these remain potential under the Compact. At its December, 1948, meeting the Southern Governors' Conference amended the Compact to empower the Board to enter into agreements with states, institutions, and agencies to provide educational services.... (Sugg and Jones, 1960, p. 21)

The signatory states included: Alabama, Arkansas, Delaware, Florida, Georgia, Kentucky, Louisiana, Maryland, Mississippi, North Carolina, Oklahoma, South Carolina, Tennessee, Texas, Virginia and West Virginia. Delaware dropped from membership in 1965. Oklahoma was not represented from 1971 to 1984 but resumed its membership in 1985. The SREB is funded annually by contributions from each state. The current level of contribution is $100,000 regardless of the size of the state. The arrangements for funding are diverse. Some states treat the fee as a line budget item; other states have their higher education commission pay the fee.

Sugg and Jones (1960) and Sugg (1963) are the best available histories of SREB. Robb (1952) is also a significant source for assessing the importance of SREB to educational development in the South. Among SREB's early accomplishments, Robb cites:

> (1) Cooperation among states and institutions for educational purposes has become more than a nice theory and desirable goal.... (2) The program has been financed.... (3) The program has support. Educators, officials of state and local governments, students, and many citizens have expressed their readiness to support a regional program of education.... (4) The longest step yet taken by any region in the total integration of its resources for educational purposes has been

made.... (5) Money is being saved by states that can ill-afford to duplicate the expensive facilities already existing in other states of the region.... [and] (6) The south has at last taken the lead in a major educational development, a fact of some psychological as well as social and economic importance. (1952, pp. 44-45)

The list continues, including the significant fact that Meharry Medical College was saved due to money channeled to it by the regional board.

Robb also cites a number of issues and problems faced by SREB. Most of these had to do with articulating vested interests in higher education in member states, the decision of some higher education institutions to develop graduate programs on their own, and questions about the depth of public support for the work of the board. The most significant point on the list, however, returns to America's overriding educational issue: "Segregation of the Negro remains an issue involving tension which could flare-up to the detriment of the regional plan" (Robb, 1952, p. 46). He also argues that SREB determined early "to divest the regional plan of any aura of segregationism" (p. 43).

While these comments comprise little more than a note on the development of SREB, they are sufficient to establish: (1) SREB's early history is associated with political turmoil as racism and desegregation dominated southern politics; (2) SREB's functions grew out of an awareness "that the Southern institutions of higher learning...still lacked much that was to be desired" (Sugg and Jones, p. 3); (3) the agency was influential "in the formation of the Western Interstate Commission on Higher Education and of the New England Board of Higher Education" (Sugg and Jones, p. vi); and (4) SREB's functions have been consistent with the goals of those who argued at its inception that the agency should provide services to its member states. In keeping with its history, a recent annual report summarized SREB's functions:

> Providing assistance to the educational and governmental leaders responsible for policy decisions regarding education in the schools and colleges of member states has always been one of its major functions. As it has over the last 40 years, SREB continues to demonstrate its ability to identify new educational issues on the horizon and to initiate meaningful efforts to help states "meet them head-on" or, as is often the case, "head them off." (SREB, 1989, p. 7)

SREB AND TEACHER EDUCATION

The Southern Regional Education Board's early activities were not focused on teacher education. In their 1960 study, Sugg and Jones list the board's publications. Other than a 1955 monograph titled "Teachers for the South's Handicapped Children," the majority of the publications deal with higher education matters. Programs of public and mental health, veterinary medicine, educational television, college enrollments, doctoral programs, nursing education, and agricultural programs are among the topics listed. Several publications, expectedly, are progress reports on the work of the interstate compact.

In his 1963 monograph, Sugg examines in more detail the topics on which SREB focused. Changing conditions and opportunities in member states guided SREB's work, a condition prevalent to this time. A five-page segment of Sugg's study is devoted to teacher education. He writes: "In teacher education, SREB's policy is to limit staff involvement to selected, critical areas rather than attempt a broad program approach to the total field" (Sugg, 1963, p. 50). He discusses the 1962 publication *The Gifted Student* with implications for teacher preparation. In the same year, a project was initiated to strengthen the preparation of teachers of emotionally disturbed children. In a related activity, the board collaborated with the United Cerebral Palsy Research in Education Foundation. In the same period, SREB collaborated with directors of emerging Master of Arts in Teaching programs at southern universities. In 1963, a workshop was to be held for deans of teacher education on the uses of instructional media. Overall, SREB's interests in teacher preparation were particularistic; it did not encompass major policies during its initial fifteen years. This conclusion is reinforced by the fact that its 1965 publication, *M.A.T. Programs in the South*, is a state-by-state outline of MAT programs, listing admission requirements and other program details. The monograph's introduction states that it is directed to college seniors not in teacher education but who might be interested in becoming teachers: "Already these programs are increasing significantly the supply of able young persons embarking upon careers in teaching that will lead to leadership positions in education" (SREB, 1965, p. iii). Other than this mild endorsement of the Master of Arts in Teaching, there is no discussion of how this approach enhanced (or was a threat to) established teacher education programs.

Of particular interest is the fact that SREB appointed a commission in 1966 to improve postsecondary educational opportunities for African-Americans. Its 1977–78 annual report gives an account of SREB's activities:

> Perhaps SREB's most important activities in this area in recent years have been in regard to achievement of racially unitary systems of higher education in the South. In the early Seventies, the board adopted a policy statement that stressed the necessity for full compliance in the movement toward unitary systems, but urged that this be done in ways both legally and educationally sound, giving careful attention to the differences among states in the structure and administration of public higher education.
>
> The board's work in the compliance area has sought to relate federal policies to widely differing local situations and to provide a means for states to make such conditions known and understood, while at the same time encouraging states and institutions to meet their responsibilities. (SREB, 1978, p. 14)

Its 1977–78 annual report also comments on SREB's long-standing interest in nursing education and on efforts to combat adult illiteracy. Considerable emphasis was placed on improving undergraduate education, with programs underwritten by a grant from the Carnegie Corporation. The uses of computers were another interest. Mental health and human service programs also were given attention. The preparation of teachers, however, is not mentioned as a major interest even during the agency's third decade of work. This condition was to change rapidly in a year or two.

It is safe to conclude that during its initial thirty years SREB's focus was primarily on professional fields other than teacher education, with most of its energy and resources being focused on postsecondary education. This work was consistent with the original intent of the compact. The Southern Regional Education Board's lack of major attention to teacher education is not posited as a negative comment. The board's work reflected the tenor of the times. The quality of teacher education was not a dominant concern despite the publication of books critical of teacher preparation by Bestor, Koerner, and Conant in the 1950s and 1960s. When attention was given to teachers, it had a limited focus, such as the improved use of instructional media by teachers. The process of preparation and the overall quality of teaching was yet to emerge as a major issue.

The one notable exception to the general avoidance of teacher education in the 1970s was the conferences designed to encourage black colleges to review their teacher preparation programs. The 1975–76 annual report states: "The annual Teacher Education Conference continues to serve as a forum for Black colleges and universities to renew their teacher preparation programs in light of new trends, issues and needs" (SREB, 1976, p. 13). A total of six conferences were held between 1971 and 1976. As early as 1970–71, the SREB reported "...on the cooperative program between Norfolk State College, a black institution, and Old Dominion, a white institution, to train teachers for integrated classroom situations" (SREB, 1971, p. 11).

A Focus on Teacher Education

It is difficult to identify the factors that brought about SREB's interest in teacher education. It appears to have been less a deliberate decision and more a reflection of issues in selected states. The fact that during the 1970s several southern states utilized tests to assess the quality of their teaching force may have been the key factor. In Arkansas, Alabama, and South Carolina, the testing of experienced teachers became a highly controversial issue. This practice created the highly charged atmosphere in which SREB's staff began to examine teacher preparation.

A colleague has suggested a related but stronger hypothesis. So long as white teachers taught white children under the separate but equal doctrine, the quality of the teaching force was not a central concern. With desegregation, some white children were taught by African-American teachers. The testing of experienced teachers, heightening attention on African-American teachers, and demands for strengthening teacher education began to grow. The fact that these demands were strongest in the SREB region support this hypothesis. The fact that concerns about teacher quality are national in scope weaken the hypothesis. Given the South's history of African-American subjugation, the assertion that racism was a factor in concerns about the teaching force cannot be dismissed. Whatever the causes, and however subliminal their nature, the quality of teachers in the South became central to the education reform movement. This line of analysis in no way applies to persons or decisions at SREB. Rather, it underscores deep historical currents and the legacies of slavery.

The 1979–80 annual report signals the increased interest of SREB in the availability of and quality of teachers: "Two recent SREB studies have examined current state action to improve teacher certification and teacher education programs as well as future supply and demand..." (SREB, 1980, p. 20). The two reports were: *The Changing Labor Market for Teachers in the South* and *Teacher Education and Certification: State Actions in the South.*

In the latter document, Stoltz speaks pointedly to quality controls in teacher preparation:

> ...Professional educators have had an aversion to embracing the language of commerce to describe their activities. Nevertheless, pipeline and quality control may well be the most appropriate terms to describe the movement today to make sizeable changes in that rather entrenched process called teacher certification. (1979, p. 1)

Commenting on declining test scores among college students, he asks:

> Isn't it just as reasonable to believe that a share of the blame should rest with the schools and teachers? And, when we get to teachers, isn't it possible that in this latter group there might be some who are weak or downright incompetent? If a state administers a competency test to all of its high school graduates and finds an unacceptably large number are failing the test, isn't it quite possible that poor teaching might have been a contributor to that failure? (p. 1)

It can be assumed that teacher educators were not pleased with the directness of this report, particularly when it continues: "...Something might be wrong with those programs that are designed and advertised as being able to produce educated teachers who ought to be able to reach and pass these cutoff points" (p. 1). The latter comment does not highlight the damaging fact that where experienced teachers were tested, the cutoff scores were low. Somewhat prophetically, the report adds:

> It would be easy, and comforting to some professional educators, to dismiss the whole furor over teacher certification as just another fad. But that would probably be wrong. There is a feature to these recent changes in the certification process that removes them from the fad category—namely, a strong direct or implied legislative endorsement accompanied by specific statutory requirements, frosted over with no small amount of quantitative and qualitative reporting requirements. (p. 2)

The report also examines changes in the teacher preparation pipeline in five states: Georgia, Florida, North Carolina, Louisiana, and South Carolina. The author concludes:

> The SREB states seem to be moving briskly, if unevenly, toward a still loosely defined common goal—the improvement of teacher quality. If they move totally independently of each other, they run the risk of rediscovering the wheel many times over, repeating mistakes needlessly, and spending much more for the development of a tool or service than would be required if the cost or experience were shared. In this situation, the states might wisely consider how cooperative undertakings might be developed to reduce end-product cost and lessen expenditures of time, funds, and talent. Carefully developed, such could occur in cooperative settings that would in no way infringe on the very legitimate demand that each state develop a unique and individualized pipeline that fits its own situation best. (p. 16)

With this report, SREB established much of its teacher education agenda. The tone of the report, intended or not, could do little else but put teacher educators on the defensive. In the succeeding ten years, that stance has not altered significantly.

In 1981, Robert Stoltz authored *Emerging Patterns for Teacher Education and Certification in the South*. In this document, progress made in several SREB states is described. Five types of changes in teacher preparation are cited: (1) test requirements at or near the end of preparation programs; (2) the lengthening probationary period for beginning teachers; (3) basic skills test required for admission to teacher education; (4) strengthened student teaching; and (5) in-service requirements coupled with the probationary period. A sixth development is cited as being inadequately addressed: research and development activities designed to modify teacher preparation (Stoltz, 1981). The report ends by urging states to share their initiatives with one another. Further:

> There is no objective way now to say which is best or even which one is most effective or efficient in terms of a state's needs and expectations. For some states now is still the time to watch and learn—beginning where it seems most can be done and leaving the options relatively open. The comprehensive plans make the best sense. But complexity shouldn't be equated with goodness. One does not have to start by going off in all directions at once. (p. 16)

This second major report does not appear to have as strident a tone as the study issued a year earlier. Indeed, it is almost "conversational" in the way it addresses readers.

Between these two landmark reports, a 1980 document, *Improving Teacher Education: Academic Program Review* (Stedman), discusses campus program reviews and accreditation processes as mechanisms for improvement. Developments in Florida, Kentucky, North Carolina, Texas, and Virginia are cited. The report urges leadership from within universities as the only way to avoid external pressures for change. The tone of the report is essentially neutral.

In 1981, a highly significant report was issued: *The Need for Quality*. The report summarizes the recommendations of a task force appointed by Governor Graham of Florida to address linkages between schools and colleges "in order to strengthen education at all levels" (SREB, 1981, p. iii). The report calls for testing for admission into teacher education as well as exit examinations. It calls for regional evaluation of teacher selection procedures. It addresses the strengthening of teacher education and notes that some three hundred fifty colleges in the region were preparing teachers, despite the decline in the number of education students. It calls for strengthening student teaching experiences and stronger working relationships between education and arts and sciences. It asserts that certification codes are too complex and rigid and reviews the perennial debate between content and methods in teacher education. It reports (without passing judgment) that some colleges are considering lengthening the program of preparation, in effect moving education courses to the graduate level. It suggests that "provisional certification" be provided for arts and sciences graduates followed by an evaluation of these persons. Scarcity of mathematics and science teachers is recognized, as well as the need for vocational guidance programs. The report continues with recommendations related to school curricula, preparing youth for the world of work, certain vocational education needs, and the cooperation needed at state and local levels to bring about improved education at all levels (SREB, 1981).

The report is interesting for two reasons. First, it expands SREB's concerns about teacher preparation and sets its agenda for K–12 schools. Second, it is perhaps the only occasion in SREB's history when a task force member wrote a minority report. William Drummond, a professor of education at the

University of Florida, questioned the recommendations regarding teacher education:

> How does the call for tighter certification requirements fit with the appeal for less complex certification processes? How does the call for careful selection of candidates for teaching, academic scholarship as well as instructional effectiveness, fit with the suggestion that anyone with a degree from a college of arts and sciences should be able to enter secondary teaching? How does the call for higher academic standards and the need for greater social prestige for teaching fit with the statement that the lengthening of preparation "would be an extremely costly step"? (SREB, 1981, p. 28)

He ends his disclaimer by advocating the extension of teacher preparation to five or six year programs so that all beginning teachers are liberally educated and strongly prepared for the field. He argues: "Higher standards require longer preparation. Higher performance expectations justify higher salaries. Higher standards and higher salaries will make teaching a more attractive career choice" (p. 28).

This document coupled with a 1983 report, *Meeting the Need for Quality: Action in the South*, comprised the SREB agenda for strengthening education at all levels in the southeast. Most of the 1981 task force members also were involved in this second document, though the chair and several members were changed. Interestingly, Professor Drummond continued as a member of the task force.

The report emphasizes that university presidents must provide leadership in improving teacher education; the importance of general education to the quality of teaching is also highlighted. Teacher certification continues to be viewed as being too rigid. The recruitment of arts and science graduates to teaching is emphasized again. The report challenges the proliferation of teaching certification fields and calls for a reduction in their number. Reciprocity on teacher certification tests is recommended, as well as continuing education efforts for teachers. While not directly related to teacher education, changes in the selection of school principals are advocated, calling for persons who are leaders as well as for an internship as part of administrative preparation (SREB, 1983a, pp. 15–21).

To students of the teacher education wars, these recommendations are familiar. While the language will vary, the same recommendations are reflected in dozens of other reports issued over the past decade. What is significant here is the evolving and consistent emphasis on these ideas by SREB. There is something to be said for any agency that is consistent in its recommendations and the reports issued in the early 1980s remain SREB's canon for the improvement of teacher education.

An illustration of the agency's sense of consistency was the appointment of a Commission for Educational Quality "...to sustain and increase the momentum for educational improvement in Southern schools and colleges" (SREB, 1984, p. 8). The 1983–84 annual report states:

> Improved teacher preparation, essential to improved student performance, is the aim of a number of SREB activities. Last fall SREB convened a meeting of presidents from selected public and private colleges and universities that produce large numbers of the region's teachers to consider initiatives college presidents might take to *strengthen teacher education.* This follow-through on one of the Task Force recommendations resulted in a variety of practical suggestions for campus action, many of which are already underway. *A summary of the presidents' suggestions,* distributed to college and university presidents throughout the region, has served to initiate or reinforce campus wide considerations for desirable changes in teacher preparation. (p. 10)

The SREB's Commission for Educational Quality issued a 1984–85 report titled, *Improving Teacher Education: An Agenda for Higher Education and the Schools.* Some twenty-five recommendations are made touching on many aspects of teacher education. An intriguing recommendation proposed additional support for teacher education institutions that would take the lead in reforming their programs:

> Financial rewards should accrue to those colleges of education that are willing to make serious curriculum and structural changes to improve their programs. Colleges that are willing to embark on large-scale and meaningful reforms should be given more assistance than those that only develop one or two new courses. Those that redesign the program should be given more support than those which only superimpose courses on top of the existing program. Financial assistance should be given to the retraining of college of education faculty and to early retirement. (SREB, 1985a, p. 10)

While little support materialized, it certainly was a refreshing recommendation for many in teacher education. Without question, the recommendation that challenged teacher educators most directly was SREB's commitment to alternative certification:

> Institutions and states should explore alternative teacher education and certification models which open teaching to a wider range of talented students while maintaining standards. These alternate approaches should emphasize the development of professional teaching skills primarily in the school classroom setting. (SREB, 1985a, p. 12)

Perhaps SREB's most controversial report was published in 1985: *An Analysis of Transcripts of Teachers and Arts and Sciences Graduates*. Based on a review of over six thousand transcripts of graduates from seventeen universities in the South, the report answers the following questions:

> What kinds of courses are teachers taking in their general education component in college? How strong (or weak) is the preparation in the content they will be teaching? How much time do teachers spend in covering the pedagogy aspects? Does this time include practical applications of the theories on how to teach? (Galambos, et al., 1985, p. 2)

Among the findings: "When all teachers are considered together, they earned fewer general education credits than the arts and sciences graduates and a smaller proportion of the teachers' credits were upper level courses" (p. 79). In respect to elementary and special education teachers, the report found there is substantial variation between the education coursework taken by elementary and special education teachers, and other teachers. Those preparing for elementary assignments are taking more than half again as many credits in education as the certification regulations require, and five credits more, on the average, than their colleges specify:

> When credits in academic courses designated primarily for teachers are included with education courses, elementary and special education teachers devote 42 percent and 51 percent, respectively, to what, for them, is the major. (pp. 82–83)

The report compares findings reported by James Koerner in 1961 with those in the SREB study. Both findings are remarkably consistent and the report's writers' comment: "How little has changed!" (p. 85).

The *Atlanta Journal and Constitution* reacted to the transcript study favorably:

Its report couldn't have come at a better moment in Georgia, where educators and state officials are buckling down to implement their landmark plan to upgrade public education. Crucial to its success is the upgrading of teacher preparation programs and the SREB report points the way. ("Failing Grade," 1985)

Reactions of some teacher educators is suggested in twin stories on the report in a Louisiana paper: "Study cites weak general curriculum for education students," and "Two Louisiana university deans criticize SREB education report" (Redman, 1985a, 1985b, p. 3D).

For many teacher educators this report must have been a serious challenge. The report was formidable because it went beyond the general recommendations of task forces. The conclusions were derived from data, from college transcripts seldom brought to public attention. Granted, the analysis of transcripts has inherent limitations. The quality of what is taught and how it is learned is not necessarily reflected in course titles or grades. Such limitations, however, have little persuasive power. The transcript is well established as *the* document by which college graduates are assessed. As to grading variations from campus to campus, these inconsistencies will tend to "wash out" when a large sample of transcripts are reviewed. In this case, the examination of six thousand transcripts from seventeen universities could not be dismissed as merely a series of opinions. The study, it must be assumed, reinforced calls for the reduction of courses in education and increases in the subject matter background for teacher, especially in elementary education.

The term "caps" has come to refer to limitations placed on the number of teacher education hours required for certification, as is mandated in Virginia and Texas, for example. Interestingly, SREB has never made a recommendation to this effect. Such caps infringe on academic freedom and it may be conjectured that SREB does not wish to be caught between legislators and higher education commissions regarding the concept. As an aside, it would be interesting to probe why eighteen credits appears to be the number of hours advocated by those arguing for limits on education courses. A copycat phenomenon is obviously at work, but this fact does not explain how eighteen hours came to be originally specified as the "correct" number of hours appropriate to prepare teachers.

In 1987, the agency issued *A Progress Report and Recommendations on Educational Improvements in the SREB States.*

In the section titled "Quality Teachers for the SREB States," the report comments on conditions in the teacher workplace. This section may be viewed as indirectly linking SREB to the growing consensus that improvements in teacher education need to be accompanied by improvements in teaching conditions. It is not a strongly made connection, however. The report recommends alternate certification programs as a way of expanding the pool of teachers and for recruiting liberal arts graduates. Loan-scholarship programs are also recommended. Maintaining standards for admission to teacher preparation is acknowledged. Drummond's concerns regarding the dichotomy between calling for maintaining standards and alternative certification appear to be ignored by SREB in these later reports, as is the case in similar reports on alternative certification.

Three specific recommendations are made for strengthening teacher education:

> Teacher education, which has not been a priority for many state and educational leaders, demands immediate attention. College and university presidents should insist that arts and sciences and education faculty examine the curriculum for preparing teachers to assure a solid grounding in the liberal arts and subjects they teach.
>
> Reform of teacher education should begin with close scrutiny of four-year programs. Abolishing all undergraduate four-year teacher education programs is premature. Various kinds of extended programs should be tried on a pilot basis with careful evaluation to determine their effectiveness.
>
> States, districts, colleges, and universities should examine student teaching policies, especially those for selecting and rewarding supervising teachers. (SREB, 1987a, p. 33)

Of these recommendations, SREB's endorsement of four-year programs may have been most significant. In its 1986–87 annual report, the agency recognized the recently issued Holmes and Carnegie Forum on Education and the Economy reports which proposed five-year preparations for beginning teachers. Their view was, and apparently remains, that such a change would be drastic and premature.

The SREB reinforced its support of alternative certification in *Alternative Teacher Certification Programs: Are They Working?* The report concludes:

> Based on preliminary information, alternative certification programs are adequately preparing persons to become teachers. At present the number of persons seeking to become

teachers through these alternative programs is small. Although programs are new, they are providing standards and training for liberal arts graduates to enter the classroom. However, in states that continue to permit emergency certification that allows liberal arts graduates to enter the classroom, it seems unlikely that large numbers will enter teaching through the alternative certification programs. Small districts are often those in greatest need of teachers, but they find it difficult to develop programs because of a limited number of available persons or resources. This means that states or colleges and universities should work with districts in developing consortium arrangements. The Texas program is taking this approach. While many educators initially were opposed to alternative teacher certification programs, that is changing. Some colleges and universities, such as those in Florida, North Carolina, South Carolina, Texas, and Virginia, have developed programs with school districts. The deans of colleges of education of the research institutions in the SREB states recently issued guidelines for alternative certification programs.

Too little program evaluation is underway, especially collecting and reporting additional information on performance of the alternative certification teachers. States, districts, and colleges and universities should immediately begin efforts to confirm or deny the early indications of effectiveness of alternative certification programs for liberal arts graduates. (SREB, 1988a, p. 6)

Also in 1988, the agency issued *Selected Educational Improvements in SREB States*, a tabular, state-by-state review of selected teacher education data. Included is information on minority teachers and preservice teacher education initiatives.

It should be noted that SREB periodically publishes the *Career Ladder Clearing House*. Suggested by former governor of Tennessee Alexander (who initiated a career ladder as part of his Better Schools Program), the agency agreed to track what is happening in states that have initiated some form of career ladder or merit pay incentives. The board provides digests of activities in any state with such programs, not restricting its purview to the southern tier of states as with most of their work.

In 1988, SREB published its *Goals for Education: Challenge 2000*. It outlines indicators of progress toward effective teacher education which are both familiar and developmental in nature. That is, they reflect emphases in other SREB reports and in other associations looking to the turn of the century. SREB's indicators include:

(1) Adopting as state policy a continuing state-level emphasis on improving teacher preparation programs that includes college and university presidents and the arts and sciences and education faculty of all colleges and universities in periodic examination of teacher preparation programs;
(2) Instituting teacher licensure and program approval standards based primarily on knowledge and performance of graduates;
(3) Evaluating different approaches to prepare teachers, such as alternative certification, four-year undergraduate, and extended programs, based primarily on performance of graduates and of their students;
(4) Reducing by one-half the percentage of graduates not meeting initial teacher licensure standards;
(5) Increasing threefold the number of minorities graduating from programs to prepare teachers—this means an annual increase of approximately 20 percent each year to the year 2000;
(6) Improving the performance of beginning and veteran teachers according to assessments of principals and veteran teachers;
(7) Maintaining or exceeding the national average in the proportion of teachers qualifying for certification compared to the number who apply when national board certification is established. (SREB, 1988b, pp. 15–16)

The last indicator is particularly interesting since it is an example of the evolving nature of such goals. The comment on national board certification reflects the fact that the concept of national certification was coming to the fore in the late 1980s and SREB added the idea to its list of desirable outcomes.

Finally, SREB published *Changing the Education of Teachers* by Willis Hawley, Ann Austin, and Elizabeth Goldman in 1988. This is an appropriate document on which to end this review for it summarizes a comprehensive study of changes in the teacher preparation between 1981–82 and 1986–87. Questionnaires were sent to all 189 public colleges and universities in the SREB region and to 56 private institutions that graduate significant numbers of teachers (Hawley, et al., 1988, pp. 1–2). Deans or heads of teacher education received one form of the questionnaire, with another form going to the dean or head of arts and sciences units. The researchers also visited selected campuses and examined factors that influence change processes.

Five statements summarize the findings:

> Considerable change is taking place in the way teachers are being educated.... It is too early to know if the changes taking place in the way teachers are educated will improve the quality of teaching in elementary and secondary schools.... In our judgment the pace of change in teacher education programs is accelerating.... Critics of teacher education may conclude that institutions of higher education are moving too slowly....
> It seems worth noting that demands for change in teacher education have not been accompanied in most states and institutions by resources to facilitate change.... (pp. 18–19)

It is significant that the matters discussed are broader in scope than in previous teacher education reports issued by SREB. This is to be expected since the study summarizes ideas derived from university personnel, both in education and in liberal arts; the authors are also a part of the world of teacher education. They probe that world more deeply than authors of other SREB reports. It is perhaps the one SREB document that most teacher educators would accept as being closer to "the truth."

The Impact of SREB

One cannot determine the impact of SREB on teacher education policy without going beyond the analysis of documents and the handful of interviews that comprise the research for this paper. The best that can be offered are suggestions for determining the influence of SREB (or of any similar agency) on state policy making. Two analogies provide frameworks for such inquiry: that of a mirror, and that of a furnace.

The Southern Regional Education Board's work can be viewed as a reflection of events in its member states. In this sense, the agency follows rather than leads. Given the complex nature of higher education and the profound issues surrounding K–12 education, especially in a region where desegregation was and is an issue, SREB has reflected trends and debates. In the 1960s and 1970s, it dealt with special education issues because those were of concern in many states. Later, the agency became concerned with the quality of teacher preparation because persistent questions were raised about the quality of teachers in state after state.

Given the composition of the board, the mix of ideas brought to discussions, the changing leadership interests (and styles) of prominent board members, it is reasonable to assume that SREB would reflect what was happening throughout its region. Hence, the mirror analogy. To suggest a mirroring function in no way lessens the importance of SREB's accomplishments over its forty-two-year history. It has served the interests of its member states and this is its prime function. It would be most unusual if it did not mirror the southeastern quadrant of the nation.

The furnace analogy would suggest a more proactive stance. In this sense, the agency produces some of the "heat" in debates about education. This analogy suggests that SREB generated the topics about which it made recommendations, thus "lighting a fire" under key persons in its member states. The board would thus be an active "player" on the educational scene, an agency that stimulates activity rather than reflects that which is already occurring. To those upset by any set of SREB recommendations, this analogy would have an appeal. It is conducive to a "we/they" conception of policy making. The Southern Regional Education Board would be perceived as serving and encouraging governors or legislators determined to alter the course of teacher education; it would be an agent provocateur.

Of these conjectures, the least viable would appear to be the furnace analogy—that of an SREB belching forth reports, heating controversy, and "driving" some of the legislative actions in selected states. Obviously, persons and events generate any given SREB report. There are many layers of persons and opinions involved on any board, however. One can expect a range of views, debates, and meliorative influences on what some see as harsh views. While further inquiry might clarify the matter, SREB certainly performs a catalytic function.

It is intriguing to speculate on who reads SREB reports, pays attention to them, or acts on them. The reports are widely disseminated. It can be assumed that among the materials that inundate policy makers, SREB's recommendations carry some weight. As an established policy agency, its work is important in the southeast region. It can also be assumed, though no evidence was sought on this point, that its impact goes beyond the region. The issues addressed by SREB are hardly restricted to its member states. The key question remains: how does SREB's work actually impact on given legislation or state board of education policies? Studies are needed to determine precisely how a given SREB report has influenced key individuals, legislation, or the political process. Far beyond the scope of this preliminary inquiry, such studies could be an important contribution to the sociology of knowledge.

Yearly legislative sessions held by SREB are one vehicle for influencing policy. These are well attended and as many as 120 state legislators will participate. Rarely is a member state not represented at these sessions. At the 1989 session, for example, the following topics were on the agenda for the legislative review:

- Leadership in Setting Goals for Education—Year 2000: Trends for the Southern Regional Education Board States
- Benchmark 1990, and Beyond: Tracking the Progress of Education in SREB States
    - —School Readiness, College Readiness and Vocational Education
    - —Highlighting State Actions on Setting Goals and Tracking Progress
    - —Educational Funding: SREB Information on Teachers' Salaries, Faculty Salaries, Higher Education Tuition, and Fees
    - —Virginia's Plan to Recognize School Performance
- Leadership and Action for Reaching Educational Goals
    - —Educational Goals for a State's Schools and Universities: Tennessee Challenge 2000
    - —The SREB Leadership Academy and NCNB Leadership Awards
    - —The National Assessment of Educational Progress and Goals for Education
    - —The University of the 21st Century: Higher Education in Virginia. (Cornett, L., April 4, 1990)

Commenting on such meetings as a vehicle for disseminating ideas, one SREB staff member said: "We'll know if its a good meeting in about a year," suggesting that the answer is dependent on whether states act on the ideas discussed.

Interestingly, the development of model legislation has not been an SREB activity. In contrast, the Southern Republican Conference has published an agenda for improving education. While not an agency with the mission or scope of SREB, its initial report specifies what is wrong with education and what the conference believes needs to be done, with model legislation provided to that end (Conners, N.D.).

The Southern Regional Education Board reports do not have the same impact as, for example, a program on the preparation of teachers on national television. While SREB reports discuss the same issues reported in the press and on TV, its dissemination channels are limited. Certainly, each time a major SREB report is issued, the staff makes efforts to get the media to report its recommendations.

In discussing this matter with SREB staff members, another analogy was proposed: that of SREB staff members being akin to bees spreading pollen. As frivolous as the analogy may appear, there is much to be learned about how informal contacts between SREB staff and policy makers influence the thinking of individuals or groups. While idea dissemination takes place at formal meetings, and SREB sponsors many such events, much more can perhaps be communicated by informal comments. The latter is a serendipitous and irregular process. Studies might track, over a period of years, formal and informal contacts between SREB staffers and education and political leaders in the fifteen states. While formal presentations and reports provide the substance of SREB's work, the travel, meeting, and phone logs of SREB staff might reveal connections between the issuance of a study and specific reactions in member states.

It would also be interesting to establish which political leaders have most influenced the work of SREB in recent years. Former Governors Graham of Florida and Alexander of Tennessee (each of whom served as chairs) and Robb of Virginia would be among those persons. A full study would probe the layers of authority and responsibility for teacher education below the gubernatorial level. One would need to gather data from and interview persons in *fifteen* governor's offices, legislatures, state departments of education, state superintendents or commissioners of education, teacher education institutions in the fifteen states, and from other policy analysts in the region. As complex as this undertaking would be, it is the only systematic way to establish the impact of SREB. This would be true of any other policy agency, of course. While not an insurmountable task, it can only be suggested in this introductory assessment.

Additional SREB Staff Insights

Staff members indicate that during the 1980s, well above half of SREB's efforts were devoted to K–12 issues and teacher education. This focus is in sharp contrast to earlier decades when the agency worked on areas such as mental health, nursing education, and the common market in higher education, and gathered statistical information on higher education.

Southern Regional Education Board staff also provided insights into how the agency operates. They view as important precedents set by early SREB leaders. The fact that the agency had the same president for twenty-five years was noted. The style of management that has characterized the agency is one that keeps it from jumping from topic to topic. In contrast, groups like the National Governors Association or the Education Commission of the States must be far more responsive to yearly leadership changes. The goal of the staff is to keep close to the pulse on matters within SREB's purview, to anticipate problems and to set goals. The impression is of an agency that makes gradual rather than sharp turns in its policy inquiries.

One staff member emphasized that the agency focuses on issues rather than responding to the pressures of special interest groups. He indicated that they are careful not to "bash" any particular group and avoid becoming embroiled in arguments. The staff recognizes the controversial nature of some of their reports, however. A recommendation that no additional doctoral programs in nursing education were needed was offered as one example of a controversial matter. In education, the 1985 transcript study of teacher education graduates and the agency's support of national assessment were other positions on which SREB received criticism.

The staff sees key legislators and governors as being most active in decision making. They also recognize that early in its history, SREB's key reference groups were in higher education. By the 1980s, contacts with state departments of education became much more viable. They also noted that when the SREB board determines to pursue certain studies, it does not follow that every state in the compact has to approve this decision.

Forthcoming SREB studies will include reports in several areas. A study is being conducted on the supply of and demand for doctoral-level scientists. Minority faculty supply and demand is also under study. The impact of financial aid to students is being tracked. A study is being conducted of African-American students in white institutions and vice versa. The perennial question of the appropriateness of remedial education in higher education institutions is under analysis. In respect to teacher preparation, a transcript study of graduates in vocational education is underway.

Conclusion

The Southern Regional Education Board has had considerable impact on the struggle to improve teacher preparation. It has influenced policy making in a number of states. The board is doing precisely what it was created to do: to address educational concerns in its member states by conducting studies and disseminating recommendations.

That some teacher educators are concerned about some SREB recommendations is to be expected. A Southern Regional Consortium of Colleges of Education was organized in 1986. Deans of education from doctoral-granting institutions in the region were invited to join. At the group's initial meetings, relationships between schools of education and SREB were a prime focus of discussion. A small group of deans were selected to open a dialogue with SREB. At succeeding meetings, the consortium focused on a number of other issues, primarily the preparation of educational administrators. While an SREB staff member has attended some meetings, the Consortium would appear to be expanding its areas of interest and is not as sharply concerned with SREB's work. At the same time, a precedent and vehicle were established for continuing the dialogue between SREB and deans of education in the southern tier of states.

Any profession that receives criticism reacts defensively, even if the criticisms are privately acknowledged. For teacher educators in the southeast, SREB's work must be taken seriously. That some recommendations are controversial and sometimes internally inconsistent does not alter the need to address the agency's views. The Southern Regional Education Board is a major contributor to policies that are slowly altering the structure of teacher preparation. While some would not agree, SREB has been of service to teacher education. It has emphasized issues that need to be addressed and resolved. The future of teacher preparation is being determined by those ignoring as well as by those seeking solutions to these issues.

12

HENDRIK D. GIDEONSE

The Redesign of NCATE 1980 to 1986

INTRODUCTION

By 1978, those associated with the National Council for Accreditation of Teacher Education (NCATE) knew that serious internal and external problems existed. NCATE, the national voluntary mechanism for peer regulation of professional preparation programs for education, was then governed by a Coordinating Board composed one-third each of representatives of: the National Education Association (NEA); the American Association of Colleges for Teacher Education (AACTE); and the Council of Chief State School Officers (CCSSO), the National School Boards Association (NSBA), and a revolving group of six other specialty organizations in education. The actual work of accrediting programs and defining standards was done by the NCATE Council, a twenty-five–member body, one third from the NEA, one-third from the AACTE, one-third from the the CCSSO, NSBA and specialty organizations, plus one public member. In 1980 NCATE accredited programs in over five hundred institutions responsible for over 80 percent of the national production of educational personnel each year.

The problems were apparent. In February, 1978, the Association of Colleges and Schools of Education in State Universities and Land Grant Colleges and Affiliated Private Universities (ACSESULGC/APU) had, in effect, placed NCATE on notice that either productive change would occur within five years or ACSESULGC/APU would consider developing an alternative accreditation system; the widespread awareness of the unhappiness of this prestigious group of institutions weighed heavily on NCATE.[1] Individual institutions (for example, five in the state of Wisconsin alone) had either withdrawn from the NCATE fold or indicated a desire to "place themselves on hold" in the accreditation timetable. Some of the most prestigious universities nationally were not accredited by NCATE. NCATE's governance was proving increasingly confusing, and participation of the CCSSO and the National Association of State Directors of Teacher Education and Certification (NASDTEC) had become a serious concern (cf. *NCB* 10/22–23/79; *NCB* 5/12–13/80). Constituent elements within the teacher education community were suspicious of each other; the smaller, liberal arts, often church-affiliated programs of teacher education felt the flagship research universities were calling the shots, but many of the latter, in their turn, felt NCATE's standards and procedures were biased against them. The institutions organized in the Teacher Education Council of State Colleges and Universities (TECSCU), because of their dominant role in the actual production of teachers year after year, chafed under the larger role they saw accorded the so-called "big" deans in accreditation and other teacher education policy activities.

The increasing vigor of specialty groups (organizations like the Council for Exceptional Children [CEC], the National Association of School Psychologists [NASP], the International Reading Association [IRA], and the Association of Educational Communication and Technology [AECT]) led them to assert themselves in governance and standards matters, challenging the relatively recently established parity created between the NEA and the AACTE. (In earlier days, AACTE had held a dominant position on both NCATE's Council and its Coordinating Board.)

On July 1, 1986, however, eight years after the 1978 ACSESULGC/APU action "giving notice," NCATE began the implementation of a thoroughgoing redesign fashioned over the preceding twenty-eight months. Sweeping revisions in concept, governance, standards (in particular those bearing on specialized knowledge and relationship to the worlds of practice), and accreditation processes were achieved. These accomplishments were substantial and full of promise. The benchmarks established during those eight years of ferment and then redesign are important for succeeding generations of education professionals and those who will play accreditation roles therein to know and understand.

Antecedents to Redesign

NCATE's redesign did not, like Athena, spring full-blown from the head of Zeus. It had antecedents.

By the early 1980s, concern had been building over the substance and application of NCATE's standards, review processes, governance, costs, and duplication with state-level program reviews (Tom, 1980a, 1980b, 1981). Indeed, in 1977, the year before ACSESULGC/APU had given NCATE notice of its grave concern, NCATE had itself called for examining its own procedures and arranged for such a study by the Institute for Research on Teaching (IRT) at Michigan State University.

Completed in November, 1980, the study found both strengths and weaknesses (Wheeler, 1980). On the plus side, NCATE generally uncovered serious quality problems where they existed. Denial of accreditation, therefore, was a clear signal of inferiority. NCATE's processes were carried out professionally and with concern for objectivity. The process was generally beneficial for the institutions participating. Finally, denial of accreditation had led to some modifications in program (Wheeler, 1980).

On the negative, the study found a vagueness in NCATE's standards and their organization, and an absence of definitions of terms or specification of evidence sufficient to meet standards. Site-visitor training respecting standards was judged cursory. A variety of constraints in working conditions impeded the ability of site visitors and NCATE Council members to evaluate programs completely and thoroughly. Institutional influences over team composition were judged inappropriate. The report noted some in-depth examination of program but, far more often, a reliance on the presence/absence approach (that is, if there were any evidence presented against a standard, it tended to be deemed met). Wheeler raised the question "whether NCATE's stamp of accreditation [was] a meaningful indicator of quality." His study "showed that NCATE's effect on program quality [was] very limited" (1980b, p. 6). The Wheeler report was received by NCATE at its October, 1980, meeting but, for a variety of reasons, the NCATE Council was not overly responsive, if not actually a bit defensive (NC, 10/20/80).

In the spring of 1981 NCATE staff undertook discussions on the implications of the IRT study for changes in NCATE. Those discussions ultimately led in October, 1981, to a staff report to NCATE's Council (NCATE Staff, 1981). The document proposed creating a single board of directors for NCATE and two accrediting commissions (one for basic professional preparation and one for advanced) which would directly elect the board of directors. The financial base of the council would have been broadened, the number of accreditation meetings reduced, and the period of accreditation set at seven years.

The size of visiting teams would have been sharply reduced, the focus of accreditation shifted from programs to institutions, and the amount and availability of information about accredited institutions expanded in the annual list. The Executive Committee received the report and scheduled an hour for council discussion (*NC*, 2/3–5/81), but participants in that dialogue agree that the conversation signaled little movement.

One last pre-redesign activity was a 1981–82 TECSCU examination of NCATE accreditation. TECSCU endorsed a two-level system of accreditation. States should assume responsibility for institutional accreditation. The states, in turn, would be accredited by a national accreditation body (TECSCU, 1982). While the document was circulated within AACTE and delivered to NCATE, it was not acted upon (*NC-EC*, 6/17/82).

IMMEDIATE STIMULI AND CHRONICLING REDESIGN

The immediate stimuli for redesign were the absence of action by council on the IRT report and the perception of several who attended the October, 1981, meeting of council (at which the staff's redesign document was discussed) that needed reform would not be forthcoming from within NCATE. A shared sense of frustration over the lack of movement culminated in a message that if something was going to happen, AACTE would have to take the initiative. Dale Scannell (Dean of Education, University of Kansas) and three colleagues, William Gardner (Dean of Education, University of Minnesota), Hans Olsen (Dean of Education, University of Houston–Clear Lake City), and Richard Wisniewski (Dean of Education, University of Oklahoma) posed the idea of preparing an alternative accreditation process to David Imig, AACTE's executive director, who shared it with the AACTE Executive Committee. AACTE President Dean Corrigan (Dean of Education, Texas A&M) created what would become known as the Committee on Accreditation Alternatives (CAA) (D. C. Corrigan, October 23, 1981). Corrigan charged Scannell and his colleagues with the task they had proposed, and more specifically, to develop a rationale for the effort, a design for a new system, a discussion of governance and participation, and a timeline and process for adoption and implementation. His charge left it open whether the alternative should replace NCATE or "be seen as an organization/process model that would significantly modify but not replace the existing Council." (Signaling the increasingly cooperative relationship developing between AACTE and NEA, after the initial meeting of the CAA Willard McGuire [NEA president and chair of the Coordinating Board] suggested Catherine Sullivan, a long-term, committed, and respected NEA member of the NCATE Council, be added to the group, and she was.)

The CAA worked for a little more than a year, maintaining continuing contact with AACTE's Board of Directors, with constituent elements of AACTE (TECSCU, the Association of Independent Liberal Arts Colleges of Teacher Education [AILACTE], and ACSESULGC/APU), and with the NEA. The final version of the CAA report, completed in January, 1983, proposed six principles to guide reformulation of national accreditation:

1. Accredit teacher education units, not programs.
2. Replace re-accreditation with continuing accreditation.
3. Articulate national accreditation with state approval.
4. Create a board of examiners skilled in NCATE standards, processes, and evaluation skills, from which to draw visiting teams.
5. Replace six families of standards applied to programs with five unit-focused standards.
6. Expand the annual list to describe the unit and indicate the support level for its programs.

Copies of the CAA report were made widely available at the AACTE annual meeting (February, 1983), but a resolution endorsing the principles was tabled before much discussion could occur. In a courageous but not universally approved statement immediately at the point of tabling, then AACTE president, Jack Gant, spoke to the meaning of the tabling; in the presence of the silence from the membership created by the tabling, he told the assembly, the matter would revert to the AACTE Board of Directors. His implication was clear; the board would continue the leadership course on which it had embarked. No one in the audience objected to that conversation. Anne Flowers, Gant's successor as AACTE president, in a March 9, 1983, memo to AACTE's chief institutional representatives, communicated her decision, after extensive consultation, to advise the AACTE staff "to move forward with the introduction of an appropriate motion at the March 4–7 NCATE Council Meeting. During the Philadelphia Meeting of the NCATE Council a motion was made to accept the Proposal of the AACTE Committee on Accreditation Alternatives. That motion was unanimously adopted by the Council..." (A. Flowers, March 9, 1983). The process of redesigning NCATE had begun.

Flowers's formal announcement suggested little of the behind-the-scenes work prior to the NCATE Council meeting. Careful work beginning with Sullivan's appointment to the CAA assured that the NEA delegates were on board. The community of interest worked out over the years, moving safely past periods of strife in the early 1970s between NEA and AACTE over perceived lack of parity on NCATE's governing bodies and relative responsibility for financial support, was reflected in the vote to set up an ad hoc multiconstituency committee of six to review the CAA report and recommend to the council how it should proceed.

The ad hoc committee undertook its work that spring and brought a recommendation before the council at its June, 1983, meeting to adopt the six CAA principles, define a process for undertaking redesign, and address the role of specialty guidelines. An attempt by specialty group representatives to consider the statements associated with specialty guidelines as principles equal to the CAA six was defeated (again a manifestation of the understandings forged between NEA and AACTE representatives in advance of the meeting), and the entire package was approved twenty-one to three (*NC*, 6/17–20/83), the only negative votes being cast by representatives of specialty organizations.

Meanwhile, changes were in the offing in the composition of NCATE's staff officers. Lyn Gubser's resignation as NCATE's executive director became effective July 1, 1983. George Denemark, former dean of education at the University of Kentucky, was enlisted to serve as Interim Executive Director. He presided over a process wherein members of the NCATE Council chaired ad hoc committees sponsored by the council's standing committees, each charged with further investigating aspects of the CAA principles.

The pressure on NCATE's scarce resources led to two decisions. One was to have the council itself do the work; there was no money to support travel and subsistence for additional committee members at NCATE's expense. The second decision was to seek to augment the council's human resources with volunteers. Letters were dispatched to a variety of organizations and agencies. The responses were favorable; volunteers and "conscripts" alike were enlisted and supported to attend to a variety of redesign tasks.

A March, 1984, meeting in Memphis generated great amounts of material and brought a substantial number of volunteers, at their own or their organization's expense, to participate in the redesign effort. Materials growing from the deliberative session were reproduced and widely circulated for review and comment (Marjorie Pike, April 4, 1984). In the meantime, AACTE members and staff were very busy working on redesign, including sponsorship of a number of hearings around the country soliciting input on the principles guiding redesign and on the developing ideas and materials contributory to the effort.

Richard Kunkel, dean of education at the University of Nevada–Las Vegas and chair of ACSESULGC/APU's 1982–83 Task Force on Accreditation, became the new executive director of NCATE July 1, 1984. Joined by Donna Gollnick, AACTE liaison to NCATE, and John Leeke, staff liaison from the NEA, Kunkel and Gloria Chernay, assistant executive director of NCATE, immediately set about the task of preparing a comprehensive redesign draft from the disparate pieces then in hand. The draft was completed in August.

Council reviewed the document and undertook a Likert-scale assessment of issues that, as yet, remained unresolved (NC, October 13–15, 1984). The Council judgments fed into a widely distributed December draft.

In February, 1985, a meeting was held in Atlanta of Coordinating Board and Council representatives that successfully addressed fundamental governance questions for redesign (R. L. Saunders, February 15, 1985). In March, at a Council meeting in Cincinnati, testimony on redesign was taken from representatives of ACSESULGC/APU, AILACTE, TECSCU, AACTE, NEA, NASP, and the Council of Learned Societies in Education. Following further discussion, straw votes on remaining issues were taken to guide yet a third rewrite of the redesign document (NC, March 10–11, 1985).

At its June meeting, with a sense of excitement tempered by the death only days before of George Denemark, the council considered and acted on the April draft of redesign. Despite the months of work and negotiation, participants remained nervous until the very end for fear that a very fragile coalition of supporters might come undone. The April document was accepted as a final draft, the standards section to be ratified the following October after consideration of any written comments, and necessary directives were given to the Task Forces on Governance and on Finance to work with the Constitution and Bylaws Committee to prepare a new constitution and bylaws for action at the October meeting (*NC*, June 7–10, 1985).

At the October meeting the requisite approval to the standards was given by council and extensive consideration was given to the proposed constitution and bylaws (*NC*, October 10–14, 1985). Four months later, the council unanimously adopted the proposed changes in governance and structure plus a Transition Document outlining an orderly transfer from the old NCATE to the new. It authorized staff to draft appropriate implementation documents to assist the small set of institutions who would volunteer to pilot the new standards and to assure that "the learnings from these visits will be systematically reported to the Unit Accreditation Board [which would assume the accreditation responsibilities formerly undertaken by the council] and the Executive Board [which would assume the governance responsibilities which had formerly been held jointly by council and the Coordinating Board]..." (*NC*, March 8–10, 1986, Attachment B). Implementation would formally begin with the July, 1, 1986, advent of the newly configured NCATE.

Major Themes of Redesign

The kinds of changes brought about and the sequence of events, while important, provide only the thinnest of outlines to explain the significance of what happened in the four years from the creation of the CAA through redesign itself to the formal launching of implementation. Five themes emerge as especially powerful frames.

Greater Efficiency and Effectiveness

Many of the concerns and issues leading to redesign can be grouped under the general heading of improving efficiency and effectiveness. The great burden perceived by institutions and the states of two separate and overlapping program reviews is one example. Institutions *needed* state approval in order for their graduates to be licensed to teach; they *wanted* national accreditation because of the perceived professional value of the peer recognition. The burden, however, of two independent reviews was substantial.

The IRT study had documented the inadequacies of using NCATE's standards on a purely presence/absence basis. But as the CAA had proposed, there were some criteria for approval that could be judged in that way. Distinguishing between criteria that can be satisfied on a presence/absence basis and those that require in-depth examination and professional judgment speaks to another dimension of efficiency (Wheeler, 1980; Scannell, et al., 1983).

The size of visitation teams was also a concern because of cost and logistics, but one of the problems with the recommendations forthcoming from the IRT study had been its programmatic (as contrasted to institutional or unit) focus. The IRT report had left the impression that teams even greater in size would be required. The large pool of visitors under the old system, the thinness of their training (especially respecting the standards themselves) and the de novo construction of each of the site-visit teams constituted additional drains on the system. Confusion among some site visitors as to what the standards were further complicated the matter.

There was no agreement on where to go with all these matters. Specialty groups were understandably concerned that the curriculum standards that NCATE had approved be applied; in their view it was program quality that ultimately assured the entry of quality graduates into the profession. On the other hand, deans and directors, especially of the larger teacher education institutions, understandably viewed the cumulative effect of individually approved program curricula as particularly burdensome. Some NASDTEC representatives, however, tended even more strongly in the exact opposite direction, contending that NCATE was not, in its pre-redesign form, evaluating programs but rather *categories* of programs (for example, not each individual secondary certification area but *all* such areas in tandem), and they were critical of NCATE for having teams that were too small to evaluate everything rather than too big.

Two key conceptual breakthroughs and some political compromises were required to resolve these puzzles. Prior to the CAA effort, two formulations of unit (as compared to program) accreditation had been developed. The first was in the NCATE staff document shared with the council in October, 1981, a formulation growing out of conversations earlier that spring between Gubser, William Gardner, Edell Hearn, and David Poisson (who had been influenced by his knowledge of accreditation procedures in other fields). The second antecedent was the TECSCU proposal for state approval of institutions reserving national accreditation for the review of state evaluation procedures (TECSCU, 1982). The unit focus emerged as a key simplifying assumption. It enabled the clarification of NCATE's domain (units) relative to the states' (programs), and set the stage for further negotiations with specialty groups on how their concerns would be addressed.

The decision to opt for unit accreditation dovetailed neatly with a variety of options for addressing concerns respecting the mechanics of evaluation. Presence/absence criteria (e.g., was there a unit, did it have a director, was the institution regionally accredited and approved by the state for teacher education, had evaluation studies of program been conducted, etc.) could be applied independently to a unit as preconditions well before a site visit. Indeed, having a visit would become contingent upon such preconditions having been met. The submission and evaluation of program portfolios against NCATE-approved guidelines could be accomplished at that time.

Furthermore, teams could be considerably smaller because of the unit focus; therefore, NCATE could afford to be more selective of site visitors, could train them more thoroughly, and could establish means whereby, functioning as continuing cohort groups, they could develop experience with one another as examiners, thereby reducing substantially on-site "socialization" functions needed for them to carry out their responsibilities efficiently. Finally, distinguishing and delineating NCATE's orientation from that of the states opened the opportunity for differentiation of function, articulation between the two, and the invention of a governance function within NCATE to address state responsibilities (the State Recognition Board). It also would allow a further elaboration, beyond their role in defining preconditions for visitation, of the states' use of specialty guidelines as a basis for conducting their program evaluations.

Embracing and Extending the Family

To create a peer evaluation mechanism for professional preparation in education one must first define the profession. Governance, therefore, is central.

Securing the appropriate involvement of all the constituent elements of the profession in the accreditation function was fundamental. During the preceding decade a long-standing tension between AACTE and NEA had been resolved by the establishment of parity between the two on the NCATE Council and the Coordinating Board (eight seats apiece). In the intervening years, however, specialty groups had begun to assert and engage themselves, but a reverse phenomenon had begun to develop with CCSSO and NASDTEC—failing to pay their assessments or to send their representatives to attend meetings. Tensions existed within the teacher education community itself between research-oriented, state college and university, and liberal arts teacher education programs. Finally, NEA's role as the only teacher organization involved in NCATE began to appear increasingly untenable.

The linchpin to this interlocking set of issues was the rekindling of the involvement of the CCSSO. That rekindling long antedated redesign itself. It began with Lyn Gubser's 1978 conversations with CCSSO's then-new executive director William Pierce. It extended through the emergence, within CCSSO, of a new interest in the chiefs' role in teacher education, despite a lingering coolness (if not hostility). In fact, the chiefs almost split with NCATE entirely, but the president, Robert Benton (Iowa), believed in the importance of teacher education, and he simply chose not to act; a letter that would have severed connections never went out.

Calvin Frazier (Colorado), the 1983-84 CCSSO president, was also interested in teacher education. Frazier wanted an energetic and committed successor to complete the work of a CCSSO Ad Hoc Committee on Teacher Certification, Preparation, and Accreditation which had been chaired by Robert Scanlon (Pennsylvania), and in Ted Sanders (Nevada) he found that person. Sanders, as Frazier, had been influenced by a 1983 policy essay on the role of inquiry in educational reform (Gideonse, 1983), in particular a recommendation that chief state school officers had a special obligation to orchestrate connections and relationships among all the elements of the education family.

A series of rapid-order events followed. Richard Kunkel's selection as NCATE's executive director effective July 1, 1984, had been announced in December, 1983. (As the University of Nevada-Las Vegas dean of education, Kunkel had enjoyed a close working relationship with Sanders as the two had sought better to articulate NCATE accreditation with state-level program approval.) The report of the chief's ad hoc committee, *Staffing the Nation's Schools: A National Emergency*, was released in January, 1984. Conversations between Kunkel, David Imig, J. T. Sandefur, and Frazier led Frazier to ask Sanders to represent the chiefs at the Memphis redesign meeting in March, 1984, also attended by Kunkel as executive director-elect. Later conversations between representatives of the NEA, AACTE, the chiefs, and Kunkel resulted in a mutual understanding between the constituent elements. Formal reconnection of the CCSSO could be secured if a number of points could be agreed upon, including matters pertaining to debts and dues, governance, the expansion of NCATE to include AFT, and facilitating notification to the states of NCATE accreditation decisions.

CCSSO acted on its part of the bargain November 13, 1984 (T. Sanders, 29 November 1984). At the same time that these events were taking place within CCSSO, conversations that began the preceding June between Sanders, Pierce, Marjorie Pike and Beth Bond (both of the NEA), Imig, Robert Saunders (AACTE President, 1985–86), and Kunkel had culminated in a AACTE/NEA/CCSSO discussion paper on the future governance of NCATE. There for the first time was laid out, not only an early version of the provisions on which CCSSO would act in November, but also the delineation of the distinction between national accreditation of professional preparation units and state approval of certification programs. The future structure of NCATE was defined—a board of directors of NCATE, and three subsidiary councils responsible for (1) unit approval, (2) specialty guidelines, and (3) development of a program, process, and standards to nationally recognize quality state approval systems (R. Saunders, et al., 1984).

The second key "family" issue was how to extend a governance role to AFT. More than a half-dozen state chiefs, because of the characteristics of their particular jurisdictions, were oriented more to the AFT than the NEA; for those chiefs, the exclusive role for NEA in NCATE represented a serious shortcoming. AACTE representatives, particularly Imig, as well as Kunkel, supported the "entire family" concept, too. Ultimately, agreement that NCATE would favorably entertain an AFT request to become fully involved was facilitated by AACTE's willingness to compromise on an essentially unrelated issue: what role would the Association of Teacher Educators (ATE) play in the new NCATE? If one of the teacher education seats on the board could go to an individual affiliated with the ATE board, this would be seen as a significant gesture of compromise, a gesture that eased any remaining reluctance of NEA figures to entertain the anticipated forthcoming petition from AFT to participate fully in NCATE affairs.[2]

The governance proposals worked out in conversations between the chiefs, NEA, and AACTE officials still had to be tested more broadly. That test came at the February, 1985,

Atlanta meeting, later widely regarded as among the most satisfying of participants' professional lives. Two groups of attendees recall working independently, then discovering that they had arrived at the same place, namely, that the existing conceptualization of the governance of NCATE having three parts—teachers, teacher education, and others[3]—should more accurately be understood as a fourfold break embracing teachers, teacher education, specialty groups, and the public policy and related governing elements including the chiefs. The realization that the conclusion met with deep acceptance by those assembled released participants' energies to flesh out the emerging details of the overarching governing structure. An Executive Board composed one-fourth of each of the four constituencies would govern three operating bodies, one responsible for the Board of Examiners and unit accreditation, one for the approval of specialty guidelines, and one for administering a process for recognizing the quality of state program approval mechanisms. Each of the three operating bodies of NCATE would have a membership composition corresponding to the relative stakes of the constituent members in the activity in question. Following Atlanta, it was only necessary to work out the details.

Knowledge Bases

NCATE's focus on knowledge bases for professional education is a signature element of the redesigned standards. The shift from the preexisting curriculum standard, together with the standards obliging units to relate to the empirical realities of the world of practice has spawned what Kunkel has called a high organizational development effort for teacher education. How did it come about?

Antecedents abound. Great increases in educational research and development had occurred in the sixties and seventies, accompanied by a cumulative development of a research and scholarly awareness in some sectors of the professional education community. A more specific stimulus, however, very much like the feelings that launched the CAA, was an immediate sense of frustration arising out of the 1979 annual meeting of AACTE that led to the coalescing of the so-called "Salishan Deans." The teacher education community in 1981 was stirred by the Salishan Deans' public challenge that future professional education be strongly grounded in research, scholarship, and the knowledge bases of the profession (Tucker, 1984). "Alumni" of the group who later became deeply involved in NCATE's redesign included: Jack Gant, who organized an annual meeting of AACTE dedicated wholly to essential knowledge for beginning educators; Richard Wisniewski and William Gardner, members of the CAA (where Wisniewski played the key role in pressing the knowledge bases formulation); and Hendrik Gideonse whose inquiry monograph impacted two of the chiefs and Kunkel in their NCATE redesign roles and who, as president of ACSESULGC/APU in 1983–84, responded to Denmark's call for redesign volunteers.[4]

None of these influences, of course, could have succeeded by itself if they had not each touched emergent understandings in the larger professional community. Nor could the impact of redrafting the standards to focus on knowledge bases have had the developmental effect on the field that it did had not parallel projects been undertaken (for example, the 1986 publication of the American Educational Research Association's third edition of *The Handbook of Research on Teaching* [Wittrock, 1986] or AACTE's vigorous pursuit of a variety of seminal efforts including a faculty development knowledge base seminar and sponsorship of the synoptic volume, *Knowledge Base for the Beginning Teacher* [Reynolds, 1989]).[5]

The Developmental Posture

A fourth feature of redesign, what came to be called NCATE's "developmental posture," contributed prominently to the success of initial implementation. From its inception NCATE's redesign process was an open and evolving one. Even the six principles advanced by the CAA were subjected to preliminary review by an ad hoc committee before being submitted to council for endorsement in June, 1983. The combination of financial necessity and the realization that more human talent would be required led council to solicit volunteer help, to prepare draft materials, and to send them out for public reaction. Hearings were held and input reported and then brought to bear on the deliberations.

Understanding grew that closure would never be achieved if everyone was expected to agree with everything. Instead, what was needed was agreement on directions and principles and the development of trust that a continuous process of adjustment would be followed consistent with those directions and principles. The decision was made to have the new standards and processes tested in pilot fashion by a handful of institutions and to have a one-year moratorium on accreditation visits during which time the first cadre of examiners would be trained. The evaluative, self-corrective stance continues in NCATE to the present.[6]

Convincing intellectually though it might be for educators to adopt a learning posture in respect to implementation, it is still to the credit of the participants that they were willing to tolerate the ambiguity of working toward a moving target in the interest of both modeling sound practice and achieving an ever-higher standard of accreditation and institutional performance.

The Personality of Reform

The redesign of NCATE had a personality, as is suggested by the preceding sections, but it also had personali*ties*. Its accomplishment could not have occurred absent a variety of modes of carrying the work forward and a rich cast of characters.

Not all of redesign was done in formal meetings and sessions; much of the absolutely vital work took place in two- and three-person conversations and in formal and informal caucuses. Some of the work that turned out to be of crucial long-term significance occurred outside of redesign itself, either preceding or paralleling it.

A vigorous caucus system was clearly enabling. Like-minded individuals, or persons representative of the same organization, would convene themselves to explore ideas, develop tentative statements, and the like. Such activity was not unknown in NCATE before redesign. The NEA representatives to NCATE had long used the technique, as, in more recent years, had AACTE. Some of the NCATE family were clearly worried by NEA's caucus practices; those who were tended to advocate others' use of the technique as an important defensive strategy against what they perceived (inaccurately, according to several close observers) monolithic behavior on the part of NEA. But over time it became clear to virtually everyone that caucuses were important, not as attempts to control, but as ways of engaging in unfettered, friendly exploration of ideas and issues in a nonthreatening and nonprovocative environment, a way of testing conceptualizations and approaches that led to better results overall. The importance of these kinds of discussions actually helped to create an entity, the Coalition of Organizations for the Professional Preparation of Educators (COPPE), when James Eikeland, Jack Cassidy, and William Grady realized that the specialty groups needed a mechanism that would allow them to function effectively in the emergent governance structure of the new NCATE.

Constituent organizations (e.g., NEA, AACTE, CCSSO), temporary systems (e.g., the CAA, the ad hoc redesign committees, and the 1984 summer writing group), and the caucus system were all important elements. But there is another way to look at these permanent and temporary systems. They were vehicles for the work of a collection of individuals whose particular contributions are credited with major roles in NCATE's redesign. Many have been identified in the narrative and analysis above, but the overall story would not be complete without special attention. There were scores of such people, and their volunteered contributions were repeatedly praised by the interviewees; here special mention is given to a few.[7]

Three individuals stand in the front rank. Dale Scannell, brimming with professional passion and more than occasionally deeply frustrated over the pace of improvement, played the critical leadership role in the CAA initiative. Richard Kunkel was able to communicate and sustain a belief in redesign to others. He appreciated the complex political realities, resolved issues, and facilitated compromises. His skills in organizational development led to the successful incorporation of NCATE's "developmental posture." His friendship and close working relationship with Ted Sanders, the third kingpin, were crucial. Chief state school officer in Nevada at the start of redesign and, later, the chief in Illinois, Sanders was committed to the improvement of teacher education, to the redesign of NCATE, and to the reinvolvement of a strengthened CCSSO role in NCATE.

Just behind the "big three" were five others. William Gardner employed the skills of diplomacy and persuasiveness to allow deeply committed people of divergent views "to agree and disagree agreeably." David Imig carried the message of frustration back to AACTE, facilitated the creation of the CAA, and worked to assure Mary Hatwood Futrell's understanding and support within NEA (as he did with Ted Sanders and CCSSO). Behind the scenes he helped assure that the right people from AACTE institutions served in all the capacities required. Willard McGuire, a former president of the NEA and a longtime, multiple-role NCATE person, "knew the territory." He is widely credited with a willingness to see a totally new situation and respond to it in new ways. He was a conciliator, willing to work on the smallest details, and also instrumental in getting

Futrell deeply involved in NCATE. Marjorie Pike, also experienced in NCATE affairs, was an informed leader in the NEA caucuses and, like McGuire, was a conciliating and integrating force. Finally, Mary Hatwood Futrell, president of NEA beginning in 1983, was critical to the larger public acceptance of the redesign effort. She saw to it that redesign happened in the NEA context and helped bring the conversation within NCATE itself to a higher level. Her willingness to work toward an accommodation of the chiefs regarding the participation of AFT in NCATE, despite strong lingering feelings within the NEA itself, was crucial.

Four people played important political roles in legitimizing and sanctioning redesign within the teacher education community. George Denemark, as interim executive director of NCATE in 1983-84, played a "white knight" role, keeping NCATE alive during a very difficult time. He begged volunteer resources, healed wounds, focused energies, and served as a kind of political umbrella. J. T. Sandefur's role was similar, but perhaps he pursued it with a bit more intensity. He "educated all the new people." Powerful, diplomatic, he maintained linkages with both AILACTE and TECSCU, but did not shrink from taking a leadership role when some of his colleagues were more inclined to raise problems than to seize opportunities. Edell Hearn played a role early that helped lay groundwork for the unit accreditation concept. While some judged him opposed to redesign because of his motion to table at the February, 1983, AACTE meeting, his access to the process and his willingness to continue working on it even after moving to table, helped legitimize the effort with his peers. Finally, Robert Saunders's role at the Atlanta meeting and his trust in McGuire made possible the compromise on governance that ultimately would lead to the full involvement of, first, the CCSSO and, then, AFT. Three individuals emerge from the specialty groups. James Eikeland (NASP) was savvy; he possessed good process skills, and didn't let criticism from his teacher education colleagues dissuade him from pulling the specialty groups together through redesign. William Grady (AECT), working the same arena and agenda, was always vocal and persuasive; even though he voted against redesign in June, 1983, he "shut up and went to work." Jack Cassidy contributed heavily to the effort on behalf of specialty groups.

Interviewees referred to special roles played by five others. Alan Tom (Washington University, St. Louis) led through his critiques of NCATE. Richard Wisniewski (University of Tennessee) used his low-key intensity to promote the need for redesign and press hard the role of knowledge bases in the revised standards. Hendrik Gideonse (University of Cincinnati) pressed the knowledge base claim, too, assured ACSESULGC/APU involvement in redesign, and, through the 1983 inquiry essay, influenced key chiefs and Kunkel. Steve Lilly was a thoughtful, reasonable advocate whose combined perspective as, first, a specialty group representative and, then, a unit head was instrumental in achieving important compromises as redesign shifted NCATE from program to unit accreditation. Finally, Cathy Sullivan's long-term role with NCATE and her participation on the CAA were of great political importance.

Four association staff officers were seen as instrumental. William Pierce (Executive Director, CCSSO) materially aided in the important groundwork for reinvigorating the CCSSO role. Bernie McKenna as staff liaison orchestrated a meticulous consideration within NEA of all the elements of redesign. Marilyn Sheahan (now Scannell), as AACTE staff liaison to the CAA was an essential catalyst for the emerging CAA document. Finally, Donna Gollnick, as staff liaison to NCATE from AACTE (and, then, after July, 1986, Deputy Director of NCATE to Kunkel) gave maximum effort to the initial and subsequent drafting of the redesign document, integrating, and identifying holes and potential and actual conflicts.[8]

Conclusion

NCATE's redesign is a case study of great political, organizational, and professional complexity. It is a story of organizational commitment and personal initiative, imagination, and steadfastness of purpose. NCATE's redesign shows a profession responding to its own perceived needs to change, to be sure, not always as fast as some of its members would like. In the context of a different perception—that it took public notice to stimulate reform beginning in April, 1983, with *A Nation at Risk*—it is important to note that America's teacher education leadership's internal moves culminated in a decision to launch redesign well before the explosion of public interest in things educational. In sum, this story suggests teacher educators possess more of a reality principle and greater public mindedness than they have been credited with in recent years.

The large number of individuals involved and the depth of their engagement is compelling; it speaks well of the teaching profession writ large. The complexity of the issues, however, clearly suggests the importance of being prepared to challenge overly simple solutions that may be proffered respecting the improvement of teaching and teacher education. On the other hand, the very complexity of the task probably contributed to its successful completion. With so many variables at work, the likelihood was increased that creative, committed people could find compromises that would allow the task to go forward.

Finally, proponents of reform can take several useful lessons from the NCATE story. Reform takes large numbers of individuals orchestrating themselves in more or less coordinated ways, prepared to compromise on specific matters, in order to achieve shared ends on which they are not prepared to compromise.

A second lesson is that all reforms have roots in what has gone before. Ideas can be found in earlier position statements that at the time appeared to go nowhere. Past working relationships may suggest affinities and experiences that can be called upon to fuel the new work, and because the homework of building trust and familiarity in working styles has been done, otherwise draining "overhead" costs of starting up can, in some measure, be bypassed.

Third, as important as the formal settings for work of this kind are, informal interactions and "safe environments" like those the caucuses provided are essential for the nonprovocative and nonthreatening testing of ideas. Any inclination to see such gatherings and colloquies as "controlling" or "organizing behind the scenes to gain unfair advantage" ought to be discounted, unless, of course, there is solid evidence to the contrary. Assuming the ultimate aim is, in fact, shared, the best defense is for all elements to use such processes in the interests of undertaking the most systematic analysis of reform alternatives to the end of contributing to the dialogue.

NCATE's redesign was a major undertaking. It is still unfolding, a testimony to clear intentions, hard work, the ability to compromise, and the construction of a system capable of learning from its own processes.

CASE STUDY INTERVIEWEES, NOVEMBER, 1989–MARCH, 1990

Name	Redesign or Related Role
Herman Behling	President, NASDTEC, 1984–1985
Robert Benton	Superintendent, Iowa; President, CCSSO 1980–1981
Jack Cassidy	NCATE Council (Spec. Group, IRA), 1983–1986
Gloria Chernay	Assistant Director, NCATE 1982–1984
Doran Christensen	Deputy Director, NCATE 1972–1984
James Eikeland	NCATE Council (Spec. Group, NASP), 1980–1986 (Chair, 1986)
Robert Fisher	NCATE Council (Spec. Group, NSTA), 1982–1986
Calvin Frazier	Colorado Commissioner of Education, 1973–1987; President, CCSSO, 1983–1984
Mary Hatwood Futrell	President, NEA, 1983–1989; NCATE Council, 1983–1986
William Gardner	NCATE Council (AACTE), 1980–1983 (Ch., 1982); President-Elect, AACTE, 1986–1987; CAA Member
Jane Godfrey	NCATE Council (AACTE), (1978–1981); Board of Directors, AACTE (1981–1984)
Donna Gollnick	AACTE Staff NCATE Liaison until 1986; Deputy Director, NCATE 1986–present
William Grady	NCATE Council (Spec. Group, AECT), 1976–1983 (Ch., 1982–1983); Coordinating Board 1983–1986
Lyn Gubser	Executive Director, NCATE 1978–1983
Edell Hearn	NCATE Council 1979–1981; NCATE Coordinating Board, 1981–1986
Harold Heller	NCATE Appeals board (Spec. Group, CEC), 1980–1982
David Imig	Executive Director, AACTE, 1980–present
Richard Kunkel	Executive Director, NCATE 1984–1989
John Leeke	NEA Staff

Name	Redesign or Related Role
Stephen Lilly	NCATE Council (Spec. Group, CEC, then AACTE), 1981–1986
Bernard McKenna	NEA Staff Liaison, 1975–1984
Willard McGuire	President, NEA, 1979–1983; NCATE Coordinating Board (NEA), 1974–1986
Hans Olsen	Member, CAA; NCATE Council, 1975–1981; Coordinating Board, 1981–1984
William Pierce	Executive Director, CCSSO, 1978–1987
Marjorie Pike	NCATE Council (NEA), 1981–1986
David Poisson	Associate Director, NCATE, 1979–1981
Shirley Richner	NCATE Council (AACTE), 1983–1986; Chair, Knowledge Base Subcommittee
J. T. Sandefur	NCATE Council (AACTE), 1982–1986, Chair, 1985–1986; NCATE Coordinating Board (AACTE) 1978–1979
Ted Sanders	Superintendent, Nev. (to 1985), Ill. (1985–1989); Chair, CCSSO Teacher Education Committee; NCATE Council 1985–1986
Robert Saunders	President AACTE, 1985–1986; NCATE Coordinating Board (AACTE), 1984–1986
Dale Scannell	Coordinating Board, 1981; Chair, CAA
Alan Tom	NCATE "critic"; AILACTE board 1980–1987
Christopher Wheeler	Principal Investigator, IRT Study
Joanne Whitmore	NCATE Council (AACTE), 1981–1986
Richard Wisniewski	NCATE Council (AACTE), 1980–1982; Member CAA

PART IV

OVERVIEW

13

David L. Clark

Leadership in Policy Development by Teacher Educators:

Search for a More Effective Future

The outcome of teacher education policy decisions in the 1980s is viewed negatively by most teacher educators. External control of teacher education curricula increased. Testing teacher education graduates to insure minimal competency became commonplace. Several states placed caps on the number of hours in education courses that could be required in accredited programs for teacher certification. Alternative models and programs for entry to the teaching profession were approved. Even policies that would have been viewed as progress by most teacher educators, e.g., requiring an undergraduate major in an academic field, increasing standards for admission to teacher education programs, were approved in a context that was obviously critical of existing programs. The requirement of an academic major was typically linked to restrictions on the number of education courses and the demand for increased entrance standards was an antidote to the perceived low quality of students in the field.

A striking feature of the recently popular policy actions and initiatives in teacher education is the anomalous relationship between them and other emerging issues and reform efforts in education generally and teacher education in particular, e.g:

1. Almost all of the cases in this volume[1] noted that in the period from the late 1960s to the 1980s educational research and development began to produce a convincing conceptual and technical knowledge base about teaching.
1.a. However, the policy outcomes of the 80s de-emphasized the importance of knowledge about pedagogy in the professional preparation of teachers.

2. The recent increased concern for dropouts and at-risk students, expanded educational opportunities for handicapped children in regular classroom situations, and extended educational opportunities to preschool populations would all seem to suggest highly specialized technical training for teachers. Demographic projections for the next two decades indicate that the proportion of minority and poor children who are least well served in current schools will increase exponentially.

2.a. Despite the fact that teaching a student population with special learning needs will surely require more pedagogical expertise, the policy initiatives have focused on increasing the subject matter background of teachers while reducing technical training.

3. The teacher education community, supplemented by leaders from national professional associations, private foundations, government, and higher education have been active during the 1980s in proposing major changes in the design and operation of teacher education programs. The most prominent of these reform efforts, the Holmes Group (1986) and the Carnegie Forum (1986), agreed on the necessity of six basic changes: (a) require an academic major and a bachelor's degree in the arts and sciences for all teachers; (b) develop a new, extended, more valid and rigorous program of professional studies for teachers; (c) integrate the professional curriculum with internships and residencies in schools; (d) restructure schools to provide a professional environment for teachers; (e) increase markedly the number of minorities prepared for teaching careers; (f) modify the structure of teacher licensing to provide for career or lead teachers who can assume broader roles in the redesign of schooling.

3.a. However, with the exception of an increased emphasis on an academic major and school restructuring, the state-based policy initiatives have ignored the reform agendas of the national groups. The most popular state policies have been: (a) testing to control entry to teacher education or teaching; (b) restricting the number of credit hours required in the professional curriculum; (c) providing alternative routes to teacher certification that bypass professional requirements; (d) increasing internship and student teaching require-

ments. State policy initiatives in teacher education have not only ignored the national reform recommendations but have generated several initiatives that conflict with them.
4. Major national structural initiatives are underway to strengthen the accreditation of teacher education programs (National Council for Accreditation of Teacher Education) and the certification of career teachers (National Board for Professional Teaching Standards).
4.a. In contrast, the State of New Jersey debated seriously whether a five-day orientation to the school and to all the important information about teaching was sufficient to launch prospective teachers on their provisional year in the classroom as a regularly salaried teacher (Cooperman, Webb, and Klagholz, 1983). In its final version the requirement turned out to be a twenty-day orientation period. Eighteen-hour caps on professional training (e.g., Texas, Virginia) make the investment of millions in improving accreditation and certification seem unnecessary.

Lifelong educationists, such as I, are inclined to debate these substantive issues that bedevil the field, supporting the initial propositions noted above and attacking the counterassertions. But the purpose of the cases in this volume, and this chapter in particular, is not to assume substantive positions but, rather, to try to understand the policy process that has led to these anomalous results in the expectation that teacher educators might be more effective participants influencing the policy process in the future.

CONTEXT OF TEACHER EDUCATION POLICY IN THE 1980s

The contemporary policy context for education in the 1980s was influenced by a change in Federal educational policy with the election of President Reagan in 1980, but also reflected longer term public and professional attitudes toward teacher education.

Lack of Public Confidence

Wisniewski's citation of Stoltz' (1979) comments in a study by the Southern Regional Education Board (SREB) captured the public mind of the 1980s regarding teacher education:

If a state administers a competency test to all of its high school graduates and finds an unacceptably large number are failing the test, isn't it quite possible that poor teaching might have been a contributor to that failure? (1979, p. 1)

Stoltz, and the public generally, believed that the answer to that question was yes and that the cause of the poor teaching was attributable, at least in part, to the system of teacher education (admission, training, certification) that produced them. Whether the public and the policy makers were right or wrong it seems clear that confidence in the system of teacher education in the United States was low—so low, in fact, that policy makers could sustain the argument that less attention to pedagogical content would improve the education of teachers. This lack of confidence also reduced the credibility of any proposals for reform that were viewed as originating with the teacher education community. The basic policy position of the field was one of vulnerability.

Criticism by Clients

Supporting the low public confidence in teacher education was the criticism of teacher training by teachers in the field. In Oregon, for example, "only 10 percent of the teachers surveyed felt they had experienced a truly excellent teacher education program" (p. 113). Legislators always place high confidence in negative comments from insiders. In fact, Biddle's and Joseph's question from the chair of the education committee in Ohio reflects a problem plaguing the field, "don't you [teacher educators] have any friends?" (p. 102). If the individual client of schools, colleges, or departments of education (SCDEs) is the teacher, their corporate clients are school boards, school administrators, and professional associations of teachers. However, in the several state cases, associations representing school boards and administrators were almost always critical of institutions of higher education and both the state affiliates of the National Education Association (NEA) and the American Federation of Teachers (AFT) were mercurial allies. Teacher educators could not rely on the educationist community to join with them to parry legislative incursions into the field.

Low Status Within the University

An even stranger problem to outsiders is the lack of support for teacher education within the university community. Arts and sciences faculties are routinely critical of professional departments and schools of education. University administrative officers buckled in state after state (e.g., New Jersey, Ohio, Texas, Virginia, Wisconsin) when the interests of the university budget or legislative program appeared to be jeopardized by a defense of the interests of the school of education. Teacher education is a low-status program on college campuses. As an example, contrast what happened to attacks on the academic integrity of teacher education programs to the university's response when the Professional Standards Commission in New Mexico foolishly undertook to cut back on academic field requirements for teachers (see Colton and Simmons). The most dramatic example of the tenuous status of education schools and colleges within the university is provided in the brief update on developments in Oregon. Faced with budgetary reductions, the president of Oregon State University proposed closing the college of education altogether. At the University of Oregon, the teacher education program was dropped. The chancellor of the Oregon State System of Higher Education stated that Portland State University (an obviously lower-status academic setting) would become the major education program in Oregon.

Divided Teacher Education Community

What would seem to be the last bastion of support for the interests of teacher education? How about teacher education academic units themselves? Unfortunately, from at least a political point of view, the teacher education community is so widespread and diverse that any proposed policy change advantages or disadvantages a significant number of participants. The qualitative improvements proposed by the Holmes Group and Carnegie Forum (e.g., the establishment of professional development schools) threatened the status quo in a larger number of SCDEs than the caps on credit hours in teacher education. When states attempted to put together alliances of their state-based associations of colleges for teacher education they discovered, for example in Ohio, that subgroups, in that case the Ohio Association of Private Colleges for Teacher Education, would not oppose the threatening legislation. With teacher education programs spread across 1300 higher education sites in the United States, in institutions that range from baccalaureate level to research-oriented doctoral study, it is unsurprising that this diversity breeds remarkable divisiveness on policy issues in the field.

Position of Hierarchical Subordination in State-Level Policy Development

An often overlooked contextual feature of SCDEs is their legal and organizational subordination in the hierarchical structure of education as a state function. As the faculty and administration of the University of Wisconsin learned, the state certifies teachers and accredits teacher education programs. If they happen to loosen the reins on teacher education units in one period of time, it is the choice of the state policy maker to have done so. The authors of the Virginia case commented on the "essential powerlessness of the teacher education community." That is true and it derives in the final analysis from a well-defined organizational position in the hierarchy. Schools, colleges, and departments of education are subordinate in teacher education policy to state boards of education, governors' offices, state legislatures, in some states to higher education commissions, and, in most states, to some units within the state department of education or, as in California, to an independent regulatory commission charged with responsibility for teacher preparation and licensing. On campus, of course, they are subordinate to the president's office and usually the graduate school.

New Popular National Agenda for Educational Improvement

A peculiar characteristic of the 1980s was the uniformity in educational policy across states that was provoked by the federal government's decision to foster devolution in its programs and policies. Devolution was expected to foster diversity. In practice, although devolution stimulated vigorous action in educational policy at the state level, relatively uniform national trends developed. A part of the reason for this was that national organizations of state officials moved educational policy to the top of their agendas, i.e., National Governors Association, National Conference of State Legislatures, and the Education Commission of the States, so that interstate agreements on the direction of educational reform were negotiated. A part of the reason was that although the federal government withdrew from the administration and control of some educational programs, it continued to assert and support solutions to educational problems from its available "bully pulpit." In teacher education, then, state activity commonly included higher requirements for entering teacher education programs, alternative routes to teacher education, teacher competency testing, career ladders for teachers, reduced instructional hours in pedagogy, and, more recently, restructuring schools—especially site-based management.

Wisniewski's discussion of the role of the SREB in shaping the policy agenda for change in the southern states in the 1980s illustrates how interstate policy grows, spreads, and reflects the national mood in educational policy. The Southern Regional Education Board along with other policy analysts and agencies: (a) reflected the public mood, (b) disseminated and added credibility to existing solutions that were being tried in several locations, (c) validated the severity of problems in the affected area, and (d) conjectured about alternative solutions (sometimes outright inventions) that enriched the pool of available alternatives. Since policy analysts tend to read one another's reports, even when policy makers are ignoring them, the analysts do arrive at an early consensus about the range of viable solutions that are worth disseminating. There is, as Wisniewski noted, a touch of the "agent provocateur" in the world of the policy analyst as they inventory, invent, predict, and assess future options in a field.

Complex Intraprofessional Agenda for Improvement in Teacher Education

There is a final characteristic of the teacher education field in the 1980s that seems to have affected what occurred. The external changes imposed on the field had greater currency than any agenda being developed by the profession itself. The package of external solutions had an integrality, simplicity, and feasibility that was appealing to policy makers. The problem was defined as inadequate preparation programs for teachers and below-average candidates for teacher education and teaching. The solution was to reduce or replace the training programs, test at entry and exit points, and tap pools of potential candidates who had not previously been recruited to the field. The vehicles to carry out the solutions fitted policy options that can be exercised at the state level, i.e., manipulate entry and exit standards, specify program quantity and emphasis, and establish alternative routes to teaching for new sources of candidates. Overall, the solutions had an efficacious side effect to those who lacked confidence in teacher educators, i.e., control of teacher education was wrested from those who had messed it up in the past.

The internally generated reform agendas exhibited integrality but scored low on currency, simplicity, and feasibility. The profession's most visible national agenda was represented by the Holmes and Carnegie reports. These ventures called for enrichment and improvement of pedagogical content rather than its reduction, intricate restructuring of the field-based component of teacher education, an extended and more expensive period of training and, most problematically, institution-by-institution reform in the hands of those who were perceived as having failed in the first place. The intraprofessional agenda was also obviously more costly than current practice to both training institutions and trainees, while the extra-institutional proposals were low to no cost.

The contextual characteristics within which teacher education policy was played out in the 1980s included:

1. A "public mind" that had little confidence in the process or products of the system for teacher preparation in the United States, coupled with great concern about the consequences of a low-quality public education system.

2. A divided educationist community that reinforced the public mind with its own doubts about how teachers were being prepared.

3. A higher education setting in which teacher education has always been defined as a low-status endeavor.

4. A teacher education community characterized by divisiveness about how to operate and/or change the structure and content of teacher education.

5. A field that is legally and organizationally vulnerable to control within the college and university in which it exists and within the state that sanctions its processes and products.

6. A national agenda for change in teacher education that developed during the decade and included a set of solutions to existing problems that appeared to be simple, feasible, and effective.

7. A competitive professional agenda for change in teacher education that did not fit the public mind toward teacher education and appeared to be complicated, difficult to implement, expensive, and problematic in effectiveness.

Procedural Features of Teacher Education Policy in the 1980s

The case studies dramatized a range of processes that occurred repeatedly across states as teacher educators attempted to involve themselves in policy development in the reform of their field. Some of these features are generic to policy processes in any era or any field; others seem either time bound or particularly characteristic of the teacher education community.

Accepting a Defensive Posture in the Policy Debate

Political reformers need weaknesses and enemies on which to focus. Ishler, for example, noted that Ross Perot's enemy in the school battle in Texas was school administration, particularly superintendents and school boards. Teacher educators just "popped up" in that instance as teachers in the field complained about the quality of their training. Teacher educators were such easy targets as the key reason for low-quality teaching that anyone interested in improving teaching would have been foolish to pass them by. They could be isolated as a target without attacking two million teachers and two national teachers' associations. They were low-status operatives in their own institutions. They were self-interested participants in the policy debate. None of the cases in this volume discovered an actor in the political scene soliciting suggestions or recommendations from an education professor or school of education. When they did testify or publish a policy paper, it was to rebut or redirect the flow of popular solutions already under consideration. The last presidential election stands as a convincing example of the impossibility of operating from a defensive posture. There is always one more charge with which to deal—one more instance in which your credibility and trustworthiness can be challenged.

Inheritance of the Agenda of Issues

Off the base of a defensive posture, the opposition is always framing the issues. If low-quality teaching is the problem, is an alternative route to teaching the solution? That is probably not the first solution that would occur to most people. However, if the framer of the issue finds alternative routes an interesting proposal, (s)he will attach it to core problems. For example, in the New Jersey case the state education agency linked the alternative route to qualitative improvement in teacher preparation. Proponents claimed that the alternate route would attract better candidates and would guarantee that even teachers employed under New Jersey's emergency certification procedure would get some formal preparation. Alternate route proposals were attached to positive symbols, i.e., competition, economy, reform. Teacher educators were left with monopoly, high expense, the status quo. In case after case the issue was framed by those who were dissatisfied with the status quo and were outside the establishment. Those inside the establishment who were equally dissatisfied with the existing conditions found themselves arguing against an eighteen-hour cap rather than arguing for an extended program in pedagogical studies.

Malfunctioning Early Warning System

If teacher educators had an early warning system that would have caused them to be alert to legislative incursions in their territory, it was malfunctioning. In case after case the reports are similar, e.g., the teacher education community was caught off guard, came in too late; the deans were incredulous that anyone would challenge the accepted ways of handling teacher licensure; by 1988, the handwriting was on the wall but most were not looking; school of education faculty and administrators heard what they wanted to hear. The signals of dissatisfaction were not difficult to discern. The several SREB reports issued from 1979 to 1981 predicted almost all of the challenges that teacher education would confront in the coming decade.

Nonetheless, teacher educators were unprepared. They squandered response time by misassessing the scope of the threat. They arrived at the game too late, with too little. This confirmed their position on the defensive and made them appear to be obstructionists when they attempted to reframe issues or suggest solutions.

History of Program Ineffectiveness and Conservatism

Teacher educators were carrying a history of ineffective program performance and resistance to change into these policy discussions. How difficult it must be for policy makers to understand the extremely negative reaction of teacher educators to the eighteen-hour cap on education courses when that has been the mode in secondary education teacher preparation for fifty years. If there was a need for expanded life space for pedagogical instruction in the teacher education curriculum, why had teacher educators been unable to convince their academic colleagues on campus of the need? If teacher educators were concerned about the quality of teachers and teaching why had admission standards to teacher education been set so low? Why had program standards been so low that, almost literally, any college or university that wished to have a professional curriculum in teacher education could obtain state program approval and national accreditation? If pedagogical instruction was important in classroom performance why did almost all states have a history of meeting teacher shortages by emergency certification that waived teacher training requirements? Why did teacher educators stand on the sidelines in the debate over academic majors and liberal arts education for teachers? Did they actually believe that academic preparation equivalent to that at the baccalaureate level was unnecessary for teachers? The author of the Oregon case lamented that even in the mid-1980s "education faculties were extremely slow to respond to the growing external demands for reform" (p. 119).

Of course there were intraprofessional reformers who were active during this same period. The Holmes and Carnegie reports sided with those who sought to upgrade academic standards. The redesign of the National Council for the Accreditation of Teacher Education (NCATE) was underway throughout the decade. However, policy makers are impressed by accomplishments not promises of accomplishment. They observed the divisiveness of the teacher education community around its own reform proposals. A practical policy maker had to believe that intraprofessional reform was less likely to occur than reform imposed on the field.

During the 1980s, teacher educators were hard pressed to defend themselves against the basic charges leveled at the field, i.e., they accept weak candidates, many of them pursue less rigorous curricula than their liberal arts counterparts, and many of the 1200 to 1300 state-approved programs are operating with minimal resources on low-status campuses and are routinely held in low regard by university departments on major campuses.

Paucity of Relevant Counterevidence

As Gideonse noted in the preface to this document, what teacher educators did not know weakened their policy stance as alternative policies arose. Bits and pieces of crude data, e.g., SREB's *An Analysis of Transcripts of Teachers and Arts and Sciences Graduates*, became influential sources in support of caps on education courses and increases in academic studies. Those data were used not only to support alternative policies but to suggest the lack of responsiveness to change in teacher education. In contrasting the findings with a 1961 report, the writers noted, "how little has changed" (Galambos, Cornett, and Spitler, 1985, p. 85).

Barr observed that "teacher educators have...failed to use their research and evaluation skills to document their successes, identify problems, and improve their programs" (p. 127). From whatever perspective one examines teacher education, there are massive deficits in data:

- Routine demographic data are unavailable.
- Evaluation studies on program outcomes are rare.
- Research studies on teaching behaviors of program graduates across programs and between trainees in regular and alternative programs are unavailable.
- Policy studies that would clarify the likely consequences of policy choice options are missing.
- In-depth descriptions of programs that could be used to increase public and professional understanding of what goes on in programs at varying quality levels have been unavailable.
- Routine studies of cost and output in teacher training have been rare.

Teacher educators in the 1980s found themselves debating the efficacy of their practices with an information base that was lean, seldom applicable directly to individual state situations, incomplete, and not designed for policy makers. Confronted with straightforward requests for data they were responding with inadequate and often obscure guesses.

Educational Value Changes

The Reagan administration brought a set of value changes in education to the federal level that were reflected in state-level educational policy. The new administration eschewed educationists. They focused concern on achievement in a narrowly defined set of "hard" subjects. Equity and access were deemphasized as policy objectives in favor of excellence and selectivity. When teachers and teaching were on the agenda the topics were likely to be career ladders or merit rating or the negative effect of teacher unions on educational productivity. Parental choice of schools was of greater concern than the condition of the country's common school heritage. Standardized testing was assumed to be the bottom-line measure of school and student success. Competition was encouraged among students, teachers, schools, and the public and private sectors in schooling. Alternate routes to teaching and administrative positions were encouraged and supported with examples drawn from successful private school settings.

The Reagan preferences in education were not the president's invention. They were consistent with expressed preferences about educational policy choice options in public opinion polls dating back to the late 1960s. The populist support for the general educational reform called for in *A Nation at Risk* lent strength to state level proposals designed to emphasize testing, mandated achievement levels, concentration on core content courses, and competition. Educationists, as a group, were out of synchronization with these new policy directions since they had worked for a quarter century with a liberal coalition at the federal level that had emphasized what had now become minority policies.

Lobbying Without Lobbyists

The cases noted the disadvantage confronting teacher education advocates because they were not available, or not included, or not prepared to put together data for a rebuttal overnight. At the state level many educationist groups are represented routinely in the legislature—universities and colleges, classroom teachers, school boards, and school administrators. Most of these groups express casual and sporadic interest in teacher education policy. Teacher organizations have been the one state-level lobby most likely to evidence interest. Their chief concern since the mid-1950s has been the establishment of boards of professional standards and the development and enforcement of basic qualifications for the teaching license. In the current cases, they were as likely to be supporting a policy opposed by teacher educators as one advocated by teacher educators. Higher education lobbies are drawn into teacher education policy occasionally but it is a topic of sufficiently low priority on their agenda that they often withdraw from the fray or compromise the specific interests of their teacher education faculty when the going gets tough.

Direct representation of the teacher education community in policy debates at the state level has been unusual. Where it has occurred the lead has typically been taken by a single dean of education or a small group that remained active for a short time, e.g., the pivotal role played by one influential dean and the Ohio ACTE in that state's teacher education reform in the 1970s. State-based associations of colleges for teacher education are loosely knit groups without full-time executive staffs. When legislators seek timely information on educational policy or when they are provided with timely information or positions of advocacy, they are seldom meeting with school or college of education representatives. Part-time lobbyists suffer from a fatal flaw—"not being there."

Dealing with Absurd Solutions

Colton and Simmons caught the flavor of many of the recent policy discussions at the state level in their quotation from an Albuquerque newspaper satirist, Jim Arnholz (1989):

> Do I have that right? The Board of Education says the University of New Mexico and New Mexico State exceed state standards, which leaves the Board of Education only one option: It won't certify teachers who know too much about the subject they teach.... That has a certain appeal for me. I'm comfortable with it. I'm beginning to feel like I'm back home.

Any interest group that is confronted with solutions which seem orthogonal to the problems in its field of interest is likely to be disoriented, for a time, in its response. This circumstance often leads to dysfunctional reactions while the interest group searches for a common ground for debate that takes into account the group's concerns for improvement and change.

Much of the confusion exhibited by teacher educators in recent policy discussions is rooted in the anomalies cited at the beginning of this chapter. Most teacher educators assumed that everyone knew that a central problem in the preparation of education professionals was insufficient pedagogical course preparation and extremely limited field experience and internships. Life space for teacher education, especially at the secondary school level, has been a part of the reform debate within teacher education for three decades. But in the midst of the effort to extend the preparation of teachers state policy makers injected a new solution—one that seemed orthogonal to the problem, i.e., restrict pedagogical training. Teacher educators were so distracted by solutions such as the cap on education courses and the advocacy of alternate routes that they lost the capacity, temporarily, to offer solutions that focused on what they would define as central to improvement in teacher training. There is a touch of the quixotic in the teacher educator who jumps into a debate on an eighteen-hour cap with the suggestion that this conversation should be about a five-year program of preparation, advanced pedagogical training that is subject specific, a full-year internship, and professional development schools. Recent contacts between state policy makers and teacher educators have been ripe sources of satire and parody since neither could discover easily the problems to which their solutions were attached.

To add to the contextual characteristics noted earlier, teacher education policy processes in the 1980s saw:

1. The teacher education community consistently on the defensive, seeming to play out a posture of self-interest, protecting the status quo.
2. The issues framed by policy makers with little or no input from teacher educators.
3. Teacher educators running to catch up, consistently caught off guard and uninformed about policy options under consideration.
4. Teacher educators reaping the negative effects of having operated low-cost, open-entry, minimal programs for decades. The past inability to mount intraprofessional reform was used to justify the exclusion of teacher educators from the policy debate.
5. Discussions proceeding with little data and information not only because expertise was not solicited but also because the field is data poor.
6. A change in policy preferences at the federal level that de-emphasized professional participation in policy making and refocused the targets of national educational priorities.
7. The disorganized state of lobbying by teacher educators limiting the possibility of effective participation in crucial policy confrontations.
8. The distance between the policy solutions being offered by policy makers at the state level and the policy solutions being advocated by intraprofessional teacher education reformers being too great to allow useful debate and compromise between the groups.

Policy Making in an Organized Anarchy

Thirty years ago Charles Lindblom in "The Science of Muddling Through" (1959) argued that the rational-comprehensive conception of policy development, based essentially on a traditional problem-solving model, missed most of what occurred in the policy process. He noted that the selection of goals and the analysis of needed and feasible actions occur simultaneously; that since means and ends are intertwined they cannot be analyzed sequentially; that the test of a "good policy" is more likely to be agreement on means by policy analysts and policy makers than a demonstrable relationship between the selected means and desired ends.

This argument was pushed further by Graham Allison in *Essence of Decision* (1971). Allison described the traditional view of policy development as the "Rational Actor Model." This view is based conceptually on the existence of consensual goals, clear technology, linear causality, and rational choice. Allison argued, and most participants in the policy process would agree, that the traditional model fails to account for the murky circumstances that surround policy development in the real world. A consensus around goals is infrequent. Individual actors hold tight to parochial goals. Organizational units arrive at goal consensus across units by agreeing to include multiple, parallel goals with which no unit would agree except by necessity. The means available to move toward goals are often uncertain. They are constrained by limits on resources to implement them. They are compromised by the organizational and institutional advantage attached to particular means. In the final analysis means are as often chosen to avoid potential negative consequences as to optimize goal attainment. Allison proposed that an understanding of the policy process could be enhanced by models that included what is known about the organizational process and governmental politics.

The interpretation of what is happening in a policy process and the significance of policy decisions is influenced by the observers' conception of policy development. The traditional or rational model highlights the anomalous nature of the four propositions stated at the beginning of this chapter. If a traditional problem-solving model had been employed by teacher education policy makers in the 1980s, the choice of policy options would have been made after needs and feasible actions had been assessed. In the alternative views suggested by Lindblom and Allison, it should have come as no surprise that the choice of policy options seemed, in some instances, to be only remotely connected to problems in the field. The choice among available options is influenced by such factors as: feasibility, cost, confidence in a particular individual or agency, relative advantage to the proposer, political advantage or disadvantage to needed supporters, the personal influence of a key figure.

Policy options come neither in a predictable sequence nor at the most propitious time. The policy maker or agency interested in raising the quality of entrants into teaching may be confronted not with an analysis of that problem but with an enthusiastic, convincing advocate of alternate routes to teaching who suggests a solution that is attractive to the policy maker. The next step in the process is often rationalizing the solution as germane to the problem. The policy process then is fitting the problem to the solution. If the solution is, on its face, unattractive to some audience, e.g., teacher educators, the exclusion of that group from a discussion of the new solution and the redefined problem may reflect on the attitude of the policy maker toward that group. In this particular example one thing would be certain. Teacher educators would be a bad group with which to start to build a coalition in support of that particular policy option. Pragmatically they would be excluded from the policy process by the advocate of alternate routes to teaching unless there was a compelling personal or political reason for her/him to include them.

A Decision–Making Model

Cohen, March, and Olsen (1976) introduced a decision-making model that reflected the same arational conditions represented by Lindblom's and Allison's alternative views of policy development. Their basic argument was that, "we often have underestimated the extent to which choice situations in organizations involve problematic goals, unclear technologies, and fluid participation" (Cohen, March, and Olsen, 1976, p. 25). Under such conditions, they suggested that the decision process is characterized by the interrelationships of four relatively independent streams of activity, i.e:

1. Problems. In the political context of the teacher education case studies the issues or concerns that represented this category would include, e.g., shortages of teachers, inadequately prepared teachers, the cost of teacher education, inadequate elementary or secondary school achievement that might be linked inferentially to poor instruction.

2. Solutions. Cohen, March, and Olsen defined a solution, in organizational terms, as "somebody's product." The interesting feature of a product is that it seeks a use and a user. In the cases just examined the solutions abound: alternate routes to certification, caps on pedagogical instruction, an academic major, highly selective admissions procedures, entrance examinations, exit testing, improved program accreditation processes and standards, five-year or fifth-year teacher education programs, tightened controls over teacher education programs, extended internships. Solution makers scan the horizon for problems to which their solution can be attached usefully. The match may be less than perfect. The consequences of the attachment may be ignored, obscure, problematic.

3. Participants. Individual players in the actions taken in these cases vary on several grounds. Some of the participants, lobbyists, and legislators are around all the time. Most of those affected are not. However, the full-time players vary in their interest in discrete problems and solutions and their interest may have little to do with the substance of either. Some of those affected, for example university presidents, found that their interest in substantively unrelated but politically linked issues, e.g., the university budget, preempted their concern for their teacher education faculty. Participants float in and out of the decision process in patternlike but unpredictable ways.

4. Choice opportunities. Although opportunities to exercise choice arise consistently, the occasion for most choices is seized sporadically. In legislative and executive actions some decisions have arbitrary time limits, most do not. The condition for choice is described by Cohen, March, and Olsen as "a somewhat fortuitous confluence. It is a highly contextual event, depending substantially on the pattern of flows in the several streams" (1976, p. 27). An influential solution carrier, for example, has access to a much wider range of problems to which the solution will be perceived as applicable. Under such a circumstance (e.g., Ross Perot in Texas or Governor Kean and Commissioner Cooperman in New Jersey) the occasions for exercising choice are multiplied and accelerated. Cooper and Tate noted that the rapid move to change teacher education in Virginia was attributable to maintaining "a consistent cast of authoritative players" (p. 155) throughout the process. Gideonse placed focal emphasis on a set of characters who held the redesign process of NCATE together during a period in which most observers would have guessed that choice opportunities would have been missed rather than grasped. Mastain and Brott contended that the history of reform in teacher education in California can be traced to influential individuals (Fisher, Ryan, Bergeson, Hart) and, equally important, the politics of promoting the legislation required a cluster of key influentials operating across several agencies of government (p. 65).

In a subsequent discussion of organized anarchies as the setting for decision making, Cohen and March argued that decision making in such settings has five basic properties:

1. Most issues most of the time have low salience for most people. A major share of the attention devoted to an issue is linked less to content than to symbolic significance.
2. The total system has high inertia. The energy needed to exercise a choice option is in low supply.
3. Any decision can become a "garbage can" for almost any problem—or for almost any solution.
4. The processes of choice are subject to overload.
5. The system has a weak information base—both historically and currently. (1986, pp. 206–207)

The purpose of introducing arational models into the discussion of case studies of policy in teacher education is threefold. Firstly, to suggest to the reader that efforts to interpret policy processes employing rational models may, probably will, lead to misinterpretations of what has occurred and what might be done about it. Secondly, the context of teacher education makes it vulnerable in the policy process to the serendipitous intrusions described in the Cohen and March model. Teacher education is a low-status field, with amorphous boundaries, claiming a weak knowledge base, operating with a divisive intrapolitical structure, maintaining a tenuous connection to the formal political decision-making process that affects it, while representing a popular, public political theme. Such a set of conditions ought to be characterized by problematic goals, unclear technologies, and fluid participation in decision making. And thirdly, these arational models add a dimension to the description of the contextual and procedural features of teacher education policy in the 1980s.

Leadership in Policy Development in Teacher Education

Three premises undergird this section:

- The results of teacher education policy choices in the 1980s were, on the whole, ineffective choices in support of the improvement of teacher preparation.
- The best-informed, most effective members of the teacher education community were excluded from, or at least uninfluential in exercising, leadership in the debate over policy options in teacher education at the state level.
- The intraprofessional reform movements of the 1980s hold out promise for improvement in the field although they had little affect on political decisions about teacher education policy. They include proposals that are worth the effort that will be required in the current decade to influence public policy in this field.

The intent of this section is to think about ways in which teacher educators who are committed to change can function as leaders in the continuing process of defining and choosing policy options for teacher education at state and national levels. Chart 1 displays two types of features that affected teacher education policy in the 1980s and the properties of decision making that Cohen, March, and Olsen argued were characteristic of complex, arational decision situations. All three sets will be used in conjecturing about tactics and strategies for educators to exercise policy leadership in teacher education. They may suggest much more innovative and interesting proposals to the reader.

Expanding the Political Base

There is no possibility that teacher educators will be a singular, effective political force nationally or at the state level. An example of a coalition that might be successful is provided in the NCATE redesign case study. Teacher educators were joined by the organized teaching profession (both the NEA and the AFT), the state education commissioners (CCSSO), specialty groups within education, and key associations of school administrators (e.g., American Association of School Administrators). The view adopted by NCATE was that an effective governance structure needs four parts—"teachers, teacher education, specialty groups, and public policy and related governing elements" (p. 257). The Congress of Education Organizations suggested in the Ohio case study is another example of a move in this direction and includes all but the public policy participants.

CHART 1
Features Affecting Teacher Education Policy in the 1980s

Contextual Characteristics	Procedural Characteristics
1. Lack of public confidence	1. Acceptance of a defensive posture in the policy debate
2. Criticism by clients	2. Inheritance of the agenda of issues
3. Low status within the university	3. Malfunctioning early warning system
4. Divided teacher education community	4. History of program ineffectiveness and conservatism
5. Position of hierarchical subordination in state-level policy development	5. Paucity of relevant counterevidence
6. New popular national agenda for educational improvement	6. Educational value changes
7. Complex intraprofessional agenda for improvement in teacher education	7. Lobbying without lobbyists
	8. Dealing with absurd solutions

Properties of Decision Making in Organized Anarchies

1. Most issues have low salience for most people.
2. System with high inertia.
3. Any decision can become a "garbage can" for any problem or solution.
4. The choice process functions routinely in a state of overload.
5. The system has a weak information base both historically and currently.

Another alternative or complementary possibility is the organization of a broad-based coalition on a regional basis. Southern Regional Education Board is a good example of the effectiveness of regional policy development. The problem for teacher education in relying on a regional education board is the low status and low public and academic confidence in the field. Regional education boards are very unlikely to serve as effective forums for teacher educators. However, a regional coalition for teacher education, involving some of the same participants represented in the NCATE example, provides a forum for the exchange of information, the assessment of problems, the discussion of alternative solutions that might modify the views of some of the field's most troublesome antagonists. Broadening the scope of the consortium beyond the geographic limits of a single state holds the possibility of involving CSSOs much as they have become involved in the governance structure of regional laboratories.

Linking Teacher Education and Teaching

Political coalitions may provide a forum for political activity and deal with the matter of increasing the salience of teacher education issues within the education community, but they become process without substance if there is not a convincing intellectual and practical linkage between teacher preparation and teaching. The field simply has to press ahead with the functional involvement of teachers in teacher education and teacher education in schooling. Professional development schools, or their equivalent, need to be a part of every training program. Teacher education institutions have to be involved directly in career-long professional development. For so long as teachers and teacher educators seem to be two loosely related communities of practice, each will be beleaguered by criticisms from the other. The heavier loser will be the teacher educator for nothing will be as convincing to policy makers as the assertion by clients that the work of the service provider is either irrelevant, ineffective, or both.

Developing a Reform Platform Within Teacher Education

No one who has ever attempted to achieve this end takes the task lightly. The American Association of Colleges for Teacher Education (AACTE) has struggled to adopt reform measures throughout its history. The Holmes Group has adopted a reform agenda that is national in breadth of representation by institutions but is obviously not a consensus platform among even the eight hundred–plus members of AACTE to say nothing of the total population of 1200 to 1300 SCDEs.

Despite past evidence of lack of success in creating such a platform, this may be the right time to do so. In fact, the Holmes Group may be closer to this end than many of its critics will allow. What does such an agenda need? Firstly, the agenda has to be attuned to some of the contemporary, popular issues in education. As a simple beginning, there is no point in debating the efficacy of requiring a liberal arts education or a subject matter major as the minimal expectation for the preparation of a teacher. Teacher educators who want to engage in that debate have to be ignored, convinced, or beaten politically. The public wants more academic preparation.

Teacher educators who argue against it tarnish the field with an anti-intellectual stance. A few of the popular elements would be less popular with leading teacher educators, for example, entrance and exit examinations and alternate routes for experienced applicants. The agenda has to include these "solutions" in the form least likely to produce negative consequences, e.g., testing that is sensitive to diverse populations and employs multiple modes of gathering evidence; alternate routes that are designed for mature adults, but brook no avoidance of pedagogical instruction and field experience.

Secondly, the agenda must be appealing and defensible from a professional viewpoint. This would call for an expanded rather than a contracted period of pedagogical training, an intensive and extended period of field experience, and an interactive relationship between the university and the schools. These requirements would also raise objections by some teacher educators but the proposed changes have to meet qualitative criteria for improvement that are credible among teachers, university colleagues outside education, and policy makers. Flexibility can be built into implementation of the reform platform while still attacking the issues of public confidence, client satisfaction, and enhanced status in the university.

Two of the properties of decision making should be kept in mind in considering the feasibility of such an agenda, i.e., low salience and high inertia. For example, smaller, baccalaureate institutions have often been described as unable or unwilling to support extended pedagogical training or a mandated academic minor. Examining this issue with the presidents, academic officers, and arts and sciences faculties of such units elicits quite different responses than talking to the two or three faculty involved directly in teacher education. The former audience just does not care much one way or the other if the implementation of the change does not interfere with their recruitment of high school seniors. However, the insistence by a small number of affected teacher education colleagues that such proposals would loose a storm of protest in the higher education community blocks action in a low-inertia system. The actual impact would probably be no stormier than university presidents' reactions to the public policy changes in teacher education of the 1980s. Leaders in teacher education must slough off the appearance and reality of low-quality, low-performing systems or their proposals will atrophy in unnecessary, intra-field compromise and inertia.

Linking Teacher Education to Educational Outcomes

Most policy makers concerned with teacher education have operated on the basis of hearsay and examples. Hearsay needs to be supplanted by evidence. Teacher educators must employ their in-house expertise in evaluation and educational research and development to supply this evidence. Policy makers need descriptions of good and bad teacher education programs. They need depictions of what well-trained teachers can do in the classroom and, especially, how this affects learning and behavior among least well-served student populations. They need evaluation data on the effectiveness of graduates of extended programs. They require testimony from teachers who benefited from training and teachers who are working with students in training programs as mentors. They need to have documentation of the common-sense observation that training improves performance—and this documentation has to provide them with examples they can understand and use in talking to and negotiating with others.

Researchers and evaluators are typically not excited about the pursuit of weak hypotheses. In this instance, however, the pursuit is justified since public policy in teacher education is embracing the weak hypothesis that training in pedagogy is unrelated, or negatively related, to teaching performance. Teacher educators need to spend time and effort preempting the weak current information base in the field and reminding policy makers of past achievements that are jeopardized by current policy decisions.

Committing to the Policy Arena over Time

Policy making is being there. Choice opportunities occur fortuitously as well as planfully. Gearing up to defend oneself in a time of emergency places the actor or agency on the defensive, by definition, and in the position of dealing with adversaries who are strangers.

Teacher educators are not at a stage of professional development where it is self-evident that policy makers will value their services highly or trust their self-assessment of the necessity of their services. Neither are they housed in freestanding entities (as for example universities or school systems) that can present their needs directly to governors and legislators through association representatives. They are dependent units in the university and state education system hierarchies. What does this mean in strategic terms in the policy arena? Teacher educators need multiple points of entry. They need consistently and persistently to work and talk with state education agency (SEA) personnel who are directly involved in certification and accreditation. They need similar entry and dialogue with academic administrators on campus and the legislative liaison personnel in the university. With or without a formal state coalition for excellence in teacher education, representatives from the teacher education community must work continuously with their allies (perhaps, first, by proving they are allies) in state-level professional agencies that maintain full-time educational policy agendas and lobbyists, e.g., teacher, administrator, and higher education organizations.

Where will the energy and interest come from to take on this level of involvement? That is a central concern of policy making in an organized anarchical system. Cohen and March argued that in a system that suffers from a shortage of decision-making energy, the individual or agency that invests time reaps rewards:

- By providing a scarce resource (energy), [it] lays the basis for a claim.
- By spending time on the homework for a decision [it] becomes a major information source in an information poor world.
- By investing more of [its] time in organizational concerns [it] increases [the] chance of being present when something important...is considered. (1986, pp. 207–208)

The energy comes from commitment. The commitment derives from the dual proposition that what is being lobbied is worth the effort and that the health of the field if not its existence is dependent upon public, political support and acceptance. Teacher educators seem currently not to be at that point of commitment in the deployment of their energy in support of reform or political action. That is a dangerous contemporary posture.

Employing Effective Tactics as well as Strategies

There are points in the discussion of policy-making processes when the entire activity appears to take on the structural characteristics of a game. In fact, a game may be a useful metaphor in examining tactics if it is kept clear that public policy consequences are not at all gamelike in the sense of a pastime or diversion. Throughout this document the authors of the case studies have reflected on tactics that work (or do not work) in the policy arena. A final reminder of a few of these effective tactics is in order:

1. Never fall back on status or reputational expertise as a reason why policy makers should pay attention to an argument.
2. Maintain flexibility in negotiating positions. Assume nothing as self-evident.
3. Never give up. Today's policy setback is nothing more than a redefined position for future negotiation.
4. While maintaining flexibility in negotiation be a true believer in the efficacy of your product.
5. Involve policy makers and dissidents within the profession in discussions of the problems and issues of the field. Their participation will soften rather than harden their position.
6. Overprepare for casual as well as formal meetings with policy makers. Assume that they are very smart but not very knowledgeable.
7. Find ways to divert pet solutions by attaching them to relatively unimportant problems instead of trying to beat them down publicly.
8. Try to discover, foster, and work with influential sponsors as well as casual supporters. Over the long haul inside informants and power brokers are needed.
9. Establish teacher educators as the official historians of teacher education and interpret that history to lend credibility to the field. Policy makers prefer documented achievers and problem solvers to either promisers or those who identify problems.
10. Combine exhortation and argumentation with concrete evidence of reform and improvement. Influencing policy making with mirrors has a short life.

An End Note

These cases have presented a picture of teacher education at a turbulent period in its history. No professional can take comfort from actions by policy makers that challenge the basic utility of their professional activity. To suggest that less pedagogical instruction will improve teaching is a challenge that cannot be left uncontested.

On the other side of the ledger there are concrete examples that the field is about the business of reform. NCATE redesign is in process. The National Board for Professional Teaching Standards (NBPTS) is an established entity. The case description of local action based on the Holmes Group recommendations could have been multiplied by a score or more institutions in which the changes being affected reflect the dual concern of excellence in subject matter and pedagogy. The Holmes Group is mounting a statewide demonstration of professional development schools and has a national network of reform-minded universities. Ishler was correct in asserting that, "Our current plight is due to our unwillingness to change teacher education while we were more in control of the process and were not in crisis" (p. 19). But it appears that the lethargy and conservatism of the field is cracking. Reform opportunities exist now that provide teacher educators with a chance to seize the moment, to lead rather than respond, to move ahead rather than to defend an admittedly vulnerable past.

The best prediction is based upon past experience. The best prediction is that teacher educators and teacher education as a field will "miss the moment." AACTE, NCATE, NBPTS, the Holmes Group, the organized teaching profession, and other reform groups pressing for basic restructuring of the teacher's workplace will form independent solution streams that will not find points at which their solutions become viable choice options that can improve the education of teachers. All of us should struggle against that prediction. The teaching profession and teacher educators need to be a unified profession of practice from the point of the selection of entrants through the content and practice of preservice instruction to lifelong professional development. Teacher empowerment and teacher education are linked inextricably. School restructuring and the restructuring of teacher education are dependent on one another. Perhaps it is time for a serious national convocation on teachers, teaching, and teacher education for and by teachers.

Teacher educators need to do much more than improve their skill at the policy-making process. They need a substantive platform for reform that is national in scope, state by state in adoption and adaptation, and district by district in implementation. They need to be an integral part of a redefined profession of teaching.

NOTES ON CONTRIBUTORS

DONALD P. ANDERSON has been Dean of the College of Education, the Ohio State University, since April 1984. He is a Professor of Educational Administration and has served on the dean's staff since 1967. He earned his B.S. degree in mathematics and physics from St. Cloud State University and completed the master's and Ph.D. degrees in educational administration at the University of Minnesota. He serves as Vice-President and Midwest Region Coordinator of the Holmes Group, as Treasurer of the Association of Colleges and Schools of Education in State Universities and Land Grant Colleges, and on the Executive Committee of the North Central Regional Education Laboratory. His current professional and scholarly interests are in the areas of professional development and organizational change.

ROBERT D. BARR is Dean, College of Education, Boise State University, a post he has held since August 1991. Immediately prior to appointment he was, for nine years, Dean of the Oregon State University College of Education. He earned his bachelor's degree from Texas Christian University and his doctorate from Purdue University. Prior to going to Oregon, he was Professor of Education and Director of Teacher Education at Indiana University. His books include *Defining the Social Studies*, *The Nature of the Social Studies*, and one of the *Phi Delta Kappan* bicentennial series, *Alternatives in Education*. He has received two national awards for Oregon's Beginning Teacher Warranty Program.

JAMES BIDDLE, Associate Professor of Education at the University of Dayton, has been an active participant in Ohio's teacher education policy discussions since 1976. He earned his baccalaureate degree at Bob Jones University, his M.Ed. at the University of Cincinnati, and his doctorate at the Ohio State University. Having served as president of the Ohio Association of Private Colleges for Teacher Education, chairperson of the Ohio Teacher Education and Certification Advisory Commission as well as a member of three State Department of Education task forces, Dr. Biddle has recently become president-elect of the Ohio Association of Colleges for Teacher Education (OACTE). He also serves on OACTE's Government Relations Committee.

RALPH BROTT is the Curriculum Director at the American School Foundation in Mexico City. He has over twenty years of administrative and teaching experience in middle and high schools in the San Francisco Bay Area and abroad. He holds a B.A. in chemistry and a M.A. in physical sciences from San Francisco State University and a Ph.D. in educational administration from the University of California, Berkeley. Dr. Brott originally started studying California's teacher credentialing system in 1983 while working as a research associate with the PACE project and continued his research in writing his dissertation, "The Cyclical Nature of Education Reform: A Case Analysis of Educator Certification in California" (1989).

KEN CARLSON is an associate professor in the Graduate School of Education, Rutgers University. He has B.S. and M.S. degrees from the State University College at Buffalo, New York, and an Ed.D. degree from the State University of New York at Buffalo. He has been Rutgers' Associate Dean for Teacher Education and recently authored, with Jack Nelson and Stuart Palonsky, *Critical Issues in Education* (McGraw-Hill, 1990). He has been Chair of the Rutgers University senate and faculty representative to the Board of Governors, and has also served as President of the New Jersey Conference of the American Association of University Professors. His scholarly and professional interests now focus heavily on equity issues.

DAVID L. CLARK is Professor of Education in the Department of Educational Leadership and Policy Studies of the School of Education, University of North Carolina. He is a graduate of the State University of New York at Albany (B.A. and M.A.) and he completed his Ed.D. at Teachers College, Columbia University. Dr. Clark has served in a variety of professional positions including professorial and administrative roles at the Ohio State University, Indiana University, where he was Dean of the School of Education, 1966 to 1974, and the University of Virginia. His continuing scholarly interests are in organizational theory and policy studies. His research and publications in teacher education have focused on the organization and governance of the field.

DAVID L. COLTON, Professor of Educational Administration, was Dean of the College of Education at the University of New Mexico 1982–1990. He holds a bachelor's degree in history and government and a master's degree in social studies education from Harvard University and has a Ph.D. in educational administration from the University of Chicago. Colton was a faculty member in the Department of Education at Washington University in St. Louis (1966 to 1982) and Director of the Center for the Study of Law Education (1977 to 1982). His publications include *Teacher Strikes and the Courts*, "*Brown* and the Distribution of School Resources," and "Enrollment Decline and School Closings in a Large City." Colton has served on the national board of the Holmes Group and chaired the Government Relations Committee of the American Association of Colleges for Teacher Education.

JAMES M. COOPER is Commonwealth Professor and Dean of the Curry School of Education at the University of Virginia. He received four degrees from Stanford University—two in history and two in education, including his Ph.D. in 1967. He has written or edited nine books, including *Those Who Can, Teach* and *Kaleidoscope: Readings in Education*, co-authored and co-edited with Kevin Ryan; and *Classroom Teaching Skills*. His books and articles address the areas of teacher education, supervision of teachers, and teacher education program evaluation. His articles have appeared in such journals as *Phi Delta Kappan, Journal of Teacher Education, Educational Leadership, Elementary School Journal, Elementary English, Journal of Research and Development in Education, Theory into Practice,* and *Education and Urban Society*. He was previously on the faculties of the University of Massachusetts and the University of Houston.

HENDRIK D. GIDEONSE is University Professor of Education and Policy Science, University of Cincinnati. From 1972 to 1986 he also served as Dean of Cincinnati's College of Education. Between 1965 and 1971 he was Director of Program Planning and Evaluation for the research programs of the United States Office of Education. He has taught at Wheelock and

Bowdoin Colleges and served for a year as professional staff with the U.S. Senate. Professional service has included the presidency of the Association of Colleges and Schools of Education in State Universities and Land Grant Colleges (1983), membership on the Government Relations Committee of the American Association of Colleges for Teacher Education, and appointment to the Unit Accreditation Board of the National Council for Accreditation of Teacher Education (1986 to 1990). His current scholarly and professional interests include standards, curriculum, policy, and reform issues in teacher education, especially the application of specialized knowledge and explicit professional values.

RICHARD E. ISHLER is Dean of the College of Education at the University of South Carolina–Columbia. He received his B.S. degree from Lock Haven University, Pennsylvania, and his Ed.M. and Ed.D. degrees from the Pennsylvania State University. Dr. Ishler has served as President of the American Association of Colleges of Teacher Education units in Ohio, Kansas, and Texas and is a former President of the Teacher Education Council of State Colleges and Universities. He served as Dean of the College of Education at Texas Tech University from 1983 to 1989 during the time the legislation described in his chapter was enacted. Dr. Ishler's current scholarly and professional interests include teacher education reform and school/university collaboration.

ELLIS A. JOSEPH has been Dean of the School of Education at the University of Dayton since 1972. He completed his baccalaureate, master's, and Ph.D. degrees at Notre Dame. He has served as Chairperson of the Ohio Teacher Education and Certification Advisory Commission and as President of the Ohio Association of Colleges for Teacher Education (OACTE). He currently chairs the OACTE Government Relations Committee.

RICHARD K. MASTAIN retired as the Executive Director of the California Commission on Teacher Credentialing in September 1989. He edited the 1988 *Manual on Certification and Preparation of Educational Personnel in the United States* for the National Association of State Directors of Teacher Education and Certification (NASDTEC). He has recently completed the 1991 NASDTEC manual, and is also chairing the Decade of Education, a California nonprofit public benefit corporation, whose purpose is to promote the status of teachers. He graduated from Northwestern University (B.S.), Whittier College (B.A.), Claremont Graduate School (M.A.), and the University of Southern California (Ed.D.).

NONA A. PRESTINE is an Assistant Professor in the Department of Administration, Higher and Continuing Education at the University of Illinois at Urbana–Champaign. Her doctoral degree was completed in 1988 at the University of Wisconsin–Madison with a major in educational administration and minors in curriculum and instruction and educational psychology. Dr. Prestine's dissertation, "Systems Theory and the Struggle for Control of the Governance of Teacher Education: A Case Study," received the AERA Division A Annual Dissertation Award in 1989. Current research interests include cognitive learning theory implications for educational administrator preparation and Essential Schooling restructuring.

MAYNARD C. REYNOLDS is Professor Emeritus, Department of Educational Psychology (Special Education Programs), University of Minnesota. In 1990–91 he held the Guglielmo Endowed Chair in Special Education at the California State University, Los Angeles. His B.S. degree (1942) is from Moorhead State University, and his M.A. (1947) and Ph.D. (1950) are from the University of Minnesota. He was Director of the federally supported Leadership Training Institute in Special Education and of the National Support System for Deans Grant Projects. He is the editor of *Knowledge Base for the Beginning Teacher*, sponsored by the American Association of Colleges for Teacher Education. He is a former President of the International Council for Exceptional Children (1965–66) and recipient of the Wallin Award from the council in 1971.

BARBARA M. SIMMONS, Dean of the College of Education at New Mexico State University at Las Cruces, holds a bachelor's degree in elementary education from Texas Woman's University and master's and doctoral degrees in elementary education from Texas Tech University. Before going to NMSU in 1985, Dr. Simmons was Professor and Associate Dean of the Graduate School at Texas Tech University. Simmons has taught grades K–6 and been a speaker, panelist, and consultant in over two hundred educational settings. Her areas of interest include early childhood education, children's literature, and women in administration. Dr. Simmons' publications include four books, more than seventy journal articles, computer software, and professional photographs. She currently serves on several national committees and is the South Central Region Coordinator for the Holmes Group.

PHILIP M. TATE is Assistant Professor, School of Education, Boston University. He was a researcher in the Commonwealth Center for the Education of Teachers and Assistant Professor in the Curry School of Education at the University of Virginia. He received degrees from the Wake Forest University and Duke University and is finishing his Ph.D. at the University of Chicago. He has published and presented papers on teacher education policy in the *Journal of Teacher Education* and at meetings of the American Educational Research Association and the American Association of Colleges for Teacher Education. Other research interests include the use of case methods in teacher education, definitions of excellence in teaching, teacher evaluation, and the application of theories from sociology and political science to educational studies.

RICHARD WISNIEWSKI is the Dean of Education at the University of Tennessee, Knoxville. He has held faculty appointments at the University of Oklahoma (where he also served as Dean of Education), the University of Wisconsin–Milwaukee, the University of Washington, and Wayne State University. He was also a teacher and counselor in the Detroit public schools. Dr. Wisniewski's doctoral work was in the field of educational sociology, and he has a particular interest in qualitative studies of educational institutions. His research interests include moonlighting among teachers, the education professoriate, and the reform of teacher education.

NOTES

NOTES TO PREFACE

1. They included James Cooper (Virginia), Penelope Earley (Washington, D.C.), Stephen Hazlett (Indiana), Ellis Joseph (Ohio), Steve Lilly (Washington), and Richard Wisniewski (Tennessee).

2. AACTE maintains an important resource the most recent product of which is *Teacher Education Policy in the States: A Fifty-State Survey of Legislative and Administrative Actions*, American Association of Colleges for Teacher Education: Washington, D.C., June, 1990.

3. The concept of "evil" does, however, suggest something of the real stakes, professional and personal, that teacher education politics entail. While for obvious reasons it is not possible to mention specifics, the very process of seeking out and maintaining collaborators for this volume on more than one occasion floundered—and even foundered—on perceived threats to position or institutional circumstance as a consequence of participation in preparing chapters. Indeed, some of the perceived or actual intimidation even raised troubling questions about academic freedom as it applies to the analysis of public policy issues in the teacher education domain. Diligent spadework, however, and a willing professional network managed to assure that many of the most salient of the teacher education policy stories could still be covered in this volume.

4. The original design called for four, but administrative pressures prevented the completion of two that would have broadened the types of institutions covered.

NOTES TO CHAPTER 1

In the preparation of this case study, the author conducted a literature search of Texas legislation that had implications for or that directly mandated requirements for teacher education. Recent legislation, specifically House Bill 72 and Senate Bill 944, is analyzed and described in detail. The author was a dean of education in Texas during the period when these bills were passed and implemented. As a result, he actually lived much of this case study. Drafts of the chapter were read and critiqued by Dr. Charles Funkhouser, Director, Center for Professional Teacher Education, University of Texas at Arlington and Dr. Doyle Watts, Chair, Department of Professional Pedagogy, College of Education, Lamar University, Beaumont, Texas.

Notes to Chapter 2

As Graham Allison magnificently demonstrated in his classic *Essence of Decision: Explaining the Cuban Missile Crisis*, actors involved in public policy issues ineluctably construct their own views of the nature of the policy problem, the motives of the individuals and entities involved in it, and the strategies appropriate to the situation. In the present case, the authors were primary players in a policy dispute. We were the college of education deans in New Mexico's two comprehensive research universities. Our colleges were NCATE-accredited. We were personally active in the Holmes Group and in AACTE and the Land Grant Deans group. During most of the period under consideration one or the other of us was chairperson of the NMACTE. Such affiliations shaped our views, sensitized us to some matters, blinded us to others, and affected our aspirations and actions. Our account of the New Mexico dispute is role-bound. We describe the dispute as we experienced it. That is both the strength and the limitation of our account. Other actors in the same dispute saw it differently and experienced it differently. It simply is not possible for us to present an "objective" or "unbiased" account. We have not tried to do so. However, we have tried to be objective about our own perceptions, i.e., to render them accurately. Such objectivity as we have been able to summon arises from several methodological considerations. First, by writing together we have sought to minimize the reporting of our personal feelings and to focus instead on the role-defined aspects of the issue. Second, wherever possible we have anchored our perceptions in the written record; citations of board minutes, correspondence, reports, and newspapers articles at least provide readers with a sense of the "realities" to which we were responding. Third, we have asked other actors in the dispute to comment on our report—not to assess whether we saw it "correctly" or "objectively" and not to ascertain whether others saw it similarly, but rather to estimate whether our rendition of our perceptions and our actions corresponds with what others thought we saw and did—however weird or unreasonable we may have appeared to them. Accordingly, we thank Don Ferguson, retired NMSU faculty member and dean, and Associate Superintendent Jeanne Knight for reading and commenting on our report. The fact that they did so in no way implies that they concur with our constructions of events or of their significance.

Despite these precautions, the reader still must deal with what is, in the end, autobiography. What we have written is not an account of events; it is an account of our construction of events. Neither more nor less should be imputed.

NOTES TO CHAPTER 3

We gratefully acknowledge reviews of a draft of this chapter by Dr. Irv Hendrik, Dean, School of Education, University of California-Riverside and former exofficio commissioner representing the University of California, and by Dr. David Levering, former chair and member of the commission representing higher education faculty.

1. The Ryan Act also restricted the professional preparation components to not more than one-fifth of a five-year program and made provisions for candidates to complete their initial requirements in four years.

2. CTA President Marilyn Bittle had charged that the bill was "anti-teacher," that most teachers already take in-service on a monthly basis, and that they "need assistance and support, not increased insecurity and pressure" (*Sacramento Union*, 11 August 1982).

3. Behind the scenes at the staff level worked a number of influential people. The competence and persistence of David Wright was a critical factor in advancing the commission's position. Senate Education Committee consultant Linda Bond was central to advancing the Commons Commission position, and Senator Bergeson's staffer Gary Jerome was instrumental in gaining compromise and guiding the legislative proposals advanced by the Commons Commission through the legislature.

NOTES TO CHAPTER 4

The author was the associate dean for teacher education and teacher certification officer for the State University of New Jersey–Rutgers during most of the events recounted in this case. He was a recipient of all the state directives concerning the college certification programs and a frequent witness against the alternate route proposal at educational fora, including state board of education hearings. He wrote numerous critiques of the proposal, most notably a seventy-two-page report for the National Commission for Excellence in Teacher Education (Carlson, 1984). The author continues to track the evolution of the alternate route and reviews the reports on it. For the case study presented here, an effort was made to be descriptive and avoid editorializing. The reader can judge the success of that effort. Individuals who reviewed drafts of the chapter included: Catherine Becker, Professor of Education, Montclair State College, and President of the New Jersey Association of Colleges for Teacher Education; William Guthrie, Associate Dean, School of Education, Rider College; Jerome Megna, Dean, School of Education, Rider College; Nicholas Michelli, Dean, School of Professional Studies, Montclair State College; Robert Pines, Director of Field Studies, Montclair State College; and Joseph Smith, Professor of

Educational Administration and former Director of the Alternate Route Academic Seminar, Trenton State College.

1. In time, special education was dropped from the proposal because of protests by advocacy groups that its inclusion defied reason. Early childhood education was added explicitly to the proposal a year later, after being treated implicitly as though it was indistinguishable from elementary education. On January 7, 1990, Cooperman finally succeeded in having early childhood and elementary education combined into a single N–8 certification program.

2. Cooperman told a group of education deans in his office on January 24, 1984, that Governor Kean had directed him to develop the proposal in-house and keep it secret until its formal announcement. The secrecy was such that not even the State Board of Examiners was consulted on the proposal. This board traditionally served as a recommending body for changes in certification requirements, and was comprised of an assistant commissioner, two state college presidents, one county superintendent, two district superintendents, a high school principal, an elementary school principal, a librarian, and four teachers. However, in the month preceding the announcement, business and civic leaders were given private briefings on the proposal (Green, 1984; Woodford, 1984). Several of these leaders endorsed the proposal immediately upon its issuance.

3. During the late spring and the summer of 1984, this writer contacted the members of the Boyer Panel to get their reaction to the alternate route proposal as it was taking final form. All the members said that they felt bound by the promise they had made to Cooperman to avoid becoming embroiled in the debate.

4. Other members of the Jaroslaw Commission were: Robert Marik, vice-president for public affairs at Merck Pharmaceuticals; Jann Azumi, a researcher for the Newark Public Schools; Harold Eickhoff, the president of Trenton State College and the first state college president who had endorsed the proposal; Frank Esposito, dean of education at Kean College and a member of the Kean gubernatorial campaign; Laurie Fitchett, president of the New Jersey Congress of Parents and Teachers; Edithe Fulton, president of the New Jersey Education Association; Bernard Kirshtein, president of the New Jersey School Boards Association; Beth Kitchen, owner of Kitchen and Associates Architectural Services; Marco Lacatena, president of the New Jersey State Federation of Teachers; Clark Leslie, vice-president for operations at Ethicon Pharmaceuticals; Monsignor Thomas Leubking, superintendent of the Trenton Diocesan Schools; Allan Markowitz, a supervisor with the Parsippany–Troy Hills Public Schools; Thomas Niland, principal of Pomona Elementary School; Murray Peyton, board secretary to the Dunellen Public Schools;

Verdell Roundtree, vice-president of the United Negro College Fund; Mark Smith, superintendent of the Chatham Borough Public Schools; James Van Hoven, president of the Independent and Private Schools Association; Helen Walsh, president of Worthington, Walsh and Dryer; William Walsh, president of the Robert Wood Johnson Foundation; and Edward Watts, president of the New Jersey Principals and Supervisors Association.

NOTES TO CHAPTER 5

The authors, as Goetz and LeCompte (1984) suggest, wish to clarify their social relationship with participants and events investigated. To a great extent the authors are participant observers in this study. Therefore, this study represents a relatively narrow perspective. Studies of teacher education development in other states, however, may be reviewed to ascertain a degree of comparability, especially if such studies were conducted by individuals who had roles similar to those of this study's authors.

The authors utilized field-note narratives as artifacts. Participant observations were analyzed, documents were reviewed, and in-depth focused interviews were conducted.

Interpreting qualitative research requires "researchers to shift gears and think in new ways, it forces them to take a stand on the significance of their activities of the past months and years" (Goetz and LeCompte, 1984, p. 197). Thus, the authors of this study have gone beyond a mere recitation of bare facts.

Interviews and reviews were conducted with: Mr. M. B. Morton, formerly Assistant Superintendent of Public Instruction in the Ohio Department of Education; Mr. Robert Ritchie, formerly Superintendent of Fairborn Schools; and Mr. Paul Ressler, formerly Director of Personnel, Dayton Public Schools. These three individuals represent living attendees of seminal teacher education policy conferences held 30 years ago.

NOTES TO CHAPTER 6

A survey was conducted in which all of the major reports, surveys, and documents were collected and interviews held at the Teacher Standards and Practices Commission, the Oregon State System of Higher Education chancellor's office, the Oregon Legislature, and the Oregon Education Coordinating Commission. The author relied heavily on his personal files and notes. During the 1980s, the author served two terms as the representative of the Oregon State System of Higher Education on the Teacher Standards and Practices Commission, a position that placed him in close working relationship with most of the influential individuals in Oregon involved in teacher education reform. Holly Zanville, Associate Vice-Chancellor for Academic Affairs, the Oregon State System of Higher Education, and David

Myton, Executive Director, Teacher Standards and Practices Commission, read and critiqued the chapter in draft form.

Notes to Chapter 7

James W. Dyke, Secretary of Education, Commonwealth of Virginia, and Thomas A. Elliott, Division Chief for Compliance Coordination, Virginia Department of Education, read and reviewed this chapter in draft form.

Notes to Chapter 9

I gratefully acknowledge the contributions of Dr. Thomas Stephens and Dr. Victor Rentel, both Associate Deans of the college of education, Ohio State University, who read and critiqued drafts of this chapter.

Notes to Chapter 10

The development of this paper had the advice of Edwin Martin, formerly head of the Bureau of Education for the Handicapped and presently, President, National Center on Employment and Disability, Albertson, NY; and of Evelyn Deno, formerly Director of Special Education, Minneapolis Public Schools and Professor, Special Education, University of Minnesota. Their suggestions are gratefully acknowledged, but they should not be held accountable for what is said in the paper, which is totally the responsibility of Maynard Reynolds.

1. Federal law now mandates special education and related services for handicapped students ages three through twenty-one; in addition, federal funds are available to help support programs for children below age three down to birth, on a permissive basis.

2. The exact reference of the "eight million" is not fully clear. To the extent that it referred to all children newborn through age twenty-one, it may have been realistic. If it referred only to school-age children, the figure was very high.

Notes to Chapter 11

My thanks to Mark Musick, President of SREB, Lynn Cornett, Vice President for State Services, and Robert Stoltz, Vice President for Educational Policies, for sharing their perceptions of the agency's history and work, and especially to Lynn Cornett for assembling SREB's documents on teacher education. Dean Alphonse Buccino of the University of Georgia and Professor John Folger of Vanderbilt University also commented on the paper. None of these persons are responsible for any of the views expressed. My thanks also to Elisabeth Wright for her assistance.

Notes to Chapter 12

This case study is based on three data sources. The small amount of published material was located and reviewed. All the pertinent records of the NCATE Council and Coordinating Board and the AACTE Board of Directors were read. The third data source, tapped twice, took the form of thirty-five one-hour-plus telephone interviews with virtually every one of the principal protagonists of redesign or its antecedents (see the list of interviewees at the conclusion of the chapter). A draft version of the far more elaborate and interviewee-documented manuscript was mailed to all the interviewees. Responses were elicited and received from all. The present chapter has, for purposes of brevity and reader flow, omitted most of the specific documentation attributed to interview sources. The fully documented version of the case study from which this chapter is drawn is twice the length of the present version and has been filed with ERIC. Copies of the interview notes plus fugitive materials recovered during the course of conducting the case study have been archived at the University of Cincinnati for the reference of future scholars. The author acknowledges the responsiveness of his interviewees, initially and in follow-up. As is usual in such matters, responsibility for accuracy and interpretation are assumed by the author.

1. This document is now fugitive but it remains very much alive in the minds of key interviewees including Chernay, Gollnick, Kunkel, McGuire, Olsen, Sandefur, and Wisniewski.

2. CCSSO invited AFT to apply to NCATE in March of 1986. The petition from AFT arrived in October, 1986, was accepted by NCATE that fall, and the necessary charter amendments making AFT membership possible were adopted in September, 1987.

3. Referred to in the parlance of the day as "the third world," meaning specialty groups and others, a terminology recorded here only for purposes of historical accuracy, because the designation understandably rankled those who were covered by it.

4. A fifth and sixth members of the Salishan Deans, Robert Koff and Myron Atkin, later became deeply involved in initiating what would become the Holmes Group (teaming up with Judith Lanier and John Palmer who had served as members of ACSESULGC/APU's Accreditation Task Force in 1982–83 chaired by Kunkel). The Holmes Group was a development that must be considered exactly parallel to NCATE's redesign. The intensity of the conceptual and planning effort associated with Holmes led to very light participation of Holmes participants in NCATE's redesign; William Gardner was the single exception. The non-involvement of many who would have been perceived at that time as "unloving critics" was probably something of an enabling factor to achieving the redesign objectives in the 1983 to 1985 timeframe.

5. The process of formulating the knowledge bases standards—from modest beginnings starting with the then existing curriculum standards, through an opening wide to new ideas, to a premature narrowing of concept on process/product lines, to the eventual reopening to more pluralistic conceptions of knowledge bases—could have been the focus of a full-blown study in its own right.

6. Subsequent steps after July 1, 1986, connected with the decision to approach implementation in a learning mode were: another careful editing of the standards after pilot use but before full-scale implementation; the revision of examiner training (and the updating of the initial cadre of examiners to bring them up to the new speed); and the revision of Board of Examiner and Unit Accreditation Board evaluative procedures after initial formulation and use.

7. The complete version of this case study filed in ERIC contains a more extensive treatment of the contributions of individuals to NCATE's redesign. Each of the attributions and weightings in this section are based on the many overlapping assessments volunteered by those interviewed for this chapter. As noted, detailed documentation can be found in the extended version deposited in ERIC. Furthermore, one of the anonymous reviewers of the volume noted some discomfort with the character of the material in this section. The point is well taken; it may, indeed, remind some readers of the responses at an awards banquet. Since it so clearly captures the tenor of the interviewee responses, it remains in the text.

8. These assessments, based on the extended responses of the interviewees, may seem unduly positive. The progress of reform was not, as it turns out, completely free of interpersonal strife. During the course of the interviews, from time to time, occasional strong reactions of participants to their colleagues in redesign were revealed. The stuff of major organizational and professional change could hardly be absent such feelings and reactions; they are a part of life.

The judgment to ignore the specifics of such interactions where they emerged is a function of three considerations. First, the processes of triangulation to test the validity of such judgments led to the conclusion, in almost all instances, that the reactions revealed in the interviews were either highly personalized, explainable by differences in context and vantage point, or a function of commitments to move forward that were so deep that sometimes actions that appeared to impede generated overreactive criticisms. Second, at the time of this writing, redesign is an evolving success story, and, even should it in the future founder, it will not be because of any of the handful of sharply critical assessments held by one or more of the participants in redesign itself. Third, these comments are made here because there is an important message about such interpersonal strife in an activity as far-reaching and essentially unsettling as this. The experience of this case suggests the wisdom of reserving judgment when tempted to draw harsh conclusions about the motives or roles of active participants.

Notes to Chapter 13

1. This chapter is based upon an analysis of the twelve case studies presented in the preceding chapters. For ease of presentation, references to specific cases will be made by either author's name or the location of the case.

REFERENCES

REFERENCES TO PREFACE

Gideonse, H. D. (1990). "What we should have learned from recent state regulation of teacher education." *Teacher Education and Practice.* 6(1):7-16.

Houston, W. R., ed. (1990). *Handbook of research on teacher education.* New York: Macmillan.

Shulman, L., and Sykes, G., eds. (1983) *Handbook of teaching and policy.* New York: Longman.

Yarger, S. J. and Smith, P. L. (1990). "Issues in teacher education research." In W. R. Houston, ed., *Handbook of research on teacher education.* New York: Macmillan, pp. 25-41.

REFERENCES TO CHAPTER 1

Blanton, A. W. (1921). *Historical and statistical data as to education in Texas, January 1, 1919-January 1, 1921* (Bulletin 133). Austin, TX: State Department of Education.

Bralley, F. M. (1913). *Eighteenth biennial report of the State Department of Education for the years ending August 31, 1911 and August 31, 1912.* Austin, TX: State Department of Education.

Chance, W. (1986). *The best of educations: Reforming America's public schools in the 1980s.* Washington, D.C.: The John and Catherine T. MacArthur Foundation.

Corrigan, D. C. "Admission and graduation requirements for state approved teacher education programs," College Station, TX: Texas A and M University, November, 1983.

Cousins, R. B. (1906). *Fifteenth biennial report of the State Superintendent of Public Instruction for the years ending August 31, 1905 and August 31, 1906.* Austin, TX: State Superintendent of Public Instruction.

Eby, F. (1925). *The development of education in Texas.* New York: Macmillan.

Funkhouser, C. (1988). "For the record: An editorial review of Senate Bill 994," *Teacher Education and Practice*, 5(1):31–41.

Galambos, E. C. (1985). *Teacher preparation: The anatomy of a college degree*. Atlanta, GA: Southern Regional Education Board.

Governor's Advisory Committee on Education. (1980). *Report and recommendations*. Austin, TX: Governor's Advisory Committee on Education.

Holmes Group. (1986). *Tomorrow's teachers: A report of the Holmes Group*. East Lansing, MI: The Holmes Group, Inc.

Howsam, R. B., Corrigan, D. C., Denemark, G. W., and Nash, R. J. (1986). *Educating a profession*, Bicentennial Commission report on Education for the Profession of Teaching. Washington, D.C.: American Association of Colleges for Teacher Education.

Ishler, R. E. (1988). "Teacher education Texas style," *Action in Teacher Education*, x (3), Fall 1988.

Lindsey, M., ed. (1961). *New horizons for the teaching profession*. Washington, D.C.: National Education Association.

McNeil, L. (1987). "The politics of Texas school reform," in W. Boyd and C. Kerchner, eds., *The politics of excellence and choice in education: The 1987 yearbook of the Politics of Education Association*. New York: Falmer Press.

National Governors' Association (1986). *Time for results: The governors' 1991 report on education*. Washington, D.C.: Author.

Reynolds, M. C., ed. (1989). *Knowledge base for the beginning teacher*. Washington, D.C.: American Association of Colleges for Teacher Education.

Task Force on Teaching as a Profession (1986). *A nation prepared: Teachers for the twenty-first century*. New York: Carnegie Forum on Education and the Economy.

Texas (1987). Senate Bill 994.

References to Chapter 2

Allison, G. (1971). *Essence of decision: Explaining the Cuban missile crisis*. Boston: Little, Brown.

Arnholz, J. (3 October 1989). "Back home and playing catch up." *Albuquerque Journal*, p. B1.

Byrne, D. and Colton, D. Letter to the Professional Standards Commission. 17 November 1983.

Colton, D. Letter to A. Morgan. 12 March 1985.

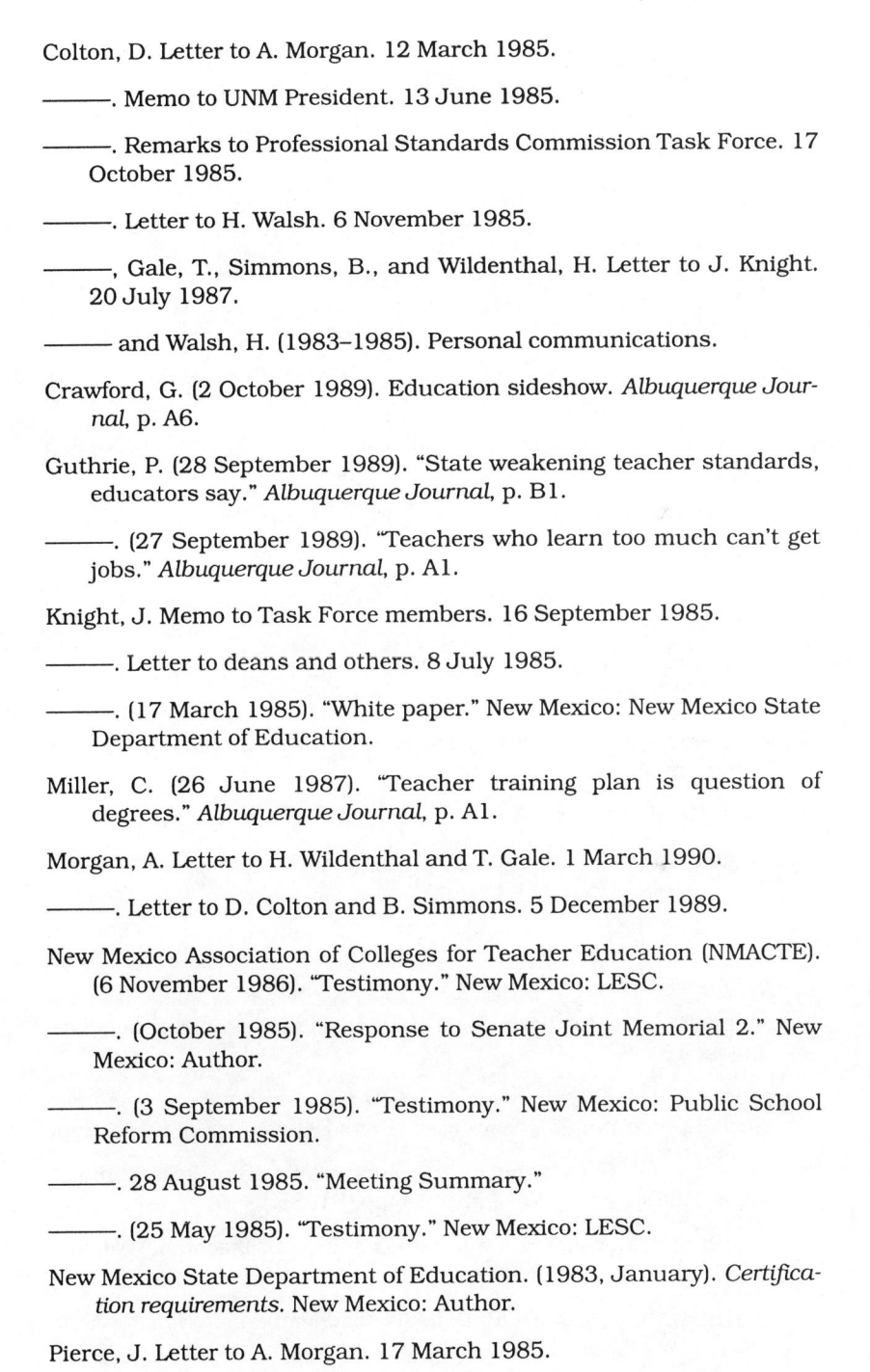

———. Memo to UNM President. 13 June 1985.

———. Remarks to Professional Standards Commission Task Force. 17 October 1985.

———. Letter to H. Walsh. 6 November 1985.

———, Gale, T., Simmons, B., and Wildenthal, H. Letter to J. Knight. 20 July 1987.

——— and Walsh, H. (1983–1985). Personal communications.

Crawford, G. (2 October 1989). Education sideshow. *Albuquerque Journal*, p. A6.

Guthrie, P. (28 September 1989). "State weakening teacher standards, educators say." *Albuquerque Journal*, p. B1.

———. (27 September 1989). "Teachers who learn too much can't get jobs." *Albuquerque Journal*, p. A1.

Knight, J. Memo to Task Force members. 16 September 1985.

———. Letter to deans and others. 8 July 1985.

———. (17 March 1985). "White paper." New Mexico: New Mexico State Department of Education.

Miller, C. (26 June 1987). "Teacher training plan is question of degrees." *Albuquerque Journal*, p. A1.

Morgan, A. Letter to H. Wildenthal and T. Gale. 1 March 1990.

———. Letter to D. Colton and B. Simmons. 5 December 1989.

New Mexico Association of Colleges for Teacher Education (NMACTE). (6 November 1986). "Testimony." New Mexico: LESC.

———. (October 1985). "Response to Senate Joint Memorial 2." New Mexico: Author.

———. (3 September 1985). "Testimony." New Mexico: Public School Reform Commission.

———. 28 August 1985. "Meeting Summary."

———. (25 May 1985). "Testimony." New Mexico: LESC.

New Mexico State Department of Education. (1983, January). *Certification requirements*. New Mexico: Author.

Pierce, J. Letter to A. Morgan. 17 March 1985.

Professional Standards Commission. *Minutes of meetings.*

State Board of Education (New Mexico). *Minutes of meetings.*

Taylor, J. P. Letter to G. Thomas. 19 September 1989.

Wildenthal, H. and Gale, T. Letter to A. Morgan. 9 February 1990.

REFERENCES TO CHAPTER 3

California Legislature, Assembly, Interim Committee on Education. Subcommittee on School Personnel and Teacher Qualification. (1967). *The restoration of teaching.* Author.

California Legislature, Senate Education Committee. (1985). Interim Hearing. 7 November 1985.

Cuban, L. (1990). "Reforming again, again, and again." *Educational Researcher,.* 19 (January–February 1990).

Kirst, M. W. (1984). *Who controls our schools?* New York: W. H. Freeman and Co.

Koerner, J. D. (1963). *The miseducation of American teachers.* Boston: Houghton Mifflin.

Schlesinger, A. M. (1963). *Path to the present.* Boston: Houghton Mifflin.

Schlesinger, A. M., Jr. (1986). *The cycles of American history.* Boston: Houghton Mifflin.

San Francisco Chronicle, 1 August 1970, p. 8.

Sacramento Union, 11 August 1982.

REFERENCES TO CHAPTER 4

"Alternate certification for teachers is examined," (1989) *Education Week,* 9(15), 11.

Bloustein, E. J. to Cooperman, S. (1984). Personal correspondence. August 10.

Boyer, E. L. (1984). *Report of a panel on the preparation of beginning teachers.* Trenton, NJ: New Jersey State Department of Education.

Braun, R. J. (1989). "Many paths point way to the schoolhouse." *Newark Star-Ledger,* November 19, pp. 81, 85.

────── (1986). "Alternate route gains as source of teachers." *Newark Star-Ledger,* November 16, p. 1.

────── (1984). "Colleges get time to fix teacher plans." *Newark Star-Ledger,* May 31, pp. 1, 16.

———. (1984). "Teacher training fails state test." *Newark Star-Ledger*, May 29, pp. 1, 14.

———. (1984). "Education chiefs settle teacher training dispute." *Newark Star-Ledger*, October 2, pp. 1, 34.

———. (1984). "Bloustein supports teacher license plan." *Newark Star-Ledger*, January 13, pp. 1, 8.

———. (1983) "Science teacher sidelined." *Newark Star-Ledger*, May 29, pp. 1, 39.

Carlson, K. (1984). *The teacher certification struggle in New Jersey*. ERIC Clearinghouse on Teacher Education (ED 250 315).

Carmody, D. (20 December 1989). "Alternate certification helps to ease teacher gap." *New York Times*, p. B8.

"Confidential PSA survey: The provisional teacher preparation program." (1986). Trenton, NJ: New Jersey Principals and Supervisors Association.

Cooperman, S. Letter to T. E. Hollander, 20 September 1984.

———. (3 October 1983). Testimony to New Jersey Assembly Education Committee and Higher Education Committee.

Cooperman, S. and Hollander, T. E. Letter to presidents of New Jersey colleges. 9 March 1984.

———. Letter to presidents of New Jersey colleges. 30 December 1983.

Cooperman, S. and Klagholz, L. (1985). "New Jersey's alternate route to certification." *Phi Delta Kappan*, 66(10):691–695.

Cooperman, S., Webb, A., and Klagholz, L. (1983). *An alternative route to teacher selection and professional quality assurance*. Trenton, NJ: New Jersey State Department of Education.

Darling-Hammond, L., Hudson, L., and Kirby, S. (1989). *Redesigning teacher education: Opening the door for new recruits to science and mathematics teaching*. Santa Monica, CA: RAND.

Gray, D. and Lynn, D. H. (1988). *New teachers, better teachers: A report on two initiatives in New Jersey*. Washington, DC: The Council for Basic Education.

Green, H. (Executive Director of School Watch). Private conversation with author, 10 July 1984.

Harris, J. Interview with author on 26 June 1990.

Jaroslaw, H. (1984). *Report of the State Commission on Alternative*

Teacher Certification. Trenton, NJ: New Jersey State Department of Education.

Larkin, R. Interview with author on 27 June 1990.

"More alternative paths lead to teaching jobs." (20 June 1990). *New York Times,* p. B7.

New Jersey Education Association. (1986). "NJEA survey of alternate route teachers reveals need for better monitoring and revisions in training." Trenton, NJ: Author.

"New Jersey, in five years, solves teacher shortage." (13 September 1989). *New York Times,* B10.

New Jersey State Department of Education. (1991). *The provisional teacher program.* Trenton, NJ: Author.

———. *Annual report on certification testing.* (1990). Trenton, NJ: Author.

———. (1989). *The provisional teacher program.* Trenton, NJ: Author.

———. (1985). *The provisional teacher program.* Trenton, NJ: Author.

"President praises state licensing plan." (9 December 1983). *The Newark Star-Ledger,* p. 1.

Remington, R. (13 January 1984). "The aid team acts for Rutgers football." *Newark Star-Ledger,* p. 1.

Saul, L. (14 December 1986) "State hails alternative teacher route." *New York Times,* p. 1, section 11.

Smith, J. Private conversation with author on 20 October 1990.

———. (1990). "School districts as teacher training institutions in the New Jersey alternate route program." Paper presented to the Eastern Educational Research Association, February 15.

Weaver, W. T. (1979). "In search of quality: The need for talent in teaching." *Phi Delta Kappan,* 61(1).

Woodford, R. (Vice-President of New Jersey Business and Industry Association). Private conversation with author on 10 July 1984.

References to Chapter 5

Bara, J. Oral remarks, Ohio House Education Committee Hearing. 11 April 1989.

Biddle, J., Gideonse, H., and Joseph, E. "Teacher education in Ohio: Chaos and complexity." Unpublished paper presented at the Ohio Association of Colleges for Teacher Education, Assembly of Chief Institutional Representatives. 19 April 1989.

Blankenship, A. H. and Marquit, L. J. (1970). *The teacher education assessment project.* Cleveland: Educational Research Council of America.

Christman, L. H. (1989). "Suggested amendments to Senate Bill 140." Columbus, Oh: Association of Independent Colleges and Universities of Ohio. Unpublished paper.

Conant, J. B. (1963). *The education of American teachers.* New York: McGraw Hill.

Earley, P. M. and Imig, D. G., eds. (1979). *State associations of colleges for teacher education and public policy.* Washington: American Association of Colleges for Teacher Education.

Essex, M. (1967). *The targets conference.* Columbus, OH: Ohio Department of Education.

Gardner, R. (1989). *Alternative certification House Bill 212.* Columbus, OH: Ohio House of Representatives.

———. (1989b). *The case for alternate teacher certification: Ohio's House Bill 212–118th General Assembly.* Memo to Ohio heads of teacher education. Columbus, OH: Ohio House of Representatives.

———. Oral remarks, Ohio House Education Committee Hearing. 11 April 1989.

Goetz, J. P. and LeCompte, M. D. (1984). *Ethnography and qualitative design in educational research.* Orlando: Academic Press, Inc.

Greene, M. F. (1967). *The Granville conference.* Columbus, OH: Ohio Department of Education.

Hairston, E. H. (1989). *Proponent testimony for Senate Bill 140.* Columbus, OH: Ohio Board of Regents.

Lindsay, M. (1961). *New horizons for the teaching profession.* Washington: National Commission on Teacher Education and Professional Standards, National Education Association of the United States.

Metz, E. C. (1967). *The Findlay conference.* Columbus, OH: Ohio Department of Education.

Office of the Governor's Press Secretary. (1988). *Governor appoints members to "Education 2000" commission.* Columbus, OH: Governor's Office.

Ohio Department of Education. (1988). *Alternative certification routes: Background information.* Columbus, OH: Ohio Department of Education.

Ohio's Education 2000 Commission. (1989). *Education 2000*. Columbus, OH: Office of the Governor.

Schechter, E. M. Oral testimony, Ohio House Ecuation Committee Hearing. 11 April 1989.

State Board of Education of Ohio. (1989). *Milestones: A history of the State Board of Education of Ohio 1956–1989*. Columbus, OH: State Board of Education.

State University Education Deans. (1973). "Ohio teacher education: A position paper." Unpublished paper.

REFERENCES TO CHAPTER 6

Barr, R. D. (1987). "Reform of teacher education and the problem of quality assurance." *Journal of Teacher Education*, September–October 1987.

———. (1985). "Inter-institutional merger: Miracle or madness." *Journal of Teacher Education*, August 1985.

Citizens Advisory Committee. (12 September 1986). *Teaching as a profession: The challenge for Oregon*. Salem, OR: Joint Interim Committee on Education, Oregon Legislature.

Davis, W. E. Personal communication with author. October 18, 1985.

Myton, D. (1985). *Averting a teacher crisis in Oregon*. Salem, OR: Oregon Teacher Standards and Practices Commission.

Office of Education Policy and Planning. (February 1990). *Staffing Oregon's schools for the twenty-first century*. Salem, OR: Author.

Oregon Educational Coordinating Committee. (October 1984). *Teacher training and teacher certification in OR: Some proposals for change*. Salem, OR: Author.

Oregon State System of Higher Education (OSSHE). (September 1989). *Information report: Four and five year teacher education preparation programs*. Salem, OR: Author.

———. (October 1988). *1986–87 education graduate survey*. Eugene, OR: Author.

———. (August 1985). *Profile of 1983–84 graduates of Oregon schools and colleges of education: One year after graduation*. Eugene, OR: Author.

———. (May, 1983). *A strategic plan for the Oregon state system of higher education, 1983–87*. Salem, OR: Author.

Schalock, H. D., and Barr, R. D. (1986). *Wingspread conference on quality assurance and teacher education.* Corvallis, OR: College of Education, Oregon State University.

Schalock, H. D., and Myton, D. "A new paradigm for teacher licensure: Oregon's demand for evidence of success in fostering learning." *Journal of Teacher Education,* November–December 1988.

Teacher Standards and Practices Commission. (1987). *Standards for master's degree teacher education programs.* Salem, OR: Author.

REFERENCES TO CHAPTER 7

Ad Hoc Committee on Teacher Education. (1987–1989). *Minutes.* Richmond, VA: Author.

Association of Colleges and Schools of Education in State Universities and Land Grant Colleges and Affiliated Private Universities (ACSESULGC/APU). (16 November 1988). *Minutes,* Attachment F.

Committee on Teachers and Teaching, Governor's Commission on Excellence in Education. (1986). *Minutes.* Richmond, VA: Author.

Corrigan, D. (1985). "Politics and teacher education reform." *Journal of Teacher Education,* 36(1):8–11.

Corwin, R. G. (1973). *Reform and organizational survival: The teacher corps as an instrument of educational change.* New York: John Wiley and Sons.

Cox, C. (10 September 1987). "More time sought for reshaping of teachers' colleges." *Richmond Times-Dispatch,* p. B5.

Cuban, L. (1988). "Why do some reforms persist?" *Educational Administration Quarterly,* 24:329–335.

Deal, T. E. (1984). "Educational change: Revival tent, tinkertoys, jungle, or carnival?" *Teachers College Record,* 86:124–137.

Drummond, W. H., and Andrews, T. E. (1980). "The influence of federal and state governments on teacher education." *Phi Delta Kappan,* 62:97–100.

Duncan, P., McLeod, A., Oehler, J., and Simon, D. (1989). "Academic prerogative vs. public policy: Will restructure result in better teachers in Virginia?" *Virginia English Bulletin,* 39(2):81–91.

Evetts, J. (1973). *The sociology of educational ideas.* London: Routledge and Kegan Paul.

Gideonse, H. D. (1984). "State education policy in transition: Teacher education." *Phi Delta Kappan,* 66:205–208.

Governor's Commission on Excellence in Education. (1986). *Excellence in education: A plan for Virginia's future*. Richmond, VA: Virginia Department of Education.

Governor's Commission on Virginia's Future. (1984). *Toward a new dominion: Choices for Virginians*. Charlottesville, VA: Institute of Government.

House, E. R. (1974). *The politics of educational innovation*. Berkeley, CA: McCutchan.

Kirst, M. W. and Walker, D. F. (1971). "An analysis of curriculum policy-making." *Review of Educational Research*, 41:479–510.

McNergney, R. F., Buckley, P. K., Herbert, J. M., Knapp, J. L., York, H. L., and Zabinski, D. J. (1988). *Should a master's degree be required of all Virginia teachers? An examination of the issue*. Charlottesville, VA: Commonwealth Center for the Education of Teachers and the Center for Public Service.

McNergney, R. F., Medley, D. M., and Caldwell, M. S. (1988). "Making and implementing policy on teacher licensure." *Journal of Teacher Education*, 3(3):38–44.

Moore, J. (1985). *Five year program of teacher education*. Charlottesville, VA: University of Virginia, Curry School of Education.

Olson, L. (14 December 1988). "Virginia institutions lukewarm on reforms in teacher training." *Education Week*, p. 8.

Ravitch, D. (1983). *The troubled crusade: American education, 1945–1980*. New York: Basic Books.

Roth, R. A. (1981). "External influences on teacher education curriculum development." *Journal of Teacher Education*, 32(5):3–6.

Smith, B. O. (1980). "Pedagogical education: How about reform?" *Phi Delta Kappan*, 62; front cover, 87–90.

State Council of Higher Education of Virginia (SCHEV). (1981). *Final report on the study of teacher preparation programs in Virginia*. Richmond, VA: Author.

Virginia State Department of Education. (1986). *Certification regulations for teachers*. Richmond, VA: Author. (ERIC Document Reproduction Service No. ED 280 848).

Walker, R. (5 May 1990). Teacher education overhaul starts to convince educators. *Richmond Times-Dispatch*, p. C6.

References to Chapter 8

Baldridge, J. V. (1983). "Organizational characteristics of colleges and universities." In J. V. Baldridge and T. Deal, eds., *The dynamics of organizational change in education* (pp. 38–59). Berkeley: McCutchan.

———. (1975). "Organizational change: Institutional sagas, external challenges, and internal politics." In J. V. Baldridge and T. Deal, eds., *Managing change in the educational organizations. Sociological perspectives, strategies and case studies* (pp. 427–448). Berkeley: McCutchan.

Berdahl, R. O. (1978). "Secondary and postsecondary education: The politics of accommodation." In E. K. Mosher and J. J. Wagoner, Jr., eds. *The changing politics of education: Prospects for the 1980s* (pp. 227–256). Berkeley: McCutchen.

Bogdan, R. C. and Biklen, S. K. (1982). *Qualitative research for education: An introduction to theory and method.* Boston: Allyn and Bacon.

Bok, D. (1982). *Beyond the ivory tower: Social responsibilities of the modern University.* Cambridge: Harvard University Press.

Carnegie Commission on Higher Education. (1973). *Governance of higher education: Six priority problems.* New York: McGraw-Hill.

Clark, B. R. (1983). "The organizational saga in higher education." In J. V. Baldridge and T. Deal, eds., *The dynamics of organizational change in education* (pp. 373–382). Berkeley: McCutchan.

———. (1976). "The benefits of disorder." *Change,* 8:31–37.

———. (1971a). "Belief and loyalty in college organization." *Journal of Higher Education,* 42:499–515.

———. (1971b). "Faculty organization and authority." In J. V. Baldridge, ed., *Academic governance* (pp. 236–250). Berkeley: McCutchan.

Corrigan, D. (1985). "Politics and teacher education reform." *Journal of Teacher Education,* 36:8–11.

Corson, J. J. (1975). *The governance of colleges and universities; Modernizing structure and processes,* rev. ed. New York: McGraw-Hill.

Curti, M. and Carstensen. V. (1949). *The University of Wisconsin: A history.* Madison: University of Wisconsin Press.

Dressel, P. L. (1980). *The autonomy of public colleges.* San Francisco: Jossey-Bass.

Easton, D. (1965). *A systems analysis of political life.* Chicago: University of Chicago Press.

Elam, S. M. (1963). "Will Wisconsin accredit NCATE?" *Phi Delta Kappan,* 44:154–159.

Epstein, L. D. (1974). *Governing the university.* San Francisco: Jossey-Bass.

Gottschalk, L. (1963). *Understanding history; A primer of historical method.* New York: Alfred A. Knopf.

Guba, E. G. and Lincoln, Y. S. (1985). *Effective evaluation: Improving the usefulness of evaluation results through responsive and naturalistic approaches.* San Francisco: Jossey-Bass.

Guthrie, J. W. (1983). "A new state model of teacher education." *Teacher Education Quarterly,* 10:1–7.

Hammond, M. F. (1986). "Teacher education and the research university." *Review of Higher Education,* 9(2):193–227.

Hawley, W. D. (1988). "Missing pieces of the educational reform agenda: Or why the first and second waves may miss the boat." *Educational Administration Quarterly,* 24(4):416–437.

Howey, K. R. and Zimpfer, N. L. (1986). "The current debate on teacher preparation." *Journal of Teacher Education,* 37:41–49.

Kennedy, M. M. (1979). "Generalizing from single case studies." *Evaluation Quarterly,* 3:661–669.

Kerr, C. (1972). *The uses of the university: With a "postscript-1972."* Cambridge: Harvard University Press.

Kirst, M. W. (1988). "Recent state education reform in the United States. Looking backward and forward." *Educational Admistration Quarterly,* 124(3):319–328.

Mason, H. L. (1982). "The current state of faculty governance: The 1966 statement revisited." *Academe,* 68:3A–5A.

McLaughlin, M. W., Pfeiffer, S., Swanson-Owens, D., and Yee, S. (1985). *State policy and teaching excellence* (Project Report No. 85–A5). Stanford, CA: Institute for Research on Educational Finance and Governance, School of Education, Stanford University.

Merriam, S. B. (1985). "The case study in educational research: A review of selected literature." *Journal of Education Thought,* 19:204–217.

Millett, J. D. (1978). *New structures of campus power.* San Francisco: Jossey-Bass.

Moran, W. E. (1972). "A systems view of university organization." In P. W. Hamelman, ed., *Managing the University: A systems approach* (pp. 3–12). New York: Praeger.

Murray, F. B. (1986). "Teacher education: Words of caution about popular reforms." *Change*, 18:18–25.

National Commission on Excellence in Education (1983). *A nation at risk*. Washington, DC: U. S. Government Printing Office.

Nickerson, J. F. and Stampen, J. O. (1978). "Political and programmatic impacts of state-wide governance of higher education." In E. K. Mosher and J. L. Wagoner, Jr., eds., *The changing politics of education: Prospects for the 1980s* (pp. 274–281). Berkeley, CA: McCutchan.

Owens, R. G. (1982). "Methodological rigor in naturalistic inquiry: Some issues and answers." *Educational Administration Quarterly*, 18(1), 1021.

Palmer, J. Letter to Wisconsin education deans and vice-chancellors of academic affairs. 18 September 1985.

Passow, A. H. (1988). "Whither (or wither?) school reform?" *Educational Administration Quarterly*, 24(3):246–256.

Patton, M. Q. (1980). *Qualitative evaluation methods*. Beverly Hills: Sage Publications.

Rist, R. C. (1982). "On the application of ethnographic inquiry to education: Procedures and possibilities." *Journal of Research in Science Teaching*, 19:439–450.

Roth, R. A. (1985). "Alternative futures for teacher education." *Action in Teacher Education*, 6:1–5.

Schotzberger, M. L. (1972). "Some reflections on higher education administration." In P. W. Hammelman, ed. *Managing the university: A systems approach* (pp. 13–22). New York: Praeger.

Schuck. R. F. (1985). "As colleges of education face the future—reflections of a friendly philistine." *Teacher Educator*, 20:2–6.

Soltis, J. F., ed. (1987). *Reforming teacher education; The impact of the Holmes Group report*. New York: Teachers College Press.

Stiles, L. J. (1963). "Reorganization accreditation for teacher education." *Phi Delta Kappan*, 45:31–37.

Teel, D. H. (8 October 1985). "Analysis of statutory authority to promulgate teacher education program approval rules." DPI Internal Memo.

Travelstead, C. C. (1963). "NCATE: Yesterday, today, and tomorrow." *Phi Delta Kappan,* 45:38–42.

University of Wisconsin–Madison. (1978). *Self-analysis report.* (Available from University of Wisconsin–Madison, Bascom Hall, Madison, WI 54706.)

University of Wisconsin System Teacher Education Task Force. (October 1984). *Benchmarks of excellence.* (Available from University of Wisconsin System, 1700 Van Hise Hall, Madison, WI 54706.)

Wallenfeldt, E. E. (1983). *American higher education: Servant of the people or protector of special interest?* Westport, CT: Greenwood Press.

Wiggins, S. P. (1964). *Battlefields in teacher education.* Nashville, TN: George Peabody College for Teachers.

Wisconsin. (1966). *West's Wisconsin statutes annotated.* St. Paul, MN: West Publishing Company.

Wisconsin. (1990). *West's Wisconsin statutes annotated.* St. Paul, MN: West Publishing Company.

Yin, R. K. (1984). *Case study research: Design and methods.* Beverly Hills, CA: Sage.

———. (1981a). "The case study as serious research strategy." *Knowledge: Creation, Diffusion, Utilization,* 3:97–114.

———. (1981b). "The case study crisis: Some answers." *Administrative Science Quarterly,* 26:58–64.

References to Chapter 9

Ackoff, R. (1970). *A concept of corporate planning.* New York: John Wiley.

Brudel, J. and Schussler, R. (1990). "Organizational mortality: The liabilities of newness and adolescence." *Administrative Science Quarterly,* 35(3):530–547.

Burkhardt, M. E. and Brass, D. J. (1990). "Patterns of change: The effects of change in technology in social network structure and power." *Administrative Science Quarterly,* 35(1):104–127.

Conger, J. A. (1990). The dark side of leadership. *Organizational Dynamics,* 19(2):44–55.

The Holmes Group. (1986). *Tomorrow's teachers.* East Lansing MI: Author.

Seider, H. (1990). *Advertising pure and simple.* New York: American Management Association.

REFERENCES TO CHAPTER 10

Ahman, J. S., Loomis, R. J., and Kelley, J. W. (1971). *The evaluation of leadership training institutes*. Fort Collins: Colorado State University, Human Factors Research Laboratory.

American Association of Colleges for Teacher Education (AACTE). (1978). "Beyond the mandate: The professional imperative." *Journal of Teacher Education*, 29(6):44–46.

Beery, K., ed. (1972). *Models for mainstreaming*. San Rafael, CA: Dimensions Publishing.

Brown, L., Nietupski, J., and Hamre-Nietupski, S. (1976). "The criterion of ultimate functioning and public school services for severely handicapped students." In M. A. Thomas, ed., *Hey, don't forget about me: Education's investment in the severely, profoundly and multiply handicapped* (pp. 197–209). Reston, VA: Council for Exceptional Children.

Brown v. Board of Education. (1954). 347 U. S. 483, 493.

Boyer, E. L. (1983). *High school: A report on secondary education in America*. New York: Harper and Row.

Campbell, D. T. (1969). "Reforms as experiments." *American Psychologist*, 24:409–429.

Corrigan, D. (1978). "Political and moral contexts that produced PL 94–142." *Journal of Teacher Education*, 29:10–14.

Council for Exceptional Children. (1971). *Basic commitments and responsibilities to exceptional children*. Reston, VA: Author.

Davis, W. E. and McCaul, E. J. (1988). *New perspectives on education: A review of the issues and implications of the regular education initiative*. Orono, ME: Institute for Research and Policy Analysis, College of Education, University of Maine.

Deno, E. (1972). *Instructional alternatives for exceptional children*. Reston, VA: Council for Exceptional Children.

Educational Policies Commission. (1948). *Education for all American youth*. Washington, DC: The National Education Association.

Gage, N. L. and Giaconia, R. (1981). "Teaching practices and student achievement: Causal connections." *New York University Education Quarterly*, 12(3):2–9.

Gallagher, J. J. (1968). Training personnel for special education. *Preparation of personnel for exceptional children*. Reston, VA: Council for Exceptional Children.

Gazvoda, M. W. (1981). "A descriptive and statistical study of Dean's Grant Projects: Federal support for change in teacher education." Unpublished doctoral dissertation. Washington, DC: The American University.

Gideonse, H. D. (1978). "Peer teaching and participation." In J. K. Grosenick and M. C. Reynolds, eds., *Teacher education: Renegotiating roles for mainstreaming* (pp. 121-142). Reston, VA: Council for Exceptional Children.

Gilhool, T. (1982). "The 1980s: Teacher preparation programs, handicapped children and the courts." In M. Reynolds, ed., *The future of mainstreaming: Next steps in teacher education* (pp. 15-25). Reston, VA: Council for Exceptional Children.

Goodlad, J. I. (1984). *A place called school.* New York: McGraw-Hill.

Grosenick, J. K. and Reynolds, M. C., eds. (1978). *Teacher education: Renegotiating roles for mainstreaming.* Reston, VA: Council for Exceptional Children.

Heller, K. A., Holtzman, W. H., and Messick, S., eds., (1982). *Placing children in special education: A strategy for equity.* Washington, DC: National Academy Press.

Howsam, R. (1983). Public education: A system to meet its needs. *Policy Studies Review*, 2(Special No. 1):85-108.

Larry P. v. *Riles.* (1972). Civil Action N. C. -71-2270,343 F. Supp. 1306. (N. D. Calif.)

Martin, E. W. (1974). "An end to dichotomous constructs: A reconceptualization of teacher education." *Journal of Teacher Education*, 25(4):217-220.

Mills v. *Board of Education of the District of Columbia.* (1972). 348 F. Supp. 866 (D. D. C., 1972).

Moore, M. T., Strang, E. W., Schwartz, M., and Braddock, M. (1988). *Patterns in special education delivery and costs.* Washington, DC: Decision Resources.

National Association of State Directors of Special Education (NASDSE). (1973). *Special education careers.* Washington, DC: Author.

National Commission on Excellence in Education. (1983). *A nation at risk: The imperative for educational reform.* Washington, DC: U. S. Department of Education.

Pennsylvania Association for Retarded Children (PARC) v. *Commonwealth of Pennsylvania.* (1971). 334 F. Supp. 1257(E. D. Pa., 1971).

Pugach, M. (1988). "Special education as a constraint on teacher education reform." *Journal of Teacher Education*, 39(3):52–59.

Reynolds, M. C. (1978). "Basic issues in restructuring teacher education." *Journal of Teacher Education*, 29(6):25–29.

Reynolds, M. C., Wang, M. C., and Walberg, H. W. (1987). "The necessary restructuring of special and regular education." *Exceptional Children*, 53:391–398.

Schofer, R. L. (1978). "Cooperative manpower planning." *Teacher Education and Special Education*, 2(1):7–11.

Sharp, B. L., ed. (1982). *Dean's Grant Projects: Challenge and change in teacher education*. Minneapolis: University of Minnesota, National Support Systems Project.

Siantz, J. and Moore, E. (1977). "Inservice programming and preservice priorities." In J. Smith, ed., *Personnel preparation and Public Law 94-142: The map, the mission and the mandate*. Washington, DC: Division of Personnel Preparation, BEH, U. S. O. E.

Sizer, T. R. (1984). *Horace's compromise: The dilemma of the American high school*. Boston: Houghton Mifflin.

Smith, B. O. (1980). "Pedagogical education: How about reform?" *Phi Delta Kappan*, 62:87–93.

———. (1975). "The growth of teacher education: Where to from here?" *Journal of Teacher Education*, 26(2):102–104.

Smith, H. (1988). *The power game*. New York: Ballantine Books.

Smith, J. (1979). *A consumer's guide to personnel preparation programs*. A report of the Teacher Education/Special Education Project, Gary Adamson, Director. Albuquerque: University of New Mexico.

SRI International. (1982). *Local implementation of PL 94-142: Final report of a longitudinal study*. Menlo Park, CA: Author.

White, C. C., Lakin, K. C., Hill, B. K., Wright, E. A., and Bruininks, R. H. (1988). *Persons with mental retardation in state operated residential facilities*. Minneapolis: University of Minnesota, Center for Residential and Community Services.

Will, M. C. (1986). "Educating children with learning problems: A shared responsibility." *Exceptional Children*, 52:411–415.

REFERENCES TO CHAPTER 11

Albright, A. D. and Barrows, John E. (1960). *Preparing college teachers*. Atlanta, GA: The University of Kentucky and The Southern Regional Education board.

Boyer, C. M. (1985). *Five reports: Summary of the recommendations of recent commission reports on improving undergraduate education.* Denver, CO: Education Commission of the State. (ERIC Document Reproduction Service No. ED 305 851).

Conners, M. (N. D.). *21st century schools: A ten year plan to reform our educational systems.* Birmingham, AL: Southern Republican Exchange.

Cornett, L. M., Vice-President for State Services, Southern Regional Education Board. Telephone conversation with author, 4 April 1990.

———. (July 1987). *Teacher education: Action by SREB states.* Atlanta, GA: Southern Regional Education board. (ERIC Document Reproduction Service No. ED 288 817).

———. (1984). *A comparison of teacher certification test scores and performance evaluations for graduates in teacher education and in arts and sciences in three southern states.* Atlanta, GA: Southern Regional Education board.

———. (1983). *Preparation programs and certification standards for teachers of science and mathematics in the SREB region.* Atlanta, GA: Southern Regional Education board.

Currence, C. (June 1985). "New report urges major reforms in teacher training." *Education Week*, pp. 1, 4.

Deighton, L. C. (1971). "Higher education, planning: Regional planning." *The Encyclopedia of Education*, 4:405.

Dowd, G. L. (November 1985). "Educational policy in transition: Teacher education and the foundations of education." [Excerpt] *Proceedings of the annual meeting of the American Educational Studies Association*, Atlanta, GA. ERIC Document Reproduction Service No. ED 268 622).

Evangelouf, J. (26 June 1985). "Panel analyzes education graduates college transcripts, finds weak grounding in liberal arts, urges twenty-five reforms." *The Chronicle of Higher Education.* 30(17):11.

"Failing grade in teacher preparation." (22 June 1985). *Atlanta Journal and Constitution.*

Galambos, E. C. (1985). *Teacher preparation: The anatomy of a college degree.* Atlanta, GA: Southern Regional Education board. (ERIC Document Reproduction Service No. ED 258 957).

———, ed. (1985b). *What works in in-service education programs for teachers?* Atlanta, GA: Southern Regional Education Board.

———. (1980). *The changing labor market for teachers in the south.* Atlanta, GA: Southern Regional Education Board.

Galambos, E. C., Cornett, L. M., and Spitler, H. D. (1985). *An analysis of transcripts of teachers and arts and sciences graduates.* Atlanta, GA: Southern Regional Education board.

Hansen, J. O. (23 June 1985). "Report urges reform in 'declining' quality of college education." *Atlanta Journal and Constitution.* p. 3A.

Haskew, L. D. (1968). "Impact of the Southern Regional Education Board in its first twenty years." SREB: The second twenty years (pp. 61–64). Atlanta, GA: Southern Regional Education Board.

Hawley, W. D., Austin, A. E., and Goldman, E. S. (1988). *Changing the education of teachers.* Atlanta, GA: Southern Regional Education Board.

Miller, J. L., Jr. (January 1967). "The Southern Regional Education Board: Continuity and change." *School and Society*, pp. 184–185.

Redman, C. (25 June 1985a). "Study cites weak general curriculum for education students." *Morning Advocate*, p. 3D.

———. (25 June 1985b). "Two Louisiana University deans criticize SREB education report." *Morning Advocate*, p. 3D.

Reed, C. B. (1978). "Competency testing's policy implications for teacher training." (An excerpt.) *Proceedings of the twenty-seventh annual SREB Legislative Work Conference: Higher Education Perspectives.* Atlanta, GA: Southern Regional Education Board.

Robb, F. C. (1952). "The south and its regional education program." *The Harvard Educational Review*, 22:26–48.

Roth, R. A. (1983). *The reform of teacher education: A review of current proposals.* Washington, DC: U. S. Department of Education. (ERIC Document Reproduction Service No. ED 233 989).

Southern Regional Education Board. (January 1990). "Paying for performance—important questions and answers." *Southern Regional Education Board Career Ladder Clearinghouse.* Atlanta, GA: Author.

———. (1989). *SREB annual report 1988–1989.* Atlanta, GA: Author.

——— (1988a). *Alternative teacher certification programs: Are they working?* Atlanta, GA: Author.

———. (1988b). *Goals for education: Challenge 2000.* Atlanta, GA: Author.

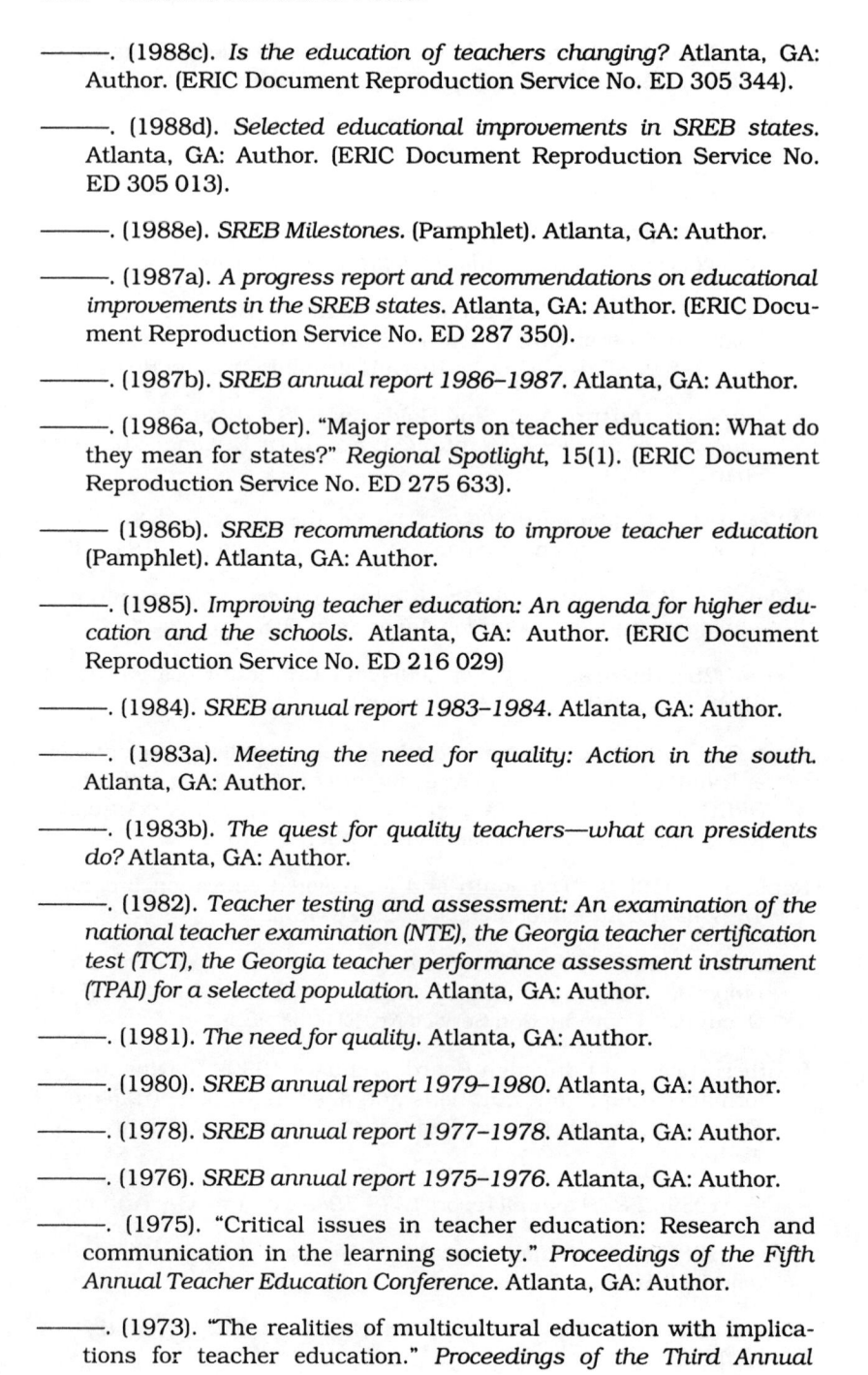

———. (1988c). *Is the education of teachers changing?* Atlanta, GA: Author. (ERIC Document Reproduction Service No. ED 305 344).

———. (1988d). *Selected educational improvements in SREB states.* Atlanta, GA: Author. (ERIC Document Reproduction Service No. ED 305 013).

———. (1988e). *SREB Milestones.* (Pamphlet). Atlanta, GA: Author.

———. (1987a). *A progress report and recommendations on educational improvements in the SREB states.* Atlanta, GA: Author. (ERIC Document Reproduction Service No. ED 287 350).

———. (1987b). *SREB annual report 1986–1987.* Atlanta, GA: Author.

———. (1986a, October). "Major reports on teacher education: What do they mean for states?" *Regional Spotlight,* 15(1). (ERIC Document Reproduction Service No. ED 275 633).

——— (1986b). *SREB recommendations to improve teacher education* (Pamphlet). Atlanta, GA: Author.

———. (1985). *Improving teacher education: An agenda for higher education and the schools.* Atlanta, GA: Author. (ERIC Document Reproduction Service No. ED 216 029)

———. (1984). *SREB annual report 1983–1984.* Atlanta, GA: Author.

———. (1983a). *Meeting the need for quality: Action in the south.* Atlanta, GA: Author.

———. (1983b). *The quest for quality teachers—what can presidents do?* Atlanta, GA: Author.

———. (1982). *Teacher testing and assessment: An examination of the national teacher examination (NTE), the Georgia teacher certification test (TCT), the Georgia teacher performance assessment instrument (TPAI) for a selected population.* Atlanta, GA: Author.

———. (1981). *The need for quality.* Atlanta, GA: Author.

———. (1980). *SREB annual report 1979–1980.* Atlanta, GA: Author.

———. (1978). *SREB annual report 1977–1978.* Atlanta, GA: Author.

———. (1976). *SREB annual report 1975–1976.* Atlanta, GA: Author.

———. (1975). "Critical issues in teacher education: Research and communication in the learning society." *Proceedings of the Fifth Annual Teacher Education Conference.* Atlanta, GA: Author.

———. (1973). "The realities of multicultural education with implications for teacher education." *Proceedings of the Third Annual*

Teacher Education Conference for Black Colleges and Universities. Atlanta, GA: Author.

———. (1972). "Strategies for facilitating self-awareness." *Proceedings of the Teacher Education Conference for Black Colleges and Universities.* Atlanta, GA: Author.

———. (1971). SREB annual report 1970–1971. Atlanta, GA: Author.

———. (1968). *Southern Regional Education Board—1948/1968.* Atlanta, GA: Author.

———. (1965). *M. A. T. programs in the south* (Catalog). Atlanta, GA: Author.

———. (1961). *Within our reach.* Atlanta, GA: Author.

Southern Regional Education Board and Florida A and M University. (1971). *Teacher Education Conference for Black Colleges and Universities Conference Proceedings.* Atlanta, GA: Author.

Stedman, D. J. (1980). *Improving teacher education: Academic program review.* Atlanta, GA: Southern Regional Education Board.

Stoltz, R. E. (1981). *Emerging Patterns for teacher education and certification in the south.* Atlanta, GA: Southern Regional Education Board.

———. (1979). *Teacher education and certification: State actions in the south.* Atlanta, GA: Southern Regional Education Board.

Sugg, R. S. (1963). *SREB: A current appraisal.* Atlanta, GA: Southern Regional Education Board.

Sugg, R. S. and Jones, G. H. (1960). *The Southern Regional Education Board.* Baton Rouge, Louisiana: Louisiana State University Press.

"Teacher miseducation." (June 1985). *Richmond Times-Dispatch.*

References to Chapter 12

For in-text citations, italicized capital letters indicate NCATE Council (*NC*), NCATE Coordinating Board (*NCB*), and AACTE Board of Directors (*ABD*) or Executive Committee (*EC*) minutes followed by the date. All other citations follow the standard APA format.

ACSESULGC/APU Task Force on Accreditation. (September, 1983). *Task force on accreditation report.* Author.

Behling, H. (1984). "Quality control of teacher preparation programs through the program approval process." Washington, DC: National Commission on Excellence in Teacher Education. (ERIC Document ED250300).

Christensen, D. (Winter, 1984–85) "The continuing quest for excellence." *Action in Teacher Education,* 6(4):17–22.

Corrigan, D. C. Letter to D. Scannell. 23 October 1981.

Council of Chief State School Officers. (1984). *Staffing the nation's schools: A national emergency.* Washington, DC: Author.

Currence, C. (24 October 1984). "NCATE debates key changes in accreditation." *Education Week,* pp. 1, 17.

Currence, C. (17 April 1985). "NCATE urges tough standards for education schools." *Education Week,* pp. 1, 16.

Currence, C. (24 April 1985). "NCATE plan praised, but some criticize its cost, standards." *Education Week,* pp. 1, 13.

Flowers, A. Letter to AACTE chief institutional representatives. 9 March 1983.

Gideonse, H. D. (1983). *In search of more effective service: Inquiry as a guiding image for educational reform in America.* Cincinnati: The University of Cincinnati.

Gollnick, D. M. and Kunkel, R. C. (1986). "The reform of national accreditation." *Phi Delta Kappan,* 68(4):310–314.

Gubser, L. (1980). "NCATE director comments on the Tom critique." *Phi Delta Kappan,* 62(2):117–119.

Lilly, M. S. (November 1983). "Redesign of the national accreditation system in teacher education." *Exceptional Children,* 50(3):219–225.

NCATE Staff. 1 October 1981. *Redesigning the governance, financing, and management of the National Council for Accreditation of Teacher Education, Inc.* Washington, DC: NCATE.

Olsen, L. (25 February 1987). "AACTE debates accreditation." *Education Week,* pp. 1, 18.

Olsen, L. and Rodman, B. (7 October 1987). "NCATE amends charter to permit A. F. T., others to join." *Education Week,* p. 4.

Pike, M. Memorandum to NCATE constituent and associate member organizations. 4 April 1984.

Reynolds, M. C. (Ed.) (1989) *Knowledge base for the beginning teacher.* Oxford: The Pergamom Press.

Roames, R. L. (1987). "Accreditation in teacher education: A history of the development of standards by the National Council for Accreditation of Teacher Education." *Dissertation Abstracts International,* 47, 3998A. (University Microfilms No. 87–04746).

Rodman, B. (18 March 1987). "NCATE revises standards to avoid duplication." *Education Week*, p. 10.

———. (9 April 1986). "Union invited to join NCATE." *Education Week*, p. 13.

———. (6 November 1985). "A. F. T. may seek membership in more demanding NCATE." *Education Week*, p. 6.

———. (15 October 1985). "A. F. T. seeks membership in accrediting organization." *Education Week*, p. 10.

———. (19 June 1985). "Accrediting group adopts stiffer standards for education schools." *Education Week*, pp. 5, 16.

Roth, R. A. (1982). "A response to Alan Tom and Richard Wisniewski." *Journal of Teacher Education. 33*(5), 32–36.

Sanders, T. Letter to D. Smith. 29 November 1984.

Saunders, R. L. Letter to NCATE Coordinating Board. 15 February 1985.

Saunders, R., Imig, D., Sanders, T., Pierce, W., Pike, M., and Leeke, J. (1984). *A discussion paper regarding governance of national accreditation: The state of the art now and in the future.* Authors.

Scannell, D. P., Gardner, W. E., Olsen, H. C., Sullivan, C., and Wisniewski, R. (1983). *A proposed accreditation system (An alternative to the current NCATE system).* Washington, D.C.: American Association of Colleges for Teacher Education.

TECSCU Accreditation Task Force. (1982). *A position statement and resolution on accreditation for teacher education.* TECSCU.

Toch, T. (21 November 1984). "Chiefs to seek major role in accreditation of education programs." *Education Week*, p. 5.

Tom, A. (1983). "Should NCATE be disaccredited? The Washington University-Maryville College experience." *Texas Tech Journal of Education, 10*(2):73–86.

———. (1981). "An alternative set of NCATE standards." *Journal of Teacher Education,* 33(6):48–52.

———. (1980a). "NCATE standards amd program quality: You can't get there from here." *Phi Delta Kappan,* 62(2):113–117.

———. (1980b). "Chopping NCATE standards down to size." *Journal of Teacher Education,* 30(6):25–30.

Tucker, S. B. (1984). "Responses to the policy inquiry on increasing the research capacity of schools of education." In H. D. Gideonse and

E. A. Joseph, eds., *Increasing research capacity in schools of education: A policy inquiry and dialogue*. Cincinnati, OH: Fleuron Press.

Warner, A. R. (1986). "A professional house divided." *Action in Teacher Education*, 8(3):19–24.

Watts, D. (1986). "Four educators comment on the redesign of NCATE." *Phi Delta Kappan*, 68(4):315–318.

———. (1983). "Four views of NCATE's role and function." *Phi Delta Kappan*, 64(9):646–649.

Wheeler, C. W. (1980). *NCATE: Does it matter?* (Research Series No. 92). East Lansing, MI: Michigan State University, Institute for Research on Teaching.

Wheeler, C. W. (1980b). *NCATE: Does it matter? (Executive summary)*. (Research Series No. 92). East Lansing, MI: Michigan State University, Institute for Research on Teaching.

Wisniewski, R. (1981). "Quality in teacher education: A reply to Alan Tom." *Journal of Teacher Education*, 32(6):53–55.

Wittrock, M. C., ed. (1986). *The handbook of research on teaching, Third edition*. New York: Macmillan Publishing Company.

References to Chapter 13

Allison, G. T. (1971). *Essence of decision: Explaining the Cuban missile crisis*. Boston: Little, Brown and Co.

Arnholz, J. (3 October 1989). "Back home and playing catch up." *Albuquerque Journal*, p. B1.

Carnegie Forum on Education and the Economy. (1986). *A nation prepared: Teachers for the twenty-first century*. Washington, DC: Author.

Cohen, M. D. and March, J. G. (1986). *Leadership and ambiguity*. Boston: Harvard Business School Press.

Cohen, M. D., March, J. G., and Olsen, J. P. (1976). "People, problems, solutions and the ambiguity of relevance." In J. G. March and J. P. Olsen, eds., *Ambiguity and choice in organizations*. Bergen, Norway: Universitetsforlaget, pp. 24–37.

Cooperman, S., Webb, A., and Klagholz, L. (1983). *An alternative route to teacher selection and professional quality assurance*. Trenton, NJ: New Jersey State Department of Education.

Galambos, E. C., Cornett, L. M., and Spitler, H. D. (1985). *An analysis of transcripts of teachers and arts and sciences graduates*. Atlanta, GA: Southern Regional Education Board.

Holmes Group (1990). *Tomorrow's schools: Principles for the design of professional development schools.* East Lansing, MI: Author.

Holmes Group (1986). *Tomorrow's teachers.* East Lansing, MI: Author.

Lindblom, C. (1959). "The science of muddling through." *Public Administration Review,* 19:79–88.

National Commission on Excellence in Education. (1983). *A nation at risk: The imperative for educational reform.* Washington, DC: U. S. Government Printing Office.

Stoltz, R. E. (1979). *Teacher education and certification: State actions in the south.* Atlanta, GA: Southern Regional Education Board.

INDEX

AACTE *see* American Association of Colleges for Teacher Education

ACSESULGC/APU, *see* Association of Colleges and Schools of Education in State Universities and Land Grant Colleges and Affiliated Private Universities

AERA *see* American Educational Research Association

AFT, *see* American Federation of Teachers

AILACTE, *see* Association of Independent Liberal Arts Colleges for Teacher Education

A Nation at Risk, 4, 6, 56, 74, 109, 159, 172, 262, 281

academic content: academic major, 12-14, 20, 36, 40, 49, 68, 119, 124, 128, 133, 138, 140-142, 144-147, 152, 168, 196, 269, 279, 290; academic preparation, 114, 235, 236, 270; advanced academic training, 8; as necessary and sufficient condition for teaching, 96; at least a minor in teaching subject, 73; elimination of, 39; prerequisite to pedagogical training, 27, 55

accreditation, XIX, 13, 15-17, 160, 209, 231, 245-266, 274, 286; *see also* NCATE

Adler, Mortimer J., 7

admission standards, 163, 236; examinations as requirement for, 118, 126, 291; increased grade point average, 119, 162, 269, 274; selective, 193, 286; too low, 137, 279

Alexander, Lamar, 237, 242

Alper, William, 6

alternative routes to certification, XII, 108, 196, 269, 270, 275, 277, 281, 283, 286, 291; New Jersey, XXI, 44, 73-90, 278; Ohio, 97-100, 105, 195; Oregon, 118; SREB, 231, 234, 236-238; Texas, 8, 12; Virginia, 134; *see also* bypass to certification

American Association of Colleges for Teacher Education: XII, XVIII, 17, 19, 22, 44, 78, 81, 204, 245, 246, 248-251, 254-256, 258-260, 262, 290, 295; Governmental Relations Task Force, XI

American Association of School Administrators, 288

American Educational Research Association, 258

American Federation of Teachers, 20, 24, 256, 261, 272, 288

Anderson, Don, 102

Andrews, L. O., 91

approved programs, 29, 31; *see also* program approval

Arnholz, Jim, 27

Aronoff, Stanley, 98, 99

Association of California School Administrators, 67

Association of Educational Communication and Technology, 246
Association of Colleges and Schools of Education in State Universities and Land Grant Colleges and Affiliated Private Universities, 143, 144, 181, 245-247, 249, 251, 258, 261; Task Force on Accreditation, 251
Association of Independent Liberal Arts Colleges for Teacher Education, 249, 251, 261
The Association for Persons with Severe Handicaps, 217
Association of Teacher Educators, 81, 256
Atkin, J. Myron, 81

Bader, Charles, 57-60, 63-65
Baliles, Gerald L., 135, 137, 139, 142, 150, 151
Bartlett, Tom, 123
Beginning Teacher Evaluation Study, 52
Behling, Herman, 264
Bell, Terrell, 143
Benton, Robert, 255, 264
Bergeson, Marian: 57, 60-66, 287; Bergeson Act, 65; Bergeson Bill, 66; Bergeson Reform, 66-69
Berliner, David, 77
Bestor, Arthur, 227
Biddle, James, 102
Bode, Boyd, 198
Bond, Beth, 256
Bowers, G. Robert, 95, 100
Boyer, Ernest: 77; Boyer Panel, 77, 81, 86, 88; Boyer topics, 77, 78
Briggs, Paul, 92
Brown, Frank, 77
Brown, Jerry, 53
Brown, John, 53, 54, 58

Brown, Lou, 217
Brown, Pat, 65
Brown v. Board of Education, 212
Bruininks, Robert, 217
Buckeye Association of School Administrators, 185
Bureau for Education Professions Development, 209, 213, 214
Bureau of Education for the Handicapped, 208-210, 214, 217
bypass of certification, 101, 105, 108; *see also* alternative routes to certification

CAA, *see* Committee on Accreditation Alternatives
California Basic Educational Skills Test (CBEST), 55, 118, 126
California: XXI, 274, 287; Commission on Teacher Credentialing, 56; Commission on Teacher Preparation, 50, 58-60, 66; Department of Education, 51, 55, 57, 60, 62, 66, 67, 70; Proposition 13, 13, 53, 57; Senate Bill 148, 62-64
California Commission on the Teaching Profession, 58; Friends of the Commission, 58, 59;
California Council for the Education of Teachers, 67
California Federation of Teachers, 67
California School Boards Association, 67
California State University, 67
California State Parent Teacher Association, 67
California Teachers Association 56, 61, 66
caps on program: California, 50; California, proposal to end limit, 57; New Jersey, 80; New

Mexico, XXI, 27-48; pedagogical preparation, XXI, 12, 15, 27, 44, 50, 80, 133, 138, 140-142, 144, 145-147, 150, 152, 235, 269, 270, 271, 273, 278, 282, 283, 286; Texas, 1-26, 44, 235, 271; Virginia, XXI, 44, 133, 140-142, 144, 145-147, 150, 152, 271; on academic content, 27-48; see also pedagogy, reduction of
career ladder, 8, 37, 96, 237, 270, 281
Carnegie Forum on Education and the Economy, 36, 112, 114, 120, 138, 147, 236, 270, 273, 276, 279
Cassidy, Jack, 259, 261, 264
CBEST, see California Basic Educational Skills Test
CCSSO, see Council of Chief State School Officers
Celeste, Richard, 98
Center for Policy Research in Education, XVII
certification, XII, XXI, 18, 229, 231, 232; administrative, California, 54; New Jersey, 79; Ohio, 95, 108; Oregon, 114, 116, 122; professional, 10; Texas, 2, 3, 8, 11-16; Virginia, 134, 135, 137, 139, 142-146, 150; Wisconsin, 160; see also credential, licensure
Chernay, Gloria, 251, 264
Christensen, Doran, 264
Clements, Bill, 10
Coalition of Organizations for the Professional Preparation of Educators (COPPE), 259
coordination between teacher education and schools, 3, 9, 11, 23-25, 70, 237, 291
Committee on Accreditation Alternatives, 248-250, 252, 253, 257, 258, 260
Commons, Dorman, 58

Commons Commission, see California Commission on the Teaching Profession
competency based, 37-39, 41, 45, 94
comprehensive system of personnel development, 203, 205, 206, 210, 220
Conant, James B., 92, 227
conditions of practice, 23, 24, 136, 236, 270
continuing education, XIX; see also inservice
Cooperman, Saul, 73, 75-81, 83-85, 87-90, 286
Corrigan, Dean, 248
Council for Exceptional Children, 206, 246
Council of Chief State School Officers, 83, 245, 246, 254-256, 260, 261, 288; Ad Hoc Committee on Teacher Certification, 255
Council of Learned Societies in Education, 251
credential: California, 49-52, 56, 66, 68, 69, 71; California, two tier, 54, 55; life credential, 53, 55-57, 59, 96; renewal, 56; two-tier, 54, 55; see also licensure, certification
Credential Counselors and Analysts of California, 58
Cross, Marilyn, 104
Cunningham, William, 66

Dale, Edgar, 198
Danielson, John, 122
Davies, Don, 209
Davis, William E., 119
Dean's Grant Projects, 210, 214-216
Denemark, George, 250, 251, 258, 261
Deukmajian, George, 56, 57, 60, 62, 64-66, 70

Dickson, George E., 96
divisions: within higher education, 35, 169; within teacher education, XVI, 47, 107, 127, 128, 148, 246, 273, 279, 287, 289; within the profession, 17, 21-23, 108, 276
Doyle, Denis, 50, 65
Drummond, William, 231, 232
due process, 203
Dyke, James W., Jr., 143, 153

Earley, Penelope, 81
Eastern New Mexico University, 28
Eastern Oregon State College, 123
Education Commission of the States, XVII, 243, 274
Education Professions Development Act, 209, 216
Educational Research Council of America, 93
Egbert, Robert, 81
Elementary and Secondary Education Act, 209
Eikeland, James, 259, 261, 264
emergency certification, 56, 96, 237, 278, 279; see also temporary certificate
entrance requirements, see admissions standards
Epps, Edgar, 77
Essex, Martin, 93
exclusion from policy process, 34, 73, 100, 277, 283, 288; by direction, XVI, 13; by omission of representation, 5, 35, 36, 787, 98, 148, 149
expertise, discounting of, XIV, 151
expanded practicum, 125
extended programs, 11, 14, 15, 213, 231, 232, 236, 238, 276, 292; fifth year, 17, 20, 49, 54, 111, 114, 117, 120-122, 123, 125, 126, 130, 131, 184, 187-189, 286; five year, 111, 112, 117, 118-120, 122, 125, 137, 144, 283; post-baccalaureate, 55; see also graduate teacher education, M.A.T.

Feistritzer, C. Emily, 77, 88
field experiences, 94, 95, 138
fifth year program, see extended program
Findlay Conference, 91-92
Findley, Donald J., 150
Fisher, Robert, 264
Fisher Act, 49, 50, 52, 67, 287; Fisher program, 52; Fisher reform, 65, 66, 68, 69
five year program, see extended program
Florio, James 88
Flowers, Anne, 249, 250
Ford, Gerald, 202
Frazier, Calvin 255, 264
Fulton, Edithe, 79
funds for teacher education, 11; for new standards, 94
Futrell, Mary Hatwood, 260, 261, 264

Gallagher, James, 209
Gant, Jack, 249, 258
Gardner, Randall, 98, 101
Gardner, William, 248, 252, 258, 260, 264
geography and policy, XV
Gideonse, Hendrik, 81, 102, 258, 262
Gilhool, Thomas 203
Godfrey, Jane, 264
Gollnick, Donna, 251, 262, 264
Goodlad, John, 7
Gottlieb, Jay, 77
graduate teacher education, 115, 119, 142, 146; see also extended programs, M.A.T.

Grady, William, 259, 261, 264
Graham, Robert, 242
Granville Conference, 92
Gubser, Lyn, 250, 252, 255, 264
Gustafson, George, 51

Hairston, Elaine, 97, 101
Haley, Bill, 5
Hart, Gary, 55-57, 60, 61, 65, 287
Hearn, Edell, 253, 261, 264
Heller, Harold, 264
Hobby, Bill, 4, 5, 6, 8
Holmes Group, XXI, 9, 14, 17, 36, 37, 39, 44, 45, 112, 114, 120, 220, 236, 270, 273, 276, 279, 290, 295; implementation of Holmes at Ohio State University, 181-198; Midwest, 193, 194
Honig, Bill, 56, 57, 70
Howsam, Robert, 204
Hughes, Teresa, 57, 65
Hughes-Hart Act (California SB 813), 57, 66

Imig, David, 78,, 248, 255, 256, 260, 264
individual effort, impact on policy, 6, 7, 65, 66, 112, 128, 150, 151, 174, 175, 242, 217, 258-263, 282, 286, 287
induction assistance, 11, 12, 68, 96, 111, 115, 135, 136; *see also* support and assessment system
inservice, 8, 54, 55, 59, 137, 230; *see also* continuing education
Institute for Research on Teaching (Michigan State University), 247, 248, 252
International Reading Association, 246
internship, 11, 17, 20, 24, 54, 55, 59, 71, 98, 232, 270, 283, 286, 291

isolation of teacher educators, 32; *see also* exclusion from policy process

Jaroslaw, Harry, 78; Jaroslaw Commission, 78, 79, 81
Jones, Grant, 5

Katz, Vera, 112
Kean, Thomas, 73, 75, 78, 88, 90, 99, 286
Kettlewell, Jan, 104
Knight, Jeanne, 28, 31, 33, 35, 37, 40
knowledge base, 19, 73, 77, 104; as basis for special and regular education, 206, 220, 221, 269; as basis for teacher education, 212, 238, 246, 257, 258, 291; encouragement to use, 98; non-mention of, 92, 93; weakness of, 287, 289
knowledge deficits for policy, XII, 279, 280, 283, 287, 289; correcting same, 292
Koerner, James D., 50, 227, 234
Kunkel, Richard, 251, 255, 256, 258, 260, 262, 264

Lacatena, Marco, 78-81
LaPointe, Archie, 77
lateness of response, XIV, 17, 279
Lakin, Charlie, 217
leaders, scarcity of, XV, 282
Leadership Training Institutes, 213, 214, 216
Leeke, John, 251, 264
least restrictive environment, 203, 213, 218
Lemmon, W. L., 140
Levering, David, 55
Lewis, Earl, 10, 11
Lewis, Gib, 4-6, 8
Lezotte, Lawrence, 77

licensure, XVIII, 278, 281; New Mexico, 29-35, 37, 42, 45, 47; Oregon, 113; *see also* certification, credential
license waivers, 28
life credential, *see* credential
life space, 15, 19, 20, 96, 213, 278, 282
Lilly, Steve, 262, 265
Lindsey, Margaret, 19, 92
LoPresti, Peter, 51

Madla, Frank, 5
Maddox, Kathryn 77
Martin, Elwin, 210
Mastain, Richard, 55, 60-63, 66
M.A.T. (Master of Arts in Teaching), 123-125, 130, 226
McGuire, Willard, 249, 260, 261, 265
McKenna, Bernie 262, 265
Meharry Medical College, 223, 225
Mehas, Peter, 62, 66
Mills v. Board of Education, 201
minorities: exclusion of by exams, 52, 118; faculty, 243; high proportion of in special education classes, 212; improvement of racially unitary systems of higher education, 227, 228; segregation of, 225
Morgan, Alan, 28, 31-35, 37, 41, 43
Myton, David, 126

National Board for Professional Teaching Standards, 40, 42, 238, 271, 295
National Commission on Teacher Education and Professional Standards, 19
National Council for Accreditation of Teacher Education, XXII, 17, 18, 44, 105, 154, 160, 245-266, 271, 279, 287-289, 295; Board of Examiners, 154, 249, 257; Coordinating Board, 245, 246, 249, 251, 254; Council, 245-251, 254; developmental posture, 258, 259; Executive Board, 252, 257; State Recognition Board, 254; unit accreditation, 249, 253, 254, 256; Unit Accreditation Board, 252; *see also* accreditation
National Council of Teachers of English, 38
National Council of Teachers of Mathematics, 38
National Education Association, XVIII, 20, 24, 245, 246, 248-251, 254-256, 259, 261, 272, 288
National Governors Association, XVII, 83, 243, 274
National Association of School Psychologists, 251
National Association of State Directors of Teacher Education and Certification, 246, 253, 254
National Conference of State Legislators, 274
National School Boards Association, 245
National Support Systems Project, 214, 215
National Teacher Examination, 83, 84, 118, 124, 135, 154
NCATE, *See* National Council for Accreditation of Teacher Education
negative assessment by graduates, 7, 8, 113, 114, 120, 147, 149, 272, 277, 289, 290
negative press, 34, 75, 80
New England Board of Higher Education, 225
New Jersey, XXI, 44, 73-90, 98,

273, 277; Board of Education, 77, 81, 82; Department of Higher Education, 79; Board of Higher Education, 81; *see also* Boyer, Ernest; Cooperman, Saul; Kean, Thomas
New Jersey Association of Colleges for Teacher Education, 78
New Jersey Education Association, 73, 75, 79, 86
New Jersey Federation of Teachers, 73, 80
New Jersey Principals and Supervisors Association, 76, 87
New Jersey School Boards Association, 76
New Mexico, XXI; Board of Education, 27, 28, 30, 31, 40, 42, 45-47; Department of Education, 28, 30, 32, 37, 38, 45-47; Governor's Commission on Public Schools, 30; Legislative Education Study Committee, 30; Public School Reform Commission, 34; Professional Standards Commission, 29, 30, 31, 33, 35, 38, 39, 41, 44-47, 273; School Reform Commission, 37
New Mexico Association of Colleges for Teacher Education, 31, 32, 34, 35, 37, 38, 40, 47
New Mexico Highlands University, 28
New Mexico State Federation of Teachers, 39, 40, 42, 46
New Mexico State University, 27, 28, 30, 35-37, 39-47, 282
Norfolk State College, 228
Normal State University, 202

Ohio, XXI, 273; Board of Education, 95, 95; Board of Regents, 95, 101; Department of Education, 91-94, 96, 97, 99, 100, 105, 182; Education 2000 Commission, 97, 98; HB 212, 97, 99, 100-102; HB 779, 104; SB 140, 98-102, 104; Teacher Education and Certification Advisory Committee, 98, 103
Ohio Association of Colleges for Teacher Education, 96, 101, 103, 104, 282
Ohio Association of Private Colleges for Teacher Education, 101, 273
Ohio Education Association, 93, 101, 104, 185
Ohio Federation of Teachers, 101, 102
Ohio School Boards Association, 185
Ohio State University, 190, 193, 194, 197, 198: Board of Trustees, 187; College of Agriculture, 182; College of the Arts, 182; College of Education, XXI, 181, 182, 184, 185, 187, 190, 192, 193, 196, 198; College of Home Economics, 184; College of Human Ecology, 182; Council of Deans, 187; President's Cabinet, 187; Professional Development Schools Policy Advisory Committee, 194; School of Music, 189, 197; Teacher Education Advisory Committee, 191
(Ohio) State University Education Deans, 100
Old Dominion University, 228
Olsen, Hans, 248, 265
oral traditions, XII
Oregon, XXI, 279: Board of Education, 112; Board of Higher Education, 112, 113, 116, 117, 122, 131; Department of Education, 128, 129; HB 3038, 122, 123; State System of Higher Education, 112, 113, 115, 116, 118-123, 128-130,

Oregon *(continued)*
273; Teacher Standards and Practices Commission, 112, 115-120, 122, 126, 128
Oregon Education Association, 111, 113, 115, 117, 118, 122, 123, 126-128
Oregon School Administrator's Asociation, 126
Oregon School Boards Association, 126
Oregon Small Schools Association 117
Oregon State University, 112, 114, 115, 118, 119, 123-125, 130, 131, 273
OSU/WOSC (Oregon State University/Western Oregon State College), 115, 127

Parker, Carl, 5, 11, 13, 14, 17, 22
parental participation, 203, 211, 281
Pearson, Mary Jane, 58
pedagogy, reduction of, 235, 269, 270, 275, 282; *see also* caps
Pennsylvania Association for Retarded Children v. Commonwealth (PARC), 201, 203
Perot, Ross, 5-8, 18, 277, 286
Petrossian, Alice, 58, 60, 62-64, 66
Phillis, William, 100
Pierce, William, 255, 256, 262, 265
Pike, Marjorie, 256, 261, 265
Poisson, David, 253, 265
policy structures, XIX; California struggle over public vs. professional authority over credentialing, 50, 51, 55-65, 66, 67, 70; New Jersey temporary systems (Boyer Panel and Jaroslaw Commission), 77-79; New Mexico Professional Standards Commission, 29; Ohio, proposed professional standards board, 97; Ohio, Teacher Education and Certification Advisory Commission, 98; Ohio, temporary systems, 94, 96; Ohio State University, role of College of Education Senate in Holmes decision, 183-186; Oregon, independent commission, 112, 113, struggle with higher education authority, 121, 122; NCATE governance of accreditation, 245, 254-257, 288; Texas proposal to appoint State Board of Education, 7; Virginia, Ad Hoc Committee on Teacher Education, 139-145; Virginia, Commission on Excellence in Education, 136-139; Virginia, original structure, 134, 135; Wisconsin, state regulatory authority vs. principle of faculty autonomy, 159-164, 167, 168
Portland State University, 130, 131, 273
probationary period, longer, 230
program approval, XVIII, 46, 52, 53, 64, 68, 113, 115, 154, 161, 162; *see also* approved program
program review, 63, 231
provisional year, 73
Public Law 94-142, XXII, 202-207, 210-213, 216-218, 221

RAND Center for the Study of the Teaching Profession, XVII
rationalistic fallacy, XVIII, 22, 105, 153, 155, 284, 285, 287
Reagan, Ronald, 50, 51, 65, 76, 77, 271, 280, 281
regular education initiative, 218, 219
regulatory reform, 32, 147, 159, 168, 176, 286; ineffectiveness of, 25, 26

research methodologies in teacher education, XIX
research and development for teacher preparation, 230
restructuring, 25, 94, 133-135, 137, 138, 140-152, 154, 270, 275, 295
rhythms, different, XII
Richner, Shirley, 265
Rickover, Admiral Hyman, 7
right to education, 201, 202, 204, 206, 218
Riles, Wilson, 51
Robb, Charles S. 135, 137, 242
Rosenshine, Barak, 77
Rutgers, State University of New Jersey, 76, 90; AAUP, 79
Ryan, Leo, 49, 50, 65, 287; Ryan Act, 50, 51, 52, 54, 67; Ryan reform, 52, 65, 66, 68, 69

Sailor, Wayne, 217
Salishan Deans, 257, 258
Salley, Robert, 53, 55, 56
San Francisco State University, 202
Sandefur, J. T., 255, 261, 265
Sanders, Ted, 255, 256, 260, 265
Saunders, Robert, 256, 261, 265
Scanlon, Robert, 255
Schlueter, Stan, 5
Scannell, Dale, 248, 260, 265
serendipity, XIV, 100, 101, 292
Shanker, Albert, 81
Shulman, Lee, 185
Sheahan (now Scannell), Marilyn, 262
Smith, Catherine, 36, 37, 41, 46
Smith, Pat, 97, 98
Snyder, Cooper, 98, 99
Sontag, Ed, 217
Southern Association of Colleges and Schools, 134
Southern Governors' Conference, 223, 224
Southern Regional Consortium of Colleges of Education, 244
Southern Regional Education Board, XVII, XXII, 18, 143, 223-244, 271, 275, 278, 280, 289; Commission for Educational Quality, 233; Teacher Education Conference, 228
Southern Republican Conference, 241
speed of policy processes, XII, 17, 33, 81, 100, 105, 106, 134, 148, 150, 170
SREB, *see* Southern Regional Education Board
standardized testing, 281
student teaching, 91-93, 121, 230, 231, 236
Sullivan, Catherine, 249, 250, 262
subject matter knowledge, *see* academic content
supply and demand, XIX
support and assessment system, 63, 64, 69; *see also* induction assistance

Targets Conference, 93
Teacher Corps, 209
Teacher Education Assessment Project, 93, 94
Teacher Education Council of State Colleges and Universities, XI, XVII, 246, 248, 249, 251, 252, 261
Teacher Education Redesign (Ohio), 94
teacher educators as foot draggers, XVI
teacher salaries, 3-5, 7, 9, 23, 24, 135-137, 237
teacher warranty, 111, 115, 116, 127
technical assistance, 213-216
Technical Assistance Development System, 214
TECSCU, *see* Teacher Education Council of State Colleges and Universities

temporary certificate, 96; see also emergency certificate
testing, XIX, 62, 71, 108, 111, 128; admission to teacher preparation, 3, 51, 52; basic skills, 55, 116, 118, 119, 124, 230, 231; basic skills test, suspended, 126; content, 73, 115, 116, 119; exit tests, 3, 17, 53, 54, 59, 68, 83-85, 96, 124, 162, 231, 232, 269, 270, 275, 286, 291; and racial factors, 228; of students and its reflections on teachers, 229; of teachers, 8-10, 12, 32
Texas, 44, 144, 147, 151, 196, 235, 237, 273, 277; State Board of Education, 4, 5, 7, 8, 12, 14-16; Commission on Standards for the Teaching Profession, 6, 15, 16, 18; early history of reform, 1-4; HB 72, 4, 5, 7, 8-10, 15-17; Higher Education Coordinating Board, 10, 14, 15, 17; SB 994, XXI, 4, 11-17, 22; Select Committee on Higher Education (SCOHE), 4, 10-13, 18; Select Committee on Public Education (SCOPE), 4-9; Teacher Appraisal System, 10; Texas Education Agency, 10, 15, 17
Texas Association of Colleges for Teacher Education (TACTE), 10, 11, 13, 17
time demands of participation in policy, XII-XIV, 47, 101, 106, 292-294
Tom, Alan, 261, 265
Tomorrow's Teachers, 183-185
transcript analysis, 18, 134, 234, 235, 243, 280
Tyler, Ralph, 198

uniform program, XXI, 101, 102
unit accreditation, 249, 253, 254, 256; see also NCATE
United States Office of Education (USOE), 210
United Teachers of Los Angeles, 67
University of California, 67
University of New Mexico, 27, 28, 30, 35-37, 39-47, 282
University of Oregon, XXI, 112, 114, 118, 123, 125, 130, 131, 273
University of Toledo, 94
University of Wisconsin: Madison, XXI, 159, 160, 161, 164, 165, 167, 175, 178, 180, 274; Madison, School of Education, 160-163, 165, 166, 168-171, 175, 178, 180; Madison, College of Letters and Sciences, 168, 170, 176; Milwaukee, 177; System, 162, 165, 175, 179; System, Board of Regents, 174, 175; System, Task Force, 166, 171
University of Virginia, 137, 139, 147, 148, 152
urban/rural conflict, 44

vested interests, XVI, 18, 21, 74, 108, 151, 152, 196, 278
Virginia: XXI, 44, 235, 273, 274, 286; Ad Hoc Committee on Teacher Education, 133, 139-147, 149-153; Beginning Teacher Assessment Program, 135; Board of Education, 134, 135, 137-140, 143, 145, 146, 149, 150, 151, 154; Commission on Virginia's Future, 137; Committee on Teachers and Teaching, 137, 146, 147, 149; Department of Education, 134, 135, 138, 140, 143, 145, 146, 149, 153, 154; Governor's Commission on Excellence in Education, 133, 136-138, 143,

Virginia *(continued)*
  146, 148, 150, 151; State Council of Higher Education, 134, 137, 139, 143, 146, 149-152; Task Force on Improving Teaching as a Profession, 136, 154; Teacher Education Advisory Board, 135, 136, 141, 146, 148, 149, 154
Virginia Association of Colleges for Teacher Education, 148
Virginia Commonwealth Center for the Education of Teachers, 136, 139
Virginia Commonwealth University, 137, 147, 148
Virginia Education Association, 139, 148, 149
Voeltz, Luanna, 217

Walsh, Herb, 28, 31-33, 35, 36
Walter, Franklin, 100
warranty, teacher, *see* teacher warranty
Wehman, Paul, 217
Western Interstate Commission on Higher Education, 225
Western New Mexico University, 28
Western Oregon State College, 115, 124, 125
Wheeler, Christopher, 265
White, Mark, 4-6, 8, 10
Whitmore, Joanne, 265
Wingspread Group, 181-183
Wisconsin: 245, 273; Assembly Education Committee, 161; Department of Public Instruction (DPI), XXI, 159-166, 169, 170, 172-178, 180; DPI Task Force, 166, 168, 171, 173, 175, 176
Wisconsin Education Association Council, 173
Wise, Arthur, 88, 185
Wisniewski, Richard, 248, 258, 262, 265